T

HISTORICAL DICTIONARIES OF INTERNATIONAL ORGANIZATIONS SERIES
Edited by Jon Woronoff

Historical Dictionary of International Organizations

WITHDRAWN

Michael G. Schechter

Historical Dictionaries
of International Organizations, No. 16

The Scarecrow Press, Inc.
Lanham, Maryland, & London
1998

SCARECROW PRESS, INC.

Published in the United States of America
by Scarecrow Press, Inc.
4720 Boston Way
Lanham, Maryland 20706

4 Pleydell Gradens, Folkestone
Kent CT20 2DN, England

British Library Cataloguing in Publication Information Available

Library of Congress Cataloging-in-Publication Data

Schechter, Michael G.
    Historical dictionary of international organizations / Michael G.
Schechter.
        p.   cm.—(Historical dictionaries of international
organizations ; no. 16)
    Includes bibliographical references.
    ISBN 0-8108-3479-0 (alk. paper)
    1. International agencies—Dictionaries.   I. Title.   II. Series :
Historical dictionaries of international oragnizations series ; no.
16.
JZ4838.S34   1998
060—dc21   98-22755
                                                        CIP

∞ ™ The paper used in this publication meets the minimum
requirements of American National Standard for Information
Sciences—Permanence of Paper for Printed Library Materials,
ANSI Z39.48–1984. Manufactured in the United States of
America.

Contents

Editor's Foreword

One of the most pervasive phenomena that distinguish the end of the 20th century is the prevalence of international organizations (IOs). There are IOs in virtually every sector: political, economic, social, educational, scientific, defense, and so forth. Some IOs have an almost universal membership, whereas others encompass states in specific regions, or subregions, or with specific interest or producing certain commodities. Some IOs are restricted to clearly defined activities and closely controlled by their members; others just grow and grow, moving into new sectors and becoming more powerful in some ways than their members. Alongside the legions of IOs whose members are sovereign states, or territories, there are masses of IOs whose members are private persons or associations. All together they number not in the hundreds but in the thousands. And yet, at the beginning of the century, hardly any existed. Even by midcentury there were few enough that specialists could be familiar with most and grasp their workings and interrelations. Today that is out of the question.

Still, if there are so many IOs, and if they are so prominent in so many fields yet so different from one another, attempts must be made at sorting things out. This *Historical Dictionary of International Organizations* is one such attempt, and here its special format is a distinct advantage. The chronology traces the progression from few and relatively "primitive" bodies to countless, often sophisticated, occasionally almost universal, and sometimes even supranational organizations of the present. The list of acronyms is indispensable in reading about them, here or elsewhere. The introduction delineates the broader context, while the dictionary goes into specifics. Some entries present the more important IOs, what they do, how they function, who belongs, and where they fit in. Others explain the rationale and workings of IOs in general. Organizations are nothing without leaders, and some of the most significant are introduced, including philosophers, pioneers, founders, and officials. Obviously, neither this book nor the fifteen volumes already published and another dozen on the way in the series of Historical Dictionaries of International Organizations could cover the whole field. So the comprehensive and carefully structured bibliography is particularly useful for those who want to know more.

In certain ways, this volume was the hardest to write in the series. It was necessary to have a broader view—to describe more different organizations and to explain how they form a whole. Since it was patently impossible to include everything in any one book, no matter how large, it was necessary to select and discard. This has been done very ably by Michael G. Schechter, professor of international relations at James Madison College of Michigan State University. He has written widely on global governance and was recently a project director for the United Nations University's Multilateralism and the United Nations System programs. This knowledge and experience were essential in producing an informative and accessible foundation for the rest of the series.

Jon Woronoff
Series Editor

Acronyms and Abbreviations

AACC	All Africa Conference of Churches
AAD	Arab Accounting Dinar
ACC	Administrative Committee on Coordination
ACCT	Agence de Coopération Culturelle et Technique
ACHR	Asian Coalition for Housing Rights
ACORD	Agency for Co-operation and Research in Development
ACP	African, Caribbean, and Pacific
ADB	African Development Bank, Asian Development Bank
ADRA	Adventist Development and Relief Agency
AFAED	Abu Dhabi Fund for Arab Economic Development
AFTA	Asian Free Trade Area
AI	Amnesty International
AIJD	Association Internationale des Juristes Démocrates
AIOEC	Association of Iron Ore Exporting Countries
ALADI	Associación Lationoamericana de Integración
AMU	Arab Maghreb Union
Ancom	Andean Common Market
ANRPC	Association of Natural Rubber Producing Countries
ANZUS	Australia, New Zealand, United States
APEC	Asia Pacific Economic Cooperation
ARC	American Refugee Committee
ASEAN	Association of Southeast Asian Nations
ASTRO	International Association of Trading Organizations for a Developing World
ATPC	Association of Tin Producing Countries
BADEA	Banque Arabe pour le Développement Economique en Afrique
BCEAC	Banque Centrale des Etats d'Afrique Centrale
BEAC	Banque des Etats d'Afrique Centrale
BENELUX	Belgium, Netherlands, Luxembourg
BINGOs	Business International Nongovernmental Organizations

BIS	Bank for International Settlements
BSEC	Black Sea Economic Cooperation
CAA	Community Aid Abroad
CABEI	Central American Bank for Economic Integration
CACM	Central American Common Market
CAP	Common Agricultural Policy
CARE	Cooperation for American Remittances to Europe
CARICOM	Caribbean Community and Common Market
CARIFTA	Caribbean Free Trade Association
CBD	United Nations Convention on Biological Diversity
CBSS	Council of the Baltic Sea States
CCC	Customs Co-operation Council
CDB	Caribbean Development Bank
CEAC	Commission Européenne de l'Aviation Civile
CEAO	Communauté Economique de l'Afrique de l'Ouest
CEBM	Organisation Européenne de Biologies Moléculaires
CEDEAO	Communauté Economique des Etats de l'Afrique de l'Ouest
CEEAC	Communauté Economique des Etats de l'Afrique Centrale
CEMAC	Communauté Economique et Monétaire de l'Afrique Centrale
CENTO	Central Treaty Organization
CEPGC	Communauté Economique des Pays des Grands Lacs
CEPT	Common Preferential Tariff
CERN	Organisation Européenne pour la Recherche Nucléaire
CFSP	Common Foreign and Security Policy
CIEC	Conference on International Economic Cooperation
CIPEC	Conseil Intergovernemental des Pays Exportateurs de Cuivre
CIS	Commonwealth of Independent States
CITES	Convention on International Trade in Endangered Species of Wild Fauna and Flora
CLISS	Comité Inter-Etats pour la Lutte Contre la Secheresse au Sahel
CMEA	Council for Mutual Economic Assistance
CMI	Comité Maritime International
COMECON	Council for Mutual Economic Assistance
COMESA	Common Market for Eastern and Southern Africa

COMINFORM	Communist Information Bureau
CNN	Cable News Network
COPA	Comité des Organisations Professionelles Agricoles
COREPER	Comité des Représentants Permanents
COW	Committee of the Whole
CPA	Cocoa Producers' Alliance
CRS	Catholic Relief Services
CSCE	Conference on Security and Cooperation in Europe
CSD	United Nations Commission on Sustainable Development
CSUCA	Consejo Superior Universitario Centroamericano
DAC	Development Assistance Committee
DAWN	Development Alternatives with Women for New Era
EAC	East African Economic Community
EAPC	Euro-Atlantic Partnership Council
EBRD	European Bank for Reconstruction and Development
ECA	Economic Commission for Africa
ECAC	European Civil Aviation Conference
ECAFE	Economic Commission for Asia and the Far East
ECB	European Central Bank
ECCB	Eastern Caribbean Central Bank
ECE	Economic Commission for Europe
ECLA	Economic Commission for Latin America
ECLAC	Economic Commission for Latin America and the Caribbean
ECO	Economic Cooperation Organization
ECOSOC	Economic and Social Council
ECOWAS	Economic Community of West African States
ECSC	European Coal and Steel Community
ECU	European Currency Unit
ECWA	Economic Commission for Western Asia
EDC	European Defense Community
EDF	European Development Fund
EEA	European Economic Area
EEC	European Economic Community
EES	European Economic Space
EEZ	Exclusive Economic Zone
EFTA	European Free Trade Association
EIB	European Investment Bank
EMBO	European Molecular Biology Organization
EMS	European Monetary System

EMU	Economic and Monetary Union
EPC	European Political Cooperation
EPTA	Expanded Program of Technical Assistance
ERASMUS	European Community Action Scheme for the Mobility of University Students
ERM	Exchange Rate Mechanism
ESA	European Space Agency
ESC	Economic and Social Committee
ESCAP	Economic and Social Commission for Asia and the Pacific
ESCWA	Economic and Social Commission for Western Asia
EU	European Union
EURATOM	European Atomic Energy Community
EUROCONTROL	European Organization for the Safety of Air Navigation
FAO	Food and Agriculture Organization
FID	International Federation for Information and Documentation
FoEI	Friends of the Earth International
FTC	Feed the Children
G-15	Group of Fifteen
G-5	Group of Five
G-7	Group of Seven
G-10	Group of Ten
G-24	Group of Twenty-Four
G-77	Group of Seventy-Seven
GAB	General Agreements to Borrow
GATS	General Agreement on Trade in Services
GATT	General Agreement on Tariffs and Trade
GCC	Gulf Cooperation Council
GEMS	Global Environmental Monitoring Service
GSP	Generalized System of Preferences
HIAS	Hebrew Immigrant Aid Society
HIC	Habitat International Coalition
HRI	Human Rights Internet
IA	International Alert
IACF	International Association for Cultural Freedom
IACO	Inter-African Coffee Organization
IAEA	International Atomic Energy Agency
IATA	International Air Transport Association
IBA	International Bauxite Association
IBEC	International Bank for Economic Cooperation

IBRD	International Bank for Reconstruction and Development
ICA	International commodity agreement
ICAO	International Civil Aviation Organization
ICB	International Commodity Body
ICC	International Chamber of Commerce
ICCAT	International Commission for the Conservation of Atlantic Tunas
ICCO	International Cocoa Organization
ICEM	Intergovernmental Committee for European Migration
ICFTU	International Confederation of Free Trade Unions
ICJ	International Court of Justice, International Commission of Jurists
ICMC	International Catholic Migration Commission
ICO	International Coffee Organization
ICPI	International Center for Peace Initiatives
ICPRP	International Commission for the Protection of the Rhine Against Pollution
ICRC	International Committee of the Red Cross
ICS	International Chamber of Shipping
ICSEM	International Commission for Scientific Exploration of the Mediterranean Sea
ICSID	International Centre for Settlement of International Disputes
ICSU	International Council of Scientific Unions
ICVA	International Council of Voluntary Agencies
IDA	International Development Association
IDB	Inter-American Development Bank; Islamic Development Bank
IEA	International Energy Agency
IEC	International Electrotechnical Commission
IFAD	International Fund for Agricultural Development
IFC	International Finance Corporation
IFLAI	International Federation of Library Associations and Institutions
IFN	International Feminist Network
IFRC	International Federation of Red Cross and Red Crescent Societies
IFUW	International Federation of University Women
IFWL	International Federation of Women Lawyers
IGOs	Intergovernmental Organizations
IIO	International Islamic Organization
IJO	International Jute Organization

ILC	International Law Commission
ILGA	International Lesbian and Gay Association
ILHR	International League for Human Rights
ILO	International Labour Organisation
ILZSG	International Lead and Zinc Study Group
IMCO	Intergovernmental Maritime Consultative Organization
IMF	International Monetary Fund
IMO	International Maritime Organization, International Meteorological Organization
INGOs	International nongovernmental organizations
Inmarsat	International Maritime Satellite Organization
INRO	International Natural Rubber Organization
INSG	International Nickel Study Group
INSTRAW	International Research and Training Institute for the Advancement of Women
INTELSAT	International Telecommunications Satellite Organization
INTERPOL	International Criminal Police Organization
IOC	International Olympic Committee
IOM	International Organization for Migration
IOOC	International Olive Oil Council
IOs	International organizations
IOS	International Organization for Standardization
IPC	Integrated Program for Commodities
IPI	International Press Institute
IPU	Inter-Parliamentary Union
IRO	International Refugee Organization
ISA	International Seabed Authority
ISCA	(International) Save the Children Alliance
ISIS	Women's International Information and Communication Service
ISO	International Sugar Organization
ITC	International Trade Center
ITPA	International Tea Promotion Association
ITTC	International Tropical Timber Council
ITTO	International Tropical Timber Organization
ITU	International Telecommunication Union
IUOTO	International Union of Official Travel Organizations
IWC	International Whaling Commission, International Wheat Council
KFAED	Kuwait Fund for Arab Economic Development
LAFTA	Latin American Free Trade Association

LAIA	Latin American Integration Association
LLDCs	Least developed countries
MDM	Médecins du Monde
MERCOSUR	Mercado Común del Cono Sur
MFA	Multifibre Agreement
MFN	Most Favored Nation
MIGA	Multilateral Investment Guarantee Agency
MINUGUA	United Nations Verification Mission in Guatemala
MINURSO	United Nations Mission for the Referendum in Western Sahara
MNCs	Multinational Corporations
MSA	Most seriously affected
NAC	North Atlantic Council
NACC	North Atlantic Cooperation Council
NAFTA	North American Free Trade Association
NAM	Non-Aligned Movement
NATO	North Atlantic Treaty Organization
NGLS	United Nations Non-Governmental Liaison Service
NGOs	Nongovernmental organizations
NICs	Newly industrialized countries
NIEs	Newly industrializing economies
NIEO	New International Economic Order
NTBs	Nontariff barriers
NWICO	New World Information and Communications Order
NWIO	New World Information Order
OAPEC	Organization of Arab Petroleum Exporting Countries
OAS	Organization of American States
OAU	Organization of African Unity
OCIMF	Oil Companies International Marine Forum
ODA	Official development assistance
ODECA	Organización de Estados Centro-americanos
ODIHR	Office of Democratic Institutions and Human Rights
OEB	Organisation Européenne des Brevets
OECD	Organisation for Economic Co-operation and Development
OECS	Organization of Eastern Caribbean States
OEEC	Organisation for European Economic Co-operation
OIC	Organization of the Islamic Conference
ONUC	United Nations Operation in the Congo

ONUMOZ	United Nations Operation in Mozambique
ONUSAL	United Nations Observer Mission in El Salvador
OPANAL	Organismo para la Proscripción de las Armas Nucleares en la América Latina y el Caribe
OPEC	Organization of Petroleum Exporting Countries
OSCE	Organization on Security and Cooperation in Europe
OXFAM	Oxford Committee for Famine Relief
PAFTA	Pacific Free Trade Area
PAFTAD	Pacific Trade and Development Conference
PAHO	Pan American Health Organization
PAU	Pan American Union
PBEC	Pacific Basin Economic Council
PECC	Pacific Economic Cooperation Council, Pacific Economic Cooperation Conference
PBI	Peace Brigades International
PCIJ	Permanent Court of International Justice
PfP	Partnership for Peace
PLO	Palestine Liberation Organization
PSF	Pharmaciens sans frontières
RAN	Rainforest Action Network
RCD	Regional Cooperation for Development
RI	Rehabilitation International
SAARC	South Asian Association for Regional Cooperation
SADC	Southern African Development Community
SADCC	Southern African Development Coordination Council
SCF	Save the Children Fund
SCI	Service Civil International
SDRs	Special drawing rights
SEA	Single European Act
SEANWFZ	South-East Asian Nuclear Weapons Free Zone
SEATO	Southeast Asia Treaty Organization
SELA	Sistema Económico Latinoamericana
SFD	Saudi Fund for Development
SI	Survival International
SIECA	Permanent Secretariat of the General Treaty on Central American Integration
SITA	Société Internationale de Télécommunications Aéronautiques
SOLAS	Safety of Life at Sea
SPC	South Pacific Commission
SPF	South Pacific Forum
TNCs	Transnational corporations

TRIPS	Agreement on Trade-Related Intellectual Property Rights
UDEAC	Union Douanière et Economique de l'Afrique Centrale
UEMOA	Union Économique et Monétaire Ouest Africaine
UN	United Nations
UNAMIC	United Nations Advance Mission in Cambodia
UNAMIR	United Nations Assistance Mission for Rwanda
UNASOG	United Nations Aouzou Strip Observer Group
UNAVEM	United Nations Angola Verification Mission
UNCDF	United Nations Capital Development Fund
UNCED	United Nations Conference on Environment and Development
UNCHE	United Nations Conference on the Human Environment
UNCHS	United Nations Center for Human Settlements
UNCIO	United Nations Conference on International Organization
UNCITRAL	United Nations Commission on International Trade Law
UNCLOS	United Nations Conference on the Law of the Sea
UNCRO	United Nations Confidence Restoration Organization in Croatia
UNCTAD	United Nations Conference on Trade and Development
UNDC	United Nations Disarmament Commission
UNDOF	United Nations Disengagement Observer Force
UNDP	United Nations Development Program
UNDRO	Office of the United Nations Disaster Relief Coordinator
UDEAC	Union Douanière et Économique de l'Afrique Centrale
UNEF	United Nations Emergency Force
UNEP	United Nations Environment Program
UNESCO	United Nations Educational, Scientific and Cultural Organization
UNFDAC	United Nations Fund for Drug Abuse Control
UNFICYP	United Nations Peacekeeping Force in Cyprus
UNFPA	United Nations Population Fund
UNGOMAP	United Nations Good Offices Mission in Afghanistan and Pakistan
UNHCR	Office of the United Nations High Commissioner for Refugees

UNICEF	United Nations (International) Children's Emergency Fund
UNIDCP	United Nations International Drug Control Program
UNIDO	United Nations Industrial Development Organization
UNIFIL	United Nations Interim Force in Lebanon
UNIIMOG	United Nations Iran-Iraq Military Observer Group
UNIKOM	United Nations Iraq-Kuwait Observation Mission
UNIPOM	United Nations India-Pakistan Observation Mission
UNITAR	United Nations Institute for Training and Research
UNMIBH	United Nations Mission in Bosnia and Herzegovina
UNMIH	United Nations Mission in Haiti
UNMOGIP	United Nations Military Observer Group in India and Pakistan
UNMOP	United Nations Mission of Observers in Prevlaka
UNMOT	United Nations Mission of Observers in Tajikistan
UNOGIL	United Nations Observation Group in Lebanon
UNOMIG	United Nations Observer Mission in Georgia
UNOMIL	United Nations Observer Mission in Liberia
UNOMUR	United Nations Observer Mission Uganda-Rwanda
UNOSOM	United Nations Operation in Somalia
UNPREDEP	United Nations Preventive Deployment Force
UNPROFOR	United Nations Protection Force
UNRISD	United Nations Research Institute for Social Development
UNRWA	United Nations Relief and Works Agency for Palestine Refugees in the Near East
UNSF	United Nations Security Force in West New Guinea
UNSMIH	United Nations Support Mission in Haiti
UNTAC	United Nations Transitional Authority in Cambodia
UNTAES	United Nations Transitional Administration for Easter Slavonia, Baranja and Western Sirmium
UNTAG	United Nations Transition Assistance Group
UNTSO	United Nations Truce Supervision Organization
UNU	United Nations University
UNV	United Nations Volunteers
UNYOM	United Nations Yemen Observation Mission
UPU	Universal Postal Union
VITA	Volunteers in Technical Assistance
WARC	World Administrative Radio Conference

WCC	World Council of Churches
WCL	World Confederation of Labor
WEU	Western European Union
WFC	World Food Council
WFP	World Food Programme
WFTU	World Federation of Trade Unions
WHO	World Health Organization
WIPO	World Intellectual Property Organization
WMO	World Meteorological Organization
WP-3	Working Party 3
WRI	War Resisters International
WTO	Warsaw Treaty Organization; World Trade Organization; World Tourism Organization
WWF	World Wide Fund for Nature; World Wildlife Fund
YMCA	World Alliance of Young Men's Christian Associations
YWCA	World Young Women's Christian Association

Selected Chronology of International Organizations and Key Related International Events

1815	Congress of Vienna, which established the Central Commission on the Navigation of the Rhine
1837	Aborigines Protection Society established
1839	British and Foreign Anti-Slavery Society established
1851	Telegraph cable laid between England and France
1855	World Alliance of YMCAs founded
1856	Danube Commission established
1863	International Committee of the Red Cross established
1865	International Telegraph Union established
December 11, 1868	Declaration Renouncing the Use in Time of War, of Explosive Projectiles under 400 Grammes Weight
1873	World Meteorological Organization begins operation (as a nongovernmental organization)
May 20, 1875	International Bureau of Weights and Measures established
July 1, 1875	General Postal Union begins operations
1878	Universal Postal Union established (formerly General Postal Union)
1883	International Union for the Protection of Industrial Property established
1884	Berlin Conference
1885	International Statistical Institute established
1886	International Union for the Protection of Literary and Artistic Works established in accordance with the Berne Convention

1889	Inter-Parliamentary Union established
1890	Pan American Union starts
1893	International Touring Alliance established
June 23, 1894	International Olympic Committee established
1895	International Institute of Bibliography (later the International Federation for Information and Documentation) established
August 24, 1898	Czar Nicholas II of Russia proposes a general international conference to consider disarmament and the peaceful settlement of disputes
1899	International Bureau for the Suppression of Traffic in Persons established
May 18, 1899	Hague Conference adopts a convention on the laws and customs of war and agrees to creation of panel of arbitrators available for the purposes of conflict resolution
July 29, 1899	Permanent Court of Arbitration established
July 1900	First Pan-African Congress (London)
1901	International Federation of Trade Unions established
1902	Permanent Sugar Commission established
1905	International Institute of Agriculture established
1906	International Electrotechnical Commission established
1907	International Health Office established
June 15–October 18, 1907	Hague Conference discusses establishment of a standing court of arbitration, immunity of private property at sea in wartime, banning of force in the collection of international debts
1909	Anti-Slavery Society International formed out of merger of Aborigines Protection Society and the British and Foreign Anti-Slavery Society
May 1910	World Congress of International Associations (Brussels), which led to the establishment of the Union of International Associations

1913	Second World Congress of International Associations (169 international nongovernmental organizations and 22 governments attend)
August 1914	World War I begins
May 1915	British League of Nations Society founded
January 8, 1918	U.S. President Wilson delivers his Fourteen Points address before the U.S. Congress
November 11, 1918	World War I ends
1919	International Chamber of Commerce established; International Research Council established; International Federation of Travel Agencies established
February 1919	Second Pan-African Congress (Paris)
April 11, 1919	International Labour Organisation established as autonomous part of the League of Nations
April 28, 1919	League of Nations Covenant unanimously approved by the Paris Peace Conference
May 5, 1919	League of Red Cross and Red Crescent Societies established
1920	Save the Children International Union established; International Federation of Christian Trade Unions established
January 10, 1920	League of Nations established; Sir James Eric Drummond takes office as its first secretary-general
January 16, 1920	First session of the League of Nations Council
March 19, 1920	First vote in the U.S. Senate to approve U.S. participation in the League of Nations
November–December 1920	First session of the League of Nations Assembly
1921	International PEN established
Summer 1921	Refugee Organization established by the League of Nations
August–September 1921	Third Pan-African Congress (London and Brussels)
September 1921	Permanent Court of International Justice established as one of the League of Nations' principal organs

October 1921	Permanent Mandates Commission holds first session
November 1921–February 1922	Washington Naval Conference
1922	International Union of Railways established
November–December 1923	Fourth Pan-African Congress (London and Lisbon)
July 24, 1924	International Institute of Intellectual Cooperation established
October 16, 1925	Locarno Pacts signed
1926	International Federal of the National Standardizing Associations established
September 8, 1926	Germany joins the League of Nations
May 1927	World Economic Conference convened by League of Nations (Geneva)
August 1927	Fifth Pan-African Congress (New York)
September 30, 1927	International Federation of Library Associations established (now the International Federation of Library Associations and Institutions
October 1927	Conference on the Abolition of Import and Export Prohibitions or Restrictions convenes and adopts convention, which never enters into force
February 8, 1928	Protocol for the Prohibition of the Use in War of Asphyxiating, Poisonous or Other Gases, and of Bacteriological Methods of Warfare (Geneva Protocol) enters into effect
August 27, 1928	Pact for the Renunciation of War (Kellogg-Briand Pact) signed in Paris
1929	Federation of International Institutions founded to assist international nongovernmental organizations with practical matters (taxes, access to the League of Nations, etc.)
January 20, 1930	Bank for International Settlements established
April 1930	London Naval Treaty
1931	International Council of Scientific Unions established, replacing the International Research Council
September 18, 1931	Mukden Incident; Japan begins occupation of Manchuria

September 22, 1931	League of Nations Council meets to consider Chinese appeal to reestablish the status quo in Manchuria
October 24, 1931	League of Nations Council passes recommendation calling for withdrawal of Japanese troops from Manchuria
December 9, 1931	League of Nations passes resolution dispatching a League Commission on Inquiry to the Far East
December 31, 1931	The Commonwealth formalized
February 2, 1932	World Conference on Disarmament opens (Geneva)
March 9, 1932	Manchukuo established as a country independent of China
September 15, 1932	Japan recognizes Manchukuo as an independent country
December 9, 1932	International Telecommunication Union established
February 14, 1933	League of Nations Assembly adopts resolution calling on its members not to recognize Manchukuo as an independent country
March 27, 1933	Japans announces plans to withdraw from the League of Nations
June 1933	Joseph Avenol takes office as the second secretary-general of the League of Nations
June 12–July 27, 1933	League-sponsored World Economic Conference (London)
October 14, 1933	Germany announces plans to leave the League of Nations
September 18, 1934	Soviet Union joins the League of Nations
December 26, 1934	Convention on Rights and Duties of States enters into force
July 1935	African Postal and Telecommunications Union established
October 3, 1935	Italy invades Abyssinia
October 21, 1935	Germany withdraws from the League of Nations
November 18, 1935	League of Nations sanctions against Italy begin
March 7, 1936	Remilitarization of the Rhineland
May 6, 1936	Italian troops occupy Addis Ababa, Ethiopia

July 4, 1936	League of Nations sanctions against Italy terminated
July 7, 1937	Sino-Japanese War begins
November 30, 1939–March 1940	Winter War (USSR and Finland)
December 14, 1939	Soviet Union expelled from the League of Nations
1939–1945	World War II
August 31, 1940	Joseph Avenol resigns as secretary-general of the League of Nations; Sean Lester, the deputy secretary-general, replaces him for the duration of the League's existence
August 14, 1941	Declaration of the Atlantic Charter
January 1, 1942	Twenty-six countries sign the Declaration of United Nations stating war and peace aims (Washington, D.C.)
May 1943	United Nations Conference on Food and Agriculture (Hot Springs, Virginia); laid foundation for Food and Agriculture Organization
October 30, 1943	Moscow Declaration (USSR, United States, United Kingdom, and China pledges cooperation for establishment of a "general international organization")
November 1943	UN Relief and Rehabilitation Administration established
	Pan-African Federation established
July 22, 1944	Bretton Woods (New Hampshire) Conference develops plans for International Bank for Reconstruction and Development, International Monetary Fund, and International Trade Organization
August 21–October 7, 1944	Dumbarton Oaks Conference (USSR, United States, United Kingdom, and China) produces plans for the peace and security provisions of the UN Charter
December 7, 1944	Convention on International Civil Aviation (Chicago Convention) adopted and International Civil Aviation Organization established
1945	International Air Transport Association

	established; World Federation of Trade Unions established
February 4–11, 1945	Yalta Conference (Roosevelt, Churchill, and Stalin agree on voting formula for UN Security Council and date for San Francisco Conference)
March 22, 1945	League of Arab States established
April 9–June 26, 1945	San Francisco Conference (50 countries negotiate and sign UN Charter)
May 7, 1945	Germany surrenders
August 6, 1945	United States drops atomic bombs on Hiroshima
August 8, 1945	Agreement for the Prosecution and Punishment of the Major War Criminals of the European Axis Powers and Charter of the International Military Tribunal (Nuremberg Charter) enters into force
August 9, 1945	United States drops atomic bombs on Nagasaki
September 2, 1945	Japan surrenders
October 1945	Sixth Pan-African Congress (Manchester, England)
October 3, 1945	World Federation of Trade Unions established
October 16, 1945	Food and Agriculture Organization established
October 24, 1945	UN Charter and Statute of the International Court of Justice enter into force
1946	International Whaling Commission established; International Hotel Association established; European Federalist Movement established
January 10, 1946	First meeting of the UN General Assembly
January 17, 1946	First meeting of the UN Security Council
January 19, 1946	Iran brings the first dispute to the Security Council (presence of Soviet troops in Iran)
January 23, 1946	First meeting of the UN Economic and Social Council
January 24, 1946	UN Atomic Energy Commission established by UN General Assembly

February 1, 1946	Trygve Lie appointed first secretary-general of the UN
February 16, 1946	UN Commission on Narcotic Drugs established; UN Commission on Human Rights established; UN Economic and Employment Commission established; UN Statistical Commission established
April 3, 1946	International Court of Justice convenes for first time
April 8–18, 1946	League of Nations dissolved
June 21, 1946	UN Commission on the Status of Women established; UN Commission on Social Development established; UN Statistical Commission established
June 24, 1946	International Bank for Reconstruction and Development begins operations
July 22, 1946	World Health Organization established
September 21, 1946	Administrative Committee on Co-ordination established
October 3, 1946	UN Population Commission established
November 4, 1946	United Nations Educational, Scientific and Cultural Organization begins operations
December 11, 1946	United Nations International Children's Fund (UNICEF) established
December 14, 1946	International Labour Organisation, Food and Agriculture Organization, United Nations Educational, Scientific and Cultural Organization, and International Civil Aviation Organization become UN Specialized Agencies
1947	Modern Commonwealth established
February 6, 1947	South Pacific Commission established
February 23, 1947	International Organization for Standardization begins operations
March 1, 1947	International Monetary Fund begins operations
March 26–April 28, 1947	UN Trusteeship Council holds its first session
March 28, 1947	UN Economic Commission for Europe established; UN Economic Commission for Asia and Far East established
April 4, 1947	International Civil Aviation Organization begins operations

April 28–May 15, 1947	First UN General Assembly Special Session on Palestine
June 5, 1947	European Recovery (Marshall) Plan begins
June 6, 1947	International Patent Institute established
July 1947	International Union for the Protection of Nature established; Committee for European Economic Cooperation formed
October 5, 1947	Communist Information Bureau (COMINFORM) established
October 30, 1947	General Agreement on Tariffs and Trade agreed to
November 15, 1947	International Telecommunication Union, Universal Postal Union, World Health Organization, International Bank for Reconstruction and Development, and International Monetary Fund become UN Specialized Agencies
November 21, 1947	UN General Assembly establishes International Law Commission
December 1947	International Committee of the Movements for European Unity established
1948	World Council of Churches established; International Road Transport Union established
January 1, 1948	BENELUX Customs Union established; General Agreement on Tariffs and Trade enters into force
February 25, 1948	Economic Commission for Latin America and the Caribbean established
March 17, 1948	Brussels Treaty signed by Belgium, France, Luxembourg, Netherlands, and United Kingdom
April 7, 1948	World Health Organization begins operations
April 16, 1948	Organization for European Economic Cooperation established
April 30, 1948	Organization of American States established
May 1948	European Movement formed
May 2, 1948	American Declaration of the Rights and Duties of Man adopted
May 14, 1948	Israel proclaims itself an independent state

August 1948	International Refugee Organization begins operations; International Danube River conference
December 3, 1948	Inter-American Treaty of Reciprocal Assistance (Rio Treaty) enters into force
December 9, 1948	Convention on the Prevention and Punishment of the Crime of Genocide approved by UN General Assembly
December 10, 1948	UN General Assembly adopts the Universal Declaration of Human Rights
1949	UN Scientific Conference on the Conservation and Utilization of Resources established; World Association of Travel Agencies established
January 25, 1949	Council for Mutual Economic Assistance established
March 1949	UN Relief and Rehabilitation Administration abolished
April 1949	International Ruhr Authority established
April 4, 1949	North Atlantic Treaty Organization established
May 5, 1949	Council of Europe established
August 1949	UN Security Council creates United Nations Truce Supervision Organization as observers in Middle East
August 12, 1949	Geneva Convention Relative to the Protection of Civilian Persons in Time of War and Geneva Convention Relative to the Treatment of Prisoners of War adopted
December 1949	International Commission on Civil Status established; International Confederation of Free Trade Unions established
December 3, 1949	Office of the UN High Commissioner for Refugees established by the UN General Assembly
December 8, 1949	UN General Assembly creates United Nations Relief and Works Agency for Palestine Refugees in the Near East
January 13, 1950	Soviet Union withdraws from UN Security Council, protesting Chinese representation
May 9, 1950	Schuman Plan published

June 1950	Expanded Program of Technical Assistance begins operations
June 27, 1950	UN Security Council authorizes a Chapter VII military operation in response to North Korean military invasion of South Korea
October 1950	Plevan Plan published
November 3, 1950	UN General Assembly adopts the Uniting for Peace Resolution
November 4, 1950	European Convention for the Protection of Human Rights and Fundamental Freedoms signed
December 15, 1950	Customs Cooperation Council established
1951	International Press Institute established
January 1, 1951	Office of United Nations High Commissioner for Refugees begins operations
January 12, 1951	Convention on the Prevention and Punishment of Genocide comes into force
April 4, 1951	World Meteorological Organization becomes UN Specialized Agency
April 18, 1951	Treaty of Paris signed establishing the European Coal and Steel Community
July 1, 1951	Colombo Plan established
July 2–25, 1951	UN Conference on the Status of Refugees and Stateless Persons
July 28, 1951	Convention Relating to the Status of Refugees opened for signature
September 1, 1951	ANZUS Council established
December 5, 1951	Intergovernmental Committee for European Migration established
December 13, 1951	Organization of American States begins operations
January 31, 1952	International Refugee Organization ceases operations
March 16, 1952	Nordic Council established
May 1952	European Defense Community treaty signed
July 1952	European Coal and Steel Community begins operations
November 1, 1952	United States detonates hydrogen bomb
November 10, 1952	Trygve Lie submits resignation as UN secretary-general

1953	International Planned Parenthood Federation established
March 5, 1953	Josef Stalin dies
April 10, 1953	Dag Hammarskjöld assumes office as UN secretary-general
July 27, 1953	Korean armistice agreement
September 3, 1953	European Convention for the Protection of Human Rights and Fundamental Freedoms enters into force
April 22, 1954	Convention Relating to the Status of Refugees enters into force
July 7, 1954	Convention on the Political Rights of Women enters into force
August 30, 1954	European Defense Community voted down by French parliament
August 31–September 10, 1954	World Population Conference (Rome)
September 8, 1954	Treaty establishing the Southeast Asia Treaty Organization signed
September 29, 1954	European Organization for Nuclear Research begins operations
October 1954	Western European Union treaty signed
October 23, 1954	Germany joins the North Atlantic Treaty Organization
1955	Central Bank of West African States established; Afro-Asian Conference on Solidarity established
February 18, 1955	Baghdad Pact signed by Iraq and Turkey
April 18–24, 1955	Bandung Conference
May 6, 1955	Western European Union begins operations
May 9, 1955	West Germany becomes a member of the North Atlantic Treaty Organization
July 15, 1955	Bank of Central African States established
August 8–20, 1955	First International Conference on the Peaceful Uses of Atomic Energy
October 10, 1955	Treaty of Friendship, Cooperation and Mutual Assistance (Warsaw Pact) enters into force
December 14, 1955	Sixteen new members admitted to UN as a consequence of East-West "package deal"
1956	Afro-Asian Organization for Economic Cooperation established
April 17, 1956	Communist Information Bureau disbanded

June 13, 1956	International Criminal Police Organization established
July 1956	Paris Club formed
July 16, 1956	Egypt nationalizes the Suez Canal
July 24, 1956	International Finance Corporation begins operations
October 23–November 22, 1956	Hungarian rebellion
October 26, 1956	International Atomic Energy Agency established
October 29–November 6, 1956	Suez crisis
November 1–10, 1956	UN General Assembly convenes Emergency Special Session on Suez crisis
November 4–10, 1956	UN General Assembly convenes Emergency Special Session on Hungarian crisis
November 5, 1956	UN General Assembly authorizes establishment of the United Nations Emergency Force
1957	Society for International Development established
March 25, 1957	Treaty of Rome establishing the European Economic Community and European Atomic Energy Agency signed
December 26, 1957	Afro-Asian People's Solidarity Organization established
1958	All-African People's Congress (Accra, Ghana)
January 1958	All Africa Conference of Churches established
January 1, 1958	European Economic Community, European Atomic Energy Agency, and European Investment Bank begin operations
February 3, 1958	BENELUX Economic Union established
February 24–April 27, 1958	First UN Conference on the Law of the Sea
March 17, 1958	Intergovernmental Maritime Consultative Organization established
April 1958	Conference on Independent African States (Accra, Ghana)
April 29, 1958	United Nations Economic Commission for Africa established
June 11, 1958	UN Security Council establishes the UN Observer Group in Lebanon

July 26, 1958	International Convention for the Prevention of Pollution of the Sea by Oil enters into force
August 1958	UN General Assembly Emergency Special Session on Lebanon and Jordan
December 1958	French Community established
January 1, 1959	Special Fund for technical assistance begins operations
April 1959	Pan-Africanist Manifesto adopted
April 8, 1959	International-American Development Bank established
May 25, 1959	Council of the Entente established
June 9, 1959	West African Customs Union established
June 23, 1959	Equatorial African Customs Union established
July 19, 1959	Community of Independent African States established
August 1959	Monrovia Conference of Foreign Ministers of Independent African States
November 20, 1959	European Free Trade Association established
December 1, 1959	Antarctic Treaty signed
1960	Second All-African People's Congress (Tunis)
March 17–April 26, 1960	Second UN Conference on the Law of the Sea
May 3, 1960	Stockholm Convention establishing the European Free Trade Association signed
June 1960	Second Conference of Independent African States (Addis Ababa, Ethiopia)
July 1960	African and Malagasy Coffee Organization established
July 14, 1960	UN Security Council authorizes UN secretary-general to deploy peacekeeping forces to Congo
September 14, 1960	Organization of Petroleum Exporting Countries established
September 17–20, 1960	UN General Assembly Emergency Special Session convenes on the Congo crisis
September 19, 1960	Indus River dispute between India and Pakistan settled with assistance of the International Bank for Reconstruction and Development
September 22, 1960	Soviet Union proposes abolition of post of

	UN secretary-general and replacement by a three-person security body
September 24, 1960	International Development Association begins operations
November 1, 1960	BENELUX Economic Union begins operations
December 1960	Brazzaville Group Conference; European Organization for Safety of Air Navigation established; European Launcher Development Organization established
December 7, 1960	Inter-African Coffee Organization established
December 13, 1960	Central American Common Market established; Central American Bank for Economic Integration established
December 14, 1960	UN General Assembly adopts the Declaration on the Granting of Independence to Colonial Countries and Peoples
December 14, 1960	Organisation for Economic Co-operation and Development replaces the Organization for European Economic Co-operation
1961	World Wildlife Fund established
January 1961	Casablanca Group Conference
March 1961	All African People's Congress (Cairo, Egypt)
March 1961	Air Afrique established
April 17–20, 1961	Bay of Pigs invasion
May 1961	South Africa leaves the Commonwealth; Monrovia Group Conference
August 15, 1961	Construction of Berlin Wall commences
August 21–31, 1961	UN Conference on New Sources of Energy
September 1–6, 1961	Conference of Nonaligned Movement (Belgrade, Yugoslavia)
September 8, 1961	African and Malagasy Union established
September 17, 1961	Dag Hammarskjöld killed in plane crash in Northern Rhodesia on way to meet leader of secessionist province of Katanga, Congo
November 3, 1961	U Thant unanimously appointed UN acting secretary-general
November 24, 1961	World Food Programme established

December 1961	African Telecommunications Union established
December 2, 1961	African Postal Union established
December 9, 1961	East African Common Services Organization established
1962	Monetary Union of Equatorial Africa and Cameroon established
May 1962	Cocoa Producers' Alliance established
May 12, 1962	West African Monetary Union established
August 1, 1962	Pan-African Women's Organization established
September 13, 1962	African Intellectual Property Organization established; African and Mauritian Union of Development Banks established
October 22–28, 1962	Cuban Missile Crisis
November 1, 1962	Central Bank of West African States established
November 30, 1962	U Thant elected UN secretary-general
1963	East African Postal and Telecommunications Corporation established
January 1963	World Food Programme begins operations
February 4–20, 1963	Conference on the Application of Science and Technology for the Benefit of Less Developed Countries
April 1963	Bern Convention on Combating and Controlling Pollution in the Rhine signed
May 14–June 17, 1963	UN General Assembly Special Session on Financial and Budgetary Problems
May 25, 1963	Charter of the Organization of African Unity signed
June 17, 1963	International Labour Organisation cancels credentials of South Africa
July 1963	First Yaoundé Convention signed
August 4, 1963	African Development Bank established
October 10, 1963	Treaty Banning Nuclear Weapons Tests in the Atmosphere, in Outer Space and under Water of August 5, 1963, enters into force
October 26, 1963	River Niger Commission established
December 18, 1963	South Africa withdraws from the Food and Agriculture Organization

1964	Group of 77 established
March 1964	African and Malagasy Union of Economic Cooperation established; European Space Research Organization established
March 14, 1964	UN peacekeepers deployed to Cyprus
March 23–June 16, 1964	UNCTAD I
May 22, 1964	Lake Chad Basin Commission established
May 28, 1964	Palestine Liberation Organization established
June 5, 1964	South Africa excluded from Universal Postal Union
June 18, 1964	African Groundnut Council established
June 30, 1964	UN peacekeepers leave Congo
August 3, 1964	Gulf of Tonkin incident
October 5–11, 1964	Conference of Nonaligned Nations (Cairo, Egypt)
December 1, 1964	19th Session of UN General Assembly, so-called "no vote" session, begins
December 8, 1964	Central African Customs and Economic Union established
December 30, 1964	United Nations Conference on Trade and Development formally established, without a vote, by the UN General Assembly
1965	Regional Cooperation for Development established
February 26, 1965	European Social Charter enters into force
March 18, 1965	International Centre for Settlement of Investment Disputes established
April 8, 1965	European Communities established
August 30–September 10, 1965	World Population Conference (Belgrade, Yugoslavia)
August 31, 1965	UN Charter amendments in force; Security Council and Economic and Social Council enlarged; change in voting majority of Security Council
November 22, 1965	United Nations Development Program created by combining Expanded Program of Technical Assistance and United Nations Special Fund
December 21, 1965	UN Convention on the Elimination of All Forms of Racial Discrimination opens for ratification

1966	Customs Union of West African States established
January 1966	Luxembourg Compromise worked out by the European Economic Community
May 1966	European Economic Community agrees on a Common Agricultural Policy
June 27, 1966	African and Mauritian Common Organization established
July 1966	France withdraws from North Atlantic Treaty Organization, remains a party to the North Atlantic Treaty
November 17, 1966	United Nations Industrial Development Organization established by the UN General Assembly
December 13, 1966	United Nations Capital Development Fund established
December 15, 1966	UN Security Council invokes Chapter VII by voting to impose compulsory economic sanctions against Southern Rhodesia, first such action by the UN
December 16, 1966	UN General Assembly unanimously approves the International Covenant on Economic, Social, and Cultural Rights and the International Covenant on Civil and Political Rights
December 19, 1966	Asian Development Bank established
February 14, 1967	Agency for the Prohibition of Nuclear Weapons in Latin America and the Caribbean established
April 21–June 13, 1967	UN General Assembly Special Session on Review of Peacekeeping Operations and Southwest Africa
May 19, 1967	UN secretary-general agrees to withdraw United Nations Emergency Force troops
June 1967	Kennedy Round of the General Agreement on Tariffs and Trade concludes
June 6, 1967	East African Community established
June 17–September 8, 1967	UN General Assembly Emergency Special Session on the Middle East Crisis
July 1967	UN Fund for Population Activities begins operations
July 8, 1967	Fighting commences along the Suez Canal
July 14, 1967	World Intellectual Property Organization established

August 9, 1967	Association of Southeast Asian Nations established
October 10, 1967	Treaty on Principles Governing the Activities of States in the Exploration and Use of Outer Space, including the Moon and other Celestial Bodies of January 27, 1967 enters into force
December 1, 1967	East African Community begins operations
1968	International Year of Human Rights; Intergovernmental Conference of Experts on a Scientific Basis for a Rational Use and Conservation of the Resources of the Biosphere (Paris)
January 9, 1968	Organization of Arab Petroleum Exporting Countries established
March 2, 1968	Organization of Senegal River States established
April 4, 1968	Arab Fund for Economic and Social Development established
April 22–May 13, 1968	International Conference on Human Rights (Teheran, Iran)
June 4, 1968	Treaty on the Non-Proliferation of Nuclear Weapons opens for signature and ratification
June 12, 1968	General Assembly proclaims Southwest Africa to be known in the future as Namibia
August 20–21, 1968	Warsaw Treaty Organization troops invade Czechoslovakia
December 20, 1968	UN General Assembly establishes Committee on the Peaceful Uses of the Sea-Bed and the Ocean Floor Beyond the Limits of National Jurisdiction
1969	Friends of the Earth established
January 4, 1969	International Convention on the Elimination of all Forms of Racial Discrimination enters into force
February 16, 1969	Arab Cooperation Council established
February 26, 1969	African and Malagasy Coffee Organization established
May 26, 1969	Andean Group established
June 1969	Bonn Agreement on combating pollution in the North Sea signed

July 1969	Second Yaoundé Convention signed
September 22–25, 1969	Organization of the Islamic Conference established
October 16, 1969	Andean Group begins operations
October 18, 1969	Caribbean Development Bank established
November 22, 1969	American Convention on Human Rights "Pact of San José, Costa Rica" adopted
December 4, 1969	Convention on Offences and Certain Other Acts Committed on Board Aircraft (Tokyo Convention) of September 14, 1963, enters into force
December 11, 1969	Southern African Customs Union established
1970	International Education Year and International Year to Combat Racism and Racial Discrimination
March 2, 1970	Rhodesia issues Unilateral Declaration of Independence from United Kingdom
March 5, 1970	Treaty on the Non-Proliferation of Nuclear Weapons enters into force
March 21, 1970	Agency for Cultural and Technical Cooperation established
May 1970	West African Customs Union dissolved
July 7, 1970	International Investment Bank established
September 8–10, 1970	Conference of Nonaligned Nations (Lusaka, Zambia)
November 1970	European political cooperation begins
1971	West African Rice Development Association established
January 1, 1971	United Nations Volunteers established
April 1, 1971	UN Fund for Drug Abuse Control established
May 1971	European Communities issue first joint foreign policy declaration
July 21, 1971	International Court of Justice rules that South Africa is illegally holding Namibia
August 5, 1971	South Pacific Forum established
August 15, 1971	United States abandons the gold exchange standard, in effect ending Bretton Woods monetary system
October 14, 1971	Convention on the Suppression of Unlawful Seizure of Aircraft (Hague

	Convention) of December 16, 1970 enters into force
October 25, 1971	UN General Assembly votes to have People's Republic of China replace Republic of China (Taiwan) at all organs of UN
December 14, 1971	General Assembly establishes the Office of United Nations Disaster Relief Coordinator
January 1, 1972	Kurt Waldheim becomes secretary-general of the United Nations
March 1972	European Communities establish the "snake"
March 11, 1972	Organization for the Development of the Senegal River established
May 1972	West African Health Community established
June 5–16, 1972	UN Conference on the Human Environment (Stockholm, Sweden)
November 22, 1972	Central African Monetary Union established
November 23, 1972	Bank of Central African States established
December 15, 1972	UN General Assembly approves creation of United Nations Environment Program
January 1, 1973	Denmark, Ireland, and United Kingdom become members of the European Community
January 26, 1973	Convention for the Suppression of Unlawful Acts against the Safety of Civil Aviation (Montreal Convention) of September 23, 1971, enters into force
February 1973	European Trade Union Confederation founded
February 12, 1973	International Telecommunications Satellite Organization begins operations
May 1973	Organization of African Unity adopts the "African Declaration on Cooperation, Development, and Economic Independence" (the Addis Ababa Declaration)
June 3, 1973	West African Economic Community established

July 3, 1973	Conference on Security and Cooperation in Europe opens (Helsinki, Finland)
July 4, 1973	Caribbean Community and Common Market established
August 9, 1973	Economic Commission for Western Asia established
September 5–9, 1973	Conference of Nonaligned Nations (Algiers, Algeria)
September 12, 1973	Inter-State Committee for Drought Control in the Sahel established
October 3, 1973	Mano River Union established
October 17, 1973–March 18, 1974	OAPEC oil embargo
November 14, 1973	West African Development Bank established
December 3, 1973	Third Law of the Sea Convention begins
December 15, 1973	Islamic Development Bank established
1974	World Population Year; Environmental Liaison Center established as liaison between international nongovernmental organizations and the United Nations Environmental Program; Nuclear Suppliers Group established; Seventh Pan-African Congress (Dar es Salaam, Tanzania); West African Economic Community established
February 18, 1974	Arab Bank for Economic Development in Africa established
May 1, 1974	UN General Assembly adopts Declaration on the Establishment of a New International Economic Order at Special Session on Raw Materials and Development
May 31, 1974	UN Security Council authorizes peacekeeping forces for the Golan Heights
June 15, 1974	African Civil Aviation Commission established
August 19–30, 1974	World Population Conference (Bucharest, Romania)
September 16, 1974	Arab Bank for Economic Development in Africa begins operations
November 1974	International Fund for Agricultural Development established
November 5–16, 1974	World Food Conference (Rome)

November 15, 1974	International Energy Agency established
December 12, 1974	UN General Assembly adopts Charter of Economic Rights and Duties of States
December 17, 1974	World Food Council established; World Intellectual Property Organization becomes UN Specialized Agency
1975	International Women's Year
January 2, 1975	World Tourism Organization established
February 1, 1975	Lomé I
March 1975	European Council meets for first time (Dublin, Ireland)
March 17–28, 1975	UN Commission on Transnational Corporations holds first session
March 26, 1975	Convention on the Prohibition of the Development, Production and Stockpiling of Bacteriological and Toxic Weapons enters into force
May 1, 1975	European Space Agency begins operations
May 19–30, 1975	International Civil Service Commission holds first session
May 28, 1975	Economic Community of West African States established
June 6, 1975	African, Caribbean, and Pacific group of states established
June 19–July 1, 1975	World Conference of the International Women's Year (Mexico City, Mexico)
August 1, 1975	Helsinki Final Act signed
August 30, 1975	Convention on the Prevention of Marine Pollution by Dumping of Wastes and Other Matter enters into force
September 1, 1975	United Nations University begins operations
September 1–6, 1975	UN General Assembly Special Session on Development and International Economic Cooperation
October 17, 1975	Latin American Economic System established
October 24, 1975	African Postal and Telecommunications Union established
November 10, 1975	UN General Assembly approves a resolution that determines that Zionism is a form of racism and racial discrimination

December 1975	Independent European Program Group within NATO formed
December 1975–June 1977	Conference on International Economic Cooperation (Paris)
December 3, 1975	Development Bank of Central African States established
December 17, 1975	Convention for the Protection of the World Cultural and Natural Heritage enters into force
December 23, 1975	Club of the Sahel founded
1976	African Solidarity Fund established
January 3, 1976	International Covenant on Economic, Social, and Cultural Rights enters into force
February 1976	Union of African Parliamentarians established
March 23, 1976	International Covenant on Civil and Political Rights enters into force, except for Article 41, permitting states to bring complaints about other states to the Human Rights Committee, which entered into force on March 28, 1979
April 27, 1976	Arab Monetary Fund established
May 1976	International Research and Training Institute for the Advancement of Women established by the UN Economic and Social Council
May 31–June 11, 1976	United Nations Conference on Human Settlements (Vancouver, Canada)
June 1, 1976	Nordic Investment Bank begins operations
June 2, 1976	African Timber Organization established
June 14–17, 1976	World Employment Conference (Geneva)
July 1, 1976	Convention on International Trade in Endangered Species (CITES) of Wild Fauna and Flora enters into force
August 16–19, 1976	Conference of Nonaligned Nations (Colombo, Sri Lanka)
September 3, 1976	International Maritime Satellite Organization established
September 26, 1976	Economic Community of the Great Lakes States established
December 16, 1976	United Nations Development Fund for Women established
1977	East African Community collapses

March 1977	First Afro-Arab Summit Conference
March 14–25, 1977	United Nations Water Conference (Mar del Plata, Argentina)
May 18, 1977	Convention on the Prohibition of Military and any other Hostile Use of Environment Modification Techniques opens for signature and ratification
June 30, 1977	Southeast Asia Treaty Organization dissolved
August 24, 1977	Organization for the Management and Development of the Kagara River Basin established
August 29–September 9, 1977	United Nations Conference on Desertification (Nairobi, Kenya)
September 9, 1977	Development Bank of the Great Lakes States established
November 1977	International Fund for Agricultural Development begins operations
November 4, 1977	Under Chapter VII of the UN Charter, the UN Security Council votes unanimously to impose a mandatory arms embargo on South Africa. First Chapter VII action against a UN member
November 19–21, 1977	Egyptian President Sadat visits Israel
December 20, 1977	UN General Assembly establishes new post of director-general for economic development
1978	African Oilseed Producers' Organization established
March 1978	United Nations Interim Force in Lebanon established; International Convention on the Carriage of Goods by Sea adopted
April 1978	UN General Assembly Special Session on Financing of UN Interim Force in Lebanon
April–May 1978	UN General Assembly Special Session on Namibia
May 1978	Gambia River Basin Development Organization established
May–June 1978	UN General Assembly Special Session on Disarmament
July 18, 1978	American Convention on Human Rights "Pact of San José, Costa Rica" enters into force

August 4, 1978	European Convention on the Suppression of Terrorism of January 27, 1977, enters into force
August 14–25, 1978	World Conference to Combat Racism and Racial Discrimination (Geneva)
August 30–September 12, 1978	UN Conference on Technical Cooperation among Developing Countries (Buenos Aires, Argentina)
October 1978	UN Disarmament Commission established
October 12, 1978	UN Commission on Human Settlements established
1979	Statute of Inter-American Commission on Human Rights adopted
February 23, 1979	International Tea Promotion Association established
March 1979	European Monetary System established
June 1979	First direct elections of European Parliament
July 12–20, 1979	Conference on Agrarian Reform and Rural Development (Rome, Italy)
July 20, 1979	International Maritime Satellite Organization begins operations
August 20–31, 1979	United Nations Conference on Science and Technology for Development (Vienna, Austria)
September 3–8, 1979	Conference of Nonaligned Nations (Havana, Cuba)
September 26, 1979	Central Treaty Organization dissolved
October 1979	Lomé II
December 27, 1979	Soviet invasion of Afghanistan begins
January 1980	UN General Assembly Emergency Special Session on Afghanistan
April 1, 1980	Southern African Development Coordination Committee established
May 1980	Economic Community of West African States adopts a defense pact
May 24, 1980	International Court of Justice rules Iran violated international law in seizing U.S. embassy and personnel
July 1980	UN General Assembly Emergency Special Session on Palestine
July 14–30, 1980	World Conference of the United Nations Decade for Women: Equality,

	Development and Peace (Copenhagen, Denmark)
August–September 1980	UN General Assembly Special Session on International Economic Cooperation
September 22, 1980	Iraq invades Iran
November 1980	Intergovernmental Committee for Migration replaces the Intergovernmental Committee for European Migration
November 21, 1980	Niger Basin Authority established
January 1, 1981	Greece becomes a member of the European Community
March 18, 1981	Latin American Integration Association begins operations
April 9–10, 1981	First International Conference on Assistance to African Refugees (Geneva)
May 25, 1981	Gulf Cooperation Council established
June 18, 1981	Organization of Eastern Caribbean States established
June 27, 1981	Assembly of Heads of State and Government of the Organization of African Unity adopts the African Charter on Human and Peoples' Rights (Banjul Charter)
August 10–21, 1981	United Nations Conference on New and Renewable Sources of Energy (Nairobi, Kenya)
September 1981	UN General Assembly Emergency Special Session on Namibia
September 1–14, 1981	Conference on Least Developed Countries (Paris)
September 3, 1981	Convention on the Elimination of All Forms of Discrimination against Women enters into force
November 15, 1981	Organization of African Unity peacekeeping troops begin to arrive in Chad
January–February 1982	UN General Assembly Emergency Special Session on Israeli Occupied Arab Territories
January 1, 1982	Javier Peréz de Cuéllar begins his term as UN secretary-general
April 2–July 15, 1982	Falklands/Malvinas War

May 22, 1982	International Maritime Organization replaces Intergovernmental Maritime Consultative Organization
June 12, 1982	Organization of African Unity orders withdrawal of its peacekeeping troops from Chad
December 1982	Third Law of the Sea Convention concludes and treaty opened for signature
1983	World Communications Year
January 1983	European Communities adopt a Common Fisheries Policy
March 7–17, 1983	Conference of Nonaligned Nations (New Delhi, India)
June 3, 1983	International Convention Against the Taking of Hostages enters into force
August 1–12, 1983	Second World Conference to Combat Racism and Racial Discrimination (Geneva)
October 18, 1983	Economic Community of Central African States established
December 1983	Eastern and Southern African Trade and Development Bank established
1984	Demise of the African and Malagasy Common Organization
January 1984	European Communities and European Free Trade Association establish a free trade area
June 1984	Western European Union agreed to as a European defense forum
July 11, 1984	Agreement Governing the Activities of States on the Moon and other Celestial Bodies enters into force
August 6–14, 1984	World Population Conference (Mexico City, Mexico)
December 1984	Lomé III
1984–85	United States, United Kingdom, and Singapore withdraw from UNESCO
1985	African Palm Oil Development Association established
1985	Economic Cooperation Organization established
March 1985	European Council agrees to a single internal market by December 1992

July 15–27, 1985	Conference to Review and Appraise Achievements of the United Nations Decade for Women (Nairobi, Kenya)
November 13–18, 1985	World Conference on the International Youth Year, 1985
December 8, 1985	South Asian Association for Regional Cooperation established
January 1, 1986	Portugal and Spain become members of the European Community
February 1986	First Francophone Summit (Paris)
February 1986	Single European Act signed
April 26, 1986	Chernobyl nuclear disaster
May–June 1986	UN General Assembly Special Session on the Critical Economic Situation in Africa
September 1986	UN General Assembly Special Session on Namibia
September 1–7, 1986	Nonaligned Movement summit (Harare, Zimbabwe)
September 15, 1986	Uruguay Round of the General Agreement on Tariffs and Trade opens
October 21, 1986	African Charter on Human and Peoples' Rights enters into force
October 27, 1986	Convention on Early Notification of a Nuclear Accident enters into force
December 11, 1986	South Pacific Nuclear Free Zone Treaty enters into force
January 1, 1987	United Nations Fund for Science and Technology for Development established
January 27, 1987	African Petroleum Producers' Organization established
February 26, 1987	Convention on Assistance in the Case of a Nuclear Accident or Radiological Emergency enters into force
March 23–April 10, 1987	UN Conference for the Promotion of International Cooperation in the Peaceful Uses of Nuclear Energy (Geneva)
June 17–26, 1987	International Conference on Drug Abuse and Illicit Trafficking (Vienna, Austria)
June 26, 1987	Convention Against Torture and Other Cruel, Inhuman or Degrading Treatment

	or Punishment of December 10, 1984, enters into force
July 1987	Single European Act takes effect
August 1987	World Commission on Environment and Development report issued
August 24–September 11, 1987	International Conference on the Relationship between Disarmament and Development (New York)
April 12, 1988	Multilateral Investment Guarantee Agency established
May–June 1988	UN General Assembly Special Session on Disarmament
August 22–24, 1988	International Conference on the Plight of Refugees, Returnees, and Displaced Persons in Southern Africa (Oslo, Norway)
September 22, 1988	Vienna Convention for the Protection of the Ozone Layer enters into force
February 17, 1989	Arab Maghreb Union established
March 22, 1989	Convention on the Control of Transboundary Movements of Hazardous Wastes and Their Disposal enters into force
April 1989–March 1990	United Nations Transition Assistance Group assists Namibian transition to self-rule
May 29–31, 1989	International Conference on Central American Refugees (Guatemala City, Guatemala)
June 13–14, 1989	International Conference on Indochinese Refugees (Geneva)
September 1989	UN General Assembly Special Session on Apartheid
September 4–7, 1989	Nonaligned Movement summit (Belgrade, Yugoslavia)
November 7, 1989	Asia Pacific Economic Cooperation Forum established
November 9, 1989	Berlin Wall collapses
November 14, 1989	International Organization for Migration replaces the Intergovernmental Committee for Migration
December 1989	Lomé IV
February 1990	UN General Assembly Special Session on Drug Problems

March 4–9, 1990	World Conference on Education for All: Meeting Basic Learning Needs (Jomtien, Thailand)
March 22, 1990	Namibia becomes independent
June 7, 1990	Warsaw Treaty Organization informally abandoned
August–November 1990	UN Security Council adopts resolutions relating to Iraqi invasion of Kuwait
August 2, 1990	Iraq invades Kuwait
September 2, 1990	Convention on the Rights of the Child enters into force
September 29–30, 1990	World Summit on Children (New York)
October 3, 1990	East and West Germany combine
October 29–November 7, 1990	World Climate Change Convention (Geneva)
November 21, 1990	Charter of Paris for a New Europe signed
January 1991	Council for Mutual Economic Assistance ceases operations
March 7, 1991	Montreal Protocol on Substances that Deplete the Ozone Layer enters into force
March 26, 1991	Southern Cone Common Market established
April 1991	UN Security Council establishes UN Iraq-Kuwait Observation Mission to monitor Iraq-Kuwait border
April 1991	UN Observer Mission for the Referendum in Western Sahara established
April 15, 1991	European Bank for Reconstruction and Development begins operations
May 1991	UN Observer Mission in El Salvador established to monitor cease-fire and human rights situation
May 2, 1991	International Convention on the Protection of the Rights of All Migrant Workers and Members of Their Families opens for signature
June 25, 1991	Croatia and Slovenia declare independence from Yugoslavia
August 20, 1991	Estonia declares independence
September 5, 1991	Convention Concerning Indigenous and Tribal Peoples in Independent Countries enters into force
November 1991	European Communities and European

	Statement of Principles for a Global Consensus on the Management, Conservation and Sustainable Development of All Types of Forests adopted
June 17, 1992	An Agenda for Peace presented to the UN General Assembly
June 25, 1992	Black Sea Economic Cooperation established
August 17, 1992	Southern African Development Community established replacing Southern African Development Coordination Conference
September 1–6, 1992	Nonaligned Movement summit (Jakarta, Indonesia)
December 1992	UN operation in Mozambique established to monitor cease-fire and electoral process and to coordinate humanitarian aid
January 1, 1993	Single European market established
February 12, 1993	UN Commission on Sustainable Development established
May 25, 1993	UN Security Council authorizes establishment of International Tribunal for Crimes committed in the former Yugoslavia
June 1993	UN Security Council establishes UN Observer Mission Uganda-Rwanda to prevent military assistance from crossing the border
June 14–25, 1993	World Conference on Human Rights (Vienna, Austria)
August 24, 1993	UN Security Council establishes UN Observer Mission in Georgia
September 1993	UN Security Council imposes sanctions against Haiti
October 5, 1993	UN Security Council establishes UN Assistance Mission for Rwanda to monitor security situation and to coordinate humanitarian aid
October 5–6, 1993	International Conference on African Development (Tokyo, Japan)
October 8, 1993	UN General Assembly lifts all previous sanctions against South Africa

November 1, 1993	European Union begins operations
December 1993	UN General Assembly creates position of UN High Commissioner for Human Rights
December 15, 1993	Uruguay Round of the General Agreements on Tariffs and Trade concludes
December 29, 1993	Convention on Biological Diversity enters into force
April 25–May 6, 1994	Global Conference on Sustainable Development of Small Island Developing States (Bridgetown, Barbados)
May 23–27, 1994	World Conference on Natural Disaster Detection (Yokohama, Japan)
March 21, 1994	United Nations Framework Convention on Climate Change enters into force
September 5–13, 1994	World Population and Development Conference (Cairo, Egypt)
October 18, 1994	International Conference on Families as part of the Year of Families
November 16, 1994	Third Law of the Sea Treaty enters into force; International Sea-Bed Authority established
November 21–23, 1994	World Ministerial Conference on Organized Transnational Crime (Naples, Italy)
January 1, 1995	World Trade Organization replaces the General Agreement on Tariffs and Trade organization, although the GATT itself continues as an agreement under the WTO; Austria, Finland, and Sweden become members of the European Community
March 6–12, 1995	World Summit for Social Development (Copenhagen, Denmark)
September 4–15, 1995	Fourth World Conference on Women (Beijing, China)
June 3–14, 1996	Second UN Conference on Human Settlements (Istanbul, Turkey)
January 1, 1997	Kofi Annan takes over as UN secretary-general
May 1997	Euro-Atlantic Partnership Council established

July 1997	NATO invites Czech Republic, Hungary, and Poland to initiate the process to become NATO members by 1999
December 1997	European Union agrees to open membership negotiations with 11 Eastern and Central European countries and engage in a strategy of rapprochement with Turkey, another applicant for membership
March 25, 1998	European Commission recommended that 11 countries met the necessary conditions to adopt the single currency, the euro, on January 1, 1999: Austria, Belgium, Finland, France, Germany, Ireland, Italy, Luxembourg, Netherlands, Portugal, Spain
May 1998	India and Pakistan test nuclear weapons

Introduction

The term *international organizations* is rarely used precisely. At times, it is even confused with the *process* of governments working together to achieve greater cooperation or world order. That is best thought of as international *organization* (in the singular).

International *organizations* (IOs), on the other hand, are the bureaucracies that often result from governments working together to solve their problems. They have letterheads, offices—often buildings—and some sort of permanent staff (the secretariat), usually paid and full-time.

The members of *intergovernmental* organizations (IGOs) are governments or predominantly government representatives. (See the chart summarizing this and other differentiating characteristics of different varieties of IOs.) The International Labour Organisation (ILO) is the most prominent example of an IGO where the representatives are not simply governments. Representatives of labor unions and management are also voting participants.

Some IGOs are called *universal* in the sense that membership is open to all countries in the world. They need not all be members to be called universal or global, however. Other IGOs are called *regional* because their membership is restricted. Only some governments are eligible for membership. These are often geographically restricted like the Organization of American States (OAS), which is restricted to countries in the Western Hemisphere. But even IGOs such as the Organisation for Economic Co-operation and Development (OECD) are referred to as regional organizations, although its members stretch from Turkey to Japan. Membership in the OECD is restricted, however. Only relatively rich countries with capitalist economies can join. Thus, it is not a universal IGO.

By tradition, IGOs have to have at least three member states. This tradition results in the omission of some quite influential and old organizations from the definition of IGOs, such as the International Joint Commission, which deals with a wide variety of water (including environmental) issues between the United States and Canada. Organizations like this are called *bilateral* organizations.

The most numerous group of international organizations is *international nongovernmental organizations*, often simply referred to as

1

Varieties of International Organizations

Type	Acronym	Geographical Coverage	Members	Source of Funding	Other Defining Characteristics	Example	Relationship to This Dictionary
Intergovernmental organizations	IGOs	Universal (open to all countries) or Regional (open only to some countries)	Almost always represent countries; by tradition more than two countries (otherwise called bilateral organizations)	Usually government appropriates (regular dues or voluntary contributions)	Not for profit	United Nations	Includes all major (current) and some prominent from the past
International nongovernmental organizations	NGOs	Often based in one country, but membership includes representatives from more than one country and/or influence transcends a single country	Represent national associations	Private membership contributions and/or from governments or IGOs	Not for profit; may or may not have consultative status granted by IGOs	Amnesty International	Most prominent included
Multinational corporations	MNCs	Often based in one country but operations are in more than one country	Corporations	Sales	Intended to make profit	General Motors	Not included

NGOs (or less often, INGOs). The variety of NGOs in this loosely defined category is even greater than that of IGOs. Some—as in this *dictionary*—exclude NGOs whose intent is to make profits. They are better referred to as multinational corporations (MNCs), transnational corporations (TNCs), or business international nongovernmental organizations (BINGOs).

Some people include in their definition of NGOs nongovernmental organizations that operate in a single country but whose *impact* affects those outside that country. In an increasingly interconnected world, that definition would seem to include almost all organizations not a part of government. Most pressure groups, for example, influence policies in other countries and in IGOs, whether they intend it or not. Thus, it seems better to limit our attention to NGOs and international NGOs whose *memberships* are from three or more countries or whose influence is *directed* at people outside the country where its headquarters are located.

Even what might seem most straightforward in this definitional maze is not: the degree to which nongovernmental organizations are independent of governments. As noted earlier, NGOs differ from IGOs because the latter are composed of government representatives. The representatives of NGOs come from a variety of countries, but they do *not* represent governments. However, funds for NGOs *can* come from governments, either directly or indirectly (e.g., from IGOs). Some NGOs shun funds from IGOs and governments—Amnesty International is an example—fearing they will lose the support of some of their constituents if they took it and thus lose global influence and respect. However, others, especially those involved in economic development and disaster relief work, are heavily dependent on government and IGO funding for their survival. It is interesting to note, in this context, that the World Bank (an IGO) has discovered that just as it has begun to see the advantages of working with NGOs, including funding them to help implement some of the World Bank's policies, some NGOs have pulled away from it. The NGOs apparently feared that working with an IGO would significantly diminish their influence, especially working with the World Bank, which has a negative reputation in many parts of the world.

To complete this point, it should be added that while most IGOs' budgets come from governments, other IGOs shun such funds. They raise money through the sale of bonds on the world's money markets (e.g., the International Bank for Reconstruction and Development, IBRD) or through voluntary contributions (like the United Nations Children's Fund, UNICEF). Clearly it is the membership that distinguishes NGOs from IGOs, not their sources of funding.

Conflicting definitions of NGOs make it impossible to estimate their number. But the figure of 20,000 would not be unreasonable, and some estimates range as high as 50,000. These include organizations with only a few members as well as those with memberships in excess of a million. This includes organizations that operate behind the scenes as they seek to influence national governments and intergovernmental organizations and those that seek and get coverage in the global media. This also includes NGOs whose home bases are anywhere and everyone, one of the consequences of the revolution in electronic communication. Traditionally their home bases were almost exclusively in the Northern Hemisphere, especially the United States. But that has changed recently. Northern-based NGOs have sponsored groups in the South and, more recently, Eastern and Central Europe. In the development field in particular, there are now large numbers of Southern-based organizations. It should also be added that while the traditional focus of NGOs has been on issues of so-called low politics (environment, economics, human rights, etc.), they now exist in all issues, including military-security.

One type of NGO is often mistakenly taken to be a representative of all NGOs. It is those that have been granted formal consultative status by IGOs, especially by the Economic and Social Council (ECOSOC) of the United Nations. But they are not representative. For example, the following sorts of NGOs are routinely excluded from being granted consultative status: (1) commercial organizations, (2) groups openly engaged in violence or advocating violence as a political tactic, and (3) groups that want to replace existing governments. Moreover, IGOs often only want to grant such status to organizations from which they can gain some benefit. This, for example, is what led the International Maritime Organization (IMO), for many years, to grant consultative status to shipping organizations but be very reluctant to grant it to environmental organizations. In addition, the United Nations (UN), in particular, prefers to grant such status to organizations that are international in scope. Obviously, an exclusionary criterion such as focusing on NGOs with consultative status granted by IGOs is unhelpful in understanding the whole range of NGOs. Thus, this definition and study are not so constrained.

On the other hand, any study of international organizations has some obvious constraints. There are simply too many international organizations to include in any single volume. The entries in this dictionary include all major IGOs that continue to operate and the most prominent of the 20th century that are no longer in operation. Thus, there are both universal and regional IGOs. Also included are a number of the most prominent NGOs. Obviously, these are only a small percentage of those that operate, but some effort has been made to include NGOs operating in a variety of issue areas and that have large memberships, have members in many countries, or have had a significant impact on key event in world history.

A Brief Historical Overview

Present-day international organizations are chiefly the product of the 19th and 20th centuries. Although examples of IGOs and NGOs existing in earlier eras can and will be cited, few of them had all of the character- istics of contemporary IGOs and NGOs.

Most notable of the early organizations are the Delian League from Greek times and the Hanseatic League that operated from the 11th to 17th centuries. The former was created to facilitate military cooperation against common enemies. The latter encouraged commerce among its members. What distinguishes both of these institutions from many oth- ers that could be noted is that they involved fairly well-developed orga- nizations; that is, they were not simply examples of international organization (in the singular). On the other hand, neither of them was succeeded by other similar institutions. In that sense, then, they were not part of any broad historical evolutionary movement.

Large governmental conferences, on the other hand, were a part of such an historical movement. In this sense, the conferences that resulted in the Peace of Westphalia of 1648 that ended the Thirty Years War and the Peace of Utrecht of 1713, for example, are more direct forerunners of modern-day IGOs. Although no international organizations were es- tablished by the Treaty of Westphalia, it marked the end of the Holy Roman Empire and thus contributed to the evolution of the modern state system, one of the essential ingredients for intergovernmental (meaning interstate) organizations. The Treaty of Utrecht, like that at Westphalia, was important because it destroyed imperial aspirations and furthered the creation of several sovereign states. Wars among these and other European states continued, however. Peace resulting from shifting alli- ances, as part of what came to be called the balance of power, was never more than temporary.

As a consequence, plans involving intergovernmental organizations aimed at stopping conflict among sovereign states proliferated in the 17th and 18th centuries. The Duke of Sully, minister of Henry IV of France, for example, suggested a confederation of 15 states. William Penn in 1693 proposed a diet of states, with voting allocated according to the foreign trade of the states. At Utrecht itself, a project developed by Abbé de Saint-Pierre for "perpetual peace" was discussed. It cen- tered on states submitting their differences for judicial decision. Refusal would result in other states uniting against them.

But it was really only with the Congress of Vienna (September 1814–

June 1815) that proposals like these, albeit much more modest, were put into practice. The conferees' primary goal in Vienna was the liquidation of unsettled political problems that had accumulated from years of warfare. This included restoring or disposing of those territories in Poland, Italy, Germany, the Netherlands, and Switzerland that Napoleon had overrun. To ensure that such political settlements were handled fairly, the negotiators had set up a statistical commission, which had made a complete census of the territories in dispute. The success of this fact-finding activity established a precedent that present-day states follow— that is, turning over authority to intergovernmental organizations to gather, collate, and disseminate policy-relevant data.

The conferees at Vienna also wrestled with a number of socioeconomic problems. For example, they declared that in the future the slave trade should be abolished. But no specific timetable was established. They dealt more definitively, however, with issues related to river navigation. For example, for the Rhine, they drafted a treaty providing for an elaborate international central control commission, the first such statute in the history of modern international organization. In fact, international rivers commissions, modeled after the Rhine Commission, were established throughout the 19th century. Some of these still exist today. More important, perhaps, the river commissions also served as important precedents for other transportation accords as industrialization spread in the 19th century.

Coming out of Vienna was also what came to be called the Concert of Europe, a commitment to convene conferences when tensions arose or hostilities broke out. The significance of this proliferation of conferences lies in the experience that governments gained from consulting in war and peacetime. Of course, the commitment to talk was not always present, nor was the commitment to talk identical to a commitment to compromise. Many of the conferences failed to achieve their ends.

Consequently, alternative mechanisms were considered. Among the most interesting were those discussed at the Hague Peace Conferences of 1899 and 1907. There the conferees issued declarations related to the rules of war and called for disarmament and the establishment of permanent means for arbitration of disputes. While the last point eventuated in the still existing Permanent Court of Arbitration, wars continued, culminating in World War I.

Intergovernmental organization progress in the 19th century, however, was not limited to or even primarily about issues of peace and security. In 1847, for example, the Association of German Railroads was established to formulate rules on transport contracts, the division of freight receipts, determination of losses or damages, track gauges, safety devices, and so forth. Although initially it was an international nongovernmental organization, it soon became obvious that to be efficient policies had to be uniform, not simply among companies but for all of the countries through which the trains passed. Building on the experience of the river commissions and looking toward a comprehensive legal convention, in 1878 Switzerland convened a meeting of representatives of other European governments. Twelve years later Germany, Austria, Hungary, Belgium, France, Italy, Luxembourg, the Netherlands, Russia, and Switzerland signed a treaty establishing a uniform law for the transport of goods by rail between their countries. They also agreed to establish a centralized office that would serve as a clearinghouse and arbitrar in case of disputes.

The 19th century also saw a revolution in communications technology. The telegraph was only a few years old when Austria and Prussia signed the first bilateral treaty regulating wire service. France took the initiative in widening the accord, in part motivated by a desire to eliminate the countless taxes that governments had initiated in conjunction with the expansion of telegraph usage. Out of this came, in 1865, a comprehensive international convention. It provided for what has become, after several name changes owing to developments in the communications field, the International Telecommunication Union. Within less than a decade, in 1874 conferees agreed on the establishment of a universal postal union, which eliminated the prior practice of paying for postage to one's own state, for sea transport, the country or countries traversed, and the delivering administration.

Even these few examples of socioeconomic organizations suggest the ways in which technological developments led to the development of intergovernmental organizations, which, in turn, contributed to greater industrial progress. Thus, the cycle continued and continues.

The elimination of time and space by modern communication and transportation benefited commerce, but it also facilitated the spread of contagious diseases. Not surprisingly then, the first international sanitary council was also established in the 19th century. But it was not until the beginning of this century that an International Office of Health was agreed to. Health has always been a very delicate subject, and few governments want their health problems widely discussed, even if such discussion is a necessary prerequisite for external assistance.

The industrial revolution also spawned the beginning of intergovernmental concern with science. For example, in 1875 an International Office of Weights and Measures was established to promulgate new standards of the meter and kilogram. Whereas the idea of granting patents and copyrights has a long history—as early as 1531 the king of France had bestowed royal privileges to persons introducing new manufacturers—it was not until the late 19th century that a group of industrialists called for the creation of an international organization for safeguarding the ownership of industrial inventions. Specifically, it was not until 1883 that 11 states met and established the Union for the Protection of Industrial Property, the ancestor organization of today's World Intellectual Property Organization (WIPO). Under the 1883 convention, citizens of contracting states began to enjoy the same advantages of the law regarding patents, industrial designs, and trademarks that had been or would be extended by any member of the Union to its own nationals.

While the focus of most of the attention on international organizational growth in the 19th and early 20th centuries has been related to manufacturing, two different sorts of organizational initiatives are worthy of note. In 1878, a union of 11 states worked together to prevent the spread of phylloxera, insects that especially attack grape crops. In a similar vein, an international convention was signed in 1902 that protected wild birds. And finally, an organization devoting itself to the general interests of agriculture throughout the world was established in 1905. The vision for what came to be the International Institute of Agriculture is credited to David Lubin, who, although a merchant himself, believed that landowning farmers also needed an organization to share in the modern industrial economy. Also worthy of note is the Permanent International Sugar Commission established in 1902. This forerunner of today's international commodity agreements was granted unprecedented powers for export control.

Although a few NGOs were established before the Congress of Vienna, the real growth in their numbers occurred after then. Many of the earliest NGOs had religious ties and were often concerned with the less fortunate in society. For example, Henri Dunant, as a consequence of his experience in helping care for the wounded from the battle of Solferino, Italy, inspired the formation of a small committee in Geneva in 1859. It eventually developed into the International Committee of the Red Cross (ICRC).

World War I ushered in a new era for international organization. For example, in the 20th century, there was an unprecedented commitment to a *permanent* agency through which countries could collaborate continuously on the problems that affected world peace. This eventuated in the establishment of the League of Nations. The founders of the League, and especially President Wilson of the United States, hoped that a collective security system, the central war prevention mechanism of the League Covenant, would succeed in preventing war in a way that the balance of power system of the Concert of Europe had not.

Along with the League of Nations, a world court was developed to supplement arbitral boards and a wide-ranging socioeconomic organization. The first took the form of the Permanent Court of International Justice (PCIJ) and the latter the International Labour Organisation

(ILO). Both of these IGOs came to be viewed as among the success stories of the period between the two world wars. As elaborated later, their success also goes far in explaining the form that intergovernmental organizations, especially the United Nations system, took in the post–World War II era. Functional agencies like the ILO proliferated and were closely tied to the UN. Regional security agencies were established to complement the UN's security system.

The real explosion in the numbers of IGOs only came in the aftermath of World War II. In part, the increase is a consequence of the broadened roles of states, and thus of IGOs in the economy. That is, states were performing more roles than they had in the past, as exemplified by government concern for population control. Thus, IGOs were set up to disseminate information, provide technical assistance, and so forth. In part, the number of IGOs increased because IGOs, especially the UN, began to create other IGOs (e.g., the United Nations General Assembly created the United Nations Conference on Trade and Development, UNCTAD). Moreover, the success of some IGOs, such as the European Economic Community (EEC), led to emulators being set up (such as the Latin American Free Trade Association, LAFTA) as well as competitors (such as the European Free Trade Association, EFTA).

As in the case of IGOs, the numbers of NGOs increased after World War I but especially in the post–World War II era. For example, both the International Chamber of Commerce (ICC) and the International Federation of Trade Unions (IFTU) were founded in the early years of the 20th century. The Save the Children International Union was established in 1920, and Service Civil International (SCI) has its roots in a work camp for reconciliation held near Verdun, France, in 1920–1921. As diplomatic and socioeconomic conditions worsened in the interwar period, the pace of this increase quickened. One estimate is that the number of NGOs rose from 400 in 1920 to 700 in 1939, still only a fraction of the number now in existence.[1]

Quite a few reasons account for the unprecedented increase in the numbers of NGOs founded in the post–World War II era. In part, the increase is a consequence of NGOs, in the North, creating other NGOs, especially in the South. The increase is also a consequence of the proliferation of IGOs and states, more targets of opportunity for them to influence. A specific and important example of the last phenomenon is the huge number of global conferences convened, especially in the 1970s and 1990s. Each of these, beginning with the United Nations Conference on the Human Environment (UNCHE) in 1972, encouraged active NGO participation. By some counts, there are literally thousands of NGOs present at such meetings, some quite small and some simply organized for the duration of the conference.

Some General Trends

Put in historical context, the adaptive nature of the precedent-setting organizations of the 19th century becomes clear. They developed at a time when central governments were expanding in their administrative competence, both relative to provincial governments and, most relevantly, in terms of issue areas within which they exercised jurisdiction (i.e., aspects of social and economic lives previously within the private sphere were now part of the public domain).

These early organizations—the so-called public international unions—served as collection points and clearinghouses for information, centers for decisions of problems common to governments, instruments for the coordination of national policy and practices, and agencies for promoting the formulation and acceptance of uniform or minimum standards in their respective fields.[2] Some—like the river commissions—had regulatory, administrative, supervisory, and adjudicatory responsibilities.

Many of these unions provided procedural precedents for the IGOs of the 20th century. For example, the Bureau of Telegraphic Union (1868) is seen as providing the precedent for the permanent international secretariats of the 20th century, most self-consciously developed by Sir Eric Drummond at the time of the League of Nations. More generally, the unions established the governance structure that typifies many contemporary IGOs. In a few, there are precedents for a variety of what came to be called weighted voting, where different members might be accorded more or less influence, based on some criterion (like levels of contributions or importance in the issue area relevant to the IGO). Valuable experience was also gained in dealing with languages, documentation, and the convening of large international conferences. This built on the Congress of Vienna's path-breaking method of coping with seating and ceremonial issues, by relying on a hierarchy based on seniority of service rather than the always debatable power of a country. Perhaps most important, the unions developed expertise in negotiating agreements—of varying degrees of legal competence and "compliance pull"[3]—for subsequent government implementation. In this sense, although the public international unions represented a new era of state cooperation, it was not necessarily idealistic or altruistic.

Also notable was that the countries' representatives in the public international unions included functional experts. Years later, representation by nondiplomats was seen as at the core of functionalism, a theory that suggested that such individuals were more likely to agree than politically conscious diplomats and that countries were more likely to agree on functional issues than political, much less military-security ones.

Over time, the theory went, states would see the advantage of cooperation on politically contentious issues.[4]

The great experiment of the beginning of the 20th century, the League of Nations, was open to all countries in the world, a universal organization. While most scholars quickly write off the League as a massive failure—having been unable to provide adequate collective security measures in its key tests of Manchuria and Abyssinia/Ethiopia, much less Nazi and Soviet expansion—more careful analysis results in a much more complex and mixed assessment. Although it is fair to conclude that its successes in the military-security realm were mainly in the smaller conflicts and its failures were in the bigger ones, its procedural innovations and its success in nonmilitary security issues are really quite impressive.

In terms of procedure, the League of Nations provided both positive examples that its successor organization, the UN, chose to emulate (such as a truly international secretariat, the potential utility of convening global conferences on pressing issues where the existing international institutional machinery was found wanting, and the value of having a world court that could reach decisions in contentious cases and give advisory opinions) and negative examples—that is, procedural innovations that did not work all that well and from which the UN's founders could learn. Included in the latter are such things as (1) the necessity to have all great powers as members, even if that meant deviating from the League of Nations's egalitarian principles of unanimity in decision making and making it difficult for countries to leave the organization on their own volition; (2) the need to give the secretary-general greater constitutional powers; (3) the need to have a more readily accessible military force of its own; and (4) the need to have provisions to encourage independence in former colonial possessions (the consequences of which were a UN trusteeship system that was much more proactive than had been the League's mandate system).

In terms of its nonmilitary security tasks, the League of Nations did some remarkably innovative and important work in such diverse areas as narcotics control, refugee assistance, and the codification of international law. While the UN's founders tried to distance themselves from the image of the failed League (e.g., by changing the names of institutions, even when they were virtually identical to what they were replacing, as with the International Court of Justice [ICJ] and the Permanent Court of International Justice [PCIJ]), the UN Charter really reflected that they had learned a great deal from the League of Nations. Perhaps as important as any of these lessons was that they wanted to ensure that the UN continued to maintain global support, even if its military security functions were found wanting. It did this by adopting the recommendations of the League's own Bruce Committee, which called for structural equality between the organs responsible for military security and nonmilitary security tasks. Thus, unlike the League of Nations, which was never given credit for the successes of the International Labour Organisation (ILO) with which it often worked closely, the UN would get such credit by having agencies like the ILO report to its main nonmilitary security organization, the Economic and Social Council (ECOSOC).

On paper, the UN and the League of Nations look quite different. In practice, the differences are less obvious.[5] For example, while the UN has been able to claim credit for the actions of its Specialized and Related Agencies, no one really believes that ECOSOC exercises oversight in anything but name only. Likewise, the UN Charter provides for a Military Staff Committee and calls on members to designate troops to be available to the UN when it needs them, but the committee has never functioned as envisaged. When the UN secretary-general finally called on members to designate troops as called for in the charter, the silence of the response, especially among those with the most troops available for such purposes, was almost deafening.

The fact that the UN has succeeded where the League of Nations did not is only partly attributable to the founders' prescient reading of the League's experience. It is also a consequence of global changes and innovative leadership. In the former regard, the most significant events were decolonization, which provided the UN with a huge new constituency (the third world became the majority in the UN General Assembly in 1960), and the ending of the Cold War, which gave the Security Council a chance to operate as the founders had originally intended. Innovative leadership allowed the UN to woo that new constituency by changing the orientation of virtually all of the UN's Specialized Agencies and shifting the balance in UN funding from military security to issues of economic development. Creative leadership also developed a number of successful activities that were not included in the UN Charter, most notably the development of peacekeeping operations.

The key debates in the UN General Assembly were also reflective of these global changes, going from U.S.-inspired Cold War rhetoric to a focus on anticolonial, antiracist, prodevelopmental, state-interventionist, and redistributionist rhetoric. None of this—the era of what some called the "tyranny of the majority"—pleased the United States very much. It walked out of the ILO and the United Nations Educational, Scientific and Cultural Organization (UNESCO) and found itself repeatedly using its veto in the UN Security Council and on the losing end of General Assembly resolutions.

But with the implosion of the Soviet Union, lost faith in planned economies, the end of South African apartheid, movements toward peace in the Middle East, and a third wave of democratization, the rhetoric in the General Assembly softened, and along with it came a modification in U.S. opposition to multilateralism in general and the UN in particular. But, as of yet, it has not resulted in financial stability for the UN system, much of which depends on a U.S. repayment of its arrears.

These self-same global changes were also reflected in the changed power relations in the various structures of the UN, going from a UN dominated by the General Assembly and the Specialized Agencies to one where, in the post–Cold War era, the long-deadlocked UN Security Council has come to dominate the organization as the UN's founders had initially intended.

The post–World War II period was also marked by the proliferation of regional organizations. The most famous and successful of these—the European Economic Community (EEC)—served as a model for all regions of the world. The purpose was economic prosperity, taking advantage of comparative advantages of size and peaceful interactions in a region noted for interstate rivalry, testing the long-standing notions of functionalism and peace through increased economic interdependence. While none of the African, Central and Eastern European, Latin American, Caribbean, or even Asian emulators has achieved the degree of success that the members of what is now called the European Union (EU) have, many have increased and coordinated trade, tariff, investment, and financial activities in a way that has contributed to the quality of life of their citizens. Other organizations have collapsed with their members vying for membership in a European Union trying to simultaneously deepen its activities, including by coordinating foreign and defense policy, at the same time that it tries to effectuate a monetary union and wean its members from the financially burdensome Common Agricultural Policy and broaden its membership.

In a similar vein, the World Bank's movement from reconstruction to economic assistance contributed to the development of a panoply of regional and subregional development banks, none of which—with the partial exception of the European Investment Bank (EIB)—operates on a scale comparable to the World Bank. All, however, have contributed to improving the lives of the citizens of the regions they are serving.

Even though their orientations often shifted to serving the interests of the poor, most intergovernmental (and international nongovernmental) organizations have their home bases in the North, and their decision-making power often reflects the global distribution of power of the colonial era. There are some noteworthy exceptions, however. Within the UN system, the most prominent exception is the United Nations Conference on Trade and Development (UNCTAD), established by the General Assembly as a counter to the General Agreement on Tariffs and Trade (GATT), perceived as an organization committed to free trade, which many in the South saw as anything but a neutral ideology. That is, free trade was portrayed as best serving the interests of the global economic hegemony and, a bit less so, other dominant global economic actors. While UNCTAD's greatest successes are probably in terms of consciousness raising and keeping the issues of economic redistribution on the global agenda, they should not be dismissed. Nor should one ignore the symbolic importance of locating the UN Environment Program (UNEP) in Nairobi, Kenya, the first UN Specialized Agency to be located in the South.

The most prominent (and notorious) intergovernmental organization articulating and effectuating policies opposed by the North is OPEC, an organization explicitly committed to interfering with the free market in petroleum. OPEC's success in rapidly raising oil prices in the early and mid-1970s led to a massive proliferation of imitator commodity organizations, all of which—in due time—proved the uniqueness of oil, as a highly prized commodity, where substitutes were expensive and hard to acquire, at least in the short run. Over the longer term, it was clearly recognized that the countries most hurt by the increase in oil prices were other third world countries. Accordingly, OPEC has provided financial backing to the International Fund for Agricultural Development (IFAD) and several regional development banks, assisting such countries in dealing with this additional burden to their negative terms of trade.

In the field of human rights, the first dramatic actions took place at the UN itself. While the U.S. delegation at the San Francisco conference was unable to get the conferees to include a bill of rights in the UN Charter, a very general commitment to basic human rights was included. There was none in the League of Nations Covenant. Moreover, there was a firm commitment that the UN General Assembly would make human rights a high-priority item on its agenda, not surprising given the global horror at discovering the atrocities committed during World War II. The General Assembly quickly endorsed the decisions of the Nuremberg Tribunal and then adopted the very comprehensive, but not legally binding, Universal Declaration of Human Rights. While the UN was deliberating over the best means for codifying the declaration— eventually taking the form of two covenants passed in 1966 and effective a decade later—the Council of Europe codified human rights in the form of the very forward-looking European Convention on Human Rights. Most important, it included options for individual petition for redress. The European Convention served as something of a model for other regions of the world, most notably Latin America and Africa. Neither Asia nor the Middle East, however, has moved very far in terms of intergovernmental organizations operating in the human rights field.

The model for regional military security was the Organization of American States (OAS). Indeed, it was on the insistence of Latin American delegates that the UN Charter provides for regional collective security and defense arrangements. But it was the North Atlantic Treaty Organization (NATO) that came to exemplify the potential for such regional accords. As in the case of the OAS, it has continued to be plagued by criticism of being excessively dominated by the United States. Partly as a consequence, both Europe and Latin America have a number of institutional competitors.

Even with this massive proliferation of universal and regional intergovernmental organizations, the UN system has periodically turned to global, ad hoc conferences as a means to highlight the need to better address particular issues. These global conferences were most evident in the 1970s and 1990s. They have successfully drawn attention to the (often interrelated) problems of food scarcity and maldistribution, overpopulation, inadequate housing, gender discrimination, desertification, and other threats to the environment. The substantive contributions of these conferences are often most pronounced in anticipation of their being convened as countries race to have positive reports to make before the globe's media. The procedural contributions are hard to overstate. Not only have many resulted in the establishment of new intergovernmental institutions—such as UNEP, the Commission on Sustainable Development (CSD), the World Food Council (WFC), and Habitat—or reinvigorated older ones—as in the case of the ECOSOC Commission on the Status of Women—but the conferences also have given rise to what some call a global civil society—that is, a massive proliferation of international nongovernmental organizations aiming to influence and implement global public policies. In some arenas, such as human rights (with Amnesty International) and the environment (with Greenpeace), it is difficult to know whether nongovernmental organizations are more or less influential than the intergovernmental ones that helped bolster and sometimes fund, compete, and overlap with them.

The Future of International Organizations

While it is always dangerous to speculate about the future, several trends look clear. First, IGOs in general and the United Nations in particular need to undergo reform to meet their multiple critics. But there are clear limits to how far the reforms will go. Powerful countries are reluctant to give up the advantages they have in an intergovernmental system that reflects a favorable distribution of global power long past. This is as true for the United States as it is for any other country. Vested bureaucratic interests also suggest that IGOs, including the Specialized Agencies of the UN, are unlikely to submit to drastic curtailment of their activities, even if they are clearly duplicative of those performed by other institutions.

Second, there will be pressure to democratize IGOs. They will respond, at least in part, by coordinating more closely with NGOs, which are often portrayed and portray themselves as being more representative of the interests and people of the countries in which they operate. Suggestions for a second UN General Assembly, with representatives of NGOs rather than states, reflect this trend. In a similar vein, there will be pressure for IGOs and NGOs to be more transparent, making public, for example, the sources of their revenue and the agreements they reach with governments.

Third, the numbers of NGOs based outside the United States will continue to increase, especially given the lack of support for many IGOs outside the North.

Fourth, but surely not finally, there will continue to be a proliferation of grassroots organizations, many of which will operate independently, in which the only transnational links will be the sharing of information and experience by electronic means. That is, we can expect an increase in a new "bottom-up" multilateralism, in which states, IGOs, and NGOs are not central decision makers but are affected by the actions of others, sometimes directed at them. While some activities like this are possible in the military security field, in the foreseeable future at least, that will not be the arena in which this is most likely to evolve. IGOs and especially states still will continue to predominate.

Notes

1. Bill Seary, "The Early History: From the Congress of Vienna to the San Francisco Conference," in *"The Conscience of the World": The Influence of Non-Governmental Organisations in the U.N. System*, ed. Peter Willetts (Washington, D.C.: Brookings Institution, 1996), p. 17.

2. Seary, "The Early History," pp. 35–36.

3. This valuable concept is used by Thomas Franck to discuss the degree to which international norms are adhered. It seems useful to apply the same concept more generally to the study of the outputs of international organizations, which include norms. See Thomas M. Franck, *The Power of Legitimacy among Nations* (New York: Oxford University Press, 1990).

4. For a wonderful summary and critique of functionalism, see Ernst B. Haas, *Beyond the Nation-State: Functionalism and International Organization* (Stanford, Calif.: Stanford University Press, 1964), pp. 3–50.

5. This is the persuasive thesis of Leland M. Goodrich's classic article: "From League of Nations to United Nations," *International Organization* 1 (1947): 3–21.

The Dictionary

A

Abu Dhabi Fund for Arab Economic Development (AFAED). The fund was established in July 1972 to provide economic assistance to Arab countries. While the fund's initial grants were portrayed as politically motivated, over time, technical considerations have gained importance. Funding focuses on projects related to economic infrastructure.

Actionaid. Created in 1972, this London-based international nongovernmental organization helps identify, fund, and manage long-term integrated rural development programs designed to overcome poverty and improve the quality of life. It seeks to work directly with children (q.v.), families, and communities in the world's poorest countries. Recent programs have been in Burundi, Ethiopia, Gambia, Ghana, Malawi, Mozambique, Sierra Leone, Somalia, Uganda, Bangladesh, India, Nepal, Pakistan, Vietnam, Bolivia, Ecuador, Peru, and El Salvador.

Administrative Committee on Coordination (ACC). To overcome some of the disadvantages of a decentralized system of Specialized Agencies (q.v.) affiliated with the UN (q.v.), ECOSOC (q.v.) authorized the formation of this committee. Chaired by the UN secretary-general (q.v.), its members include the executive heads of the Specialized Agencies. Its charge is to prevent duplication of effort, to allocate responsibilities, and to harmonize the purposes of the various agencies. Its history has been marked by frequent criticism for not living up to its charge.

Administrative Tribunal. A UN (q.v.) court of justice created to hear and pass judgment on complaints alleging nonobservance of contracts of employment or terms of appointment brought by staff members of international organizations. It was established in 1949 by the UN General Assembly (q.v.). The tribunal is open to all UN personnel and to the employees of selected Specialized Agencies of the UN. It normally reviews cases only after they have been heard by the Joint Appeals Board. The International Court of Justice (ICJ) (q.v.) acts as a court of appeals for decisions issued by the Administrative Tribunal. It was first used in 1952, when the UN secretary-general (q.v.) dismissed or suspended a number of UN Secretariat (q.v.) employees who were U.S. citizens. The grounds for dismissal was the refusal of the staff members to testify before a U.S. federal jury or before congressional committees on questions of subversion. Twenty-one of the former employees appealed their cases to the Administrative Tribunal. The tribunal awarded compensation to 11 of those dismissed.

Adventist Development and Relief Agency (ADRA). With its headquarters in Silver Spring, Maryland, this international nongovernmental organization, established by the Seventh-Day Adventist Church, maintains offices in more than 100 countries. It provides emergency relief for victims of natural disasters (see disaster relief) in less developed countries. It also provides general support to community development activities, leading to self-sufficiency. It focuses on education, medicine, food, water, and hygiene. Less than 20 percent of its funding is public in origin.

Advisory Opinions. The International Court of Justice (ICJ) (q.v.) may be requested to give advisory opinions by the UN General Assembly (q.v.), the Security Council (q.v.), and such other UN (q.v.) organs or Specialized Agencies (q.v.) as authorized by the General Assembly. Thus far no affirmative action has been taken on requests for such authorization by the UN secretary-general (q.v.). Although not binding, such opinions are authoritative interpretations of international law.

African, Caribbean, and Pacific (ACP). Refers to the 46 developing countries (q.v.) of Africa, the Caribbean, and the Pacific that signed the 1975 Lomé Convention (q.v.) with the European Economic Community (EEC) (q.v.). Most of the ACP countries were former colonies of the United Kingdom, France, and Belgium. The number of ACP countries increased as the Lomé Convention was renegotiated and with the accession of Portugal and Spain to the EEC. There are now 70 ACP countries. The basic objective of ACP countries is to establish favorable trade (q.v.) relations with the EEC (and European Union [EU] [q.v.]). The ACP agreements, which replaced the Yaoundé (q.v.) and Arusha conventions (previously referred to as Associated African States and Madagascar [AASM] countries), offered privileged access to the European market, economic development (q.v.) aid, a price stabilization fund for commodities (q.v.), and a new basis for industrial cooperation. The ACP states are allowed duty free access to the EU market for most of their products, on a nonreciprocal basis. They are also able to apply for grants from the European Development Fund (EDF) and low-interest loans from the European Investment Bank (EIB) (q.v.).

African Development Bank (ADB). Set up in 1964 to promote economic development in Africa, with its headquarters in Abidjan, the Ivory Coast, this organization is composed of all 52 African countries except South Africa, whose membership was approved in December 1995 and becomes effective when it pays in its portion of the bank's capital. Unlike other regional development organizations, membership in the ADB was originally limited to African countries, but a decision was taken in 1979 to admit nonregional members—owing to the need for additional capital—while still emphasizing its avowed set of principles aimed at preserving the bank's African character. There are now 25 non-African shareholders in the bank. The bank's primary functions are to provide loans for financing national and multinational projects, encourage public and private investment, assist member countries in improving use of their resources, enhance members' economic systems and promote the balanced growth of foreign trade, extend technical assistance, and cooperate with those economic institutions in and outside Africa that support African economic development. Accordingly, the bank has developed close links with the Food and Agriculture Organization (FAO) (q.v.), World Bank (IBRD) (q.v.), International Labour Organisation (ILO) (q.v.), Organization of African Unity (OAU) (q.v.), UNESCO (q.v.), and World Health Organization (WHO) (q.v.). The bank secures capital through its supporting unit, the African Development Fund.

Afro-Asian People's Security Conference (also known as the Bandung Conference). Organized at the initiative of President Sukarno of Indonesia and supported by Burma, India, Pakistan, and Sri Lanka, the Bandung Conference of 1955 is often seen as the first major meeting of third world states and as the origin of the Non-Aligned Movement (NAM) (q.v.). The conference was also notable because of Chinese participation and the absence of a Soviet delegation. Its final communiqué put forward resolutions on economic needs, cultural cooperation, human rights (q.v.), the search for self-determination (q.v.) by dependent peoples, and world peace. The participants declared, "Colonialism in all its manifestations is an evil which should speedily be brought to an end." The conferees also adopted the Indian *Panchssheel* or five principles of coexistence: (1) mutual respect for territorial integrity and sovereignty, (2) nonaggression, (3) noninterference in the internal affairs of others, (4) equality and mutual support, and (5) peaceful coexistence. In 1958, a second Afro-Asian Solidarity Conference was held in Cairo, setting up a permanent council to meet annually and be composed of one representative from each national committee. "Peoples" rather than states were represented. In 1965, another solidarity conference was scheduled to be held in Algiers, Algeria, but it was postponed indefinitely.

Aga Khan, Prince Sadruddin (1933–). The son of Aga Khan III, he was born in Paris and educated at Harvard, where he studied Middle Eastern history and founded the Harvard Islamic Society. Since 1958, Aga Khan has spent much of his time acting as a consultant to the United Nations (q.v.), including UNESCO (q.v.). He became increasingly concerned with issues related to refugees and humanitarian assistance. He served as the United Nations High Commissioner for Refugees (UNHCR) (q.v.) from 1965 to 1977. As a special assistant to the UN secretary-general (q.v.), he carries out special missions for and in the name of the secretary-general. For example, he was actively engaged in investigating conditions related to refugees in Afghanistan, Iraq, and Kuwait. See also UN High Commission for Refugees.

Agence de Coopération Culturelle et Technique (ACCT) (Agency for Cultural and Technical Cooperation; also known as the French Commonwealth). Established in March 1970 with headquarters in Paris to facilitate the exchange of culture, education, science, and technology among countries where French is in common use, the ACCT has been working toward the establishment of a full-fledged Francophone Commonwealth. The initial idea is often credited to Leopold Sedar Senghor, then president of Senegal. The first intergovernmental meeting, which was held in Niamey, Niger, in 1969, followed years of annual conferences among ministers in Francophone countries responsible for education and for youth and sport. The key stumbling block to the agency achieving its ultimate goal has been disagreement over Quebec and, more generally, between Canada and France, with the latter seeing the ACCT as having a pro-Canada tilt to it. Currently, both Quebec (since 1971) and New Brunswick (since 1977) have the status of "participating governments" in the agency. Discussions at the agency's General Conference, at which all members are represented, have focused on foreign assistance projects, especially to the poorest member states and the rural poor. They have also spent time discussing African members' external debts and the desirability of tying foreign aid to progress toward democracy in recipient states. The first summit conference, of heads of government, took place in Paris in 1986.

Agency for Co-operation and Research in Development (ACORD). Formed in 1974, as Euro Action, ACORD is a broad-based international consortium of European and Canadian nongovernmental organizations working together for long-term economic development (q.v.) in Africa. ACORD was created to work in those parts of Africa where local structures were weak or nonexistent. Moreover, it sought to establish an international platform for the discussion of development issues. Beginning around 1986, the emphasis turned to the support of informal, grassroots organizations, especially those working in alliances. In so doing, it hopes to promote self-reliance and equality.

Agenda 21. The term commonly used to refer to the 800-page program for managing the various sectors of the environment in the 21st century, adopted at the United Nations Conference on Environment and Development (UNCED) (q.v.), the Rio Conference. Many of the action items contained in the agenda are quite specific, often calling for degrees of protection of the environment beyond the current capacity of many countries. The protection of the atmosphere is probably the most controversial of such items. The key to the success of the agenda is its implementation, which depends on funding. Few funding commitments were made at the time of the Rio Conference itself.

All Africa Conference of Churches (AACC). Established in 1958, with headquarters in Nairobi, Kenya, the AACC coordinates the activities of African churches. It has been a strong advocate of human rights (q.v.) throughout the continent.

Amazon Pact (also known as the Amazon Cooperation Council). The pact is a 1978 treaty aimed at coordinating the development of the Amazon River basin and protecting the region's environment (q.v.) through the rational utilization of its resources. The parties to the pact include Bolivia, Brazil, Colombia, Ecuador, Guyana, Peru, Suriname, and Venezuela. The treaty's key provisions include the (1) free navigation on all rivers of the Amazon region, (2) rational use of the region's water resources, (3) right of each state to develop its Amazon territory so long as it does not cause any harmful impact on the territories of other members, (4) development of cooperative research on the river basin, (5) improvement of health and the building of a transportation and communication infrastructure, and (6) promotion of tourism. The region's foreign ministers meet as the Amazon Cooperation Council.

American Refugee Committee (ARC). Established in 1978, ARC is a nongovernmental organization that provides primary health care, training, and other services to refugees (q.v.) who have left their homes because of persecution, war, natural disasters, or other threats to their health and well-being. Its recent activities have included assistance to the Kurds in Iraq and Turkey and to returnees in Cambodia.

Amnesty International (AI). Amnesty International, an international nongovernmental organization founded in London in 1961, seeks to mobilize international public opinion to apply pressure on governments to alter their countries' inhumane policies. AI has more than 200,000 individual members from 95 countries, many of whom participate in one of its almost 3,000 local groups. AI often sends representatives to observe trials and interview individuals deemed by AI to be "prisoners of conscience." In addition to prisoners of conscience, AI focuses on the abolition of torture and the death penalty. It received the Nobel Peace Prize in 1977. See also human rights.

Annan, Kofi (1938–   ). Elected as the seventh UN secretary-general (q.v.), effective January 1, 1997, Annan is both the first secretary-general from sub-Saharan Africa (he is from Ghana) and the first career United Nations (q.v.) official to rise through the ranks. Prior to his election, Annan had served as one of the UN's under secretaries-general: he was in charge of the UN's peacekeeping forces (q.v.). Annan's election had the strong backing of the United States, and his election was seen as an opportunity for the UN to get the United States to repay its arrears. Annan's focus, throughout his career, has been on the importance of economic development to help provide people with basic needs: food, clothing, shelter, and health care. Thus, it was not surprising that one of his chief goals as secretary-general was to transfer funds saved by administrative reform into development assistance for the poorest countries.

Anti-Slavery Society for the Protection of Human Rights. Formed in 1909 out of a merger of the Aborigines Protection Society (founded in 1837) and the British and Foreign Anti-Slavery Society (founded in 1839), the Anti-Slavery Society, which has its headquarters in London, is particularly concerned with the persistence of various forms of slavery, including forced labor and child labor. In addition, it seeks to promote the well-being of indigenous peoples, by monitoring adherence to international human rights treaties and sending information of violations to the relevant governments. When that approach does not suffice to remedy the problem, it presents evidence to the United Nations Commission on Human Rights (q.v.) and its subordinate bodies.

ANZUS Council. The council was established in 1951 under the ANZUS Treaty signed by Australia, New Zealand, and the United States. The aim of the treaty, which is to remain in force indefinitely, is the collective defense and the preservation of peace (q.v.) and security in the Pacific area. ANZUS never had a formal headquarters; meetings rotated among the member states. Following a dispute in January 1985 over U.S. access to New Zealand ports and airfields, meetings of the full ANZUS Council have not taken place.

Arab Maghreb Union (AMU). While the goal of establishing an organization to strengthen the bonds among North African states can be traced back to the 1920s, it was only in 1989, with the establishment of the AMU, that this took concrete form. The union, which has its headquarters in Casablanca, Morocco, and for which the Presidential Council is the key decision-making body, has had its ambitious economic cooperation and integration (q.v.) plans thwarted by disagreements among members. These roadblocks have included disagreements about United Nations (UN) (q.v.) sanctions against Libya, the spread of the Islamic fundamentalist movement, and the political status of Western Sahara.

Arab Monetary Fund. In operation since 1977, the fund, which has its headquarters in Abu Dhabi, the United Arab Emirates, aims to assist all Arab countries in coping with balance of payments and other financial difficulties. The goal is to develop an overall policy of monetary and economic cooperation and integration (q.v.), thereby promoting economic development (q.v.). Its specific aims include (1) correcting balance of payments disequilibria among member states; (2) assisting in the elimination of restrictions on current payments between member states; (3) promoting development of Arab financial markets; and (4) studying ways to initiate the use of the Arab dinar as a unit of account, thus paving the way for the creation of a unified Arab currency. The fund operates as both a bank and a loan fund similar to the International Monetary Fund (IMF) (q.v.). It uses its own unit of account, the Arab Accounting Dinar (AAD), which is expressed in relation to the IMF's Special Drawing Rights (SDRs) (q.v.).

Arbitration. The process of dispute settlement where the parties choose an ad hoc judicial panel to impose a resolution on the parties. Both the UN (q.v.) Charter and the League of Nations (q.v.) Covenant listed arbitration among the proper methods for settling disputes between countries. See also Permanent Court of Arbitration; United Nations Commission on International Trade Law (UNCITRAL).

Arms control. See Peace, disarmament, and arms control.

Asia Pacific Economic Cooperation (APEC). APEC was formed in November 1989. Before then, the promotion of Pacific regionalism had been largely undertaken by international nongovernmental organizations. APEC, which operates as a forum for discussion of all sorts of economic issues such as market access and trade (q.v.) and investment liberalization, has its current headquarters in Singapore. U.S. President Clinton substantially upgraded APEC's role by convening in 1993 in Seattle, Washington, the first summit meeting of the APEC countries. Since then, summit meetings of the Pacific Rim countries have become an annual routine. APEC is among the world's most significant regional economic organizations, having among its members the two largest economies in the world, the United States and Japan; the most populous country, China; and the world's fastest-growing countries, the newly industrializing countries (NICs) (q.v.) and Association of Southeast Asian Nations (ASEAN) (q.v.) members. Its 18 member states comprise 53 percent of the world's economy, 42 percent of world trade, and 38 percent of the world's population.

Asian Coalition for Housing Rights (ACHR). Founded in 1988, the ACHR is an international nongovernmental organization whose purpose is to articulate and promote the concept of people's laws and rights to housing and to put an end to evictions and the displacement of people. The ACHR's secretariat, which serves the interests of three billion people in 10 countries, is located in Bangkok, Thailand.

Asian Development Bank (ADB). Established in 1966 under the auspices of the UN Economic and Social Commission for Asia and the Pacific (ESCAP) (q.v.), the ADB's headquarters are in Manila, the Philippines. In addition to 40 member countries and territories within the ESCAP region, all developing countries (q.v.) of the area, plus Australia, New Zealand, and Japan and 16 other developed countries from outside the region, including Canada, France, Italy, Germany, the United Kingdom, and the United States, are members. Taiwan is a member, under the name Taipei-China. The ADB promotes investment of public and private capital in the region but is now in serious need of a substantial increase in its capital resources, in part to offset cuts by the United States. But the Americans, among others, are openly skeptical about the need for funds to go to the ADB, given the region's ease in attracting external investment capital.

Assistance, technical and financial. Technical and financial assistance, a major activity of intergovernmental organizations for the past 35 years, is an integral aspect of the international organizations' support of economic development (q.v.) activities. Intergovernmental organizations, most notably the Development Assistance Committee (DAC) (q.v.) of the Organisation for Economic Co-operation and Development (q.v.), have played important roles in the coordination of member governments' technical assistance programs as well as providing such assistance themselves. The United Nations Development Program (q.v.) has been a major source of funds for other United Nations (q.v.) agencies, encouraging them to become active agents in providing technical expertise to member countries. This has contributed to the reorientation of various UN Specialized Agencies (q.v.). For example, the International Civil Aviation Organization (q.v.) has assisted member countries in siting and constructing airports, and the World Health Organization (q.v.) has worked with the International Labour Organisation (q.v.) in improving the health and environment of workers. While the World Bank Group (q.v.) initially focused on infrastructural assistance, it broadened its scope, especially in the 1970s and 1980s, moving into such controversial areas as education and population planning. See also Agence de Coopération Culturelle et Technique; Expanded Program of Technical Assistance; Hoffman, Paul; Kuwait Fund for Arab Economic Development; most seriously affected; official development assistance; Rotary International; Volunteers in Technical Assistance; Yaoundé Conventions.

Association Internationale des Juristes Démocrates (AIJD) (International Association of Democratic Lawyers). Founded in 1946 with its headquarters in Brussels, Belgium, the AIJD is an international nongovernmental organization whose activities include the defense and development of rights and liberties, including assistance in the development of related legislation. Members of the association often serve as trial observers in countries whose human rights (q.v.) practices have been criticized.

Association of Iron Ore Exporting Countries (AIOEC). The association was founded in 1975 at the height of the global influence of the Organization of Petroleum Exporting Countries (OPEC) (q.v.) and when the New International Economic Order (NIEO) (q.v.) was near the top of the global agenda. It aims to ensure the orderly growth of iron ore exports, to secure fair and remunerative returns so as to improve member states' terms of trade, and to contribute to the economic and social development of member countries. Its powers are purely consultative, namely to provide a forum for the exchange of information and experience relating to use issues and market conditions.

Association of Natural Rubber Producing Countries (ANRPC). Established in 1968 and reconstituted in 1982, the ANRPC coordinates the production and marketing of natural rubber, promotes technical cooperation among its members, and seeks to bring about fair and stable prices for natural rubber. Its members, which include India, Indonesia, Malaysia, Papua New Guinea, Singapore, Sri Lanka, Thailand, and Vietnam, are responsible for the production of almost 90 percent of the world's natural rubber supply.

Association of Southeast Asian Nations (ASEAN). This organization, based in Jakarta, Indonesia, aims to accelerate growth, social progress, and cultural development in Southeast Asia. ASEAN was established in Bangkok, Thailand, in 1967 at a foreign ministers' meeting of the five founding states: Indonesia, Malaysia, the Philippines, Singapore, and Thailand. Laos and Papua New Guinea have observer status. Brunei joined in 1984. Perhaps most significantly, Vietnam was granted membership in July 1995, the first communist country granted membership in an organization seen by some as being founded, at least in part, as a bulwark against communism. In a similar vein, the first meetings between ASEAN and Chinese governmental officials were held in May 1995. Laos and Myanmar became members in 1997, the latter over strong objections by the United States, which is an outspoken critic of Myanmar's human rights (q.v.) record. Plans for Cambodian membership were thwarted, owing to that country's bloody leadership crisis on the eve of the 1997 meetings. The Cambodian coup leader, Hun Sen, has agreed to allow ASEAN to assist in dealing with his country's political turmoil.

Although ASEAN's focus—consistent with its charter—is on accelerating regional economic growth, its aims have always included the promotion of political stability in the region. Indeed, the association has been criticized by some for having failed to create a zone of peace and neutrality in the region; significantly, the long-awaited South-East Asian Nuclear Weapons Free Zone (SEANWFZ) treaty was signed in December 1996. ASEAN has been successful in developing relations with other international economic organizations, but less successful in achieving economic development (q.v.) of its member states and on reducing intra-ASEAN tariffs on unprocessed agricultural goods. This is, in part, a consequence of the vast difference in levels of economic development of the member states as well as traditional differences in political and economic regime types. Nonetheless, it established an Asian Free Trade Area (AFTA) and a Common Preferential Tariff (CEPT), effective January 1, 1993. A common market remains the goal for 2015.

Association of Tin Producing Countries (ATPC) (also known as the International Tin Producers' Association). Founded in 1983, the association's key aims are to undertake research, including about the use of modern technology to lower prices and development of tin, and to reduce the involvement of third parties in the marketing of tin. The ATPC's headquarters are in Kuala Lumpur, Malaysia. Its successes have been limited by the production and sale by non-members. Its members include Australia, Bolivia, Brazil, China, Congo, Indonesia, Malaysia, and Nigeria. The recent elevation of Brazil from associate to full membership was widely hailed because of the importance of Brazil as a tin exporter. Thailand's recent departure from ATPC was characterized as a "nonevent."

Avenol, Joseph (1879–1952). Having begun his career in the French finance ministry and worked for 10 years as deputy director-general of the League of Nations (q.v.), Avenol took over as the second secretary-general of the League at a particularly difficult time. The first months of his tenure in the summer of 1933 were marked by the failure of the League of Nations-sponsored London Economic Conference, the breakdown of the League-sponsored Disarmament Conference, and the withdrawal of Germany from the League. Moreover, he was unable to win the trust or liking either of the key country delegations or of the staff of the secretariat. While Avenol was successful in terms of administrative finances, he was unable to get the council members to take the steps necessary to stand up to Japanese and Italian expansion, much less that of Hitler's Germany. Indeed, by the time he resigned in August 1940, many accused him of being pro-Axis.

B

Baker Plan. The Baker Plan was the first systematic initiative that linked multilateral lending institutions, commercial banks, and the question of third world debtor country adjustment. It was announced by then U.S. Treasury Secretary James Baker during the 1985 joint IMF-World Bank meetings, and he elaborated on it subsequently. The banks would be called to provide new money, amounting to $7 billion annually over the following three years, to 15 developing countries (q.v.) in debt difficulties. (The bulk of them were in Latin America.) There were to be new net loan disbursements by multilateral development agencies of $3 billion per year over the same time period. Furthermore, developing countries were to make serious efforts to adjust. Baker's plan was largely a set of suggested guidelines; it lacked any implementation mechanism. Because of the origins of the proposal, however, something like it was put in place but on a smaller scale than Baker had envisaged. In 1996, moreover, the World Bank (q.v.) and the International Monetary Fund (q.v.) agreed to a new program to raise the level of forgiveness that creditors can offer and, for the first time, to eliminate debts owed to international aid agencies. It was looked at as particularly important in helping out debt-ridden African countries.

Bandung Conference. See Afro-Asian People's Security Conference and Non-Aligned Movement.

Bangkok Declaration. The August 8, 1967, accord that initiated the Association of Southeast Asian Nations (ASEAN) (q.v.).

Bank for International Settlements (BIS). The Swiss government agreed, in 1930, to set up in Basel, Switzerland, what became the BIS. Early discussions focused on reparations and other problems arising out of World War I. The goal was to carry out banking functions in connection with the annual reparation payments to be made by Germany in such a way as to stimulate German exports and thereby its ability to pay. However, the BIS soon ceased to be concerned mainly with reparations and assumed the more general function of providing facilities hitherto lacking in carrying out international settlements and doing high-level (and well-respected) monetary research. More generally, the BIS aims to promote cooperation between central banks, provide facilities for international financial operations, and act as an agent in international financial settlements. It buys and sells gold on its own account and accepts custody of gold for the accounts of member central banks. It also receives short-term deposits and uses these for lending purposes. Thirty-two central banks are currently members, the U.S. Federal Reserve having only recently become a member. In the 1980s, the bank granted large-scale loans to the central banks of Latin American countries (Argentina, Brazil, and Mexico) in an effort to avoid their defaulting on international loans and to the International Monetary Fund (q.v.) to lend support to its third world loan operations. The

BIS continued this practice in the 1990s, for example, by assisting in propping up the Mexican economy.

Banking and finance. Even before World War II was concluded, it was generally agreed that there needed to be a multilateral financial system to prevent the sort of "beggar thy neighbor" policies that exacerbated interstate competition and conflict in the interwar years. That consensus led to the establishment of the International Monetary Fund (IMF) (q.v.) to cope with balance of payment disequilibria and the International Bank for Reconstruction and Development (IBRD) to assist countries needing long-term loans to assist with more fundamental, structural problems. Both organizations were seen as important supplements to the Bank for International Settlements (BIS) (q.v.). Throughout the 1940s and 1950s, the major recipients of their loans were economically advanced countries. That has changed with decolonization (q.v.). Among the major aid recipients are India, Pakistan, and, later, China. With the end of the Cold War, Russia and other formerly centrally planned economies have also been major recipients of aid.

The operations of these global institutions have been supplemented by regional and subregional banks, beginning with the Inter-American Development Bank (IDB) (q.v.). The premise behind such institutions is that regional expertise and sensitivities might ensure more desirable loan conditions. In fact, the most lenient loan conditions, concessionary for the poorest of the poor, have come from the International Development Association (IDA) (q.v.), one of the World Bank's (q.v.) affiliates. Moreover, recently there has been an upsurge in requests for loans for the private sector, always the special province of the International Finance Corporation (q.v.), the smallest banking affiliate of the World Bank Group (q.v.). See also Abu Dhabi Fund for Arab Economic Development; African Development Bank; Arab Monetary Fund; Asian Development Bank; Baker Plan; Banque Arabe pour le Développement Economique en Afrique; Banque Centrale des Etats d'Afrique Centrale; Black, Eugene; Bretton Woods System; Camdessus, Michel; Caribbean Development Bank; de Larosière, Jacques; Eastern Caribbean Central Bank; European Bank for Reconstruction and Development; European Currency Unity; European Investment Bank; European Monetary System; European Monetary Union; Gutt, Camille; International Bank for Economic Cooperation; International Investment Bank; Islamic Development Bank; Jacobsson, Per; McNamara, Robert S.; Paris Club; Preston, Lewis T.; Saudi Fund for Development; Schweitzer, Pierre-Paul; Special Drawing Rights; Union Economique et Monétaire Ouest Africaine; United Nations Capital Development Fund; West African

Development Bank; Witteveen, Henrikus Johannes; Wolfensohn, James; Woods, George.

Banque Arabe pour le Développement Economique en Afrique (BADEA) (Arab Bank for Economic Development in Africa). The BADEA was formed in 1973 by the League of Arab States (q.v.) to contribute to economic development (q.v.) in Africa. It finances infrastructural, industrial, and agricultural projects and provides technical assistance to African countries faced with the devastating consequences of high oil prices. The decision to establish the bank was reached in 1973 in Algiers at the sixth summit meeting of the Arab states. Its founding agreement was signed in Cairo, Egypt, in 1974. Some of the bank's funds have been channeled into the African Development Bank (q.v.) and to southern African liberation movements. Headquartered in Khartoum, the Sudan, 18 Arab states have subscribed, with over half of the funds coming from Iraq, Kuwait, Libya, Saudi Arabia, and the United Arab Emirates. The bank plays an active role in promoting Arab investment in Africa and in coordinating Arab assistance for economic development. Recipient Africans have been critical as to the fairness of the BADEA in channeling investment funds and economic assistance, with the Arabs being portrayed as preferring to channel funds through national institutions and to selected African Muslim states. Many African leaders have stated that the Arab states ought to channel most, if not all, of their aid through the African Development Bank, which, unlike the BADEA, has black Africans on its board of directors.

Banque Centrale des Etats d'Afrique Centrale (BCEAC) (Central Bank of the Central African States). This organization, based in Brazzaville, the Congo, was established in 1972. It serves as the exclusive issuing house for currency circulated within member states. It also helps in the planning of member states' monetary policies and monitors bank adherence to credit regulations.

Basket Three. Basket Three refers to the third of three "baskets," or sections, into which the Final Act of the Conference on Security and Cooperation in Europe (CSCE) (q.v.) was subdivided. Basket Three deals with cooperation in humanitarian and other fields, specifically advocating the freer movement of ideas, information, and people through family reunifications, binational marriages, easier travel, increased access to broadcast and printed information, and increased educational and cultural exchanges.

BENELUX Economic Union (Union Economique Benelux). The BENELUX Economic Union is a customs union ensuring the free movement of persons, goods, capital, and services among Belgium, the Netherlands, and Luxembourg. Agreement on its establishment was reached in The Hague, Netherlands, in 1958; it came into being in 1960. Its headquarters are in Brussels, Belgium. Its origins can be traced to the Customs Union Treaty of 1944 and the BENELUX Customs Union, which was formally established in January 1948. The Economic Union has abolished internal tariffs and greatly reduced trade (q.v.) quotas and other trade restrictions, in many ways leading the way in Western Europe. The Union's constitutive treaty stipulated that the three countries should eventually merge their fiscal and monetary systems.

Bilderberg Conferences. The conferences involve prominent business and political leaders of Western Europe and North America. They are held annually by invitation and in great secrecy. The conferences, whose topics range over any issue of mutual concern and interest, are named for the Bilderberg Hotel in Oosterbeck, the Netherlands, at which the first such conference was held in May 1954. All those who have attended the conferences are referred to as "Bilderbergers" or the "Bilderberg group."

Black, Eugene (1898–1992). Black served as the second president of the World Bank (q.v.), after a successful career with Chase Manhattan Bank and two years as the assistant and hand-chosen successor of the first World Bank president, John J. McCloy. During Black's extended period as World Bank president (1949–1962), the bank developed its reputation on Wall Street as a financially stable institution, one that loaned only for projects with the potential for being sufficiently profitable that the borrowing country could repay the loans and, accordingly, as a place whose bonds were worthy of investment. The bank under Black also developed its reputation for favoring "bricks and mortar" projects (i.e., large infrastructure loans) but not playing ideological favorites in terms of who was to receive loans.

Black Sea Economic Cooperation (BSEC). Established in June 1992 with headquarters in Istanbul, Turkey, the BSEC aims at promoting bilateral and multilateral economic cooperation (q.v.) among states on the Black Sea (Albania, Armenia, Azerbaijan, Bulgaria, Georgia, Greece, Moldova, Romania, Russia, Turkey, and Ukraine). The organization, which some see as competing with the European Union (EU) (q.v.) and Organization on Security and Cooperation in Europe (OSCE) (q.v.), has as its major policy-making body meetings of the foreign ministers. Its future plans include the establishment of an investment bank.

Blix, Hans (1921–   ). A professor of law and a Swedish diplomat who had served his country as foreign minister beginning in 1978, Blix was appointed as director-general of the International Atomic Energy Agency (IAEA) (q.v.) in 1981. In that position, he was unusually visible, most notably at times of crises, such as the IAEA's investigation of the Chernobyl nuclear disaster in the Soviet Union, in the aftermath of the Gulf War, and in light of the North Korean threat to drop out of the Nuclear Non-Proliferation regime. In more bureaucratic terms, Blix succeeded in resisting calls for his ouster from third world member states and dealing with severe budgetary constraints.

Bloc politics. Bloc politics is the name given to a group of states that adopt a similar position on certain types of issues, usually as a result of a caucus decision, in their voting as members of the UN General Assembly (q.v.). These coalitions were evident in the UN before blocs were formalized into caucusing groups, such as the Asian-African group. Some have portrayed them as necessary for effective negotiation. There is considerable overlap in membership of various blocs.

Boutros-Ghali, Boutros (1922–   ). The sixth United Nations secretary-general (q.v.). His first and only term began on January 1, 1992, and concluded in December 1996. As an Egyptian, he was the first secretary-general from Africa and the Arab world. Prior to his selection as secretary-general, he had served as Egyptian deputy prime minister and authored more than 100 scholarly publications. He inherited an organization plagued by financial and administrative difficulties and overcommitted in terms of peacekeeping activities. Among his most notable accomplishments was authoring (in 1992) an *Agenda for Peace*, subsequently revised and supplemented by an *Agenda for Development*. He (along with Cable News Network, CNN) is also credited with focusing the world's attention on Somalia, setting the stage for the deployment of UN troops there. His alleged inability to manage the UN's budget effectively and his willingness to take issue from time to time with the United States resulted in a decision by Washington to veto his quest for a second term. He was particularly unpopular with the United States Congress, which made clear that the United States would never repay its debt to the UN so long as Boutros-Boutros Ghali remained its secretary-general.

Brandt Commission. An independent international commission, created in September 1977 at the suggestion of former World Bank (q.v.) president Robert McNamara (q.v.) and headed by former West German chancellor Willy Brandt. The commission, which was dissolved in December 1980, gathered information on and proposed solutions to North-South problems. The two reports issued by the commission called for such things as increased foreign aid to developing countries (q.v.); international taxes on trade, ocean mining, and arms sales; limits on energy use; increased funds for the International Monetary Fund (IMF) (q.v.), including the issuance of an extra $40 billion of Special Drawing Rights (SDRs) (q.v.); and the removal of all trade barriers in developed countries on the import of tropical products. See also Palme Commission.

Bretton Woods System. The term given to the international monetary system devised at a 1944 conference convened, at President Roosevelt's suggestion, in Bretton Woods, New Hampshire. To prevent an occurrence of the economic problems that were blamed on the 1929 Depression and World War II, a system was created with rules for a foreign exchange system (a so-called fixed exchange system, based on gold but actually on the U.S. dollar), balance-of-payments adjustments, and supplies of reserve assets. The conference gave rise to the International Monetary Fund (IMF) (q.v.) and the International Bank for Reconstruction and Development (IBRD), but its proposed International Trade Organization was ultimately rejected by the U.S. government. The Bretton Woods System is generally taken to have ended in August 1971 when the United States suspended the convertibility of dollars into gold.

Bruce Report. On May 27, 1939, the Council of the League of Nations (q.v.) appointed Stanley Melbourne Bruce, then Australian high commissioner in London and a former Australian prime minister, to chair a committee to study and report on the development and expansion of the League's machinery for dealing with technical (i.e., social and economic) questions. The report, which—like the committee—came to be known for its chair, was published on August 22, 1939, only a few days before the Nazi invasion of Poland. Thus, it was too late to be relevant to the League, but it became the blueprint for the UN's Economic and Social Council (ECOSOC) (q.v.).

Bruntland, Gro Harlem (1939–). Prime minister of Norway for three terms, she chaired the World Commission on Environment and Development, widely referred to as the Bruntland Commission, whose report served as background for the UN Conference on Environment and Development (q.v.). The report, commonly referred to as the Bruntland Report, is often credited with making "sustainable development" a household term. Often mentioned as a possible candidate for UN secretary-general, she was appointed director-general of the World Health Organization, effective January 21, 1998.

Brussels, Treaty of (also known as the Treaty of Economic, Social, and Cultural Collaboration and Collective Self-Defense, and as the Western Union). Western Europe's first post–World War II collective security (q.v.) agreement. The signatories—Belgium, France, Luxembourg, the Netherlands, and the United Kingdom—agreed in 1948 to give each other "all military and other aid and assistance if any one was attacked" as well as to collaborate in economic, social, and cultural matters. The treaty was initiated by the British foreign minister, Ernst Bevin, who saw it as a temporary bridge until the United States could be persuaded to make a long-term commitment to the defense of Western Europe. It was quickly transformed from an anti-German to an anti-Soviet organization. Although the military aspects of the treaty largely overlapped those of the North Atlantic Treaty Organization (NATO) (q.v.), the commitment lacked NATO's qualifications. The Brussels Treaty Organization survived and became the basis of the Western European Union (WEU) (q.v.), with the entrance of Germany and Italy.

Bunche, Ralph J. (1904–1971). After working in the U.S. Department of State, Bunche was appointed (in 1946) to head the Trusteeship Division of the UN Secretariat (q.v.). In 1947, he was assigned to the UN Palestine Commission and became its chief mediator after the assassination of Count Folke Bernadotte. In 1950, in recognition of his accomplishments as mediator, he was awarded the Nobel Peace Prize, the first black to be so recognized. He was later promoted to the rank of UN undersecretary and served as special representative of the secretary-general to UN peacekeeping (q.v.) missions in the Middle East, the Congo, and Cyprus.

Burden sharing. A widely used term to describe the relative share of North Atlantic Treaty Organization (NATO) (q.v.) defense expenditures borne by each of the alliance's members. It is one of the most contentious issues in the history of NATO, as members have argued over each member's relative costs and benefits as well as its capacity to contribute.

C

Camdessus, Michel (1934–   ). In 1987, Camdessus was appointed as the International Monetary Fund's (IMF) (q.v.) managing director and chairman of the Executive Board. Immediately prior to his appointment, Camdessus was governor of the Bank of France. Before that he had served as chair of the Paris Club (q.v.) (1978–1984), director of the French Treasury, and chair of the Monetary Committee of the European Economic Community (EEC) (q.v.). Unlike his predecessors, Camdessus has encouraged a more open atmosphere in the IMF. He has also been an unusually public managing director and quite proactive in trying to assist in the stabilization of the Russian economy. At the same time, he has been rather critical of the size of the U.S. trade and budget deficits and of commercial banks' refusal to reschedule debts owed to them by third world countries.

Capacity Study of the United Nations Development System. A report issued in 1970 under the leadership of Sir Robert Jackson that examined the need for reform in the United Nations (q.v.) development system. The main criticisms of the UN included the proliferation of projects and agencies without relationship to broad global planning, a lack of coordination, and the failure to establish and adhere to clear priorities. The goal was progress toward more rational and coordinated UN development efforts.

CARE International. Established as Cooperation for American Remittances to Europe (CARE) in 1905, it has been calling itself CARE International since the early 1980s. CARE's purpose is to channel financial assistance to people in economically less developed countries. It tries to promote economic development (q.v.) and the use of indigenous resources, providing emergency and disaster relief (q.v.) as needed.

Caribbean Community and Common Market (CARICOM). A customs union providing for the elimination of trade (q.v.) barriers among members, a common external tariff, and the harmonization of certain domestic economic policies. It was created by the 1973 Treaty of Chaguaramas (Trinidad) and entered into by Barbados, Guyana, Jamaica, and Trinidad and Tobago. Eight other Commonwealth (q.v.) Caribbean countries acceded to full-membership status in 1974. The treaty was amended in 1976 to allow the Bahamas to join as a member of the Caribbean Community without being required to join its common market. Some regional countries have observer status.

The basic purpose of the community is to foster unity among peoples of the Caribbean through coordinated regional actions in such areas as health (q.v.), education, labor, transportation (q.v.), economics, trade (q.v.), and foreign policies. CARICOM was a successor to CARIFTA (the Caribbean Free Trade Association). Tensions have long existed in the community between stronger economies striving for free trade and the weaker economies, which are reluctant to give up protectionism. Differences on foreign investment also exist. The implementation of a common external tariff has often been post-poned. In spite of all of this, the members have pledged themselves to establish an export bank and to achieve full monetary union, with a single currency, by the year 2000.

Caribbean Development Bank (CDB). Since 1969, the CDB has fostered cooperation and integration by financing investment projects and programs of its less developed members. Accordingly, it works closely with the Caribbean Community and Common Market (CARICOM) (q.v.). It has been partly supported by funds from the World Bank (q.v.) and other international financial institutions, member countries, and the United States. Still its activities have been constrained by low levels of funding.

Caritas Internationalis (International Conference of Catholic Charities). Caritas, founded in 1951 with headquarters in Vatican City, is an international nongovernmental organization representing groups in over 100 countries dedicated to spreading charity and social justice internationally through emergency aid and disaster relief (q.v.), social development programs, and academic research.

Carter Center. Created in 1982, the Carter Center is located at Emory University in Atlanta, Georgia. It seeks to resolve conflict, promote democracy, preserve human rights (q.v.), improve health (q.v.) and fight hunger around the world. It has an active conflict mediation program, with former U.S. President Carter its most prominent mediator, and has been frequently engaged in monitoring democratic elections.

Cassese, Antonio (1937–). A renowned Italian international lawyer, Cassese is currently serving at the president of the International Criminal Tribunal for the former Yugoslavia. Following his appointment as president of the tribunal, Cassese left his full-time position at the European Institute in Florence. He continues, however, as director of the Academy of European Law. Cassese studied law at the Universities of Pisa and Frankfurt and at the Institut Universitaire des Hautes Etudes Internationales, Geneva. He was professor at the University of Pisa (1964–1974) and then at Florence, where he directed the School of International Affairs and was professor of international law at the Faculty of Political Sciences "Cesare Alfieri." He has been a member of the Italian delegation to the United Nations General Assembly (q.v.) and to diplomatic conferences on human rights (q.v.) and the international law of armed conflict. In 1987–1988, Cassese chaired the Steering Committee for Human Rights of the Council of Europe (q.v.), and he is president of the European Committee for the Prevention of Torture and Inhuman or Degrading Treatment. He has written about the law of armed conflict; conditions restricting the use of force, human rights, parliamentary control of foreign policy; and the responsibility of states for international crimes. His research pursues two themes: the role of the principle of self-determination (q.v.) of peoples in the world community, and international human rights protection, particularly by the Council of Europe.

Catholic Relief Services (CRS). Founded in 1943 as War Relief Services, the name was changed to its current one in 1955. CRS's major activities include responding to calls from victims of natural and human-made disasters, providing assistance to the poor, and working with religious leaders and groups committed to increased social equity. Funded by the Catholic community of the United States, it has field offices in over 40 countries and is active in over 70.

Central American Common Market (CACM) (Mercado Común Centroamericano). The CACM aims at the full liberalization of existing trade (q.v.) barriers between member countries: Costa Rica, El Salvador, Guatemala, Honduras, and Nicaragua. The CACM was established in Managua, Nicaragua, in 1960; its headquarters are in Guatemala City. The initial Treaty on Central American Integration was to expire in 1981, but member states agreed to keep it operative until an agreement could be reached on a new integration plan. The CACM's structure includes a tripartite Commission of Ministers and Deputy Ministers of Finance and Governors of central banks. War between El Salvador and Honduras in 1969, revolution in Nicaragua in the 1980s, serious unrest in El Salvador, and long-standing domestic problems in Guatemala and Honduras made integration a low-priority concern in member states. Still, in the 1990s, members agreed to a number of important changes in the organization, and hope appears to have returned for the region and the organization. The CACM operates the Central American Bank for Economic Integration (CABEI).

Central Commission for the Navigation of the Rhine. Europe's oldest international organization, the commission was established in 1816 to implement the principle of freedom of navigation on Europe's main international river. Its headquarters are in Strasbourg, France. It has considerable powers, including that of binding arbitration in disputes among those who use the river.

Central Treaty Organization (CENTO). A now defunct regional defense alliance against communist aggression in the Middle East aimed at the provision of security as well as the encouragement of social and economic cooperation (q.v.). It was established in 1955 when Turkey and Iraq signed the Treaty of Mutual Cooperation. The United States, which initiated the idea of CENTO, never formally joined it, owing to fear of Arab repercussions. It was known as the Baghdad Pact until Iraq withdrew in 1959, following a revolution there. The headquarters then moved to Ankara, Turkey. Combined CENTO ground, air, and naval exercises were undertaken until the 1979 revolution toppled the Shah of Iran. Weakened as an organization from the outset, because of its failure to attract Arab countries and an inability to solve domestic and international problems, its hopes for developing into a purposeful alliance ended in 1979. Still, in retrospect, it is clear that it had some success in the form of economic development (q.v.) projects, especially in telecommunications.

CERN (Organisation Européenne pour la Recherche Nucléaire) (European Organization for Nuclear Research, formerly the European Council for Nuclear Research). Founded in 1954 in Paris, France, with headquarters in Geneva, Switzerland, CERN is not concerned with work for direct military requirements. All its findings are published or made public. Currently CERN has 19 members: Austria, Belgium, the Czech Republic, Denmark, Finland, France, Germany, Greece, Hungary, Italy, the Netherlands, Norway, Poland, Portugal, Slovakia, Spain, Sweden, Switzerland, and the United Kingdom. Russia hopes to join soon. CERN has some of the world's largest accelerators and thus attracts leading nuclear physicists from around the world to carry out research. CERN's Eastern European counterpart was the Joint Institute for Nuclear Research.

Charter of Economic Rights and Duties of States. Originally proposed at the United Nations Conference on Trade and Development III (UNCTAD III) (q.v.) by then Mexican President Luis Echeverría, the Charter was adopted by the UN General Assembly (q.v.) on December 12, 1974, by a vote of 120–6 (with 10 abstentions). The charter—which as a General Assembly resolution only carries the legal weight of a recommendation—is a broad set of guidelines for the conduct of international economic relations. The most controversial provisions of the charter, and those most strongly opposed by rich, capitalist states with the U.S. in the leadership, are contained in Article 2: the right of states to absolute sovereignty over their natural resources, with compensation for nationalization of foreign business in accordance with *domestic* law.

Charter of Fundamental Social Rights (also known as the Social Charter or Social Chapter). A document prepared in 1989 by the

European Commission (q.v.) as part of the preparations for the establishment of a single internal market by the end of 1992. The basic objective was the codification, in general terms, of both what the European Community (EC) (q.v.) had already initiated and what were deemed to be desirable new goals in the field of social and employment policy. It outlined a code of practice covering living and working conditions and was directed primarily at the rights of workers: collective bargaining; training and equal opportunities (especially of women and underprivileged groups); health and safety protection; the free movement of labor. These goals were to be achieved through a harmonization of working conditions throughout the EC by raising standards in all member states up to the level of the best national practice. British opposition—especially to the provisions related to representation of workers on the management boards of industrial companies and to a maximum working week—made EC unanimity impossible.

Children. Governments have long recognized the universal concern with the plight of often defenseless children, be it as refugees (q.v.) or victims of war, natural disasters, sickness, and so forth. The key UN institution addressing the needs of children, the United Nations International Children's Emergency Fund (UNICEF) (q.v.), is one of its biggest success stories, even though its funding is voluntary and thus always precarious. Numerous international nongovernmental organizations, religious and secular, regional and global, focus on the special needs of children. See also Christian Children's Fund; Feed the Children International; Save the Children Alliance; Save the Children Fund; World Vision International.

Christian Children's Fund. An international nongovernmental organization created in 1938 to improve the condition of the world's children (q.v.) by providing education, medical care, food, clothing, and shelter. The goal of the fund, whose headquarters are in Richmond, Virginia, is to promote self-sufficiency by working through local groups for the improvement of child welfare standards and services according to need and without discrimination as to sex, race, creed, or religion.

Club du Sahel (Club des Amis du Sahel) (also known as the Friends of the Sahel and the Permanent Interstate Committee for Drought Control in the Sahel). Established in 1975 to bring together Sahelian member states' governments and public organizations with actual and potential donors to discuss means for coping with the region's problems, especially those relating to water resources, livestock, and agricultural productivity. The organization's headquarters are in Paris, France. Its members include Austria, Burkina Faso, Canada, Cape Verde, Chad, Denmark, France, Gambia, Germany, Guinea-Bissau, Italy, Japan, Mali, Mauritania, the Netherlands, Niger, Senegal, Switzerland, and the United States.

Club of Rome. The club, which now has organizational members in dozens of countries, grew out of an April 1968 meeting of scientists, educators, economists, humanists, industrialists, and national and international civil servants held in Rome, Italy. All were concerned about the consequences of global interdependence, what they referred to as the "global problematique." They are best known for noting the ecological consequences of unrestrained economic development (q.v.) of economically linked countries. Their concerns have broadened over time, including consideration of such issues as governability. Still, their most famous publication and project to date is probably their work on *Limits to Growth*.

Cocoa Producers' Alliance (CPA). Established under the terms of the Abidjan Charter of January 20, 1962, the CPA now counts among its members those who produce almost 90 percent of the world's cocoa crop. The aims of the alliance include the exchange of technical and scientific information, promotion of economic and social relations among the member states, promotion of cocoa consumption, and assurance of the proper supply of cocoa to the market at remunerative prices.

Collective security. A means of restraining aggression and ending breaches of the peace by agreement of a body of states to take common action. It assumes that one of the ways to deter aggression is joint confrontation by a pact among countries. An act of aggression against one must be recognized as an act of aggression against all. U.S. President Wilson insisted that the notion be included in the League of Nations' (q.v.) Covenant.

Collective self-defense. Article 51 of the UN Charter provides that, in the case of armed attack against a member state, nothing in the charter impairs that state's right of individual or collective self-defense until the Security Council (q.v.) has acted to restore international peace and security. Any actions taken in the name of self-defense are to be reported to the Security Council. In practice, this notification does not usually happen.

The call for self-defense permitted the emergence of various intergovernmental organizations formed for that purpose and accepted as such. These included the North Atlantic Treaty Organization (NATO) (q.v.) and the Warsaw Treaty Organization (WTO) (q.v.).

Colombo Plan for Cooperative Economic and Social Development in Asia and the Pacific. Established in 1950 in Colombo, Sri Lanka, the Colombo Plan is intended to enhance economic development (q.v.) in South Asia and the Pacific. Originating in a meeting of Commonwealth (q.v.) foreign ministers, it tries to focus global attention on the development needs of the region. The Colombo Plan is primarily an instrument for the promotion of interregional economic and social cooperation and development rather than an operating agency. Most of its development projects are funded internally. It also provides some technical assistance and, since 1973, has operated the Colombo Plan Staff College for Technical Education.

COMECON. See Council for Mutual Economic Assistance (CMEA).

Comité des Organisations Professionelles Agricoles (COPA) (Committee of Agricultural Organizations). A transnational federation of farming unions and associations, generally considered to be one of the most influential transnational interest groups related to the European Community (EC) (q.v.) and European Union (EU) (q.v.). The structure of the Common Agricultural Policy (CAP) (q.v.) and its centrality to the EC has meant that COPA is actively engaged in annual wage negotiations for the whole farming sector.

Comité des Représentants Permanents (COREPER) (Committee of Permanent Representatives). Technically, the heads of the delegations, or permanent representatives, that each member state of the European Community (EC) (q.v.) and then the European Union (EU) (q.v.) maintains in Brussels, Belgium, but more loosely used to refer to the totality of the delegations, including various committees and subgroups. Its main task is to act as a service agent and gatekeeper to the EU's Council of Ministers (q.v.). Where there is unanimity in COREPER, proposals are simply approved by the Council of Ministers without discussion or vote. Where there is disagreement on a proposal, one of the specialist groups works on it further. Given the workload, there is now a COREPER I, composed of deputies, and COREPER II, the ambassadorial-level meetings themselves. The power and influence of the COREPER are criticized by those who are leery of the power of national governments in the EU or who are concerned with issues of accountability within the EU institutional framework.

Comité Inter-Etats pour la Lutte contre la Secheresse au Sahel (CLISS). Formed in 1973, CLISS is an organization of seven contiguous states in the Sahelian region. Their goal is the coordination of relief, rehabilitation, and development activities to combat the effects of drought.

Comité Maritime International (CMI). CMI traces its origins to a meeting in Brussels, Belgium, in 1897. Currently headquartered in Antwerp, Belgium, CMI convenes periodic conferences for the purpose of drafting maritime treaties. Topics have included collisions at sea, limitations of shipowners' liabilities in collisions, and maritime oil pollution. It works closely with both the United Nations Conference on Trade and Development (UNCTAD) (q.v.) and the International Maritime Organization (IMO) (q.v.).

Commission for Social Development (formerly the Social Commission). The commission established on June 21, 1946, as the Social Commission, advises the United Nations Economic and Social Council (ECOSOC) (q.v.) on a wide range of social policy issues and social perspectives of development. Functioning under a broad mandate, the commission, which now consists of 46 member states, has met at various intervals at different locations throughout its existence. Among its major foci of attention lately have been the impacts of globalization and technological innovation, including on employment.

Committee of the Whole (COW). Created by the UN General Assembly (q.v.) in 1977 to monitor implementation of the decisions and agreements reached at the United Nations (UN) (q.v.) regarding the New International Economic Order (q.v.) and to serve as a forum on global economic problems and priorities. The committee, which is open to all members of the UN, was seen by developing countries (q.v.) as a preferred way to avoid having global economic decisions made in bodies with weighted voting (q.v.), such as the World Bank (q.v.) and International Monetary Fund (IMF) (q.v.).

Commodities. Because a large number of countries depend on the export of commodities, or often a single commodity, for a substantial percentage of their export revenue, the issue of an intergovernmental organization to stabilize the prices of commodities was on the top of policy makers' agendas in the last years of World War II. However, members of the U.S. Senate in particular were uncomfortable with the sort of market interference that commodity organizations involve. Thus, the International Trade Organization never came into being. Its replacement, the General Agreement on Tariffs and Trade (GATT) (q.v.), never had stabilizing the price of commodities as one of its goals. It was not until the UNCTAD (q.v.)-developed Common Fund for Commodities (q.v.) came into existence that the UN had an overall mechanism committed to this goal. Central to the Common Fund are a number of buffer stocks, some simply taken over from preexisting international commodity agreements (q.v.).

In addition to these producer-consumer agreements, where price and supply stability is the goal, are a number of producer only organizations, often referred to as cartels. The most well known of these is the Organization of Petroleum Exporting Countries (OPEC) (q.v.), which became something of an unreplicable model for many other commodity cartels, some of which quickly failed and none of which succeeded in raising their respective commodity prices as had that focusing on the high demand, difficult to substitute for in the short-run commodity exemplar, petroleum. See also Association of Iron Ore Exporting Countries; Association of Natural Rubber Producing Countries; Association of Tin Producing Countries; Cocoa Producers' Alliance; Conseil Intergovernmental des Pays Exportateurs de Cuivre; Integrated Program for Commodities; Inter-African Coffee Organization; International Cocoa Organization; International Coffee Organization; International Commission for the Conservation of Atlantic Tunas; International Grains Council; International Jute Organization; International Lead and Zinc Study Group; International Natural Rubber Organization; International Nickel Study Group; International Olive Oil Council; International Sugar Organization; International Tea Council; International Tea Promotion Association; International Tropical Timber Organization; MINEX; Organization of Arab Petroleum Exporting Countries; STABEX; Unión de Países Exportadores de Banana.

Common Agricultural Policy (CAP). A common agricultural policy is one of the few explicit policy obligations laid upon members of the European Community (EC) (q.v.) by the Treaty of Rome and carried over by the European Charter. But it was not until January 1962 that even an interim accord on general principles of a common policy could be reached. As it has evolved, the CAP consists of three major elements: a single market for agricultural products, with common prices; a common external tariff levied on agricultural imports into the EC; and common financial responsibility. The core of the CAP is the guaranteed price system administered by the European Agricultural Guidance and Guarantee Fund. Agricultural prices have traditionally been set high, owing to political pressure, with the result being overproduction. Surplus produce is either bought at fixed prices and stored (resulting in the so-called mountains of butter or wine lakes) or exported, with exporters receiving subsidies (or restitutions) to cover the difference between the high purchase prices and the lower prices at which they had to sell on the world market.

Thus, the CAP has contributed to increased production, self-sufficiency, and prosperity for farmers but not necessarily low prices for consumers. By the 1980s, the CAP composed two-thirds of the EC's and then the European Union's (EU) (q.v.) budget, resulting in strong criticism, especially by the British. This resonated with that of the U.S. and third world agricultural exporters, who long argued that the CAP interfered with the free market in agriculture and hurt states whose comparative advantages were in agricultural goods. Some reform measures have been implemented to lower the percentage of the EU's budget consumed by the CAP.

Common Fund for Commodities. After protracted negotiations under the direction of the United Nations Conference on Trade and Development (UNCTAD) (q.v.) secretariat, the Common Fund Agreement was concluded in 1980. The fund serves as the key instrument of the Integrated Program for Commodities (q.v.) and is charged with facilitating the conclusion and functioning of international commodity agreements (q.v.), particularly in commodities of export interest to the economically least developed countries (q.v.). The Common Fund, which has its headquarters in Amsterdam, the Netherlands, began operations on September 15, 1989. Critics are concerned that it will be perpetually plagued by financial problems because almost all commodity (q.v.) prices rise and fall simultaneously, and thus the fund will never be self-supporting.

Common heritage of mankind. In 1970, in response to the request of the Maltese ambassador to the United Nations (q.v.), Arvid Pardo, speaking for the developing countries (q.v.), the General Assembly (q.v.) created a Seabed Committee. The committee called for a moratorium on all seabed exploration, declaring the seabed beyond national jurisdiction as the "common heritage of mankind."

Common Market for Eastern and Southern Africa (COMESA). Established in 1994 with the goal of creating a common market to attain sustainable, balanced, and harmonious development. With headquarters in Lusaka, Zambia, COMESA is promoting cooperation in transportation (q.v.), communications (q.v.), finance, and marketing. It is also working toward trade (q.v.) liberalization and tariff reduction. It has pledged to coordinate its activities with SADC (Southern African Development Community) (q.v.).

Commonwealth, The. Formalized as an organization in 1931, the Commonwealth of Nations was formerly known as the British Commonwealth of Nations. It is composed of former British colonies (53, with Cameroon and Mozambique being the newest members and the most important membership change being the reentrance of South Africa in 1994). There is no Commonwealth charter, treaty, or constitution, but all members recognize the British monarch as the symbolic head of the Commonwealth. It meets and consults on a regular basis to foster common links, coordinate mutual assistance for social and economic development (q.v.), and contribute to the restructuring of international economic relations. The monarch is present at all summit sessions of the Commonwealth, but does not attend meetings.

The Commonwealth has recently been quite active in encouraging privatization efforts and in election monitoring, including the elections in South Africa. The 1997 Commonwealth Heads of Government Meeting focused on trade (q.v.), investment, and development. The Commonwealth oversees a number of important units including the Commonwealth Fund for Technical Cooperation.

Communauté Economique de l'Afrique de l'Ouest (CEAO) (West African Economic Community). Established in April 1973, the CEAO, which replaced the Customs Union of West African States, aimed at promoting trade and economic cooperation (q.v.) among its member states, the former French colonies of Burkina Faso, Côte d'Ivoire, Mali, Mauritania, Niger, and Senegal. The CEAO instituted a Regional Cooperation Tax to promote regional trade in locally manufactured goods. It also included a Community Development Fund that compensated states suffering losses from interstate trade and a Solidarity and Intervention Fund that provided development funds to the poorest member states. One of the long-standing challenges to the CEAO, which had its headquarters in Ouagadougou, Burkina Faso, was how to balance member states' trade with that of their neighboring states, which often included former British colonies. In 1994, the members gave up and disbanded the organization, concluding that there were simply too many fundamental differences to overcome, compounded by overall organizational inefficiencies.

Communauté Economique des Etats de l'Afrique Central (CEEAC) (Economic Community of Central African States). Like many such communities established in the South, the goal is to try and replicate the success of the European Union (q.v.). More specifically, the community, which was established in 1983 and has its headquarters in Libreville, Gabon, has set as its goal for the year 2000 the end of customs duties and other trade restrictions and the establishment of a common market. Thus far, it has been held back by staff problems and conflicts within various member countries.

Communauté Economique des Pays des Grands Lacs (CEPGC) (Economic Community of the Great Lakes Countries). Security concerns were among the original focus of this three-member organization (Burundi, Rwanda, and Zaire). When setting up the organization in 1976, the member states were all concerned about coordinating their policies toward South Africa. With the change of regime there, the community, which has its headquarters in Giseny, Rwanda, can focus on the promotion of economic integration. While the community has succeeded in establishing the Development Bank of the Great Lakes States and facilitating political, cultural, technical, and scientific cooperation among the various member states, the internal chaos in Burundi and Rwanda has precluded much progress in the 1990s.

Communications. Among the first intergovernmental organizations were those concerned with helping people communicate across national boundaries. These include the Universal Postal Union (UPU) (q.v.) and the International Telecommunication Union (ITU) (q.v.). Amazingly resilient organizations, they continue to exist today but have yet to evidence the validity of the major tenets of functionalism (q.v.). That is, even though they are deemed technical organizations, they have from time to time been highly politicized. Moreover, success in the communications arena has not automatically spilled over into cooperation among members in other, unrelated issue areas. More recently, the United Nations Educational, Scientific and Cultural Organization (UNESCO) (q.v.) has been the major venue for debates about states' sovereign rights to censor news and the right to limit informatics.

See also International Maritime Satellite Organization (Inmarsat); International Telecommunications Satellite Organization (INTELSAT); MacBride Commission; New World Information Order; Société Internationale de Télécommunications Aéronautiques (SITA); World Administrative Radio Conference (WARC).

Community Aid Abroad (CAA). Based in Melbourne, Australia, since 1963, CAA supports long-term community-based self-help projects for those in need in developing countries (q.v.). It also provides disaster relief (q.v.) and development education activities and lobbies for basic human rights (q.v.). At last count, it was supporting over 250 projects in more than 26 countries.

Conciliation. Conciliation—in which representatives of a group of states establish the facts in a dispute and use them as the basis for making recommendations—is one of the peaceful methods of dispute used by the United Nations (q.v.) and the Organization of American States (q.v.).

Confederation of Central African NGOs. The confederation grew out of the United Nations Conference on Environment and Development (UNCED) (q.v.). Its goal is to provide a framework for cooperation among voluntary development organizations and nongovernmental development and environmental organizations in Central Africa. The purpose is to promote popular participation in furthering the goals of sustainable development and slowing the spread of desertification.

Conference on Disarmament. This is the United Nations' (UN) (q.v.) most important negotiating agency on the subject. It is the successor agency (since 1984) to a series of similar major agencies within the UN structure. It has 40 members, including all of the permanent members of the Security Council (q.v.). Its work has been supplemented by that of a series of special sessions of the General Assembly (q.v.). See also peace, disarmament, and arms control.

Conference on International Economic Cooperation (CIEC). Often referred to as the North-South dialogue, several sessions were held between December 1975 and June 1977. The original idea for such meetings came from then French President Giscard d'Estaing. Twenty-seven countries participated in the meetings: 8 industrial states, 7 oil-producing countries, and 12 economically developing countries (q.v.). Attention was focused on energy, raw materials, development, and finance.

Conference on Security and Cooperation in Europe (CSCE). See Organization on Security and Cooperation in Europe (OSCE).

Connally Reservation. Article 36, section 2, of the Statute of the International Court of Justice (ICJ) (q.v.) provides that any party to the statute may declare that it recognizes as compulsory, in relation to any other state accepting the same obligation, the jurisdiction of the ICJ. This is the so-called "optional clause," because one can be a party to the statute without adhering to this proviso. Most members of the ICJ do not subscribe to this optional clause, and many that do have made it subject to a number of reservations. The most sweeping (and famous) of these reservations was the Connally Amendment attached to the U.S. adherence to the clause. This reservation specified that ICJ jurisdiction would not apply to "disputes with regard to matters which are essentially within the domestic jurisdiction of the United States as determined by the United States of America." This self-judging reservation, which served as a model for reservations by many other countries, effectively nullified the effectiveness of adherence to Article 36(2). In the aftermath of the International Court of Justice's decision in the Nicaraguan harbor mining case, the United States withdrew its adherence to the optional clause entirely. Cases involving the United States could still go before the court, however, either as a consequence of agreements in other multilateral treaties or by special agreement. The United States has considerable interest in many of the court's decisions, not least of all its 1996 advisory opinion that the use or threat of nuclear weapons was the "ultimate evil" and thus should be outlawed. The ICJ, however, could not decide whether they should be banned when used for purposes of self-defense.

Conseil de l'Entente (Council of the Entente). Established on May 29, 1959, with headquarters in Abidjan, Côte d'Ivoire, the council's goal is to promote economic development (q.v.) via regional cooperation (q.v.). For much of the council's history, it was perceived by the smaller member states (Benin, Burkina Faso, Niger, and Togo) as an institution promoting the Côte d'Ivoire's quest for regional political and economic predominance. More recently, however, substantive progress has been made in the areas of tourism (q.v.), infrastructure, food production, and energy. Moreover, discussions have been held on regional security.

Conseil Intergovernemental des Pays Exportateurs de Cuivre (CIPEC) (Intergovernmental Council of Copper Exporting Countries). CIPEC, founded by the Convention of Lusaka in 1967, attempted to operate as a cartel but failed, primarily because there exist close substitutes for copper. CIPEC operated thereafter, until its demise in 1992, as a copper information-gathering institution with headquarters in Paris. It collapsed, in part, because of the inability of African members to live up to their financial obligations and because of the Chilean government's commitment to market mechanisms for determining price.

Contadora Group. Following up on an initiative of the Mexican government, the foreign ministers of Colombia, Mexico, Panama, and Venezuela held a number of meetings in the mid- and late 1980s aimed at reducing tensions and conflict in Central America. The group's name comes from the Panamanian island where they first convened. They came to be identified with the view that the problems of the region result from economic, social, and political inequities rather than the East-West conflict. They favored increased foreign economic assistance and the termination of foreign military assistance as means for improving the region's military-security climate. The group is given considerable credit for helping resolve the conflicts between the U.S.-backed Contras and the Sandinistas in Nicaragua.

Convention on International Trade in Endangered Species of Wild Fauna and Flora (CITES). The secretariat, based in Geneva, Switzerland, is responsible for monitoring adherence to the CITES treaty, which aims at the protection of certain endangered species through regulating their trade across state boundaries. The convention, which has been in legal effect since 1973, has had some limited impact and is credited with decreasing the killing of elephants for their tusks. In 1997 Botswana, Namibia, and Zimbabwe requested and were granted permission to resume limited trade in ivory. It was their contention that they had too many elephants on too little land. Their position was strongly contested by other governments. Indeed, some suggest that the entire CITES approach merely increases the "black market" for the illegal killing and marketing of endangered species.

Cooperation Council for the Arab States of the Gulf (commonly known as the Gulf Cooperation Council, GCC). Formed in 1981 by Bahrain, Kuwait, Oman, Qatar, Saudi Arabia, and the United Arab Emirates (i.e., states that border the Arabian Gulf). The GCC has its headquarters in Riyadh, Saudi Arabia. It seeks to ensure security and stability in the region through political and economic cooperation (q.v.). Thus, it seeks to promote, expand and enhance economic ties, although it is not a vehicle for political and economic cooperation and integration (q.v.). All members are oil-producing states with special ties and common systems of government. Much of the GCC's time is spent discussing issues related to oil. The GCC's strained cooperation, as demonstrated during the Iraqi occupation of Kuwait, has led some to question its viability.

Corfu Channel case. This was the first case heard by the International Court of Justice (ICJ) (q.v.). The case began in the Security Council (q.v.) with the United Kingdom complaining about the loss of 44 lives aboard British destroyers that had hit mines laid by Albania in the Corfu Channel. In April 1947, the Security Council recommended that the case be taken to the ICJ. In 1949, the court held Albania responsible for the laying of the mines, upheld the right of innocent passage by the British ships through international waters, and assessed damages to be paid by Albania at £843,947. Albania challenged the jurisdiction of the court on technical grounds and never paid the monetary judgment. For years this was the only ICJ judgment that was not enforced. The case was also notable in terms of the basis of the judgment, which many saw as including a natural law element to it.

Council for Mutual Economic Assistance (CMEA) (also known as COMECON). Called COMECON in the West, the CMEA was formed in 1949 to assist in the economic development (q.v.) of and to coordinate the economic planning for Eastern European (and subsequently Cuba, Mongolia, and Vietnam, out of the region) countries in the Soviet bloc. CMEA was never as successful as its Western European competitor—the European Economic Community (EEC) (q.v.). Indeed, beginning in 1976 some CMEA members entered into bilateral trade (q.v.) agreements with individual EEC members. The EEC rejected bloc-to-bloc negotiations, taking the position that to do so would provide undue legitimacy to CMEA, which was seen by many as simply another means for the Soviet Union to maintain control over and dominate its allies. The fall of the state socialist governments of most of its European members (1989–1990) and the end of the use of the ruble as a basis for intermember trade doomed the organization. In 1991, it was dissolved.

Council of Arab Economic Unity. With its headquarters in Cairo, Egypt, the council held its first meeting in 1964. Its members are Egypt, Iraq, Jordan, Kuwait, Libya, Mauritania, Palestine, Somalia, Sudan, Syria, the United Arab Emirates, and Yemen. The aim of the council, whose headquarters are in Amman, Jordan, is to establish a customs union. To this end, members are usually represented by ministers of economics, finance, and trade at the council meetings, which are convened twice a year. While a customs union has yet to be established, the council supervises the Arab Common Market and coordinates agricultural and industrial projects. It has also made progress in improving the region's rail and road networks.

Council of Europe. An intergovernmental consultative body established in 1949 as Western Europe's first postwar political organization. It owed its inspiration to the 1948 Congress of Europe, which had sponsored the formation of the European Movement, dedicated to persuading European governments of the need for and desirability of political cooperation and integration. The council is concerned with European cooperation, rather than integration, in all areas except for defense. Permanent offices for the organization were provided by

France in Strasbourg. While the Cold War restricted its membership to Western Europe, in the 1980s it expanded to become the European organization with the largest spread of membership (aside from the Organization on Security and Cooperation in Europe [q.v.], which has a much narrower mandate). In 1996, Russia became a member, as did Croatia. They joined Albania, Andorra, Austria, Belgium, Bulgaria, Cyprus, the Czech Republic, Denmark, Estonia, Finland, France, Germany, Greece, Hungary, Iceland, Ireland, Italy, Latvia, Liechtenstein, Lithuania, Luxembourg, Macedonia, Malta, Moldova, the Netherlands, Norway, Poland, Portugal, Romania, San Marino, Slovakia, Spain, Sweden, Switzerland, Turkey, Ukraine, and the United Kingdom. Azerbaijan, Georgia, and Bosnia have also applied.

The council consists of two major institutions: the Committee of Ministers, the more important body, and the Assembly (renamed the Parliamentary Assembly since 1974), composed of delegates appointed or elected by and from members' national legislatures. Since 1952, foreign ministers have rarely met except for highly symbolic or highly sensitive issues. The assembly is essentially a discussion chamber that can only forward recommendations to the committee of ministers for consideration. The committee may, and often has, rejected or ignored these recommendations. The Parliamentary Assembly, which can debate any nonmilitary security–related issue, has developed close relations with the European Parliament (q.v.) of the European Community (q.v.) and the European Union (q.v.), with which it shares a common site. They hold joint meetings each year. The 1950 European Convention on Human Rights (q.v.) is widely recognized as the council's most important achievement. The council operates the Council of Europe Social Development Fund that assists national refugees (q.v.), political refugees, victims of natural disasters, and migrant workers. See also European Commission on Human Rights.

Council of Ministers. The key decision-making organ of the European Community (EC) (q.v.) and then the European Union (EU) (q.v.). Its wide responsibility for a broad range of policy areas means that there are, in effect, several councils, which can even meet simultaneously. If the topic under discussion is the budget, then national finance ministers meet. If it is agriculture, then the council is composed of national ministers of agriculture. At the apex is the General Affairs Council—that is, the meetings of the national foreign ministers. The direction of the council is the responsibility of its president. Member states hold the presidency in rotation. Where the council is not presented with a unanimous recommendation from the Comité des Représentants Permanents (COREPER) (q.v.), the matter can be decided by a majority vote (for minor, mostly procedural, issues), a qualified (i.e., two-thirds, currently 62 of the 87 votes) majority, or unanimously. Voting is weighted, with the countries with the largest population getting the most votes. France, Germany, Italy, and the United Kingdom have 10 each, and Luxembourg has two. The Treaty of Rome anticipated a gradual increase in the use of majority and qualified majority voting, a move blocked in 1965 by French President Charles de Gaulle. The Luxembourg Agreement (q.v.) of 1966 reconfirmed the right of a national veto when a state deems that its vital national interests are involved. While the Single European Act (q.v.) significantly extends the areas to which qualified majorities apply, member states have generally preferred to operate by unanimity.

Council of the Baltic Sea States (CBSS). Established in Copenhagen, Denmark, on March 5, 1992, by Norway and the littoral states of the Baltic Sea–Denmark, Estonia, Finland, Germany, Latvia, Lithuania, Poland, Russia, and Sweden. Its main objective is to promote economic development (q.v.) and the development of new democratic institutions in the member states that previously had few or none. Much of the focus has heretofore been to channel financial aid for economic development from Germany and Scandinavia to the poorer states of the East. The first decisions reached at the annual Council of Ministers' meetings (there is no secretariat) focused on transportation (q.v.), communications (q.v.) and the environment (q.v.). Progress has been slowed by disputes among some of the members, including the presence of Russian troops in some of the member states.

Court of Auditors. Established in 1977, this agency, composed of one appointee named by the European Union's (q.v.) Council of Ministers from each member state, examines all accounts of revenue and expenditures of all European Union institutions. While some credit it with serving as an efficient watchdog and critic of wasteful expenditure and, on occasion, of financial mismanagement, its focus of attention is on issues of illegality or at least mismanagement. Its annual reports, for example, have been particularly effective in uncovering fraudulent claims made under the Common Agricultural Policy (CAP) (q.v.). Since the Maastricht Treaty (q.v.) was ratified in 1993, the Court of Auditors has formally been the fifth European Union institution.

Court of First Instance. Established in 1989 as a backup to the European Court of Justice (q.v.) of the European Union (q.v.). It has taken over jurisdiction of some of the more minor categories of cases, especially those involving European Union employees (e.g., questions of recruitment, promotion, salaries, disciplinary measures).

Customs Co-operation Council (CCC). Established in December 1950 with its headquarters now in Brussels, Belgium, the CCC is charged with studying questions related to customs and to the promotion of cooperation in customs matters. There are currently 136 members of this little noted intergovernmental organization that is committed to trade liberalization by means of harmonizing and standardizing customs systems. Most recently, the organization—which is seeking to promote itself a bit more than in the past—has focused on policies and procedures related to smuggling and protection of intellectual property and toward further involvement of the new regimes in Eastern and Central Europe.

D

Dadzie, Kenneth K. S. (1930–1995). After a successful career in the Ghanaian foreign service, Dadzie was seconded to the United Nations (q.v.) in 1963. There he served in a number of capacities focusing on decolonization (q.v.) and development cooperation. From 1978 to 1982, he served as the director-general for Development and International Economic Cooperation and, from 1986 to 1994, as secretary-general of the United Nations Conference on Trade and Development (UNCTAD) (q.v.), the two highest positions in the United Nations system concerned with development policies and international cooperation for development. At UNCTAD, he is credited with initiating a reassessment of that organization's role, in an attempt to make it more relevant to a world in which the watchwords included capitalism, privatization, and limited interference with the free market. At the time of his death, Dadzie was serving as the Ghanaian high commissioner to the United Kingdom.

Danube Commission. Established to regulate navigation on the Danube River and to ensure the application of uniform rules. The original commission, created in 1856, sought to control and improve conditions of navigation on the "maritime" Danube, especially those relating to navigation, flood control, water power, and irrigation. Today's commission, constituted in Belgrade, Yugoslavia, in 1948, was founded by Bulgaria, Czechoslovakia, Hungary, Romania, Ukraine, the USSR, and Yugoslavia. Since 1957, at the invitation of the commission, Germany has taken part in the commission's work. Austria joined in 1960.

Declaration on the Granting of Independence to Colonial Countries and Peoples. This landmark resolution was passed by the General

Assembly (q.v.) in 1960, in the immediate aftermath of the admission to the United Nations (UN) (q.v.) of 17 formerly colonial states. The resolution, which was characterized as implementing the UN Charter, declared the rights of all peoples (left undefined) to political independence and self-rule. The following year the General Assembly created a committee to oversee the decolonization (q.v.) process.

Decolonization. One of the key differences between the League of Nations (q.v.) mandates (q.v.) and the United Nations (q.v.) trusts is that the Trusteeship Council (q.v.) was charged with assisting all of the trust territories (q.v.) in achieving the necessary requisites for independence, whereas the League's Mandate Commission expected many of the mandates to remain dependent possessions. More important in the long run, however, the members of the United Nations came to understand their charge as also including encouragement of decolonization in countries that were not trust territories. In this vein, the UN General Assembly (q.v.) passed countless resolutions urging the colonial powers to follow the U.S. example in the Philippines and grant independence to their colonies. The process was long and, in many places, bloody. But most agree that the UN's role, including the work of the United Nations Special Committee on the Situations with Regard to the Implementation of the Declaration of the Granting of Independence to Colonial Countries and Peoples (q.v.), was vital in accelerating the pace of decolonization. Other intergovernmental organizations, most notably the Organization of African Unity (OAU) (q.v.), saw decolonization as central to its mission as well. See also self-determination.

Defense. The chief purpose of the UN (q.v.) is to maintain peace and security. Accordingly, its charter clearly delimits the tasks of other agents of collective self-defense, some of which—most notably the Organization of American States (OAS) (q.v.)—predated the UN. With clear limits to what the UN could do to prevent conflict, especially in the Cold War era, regional, collective defense organizations proliferated. Many of these, such as the Central Treaty Organization (CENTO) (q.v.), have long since disappeared. But the most prominent, the North Atlantic Treaty Organization (NATO) (q.v.), continues and recently even agreed to expand its membership, admitting some members of the now defunct Warsaw Treaty Organization (WTO) (q.v.), which had actually been established to counterbalance NATO. See also Afro-Asian People's Security Conference; ANZUS Council; Brussels, Treaty of; burden sharing; EUROGROUP; European Defense Community; Harmal Report; Inter-American Treaty of Reciprocal Assistance; Ismay, Hastings Lionel Ismay; Luns, Joseph M. A.

H.; Military Staff Committee; Solana, Javier; Southeast Asia Treaty Organization; Spaak, Paul-Henri; United Nations Security Council; Western European Union; Wörner, Manfred.

de Larosière, Jacques (1929–). Prior to becoming managing director of the International Monetary Fund (IMF) (q.v.) in 1978 (where he remained in office for two full terms, until 1987), de Larosière worked as a French banking executive and in the French government. He also served as president of the Group of Ten (q.v.). De Larosière was a high-profile managing director, in part because of his personality and in part because of the times when he served. Among the major challenges of his period in office was the so-called third world debt. He was actively engaged, for example, in coping with the renegotiation of the Mexican debt. He was frequently scorned by the United States, as he was not reluctant to criticize that country when he felt its financial policies were insufficiently attentive to inflationary concerns. In addition to his service at the IMF, he has received much praise for his work as president of the European Bank for Reconstruction and Development (q.v.).

Delors, Jacques (1925–). President of the European Commission (q.v.) from 1985 to 1995. His earlier career was in economics and finance in his native France. He joined François Mitterrand's Socialist Party only in 1974 and was elected to the European Parliament (q.v.) in 1979. It was Delors who took overall responsibility for achieving the goal of a single internal market for the European Community (EC) (q.v.) by the end of 1992. Delors's vision of Europe, however, went well beyond an economic market. He was equally insistent that EC member states should work for monetary and political integration. His arguments and endeavors gained him the reputation as the most activist and influential president of the Commission since Walter Hallstein (1957–1967). Three of his most important initiatives were endorsement of a Charter of Fundamental Social Rights (q.v.) as an essential social complement to the economic structure of an internal market, the 1987 proposals for EC budgetary reform, and the 1988 proposals for Economic and Monetary Union (EMU) (q.v.). His insistence that the commission must become a "real executive" answerable to and counterbalanced by the "democratic institutions of the future Federation" was most strongly resisted by the United Kingdom, especially while Margaret Thatcher was prime minister.

In April 1989 he authored what came to be known as the Delors Report. It laid out a three-stage mechanism for the creation of a European system of central banks and then a European Central Bank as a way of instituting monetary union.

Developing countries. One of many terms used to describe countries, mainly located in Africa, Asia, and Latin America, with economies that rely heavily on the production of agriculture and raw materials and that have relatively low per capita gross national products (GNP). The term was used to replace *underdeveloped countries,* which was deemed condescending. The term *developing countries* has itself been criticized as it seems to imply that all countries are and should be headed toward development, presumably along paths similar to those already developed (i.e., industrialized.) Others have preferred to use the term *less developed country* (LDC), which many feel should be qualified by the modifier *economically* (less developed country) to underscore that many such countries are quite advanced, including in cultural terms. Some try to avoid such controversies by speaking in terms of "the South," although not all such countries are in the Southern Hemisphere, nor are all countries in the Southern Hemisphere poor.

Others have spoken of the third world or even the "fourth" and "fifth" worlds, with countries getting increasingly poor as one goes from the "first" to the "fifth." But such terminology itself was problematic because countries of the first world were distinguished from second in terms of degree of wealth, industrialization, *and* regime type. The second world was composed of centrally planned economies as contrasted to the market or mixed-market economies of the first world. On the other hand, the regime types of third, fourth, and fifth worlds were less relevant than the countries' relatively low gross national products.

The World Bank (q.v.), while acknowledging the lack of consensus within the UN system concerning the terms *developed* and *developing*, differentiates, for statistical "convenience," between "low-income economies" (those with GNP per capita of $765 or less), "middle-income economies" (with GNP per capita of more than $765 but less than $9,386), and "high-income economies" (with GNP per capita of more than $9,386). They have also subdivided middle-income economies between "lower-middle-income" and "upper-middle-income." The cutoff point is GNP per capita of $3,035. Critics of GNP per capita note that such a statistic neglects the degree of income stratification in countries, especially important in countries with relatively small populations, in which a small but very rich elite can raise the income categorization of a country where the vast majority of the population is very poor. This description fits some oil-exporting countries.

Development Alternatives with Women for New Era (DAWN). Founded in India in 1974, DAWN acts as a catalyst in international development thinking and policy making. Its goal is to focus attention on the consequences of particular development programs for women (q.v.), people of color, and those in the lower class.

Development Assistance Committee (DAC). The DAC is an 18-member committee of the Organisation for Economic Co-operation and Development (OECD) (q.v.), whose responsibilities include the coordination, monitoring, and evaluation of official development assistance (q.v.) from member countries to economically developing countries (q.v.). Major aid donor members meet on a regular and frequent basis to discuss ways in which the quantity and quality of their aid can be improved. The DAC has no formal authority over its members, but it has succeeded in specifying certain minimum standards of aid quality (e.g., relating to the financial terms and minimum "grant element" of official development assistance). It has a reputation for candid critiques. Moreover, through its secretariat, the DAC has played an important role in collecting and standardizing statistics on aid flows.

Development decades. Ten-year periods, covering the 1960s, 1970s, 1980s, and 1990s, designated by the United Nations (UN) (q.v.) for exceptional effort in the area of economic development (q.v.), including foreign and technical assistance. The first was announced in 1961 (General Assembly Resolution XVI, 1710); the chief goal was increasing economic growth in economically less developed countries by at least 5 percent per year by the end of the decade. That goal became an annual goal and was increased to 6 percent during the second decade and 7 percent during the third decade. In spite of the fact that none of the goals was attained—indeed, the gap between the rich and poor has continued to increase rather than decrease—the UN remains steadfast in its commitment to try to eradicate poverty and to achieve a fairer distribution of the world's wealth. The General Assembly (q.v.) created a Committee for Development Planning to assist in planning for each decade.

Dillon Round. The multilateral trade (q.v.) negotiations held between 1960 and 1961, under the auspices of the General Agreement on Tariffs and Trade (GATT) (q.v.). The talks were named to honor C. Douglas Dillon, then U.S. secretary of the treasury.

Disarmament. See Peace, disarmament, and arms control.

Disaster relief. An informal division of labor has evolved between intergovernmental and international nongovernmental organizations working on disaster relief, be it human made or from droughts, famine, or floods. Intergovernmental organizations, such as the Office of the United Nations Disaster Relief Coordinator (UNDRO) (q.v.), often coordinate the work of a large number of often overlapping religious and secular nongovernmental organizations. Some such as the International Islamic Relief Organization (IIRO) (q.v.) deal with all sorts of disasters anywhere in the world. Others' mandates are more circumscribed, such as that of Community Aid Abroad (CAA). See also Adventist Development and Relief Agency; Caritas Internationalis; Catholic Relief Services; Comité Inter-Etats pour la Lutte contre la Secheresse au Sahel; Médecins du Monde; Médecins sans Frontières; OXFAM; Pharmaciens sans Frontières.

Domestic jurisdiction. One of the basic principles included in the UN Charter forbids the United Nations (UN) (q.v.) "to intervene in matters which are essentially within the domestic jurisdiction of any state" (Article 2[7]). The precise meaning of the phrase has been a subject of debate from the first meetings of the UN General Assembly (q.v.), when South Africa contended that a discussion of its policies of apartheid were a violation of its "domestic jurisdiction," especially as such a discussion would inevitably lead down the slippery slope of intervention. Over time, the South African prediction appears to have been prescient, as the UN went from denouncing South Africa's policy to sending investigatory missions and eventually to providing financial support to opposition troops—a practice obviously not limited to the South African context. According to the charter, the only times that the UN could breach the domestic jurisdiction principle was when the UN Security Council (q.v.) declared a threat to international peace and security.

Drummond, (James) Eric (Earl of Perth) (1876–1951). Sir Eric was just over 40 when he was selected as the first secretary-general of the League of Nations (q.v.), but he had already worked for 19 years as an official in the British Foreign Office and was one of the principal figures there. Actually, Drummond was not the delegations' first choice: he was offered the position after it had been turned down by Sir Maurice Hankey, who had been, in effect, the secretary-general of the Paris Peace Conference. Drummond's major contribution as secretary-general was to establish a truly international secretariat, something unprecedented in the history of international organization. As secretary-general, it was Drummond's deliberate policy to keep himself and the League Secretariat in the background and to ensure that full responsibility for all decisions was taken by the League Council, Assembly, or another body to which they delegated authority. His resignation as secretary-general was greeted with genuine sadness, for member states had come to respect his integrity, judgment, and impartiality, all characteristics identified with the best of the British civil service tradition. After leaving his League post, Drummond served as British ambassador to Rome (1933–1939) and as chief of foreign policy in the Ministry of Information (1939–1940). He succeeded to his earldom in 1937 and served as deputy leader of the Liberal Party of Britain from 1940 until his death.

Dumbarton Oaks Conference. Meeting of the major powers to develop specific proposals for creating a new post–World War II international organization to replace the League of Nations (q.v.). The conference was held at an estate (Dumbarton Oaks) in Washington, D.C., in 1944 in two separate phases. At the first, conversations were among the U.S., Soviet, and British delegations; at the second, among U.S., British, and Chinese delegations. The conference adopted the following: (1) purposes—the primary purpose of the organization was to be the maintenance of international peace and security; (2) nature—it was to be based on sovereign equality of members; (3) membership—all members must be peace-loving states, and new membership was to be voted on by the Security Council (q.v.) and the General Assembly (q.v.); (4) organs—the five major bodies proposed were the Security Council, General Assembly, Secretariat (q.v.), Economic and Social Council (ECOSOC) (q.v.), and the International Court of Justice (ICJ) (q.v.); (5) competence—the Security Council was to have the primary responsibility for peace and security. With some modifications, these proposals became the UN Charter.

E

Earthwatch. A network established pursuant to the United Nations Conference on the Human Environment (q.v.) to monitor land, water, and atmospheric conditions and changes that might affect the human environment (q.v.). More than 100 monitoring stations were planned, forming a Global Environmental Monitoring Service (GEMS) linked to a central data bank in Geneva, Switzerland.

East African Economic Community (EAC). Kenya, Uganda, and Tanzania sought to guarantee the free movement of goods in their region of Africa. In line with this goal, they established the EAC in 1967 for a 15-year period to coordinate communications (q.v.), finance (q.v.), commerce, industry, and social and research services. The agreement provided for the establishment of an East African Bank and a Common Market. The East African Common Services Organization had performed these activities prior to the countries' independence. Problems of the EAC included competition for foreign investment among member states and ideological differences, especially between Kenyan capitalism and Tanzanian socialism. In addition, there were personality clashes among the country's leaders. Once considered a promising effort at international integration, it collapsed in 1977. There is now talk of its revival.

Eastern Caribbean Central Bank (ECCB). Established in 1983, with headquarters in St. Kitts-Nevis, the bank maintains a common currency between member territories and seeks to promote monetary stability and further economic development (q.v.) in the region.

Economic and Social Commission for Asia and the Pacific (ESCAP). The 1974 name of what was formerly the Economic Commission for Asia and the Far East (ECAFE), which was founded in 1947 as a regional agency of the United Nations Economic and Social Council (ECOSOC) (q.v.). It is composed of 38 Asian and Pacific states, as well as France, the Netherlands, Russia, the United Kingdom, and the United States. Its primary purpose is to initiate and participate in measures for facilitating concerted action for the economic development (q.v.) of Asia and the Pacific, including by raising the level of economic activity of the region and maintaining and strengthening economic relations among both regional and outside states. ESCAP sponsors research and studies of economic and technological problems and developments in the region. Over the years, it has set up the Asian Free Trade Zone, Asian Pacific Coconut Community, International Pepper Community, Asian Clearing Union, Asian Reinsurance Corporation, Asian Development Bank (q.v.), Regional Mineral Resources Development Center, and South East Asia Tin Research and Development Center.

Economic and Social Commission for Western Asia (ESCWA) (formerly known as the Economic Commission for Western Asia, ECWA). ESCWA aims to promote economic and social development in the Middle East. It was established in 1973 as an Economic and Social Council (ECOSOC) (q.v.) body for western Asia. Earlier plans for a Middle Eastern Economic Commission had been thwarted owing to regional conflicts. ESCWA included Egypt and the Arab countries of southwestern Asia but excluded the remaining countries of the Middle East (i.e., Israel, Turkey, and Iran). Beirut, Lebanon, was chosen at its headquarters, but they were temporarily moved to Baghdad, Iraq, and subsequently to Amman, Jordan. In its attempt to raise the levels of economic activity in the region, ESCWA emphasizes food security, integrated rural development, transfer of appropriate technology, and transportation (q.v.) and communications (q.v.).

Economic and Social Committee (ESC). The weakest of the central institutions of the European Community (EC) (q.v.). and then the European Union (EU) (q.v.), the ESC only has an advisory function in the EU. Still, both the European Commission (q.v.) and the Council of Ministers (q.v.) must consult it on a wide range of issues, and in practice the degree of consultation is extensive. Its membership of 189, which is a part-time commitment, is based on national interest groups, with each national delegation consisting of workers, employers, and representatives of other occupational groups. Most of the ESC's work is done in specialized subgroups, where its influence on potential EU policy has been greatest.

Economic and Social Council (ECOSOC). See United Nations Economic and Social Council.

Economic Commission for Africa (ECA). Founded as a regional agency of ECOSOC (q.v.) in 1958 when eight independent African states became members. South Africa was suspended as a member in 1963. The ECA's major purpose is to promote and facilitate concerted action toward the economic and social development of Africa and to maintain and strengthen economic relations between African states. It has helped establish many banking (q.v.), trade (q.v.), resource utilization, and other organizations in Africa, but its lack of resources and political problems have limited its successes.

Economic Commission for Europe (ECE). Established as a regional agency by the United Nations Economic and Social Council (ECOSOC) (q.v.) in 1947, the ECE operates through an annual plenary session, usually in Geneva, Switzerland, and meetings of its subsidiary bodies. It has changed from its initial focus on war reconstruction to economic development (q.v.). Much attention has been devoted to East-West trade and the environment (q.v.). Until the establishment of the Conference on Security and Cooperation in Europe (CSCE) (q.v.), it was the only European body where the states of both East and West met on a regular basis.

Economic Commission for Latin America and the Caribbean (ECLAC). Established as a regional agency for the United Nations Economic and Social Council (ECOSOC) (q.v.) in 1948 as ECLA, "and the Caribbean" was added in 1984. Its membership includes Latin American and Caribbean states, plus Canada, France, the Netherlands, Portugal, Spain, the United Kingdom, and the United States. Its headquarters are in Santiago, Chile. In its quest to accelerate economic development (q.v.) in the region, it created the Latin American Institute for Economic and Social Planning and assisted in the establishment of the Latin American Free Trade Association (LAFTA) (q.v.) and the Central American Common Market (CACM) (q.v.). It is often described as the most effective of the regional commissions, especially in its early years. Its executive secretary for its first 15 years was Raúl Prebisch (q.v.).

Economic Community of West African States (ECOWAS) (Communaté Economique des Etats de l'Afrique de l'Ouest, CEDEAO). The community promotes trade, self-reliance, and cooperation in the western Africa region, with the goal of a customs union and ensuring free movement of capital, services, and people. The constitutive treaty was signed in Lagos, Nigeria, in 1975; the community's headquarters are in Abuja, Niger. The initial and still chief goal of this 16-member organization is the implementation of common commercial policy and harmonization of economic and industrial policies. That is why it maintains responsibility for the establishment of the Fund for Cooperation, Compensation and Development. However, especially with the establishment of the ECOWAS Standing Mediation Committee in July 1990, the community's role in political and security issues became more pronounced. One of its long-standing challenges is that 50 percent of the membership lives in Nigeria; 60 percent of its trade and one-third of its budget are there also. Thus, there is much competition between haves and have-nots. The consequences are that there is a problem affecting even summit decisions and, at times, the community is perceived as a tool of Nigeria. An example of this was the community's controversial involvement in the Liberian civil war in 1990. The Liberian President Samuel Doe was captured and executed while the community's peace mission was in operation. There is some hope that recent institutional expansion, including the establishment of a parliamentary assembly, will lessen both of these problems.

Economic cooperation and integration. Although now contentious notions, the beliefs that free trade increases economic prosperity and contributes to peaceful interactions between countries and that large markets are vital to exploit the advantages of economies of scale has been pervasive at least since the 18th century. Thus, it is not surprising that one of the long-standing activities of intergovernmental organizations, especially in the post–World War II era, has been the elimination of trade barriers between countries. This has occurred on the international level, most notably in the General Agreement on Tariffs and Trade (GATT) (q.v.) and the World Trade Organization (q.v.) and in various regions around the world. The greatest success to date has been in Western Europe, initially with BENELUX (q.v.) and the European Economic Community (EEC)/European Community (EC)/European Union (EU) (q.v.). Indeed, in many ways, regional economic development (q.v.) efforts in Latin America, Eastern Europe, Africa, and, to a lesser extent, Asia modeled themselves after the Western European successes. There have probably been more failures (such as the East African Economic Community [q.v.] and the Council for Mutual Economic Assistance [q.v.]) than successes, but the notion that regional trading blocs attract foreign investment and afford the possibilities of specialization and comparative advantage lead countries to continue to invent and reinvent such intergovernmental organizations. See also Arab Maghreb Union; Asia Pacific Economic Cooperation; Caribbean Community and Common Market; Central American Common Market; Comité des Représentants Permanents; Common Agricultural Policy; Common Market for Eastern and Southern Africa; Communauté Economique de l'Afrique de l'Ouest; Communauté Economique des Etats de l'Afrique Central; Communauté Economique des Pays des Grands Lacs; Conference on International Economic Cooperation; Council of Arab Economic Unity; Council of Ministers; Delors, Jacques; Economic and Social Committee; euro; European Coal and Steel Community; European Commission; European Community Action Scheme for the Mobility of University Students; European Council; European Economic Area; European Free Trade Association; European Monetary Union; European Political Cooperation; Havana Charter; Junta del Acuerdo de Cartagena; Latin American Free Trade Association; Latin American Integration Association; Luxembourg Agreement; Maastricht, Treaty of; Mano River Union; Mercado Común del Cono Sur; Monnet, Jean; Santer, Jacques; Schuman, Robert; Single European Act; snake; Union Douanière et Economique de l'Afrique Centrale.

Economic Cooperation Organization (ECO). ECO is the 1992 successor organization to the Regional Cooperation for Development (RCD), which had been formed by Iran, Pakistan, and Turkey in 1964 and charged to provide economic cooperation (q.v.) and cultural exchange. The RCD was envisioned as a means of establishing a West Asian common market that would promote trade (q.v.), assist in joint enterprises, and enhance the well-being of the people of the member states. It was replaced by ECO, which is headquartered in Teheran, Iran, and includes among its members Afghanistan and the six Muslim republics of the former Soviet Union, which followed the explosion of newly independent Central Asian states. The organization now, however, is plagued by competition between Turkey and Iran for leadership in Central Asia. Its focus, however, has continued to be on improving communication among members and setting up some common institutions: a shipping line, regional banks, and an insurance company are already in place, and plans exist for an ECO airline.

Economic development. The massive expansion of international organization activity in the field of economic development came in the early 1960s—that is, after numerous newly independent African states joined the United Nations (q.v.). Countless new organizations were established, most notably the United Nations Conference on Trade and Development (UNCTAD) (q.v.), the United Nations Industrial Development Organization (UNIDO) (q.v.), and the United Nations Development Program (UNDP) (q.v.). Older organizations either rapidly expanded their funding base and activities, including the regional commissions of the Economic and Social Council (ECOSOC) (q.v.) and the regional development banks, or changed their orientation. Virtually all of the UN's Specialized Agencies (q.v.) added technical assistance roles, sometimes dwarfing their earlier tasks. The major clients of the International Monetary Fund (q.v.) and World Bank (q.v.), for example, became developing countries (q.v.). While the International Bank for Reconstruction and Development (IBRD) continued to expand, its newer affiliates, especially the International Development Association (q.v.), got much of the world's attention (and criticism). Not only did the World Bank Group (q.v.) become the globe's major source of economic development assistance, involved in every kind and phase of economic development projects, but it employs the most development economists in the world.

Not surprisingly, this massive expansion led to criticisms of duplication, waste, a bias toward very big projects and overly invasive policy recommendations. In part to counter such criticisms, intergovernmental organizations, particularly the World Bank, have begun subcontracting with nongovernmental organizations. See also Abu Dhabi Fund for Arab Economic Development; Actionaid; Adventist Development and Relief Agency; African, Caribbean, and Pacific group of states; Agency for Co-operation and Research in Development; Brandt Commission; Capacity Study of the United Nations Development System; CARE International; Community Aid Abroad; Confederation of Central African NGOs; development decades; Economic and Social Commission for Asia and the Pacific; Economic and Social Commission for Western Asia; Economic Commission for

Africa; Economic Commission for Europe; Economic Commission for Latin America and the Caribbean; Economic Community of West African States; Economic Cooperation Organization; least developed countries; Morse, Bradford; Multilateral Investment Guarantee Agency; New International Economic Order; newly industrializing countries; Organisation for Economic Co-operation and Development; Pearson Commission; Prebisch, Raúl; Prebisch Report; Sixth Special Session; Southern African Development Community; Third World Forum; United Nations Conference on Environment and Development; United Nations Non-Governmental Liaison Service; United Nations Population Fund; United Nations Research Institute for Social Development; United Nations Volunteers.

Environment. Although it is now virtually impossible to count the number of international organizations working to improve the environment, either directly or through publicity and lobbying, this is a very recent phenomenon. Neither the Charter of the United Nations (UN) (q.v.) nor the Treaty of Rome establishing the European Economic Community (q.v.) mentioned the need to clean up the environment.

Most people trace international organization involvement to the UN Conference on the Human Environment (q.v.) (also known as the Stockholm Conference, which included a parallel conference of international nongovernmental organizations). In actuality, the International Maritime Organization (q.v.), then known as the Intergovernmental Maritime Consultative Organization (IMCO), had focused on the problems of oil pollution several years prior to the Stockholm Conference. But it was only in the aftermath of Stockholm that the United Nations established the United Nations Environment Program (q.v.), countless UN Specialized Agencies (q.v.) expanded their agendas to include environmental concerns, and international nongovernmental organization proliferation occurred. Many nongovernmental organizations, like the Sierra Club International Program (q.v.), lobby governments and intergovernmental organizations about deforestation, ozone layer depletion, global warming, dangers of many pesticides, air and water pollution, and so forth. Others, sometimes referred to as environmental resistance movements, are more activist. Among the best known of this genre is Greenpeace (q.v.), including its efforts to limit the use of nuclear power and eliminate nuclear weapons testing. See also Agenda 21; Amazon Pact; Bruntland, Gro Harlem; Convention on International Trade in Endangered Species of Wild Fauna and Flora; Earthwatch; Friends of the Earth International; International Commission for the Protection of the Elbe; International Commission for the Protection of the Moselle against Pollution; International Commission for the Protection of the Rhine against Pollution; International Commission for the Protection of the Saar against Pollution; International Union for Conservation of Nature and Natural Resources—World Conservation Union; International Whaling Commission; Rainforest Action Network; Strong, Maurice; United Nations Commission on Sustainable Development; United Nations Conference on Environment and Development; World Meteorological Organization; World Wide Fund for Nature.

Euro. The single currency for Europe to be launched on January 1, 1999. In the agreement to have a single currency is the operation of a European Central Bank (ECB), the degree of whose independence from European Union (q.v.) member governments is a topic of wide disagreement. Likewise, participating countries have had to agree on how to constrain participants' budget deficits.

Euro-Atlantic Partnership Council (EAPC). In May 1997, the members of the North Atlantic Treaty Organization (NATO) (q.v.) agreed to establish the Euro-Atlantic Partnership Council as a successor to the North Atlantic Cooperation Council (NACC) (q.v.). The Partnership Council is the mechanism by which nonmember governments can consult and cooperate with member states, individually or in groups. Topics for discussion include crisis management; arms control; nuclear, biological, and chemical proliferation and defense (q.v.); international terrorism; defense planning and budgeting; and the security impacts of economic development (q.v.). Membership is open to Organization on Security and Cooperation in Europe (OSCE) (q.v.) member states and currently includes Albania, Armenia, Austria, Azerbaijan, Belarus, Bulgaria, the Czech Republic, Estonia, Finland, Georgia, Hungary, Kazakhstan, Kyrgyz Republic, Latvia, Lithuania, Macedonia, Moldova, Poland, Romania, Russia, Slovakia, Slovenia, Sweden, Switzerland, Tajikistan, Turkmenistan, Ukraine, and Uzbekistan.

EUROGROUP. The term usually used to refer to the Informal Group of European Defense Ministers within the North Atlantic Treaty Organization (NATO) (q.v.). As the EUROGROUP, the defense ministers meet on a regular basis to review documents and discuss possible initiatives on defense (q.v.) and security that are more specifically of European, rather than Atlantic or Western, concern. EUROGROUP aided in cooperation and coordination with France and Spain, which have been for a long time outside NATO's integrated military command structure.

European Atomic Energy Community (EURATOM). Created in 1958, EURATOM seeks to establish a common market among European Union (q.v.) members for nuclear raw materials and equipment, to form a technical pool and to coordinate research. Goals also include common safety standards, regular and equitable supply of ores and nuclear fuels, as well as movement toward peaceful uses of nuclear energy. It is one of the basic institutional components of the European Union (EU).

European Bank for Reconstruction and Development (EBRD). An initiative of the European Community (EC) (q.v.) and now the European Union (EU) (q.v.) to aid in the economic reconstruction of Eastern Europe after the collapse of communist political regimes. The idea originated with French President François Mitterrand in November 1989. In spite of its name, the EBRD was not conceived as a purely European enterprise; its members include Australia, Canada, Egypt, Israel, Japan, Mexico, Morocco, New Zealand, South Korea, and the United States. The EBRD, which is meant to work in conjunction with the International Monetary Fund (IMF) (q.v.) and the World Bank (q.v.), became functional in March 1991. By 1992, full membership was extended to all of the successor states of the Soviet Union, and the bank planned to direct some 40 percent of its lending to the members of the Commonwealth of Independent States (CIS). The EBRD's headquarters are in London. Its first president, Jacques Attali, was forced to resign, at least in part because of the funds being expended on executive expense accounts. Under his successor, Jacques de Larosière (q.v.), former managing director of the IMF, the EBRD has won considerable praise as a model multilateral development bank. Still, its loans for nuclear power garner criticism in some circles.

European Civil Aviation Conference (ECAC) (Commission Européenne de l'Aviation Civile, CEAC). Established in 1995 to review the development of European civil aviation to promote its coordination, better utilization, orderly development, and safety.

European Coal and Steel Community (ECSC). Formed in 1952, the ECSC placed under a single, supranational authority the coal and steel production facilities of West Germany and France and removed distributive restrictions among the then six members of the European Economic Community (EEC) (q.v.). ECSC's manifest goals were to contribute to the expansion of the member states' economies, the development of employment, and the improvement of living standards in participating states. Its latent goals included preventing another war between France and Germany and furthering the possibilities of political union in Western Europe. The ECSC was the "brainchild" of French foreign minister Robert Schuman (q.v.), who proposed it in 1950. It was a basic institutional component of the European Community (EC) (q.v.) and the European Union (EU) (q.v.).

European Commission. The highest administrative organ and, along with the Council of Ministers (q.v.), one of two executive institutions of the European Community (EC) (q.v.) and then the European Union (EU) (q.v.). Under the Treaty of Rome, the commission is responsible for the initiation, supervision, and implementation of EC/EU policies, sharing decision-making powers with the Council of Ministers. With its ability to place legislation or initiatives (including draft budgets) before the council, it has been the principal formulator of decisions. It has significant autonomy of action in the operation of the Common Agricultural Policy (CAP) (q.v.), in competition policy, and over the coal and steel industries. It was expected to serve as the engine of the integration effort. It also represents the EC/EU and the member states in several international organizations as well as in EC/EU external trade and economic negotiations and relations with nonmember countries. The five largest member states (France, Germany, Italy, Spain, and the United Kingdom) are each entitled to two commissioners; the other states are allowed one each for a total of 20. One commissioner is appointed by the Council of Ministers to serve as president of the commission. Decisions are usually by majority vote. See also Charter of Fundamental Social Rights; Delors, Jacques.

European Commission of Human Rights. A quasi-judicial body that examines charges of infringements of human rights (q.v.) as enumerated in the European Convention on Human Rights (q.v.). Established in 1953 and working under the aegis of the Council of Europe (q.v.), the commission has both a judicial and a conciliatory function. It has the right, on its own initiative or in response to complaints by states or individuals, to consider whether the convention has been violated. Where it believes the allegations have been substantiated, it attempts a resolution. If this process breaks down, as it rarely does, the commission has the right to send the case to the European Court of Human Rights (q.v.) for adjudication. Each state that has ratified the convention has the right to appoint a commissioner, who serves as an individual, not as a government representative.

European Community (EC). A term describing the collective body that resulted from the merger in July 1967 of the administering networks and structures of the European Atomic Energy Agency (q.v.),

European Coal and Steel Community (q.v.), and European Economic Community (q.v.). Its goal was closer economic and political integration. In 1993, it was succeeded by the European Union (EU) (q.v.). See also Council of Ministers.

European Community Action Scheme for the Mobility of University Students (ERASMUS). A program, adopted in 1987, of the European Community (EC) (q.v.) whereby students can spend an integral part of their studies at a university in another EC country. The European Commission's (q.v.) hope was that 10 percent of the EC student population would be participants by 1992, but the Council of Ministers (q.v.) was willing to endorse only a much more limited version of the plan.

European Convention on Human Rights. Developed by the Council of Europe (q.v.) and in force since 1953, the European Convention creates the international machinery for the protection of human rights (q.v.) in controversies arising in the signatory states. Most council members have ratified the convention; some have also ratified provisions providing individuals and private groups the right and means to seek redress at the international level. The convention's chief weapon is member states' fear of negative publicity. Most cases reach amicable out of courtroom settlements. The convention was long taken to be the most extensive international machinery for the protection of human rights in the history of the state system. See also European Commission on Human Rights; European Court of Human Rights.

European Council. Summit meeting of member states of the European Community (EC) (q.v.), the council was added to the formal EC structure in 1974. It discusses questions at the highest level, including foreign policy issues. It has overall responsibility for comprehensive European cooperation and goal setting. It set out the 1992 plan to accelerate and deepen the European integration process.

European Court of Human Rights. Judicial body of the European Convention on Human Rights (q.v.) with one judge from each member state of the Council of Europe (q.v.). They serve in their individual capacity. The court's judgments include legally binding decisions. It is the final arbiter of the convention. See also European Commission of Human Rights.

European Court of Justice. Judicial court of the European Community (EC) (q.v.) and then the European Union (EU). It interprets treaties, settles disputes, and assesses penalties. It was created in 1952 and is

located in Luxembourg. Its decisions are binding on members, EC/
EU institutions, corporations and individuals. It may also review measures taken by the EC/EU Commission (q.v.) or the EC/EU Council
of Ministers (q.v.). It can also issue advisory opinions. Some critics
complain that the court is too powerful; others, however, lament its
lack of sanctions to punish habitual offenders. The court also suffers
from a case overload.

European Currency Unit (ECU). Created in 1979 as a bookkeeping
device for, and in accordance with, the Maastricht treaty (q.v.) on
political and economic union, it is expected to be the future common
currency of the European Union (EU) (q.v.). It is the basic denomina-
tor of the Exchange Rate Mechanism (ERM) of the European Monetary System (EMS) (q.v.) and it is the basic indicator determining the
divergence of national currencies from their central rates in the EMS.
It is the basic unit of account for the intervention system of the ERM.
It is the reserve instrument for the national central banks within the
EC/EU and the means by which they make settlements between themselves. The value of the ECU is based on a weighted basket of currencies, with each EC/EU currency participating in the basket receiving
a different weight based roughly on an amalgamation of the population size and economic strength of that country.

**European Defense Community (EDC) (also known as the Plevan
Plan).** The second and ultimately unsuccessful experiment in the
early 1950s in sectoral integration sponsored by the Europe of the
Six. (The first was the European Coal and Steel Community [ECSC]
[q.v.].) It was proposed by Premier René Plevan of France as an alternative to U.S. pressure that Europe significantly augment its contribution to the North Atlantic Treaty Organization (NATO) (q.v.), in part
by a rearmament of West Germany. The focus of the EDC Treaty,
which was signed in Paris in May 1952, was a European army that
would include a West German military contingent. The treaty was
defeated in France in August 1954 on a technical vote (on whether to
discuss it) in the National Assembly. The defeat spawned two important institutional developments. First, following a proposal by British
prime minister Sir Anthony Eden, the Western European Union
(WEU) (q.v.) was formed, with responsibilities for restraining German rearmament. In addition, advances were made along the path
toward the entrance of an armed Germany into NATO.

**European Economic Area (EEA) (also known as the European Eco-
nomic Space, EES).** Projected as the world's largest trading bloc;
agreed to in 1991 by the European Community (EC) (q.v.) and the

European Free Trade Association (EFTA) (q.v.). The impetus behind this was concern, especially by members of EFTA, about the implications for them of the EC's establishment of the single internal market. The original proposal was a set of concentric rings, with the EC at the center, each distinguished by the kind of economic arrangement it had with the EC. As negotiations progressed, however, it became clear that several EFTA members really preferred full membership in the EC. As a consequence, the proposal was reformulated and renamed the European Economic Space (EES), in which there would be a single market for goods, services, and labor—largely on EC terms. Only in agriculture would EFTA states retain their own policies. See also European Union.

European Economic Community (EEC). Growing out of a meeting of the foreign ministers of six Western European countries in Messina, Italy, in June 1955 and established in 1957, it aimed to create a common market based on free trade, common social and financial policies, the abolition of restrictive trading practices, and the free movement of capital and labor. It was agreed that the organization, whose institutional structure was patterned after that of the European Coal and Steel Community (ECSC) (q.v.), would be open to any European country willing to accept the provisions of the Treaty of Rome. However each of the original six members (Belgium, France, Italy, Luxembourg, the Netherlands, and West Germany) retained the right to veto any application. When the executive and administrative networks of the EEC, ECSC, and the European Atomic Energy Agency (EURATOM) (q.v.) were merged on July 1, 1967, creating the European Community (q.v.), the acronym EEC (and the popular alternative phrase Common Market) continued to be used by many to refer to the post-1967 EC.

European Free Trade Association (EFTA). With the goal of eliminating tariffs and other trade barriers on industrial goods among its members, EFTA was established in 1957 (by the Stockholm Convention), effective 1960, as an alternative body to the European Economic Community (EEC) (q.v.) by the Outer Seven (Austria, Denmark, Finland, Norway, Sweden, Switzerland, and the United Kingdom). EFTA went into eclipse when Britain chose the European Community (q.v.) over EFTA and particularly with the development of the European Economic Area (EEA) (q.v.) and European Economic Space (EES) and the decision of Austria, Finland, and Sweden, but not Norway and Switzerland, to join the European Union (EU) (q.v.). The days of

EFTA as an independent entity seem numbered, but it will remain in existence at least until all accessions to the EU are completed.

European Investment Bank (EIB). Located in Luxembourg, the EIB, which was called for in the Treaty of Rome, finances capital investment to assist in the economic development (q.v.) of the European Community (EC) (q.v.) and then the European Union (EU) (q.v.). Most of the EIB's funds are raised on international capital markets. The EIB loans, which run from 7 to 20 years, are not intended to fully fund any project. Even so, there is high demand for them.

European Molecular Biology Organization (EMBO) (Organisation Européenne de Biologies Moléculaires). Founded by a group of biologists in Geneva, Switzerland, in 1963, this nongovernmental organization is now composed of some 900 elected biologists and has its headquarters in Heidelberg, Germany. Its goal is to promote cooperation among Europeans for fundamental research in molecular biology as well as in allied fields. Among its most concrete accomplishments is the establishment of a European Molecular Biology Laboratory.

European Monetary System (EMS). Established in 1979, the EMS aims at increasing monetary stability among the members of the European Community (EC) (q.v.) and then the European Union (EU) (q.v.). This is to be achieved, in particular, by the adoption of a common European currency and all that it implies (e.g., credit and exchange rate mechanisms to deal with balance of payments surpluses and deficits). Some EC/EU members, including the United Kingdom, have balked at the full implementation of these commitments. See also European Currency Unit.

European Monetary Union (EMU). A monetary union is the stage in economic cooperation and integration (q.v.) beyond a common market. It involves a high degree of economic coordination, including unification of the most important areas of economic policy, integration of budgetary policy, and monetary coordination based on either an unconditional fixed exchange rate with full currency convertibility or a single currency. The idea of the EMU has been on the agenda of the European Community (EC) (q.v.) and then the European Union (EU) (q.v.) since 1969. At the Hague summit in December of that year, the heads of the then six member states set 1980 as the completion date for full EMU. The move to floating currencies and the rapid increase in oil prices in the 1970s meant that by the end of the decade EMU was more or less forgotten. Indeed, it was even largely absent from the Single European Act (q.v.) of 1987.

However, in the following year, 1988, the European Council (q.v.) appointed a committee headed by Jacques Delors (q.v.) to consider the issue. The Delors Committee reported in 1989, outlining a three-stage sequence for the achievement of the full EMU, though without specifying dates for the completion of each phase. The plan called for all member states to be brought into the Exchange Rate Mechanism (ERM) of the European Monetary System (EMS) (q.v.) as a first step. The second step would involve EC limits on national budget deficits, a reduction in the currency fluctuation limits in the ERM, and planning for a European central bank. These were portrayed as necessary if the internal market were going to be truly effective. The Delors proposals were accepted by the European Council (q.v.) in June 1989, with July 1990 set as the date for launching the first stage. The Maastricht Treaty (q.v.) of December 1991 committed the EU to establishing the full EMU by 1999. See also euro.

European Organization for the Safety of Air Navigation (EURO-CONTROL). Established in December 1960 but not effective until March of 1963, this intergovernmental organization based in Brussels, Belgium, has fallen short of its goal: a common European air control system. Most member countries still wish to control their air space when it comes to military planes. Still, the organization has been successful in dealing with much of the air congestion that long plagued Europe, especially Western Europe, by providing air traffic control services without concern for national boundaries. There is some hope for the beginning of the implementation of an Air Traffic Management System by the year 2000.

European Parliament. The Treaty of Rome, which set up the European Economic Community (EEC) (q.v.), stated that eventually election to the European Parliament would be made directly by the people in the member states. That did not occur until 1978, 20 years after the parliament was set up. Moreover, its powers were quite limited until the so-called Maastricht Treaty (q.v.). They provide that parliamentary assent is required for the passage of mainstream legislation. While there is no limit to what the parliament can discuss in its monthly sessions in Strasbourg, France, and in its committee meetings and "miniplenaries" in Brussels, Belgium, it has always played a significant role in the approval process, but not the formulation of the EEC's budget. Among the topics to which it has devoted considerable time are human rights (q.v.) and the environment (q.v.). It is currently composed of 626 members elected every five years. Germany has the largest number of seats (99), and Luxembourg has the fewest (6). Seats are allocated in line with the percentage of European

Union (EU) (q.v.) population each member state has. Adding to the challenges of a body that meets in two different countries is the fact that the parliament's 3,800-person secretariat is located in Luxembourg.

European Patent Organization (EPO) (Organisation Européenne des Brevets, OEB). The EPO was established in accordance with the European Patent Convention, which was signed in Munich, Germany, in 1973 and entered into force in 1977. The EPO aims at the harmonization of patent legislation in accordance with the Patent Convention's provisions. It is also responsible for the granting, administration, limitation, and revocation of community patents within the European Community (EC) (q.v.) and later the European Union (EU) (q.v.). When fully operational, there will be a Common Patent Appeals Court to assure the convention's application in the EU. Since 1993, the EPO has concluded extension agreements with nonmember countries.

European Political Cooperation (EPC). This phrase is used to describe the efforts of the members of the European Community (EC) (q.v.) and later the European Union (EU) (q.v.) to collaborate on foreign policy. The origins of the EPC lie in the so-called Davignon Reports of the early 1970s, which called for foreign policy harmonization. The EPC has been most evident in coordination of EC/EU policy in other international fora, including the United Nations (q.v.).

European Space Agency (ESA). The ESA was formally established in October 1980, but it operated in a de facto fashion long before that and was even provided for in a 1962 convention that went into force two years later. The purpose of this Paris-based agency is to provide and promote space research and technology for peaceful purposes. Stated otherwise, it is to "Europeanize" the national space programs in Europe. Its major successes to date have focused on the Ariane missile system. It has made strides in the area of space technology, meteorology, and telecommunications.

European Trade Union Confederation. The confederation, which has its headquarters in Brussels, Belgium, was founded in February 1973 by trade unionists from 15 Western European countries. Their goal is to deal with the interests of European working people, both those who live within and outside of the European Union (q.v.). There are currently 45 million members in 21 countries.

European Union (EU). The EU was established on November 9, 1993, with the entering into force of the Treaty of European Union, commonly known as the Maastricht Treaty (q.v.). According to the treaty, the Union's objectives include the promotion of economic and social progress, in particular through the creation of an area without internal frontiers, and the assertion of Europe's place in international affairs, through a common defense and foreign policy. In addition, the EU is called upon to follow the principle of subsidiarity. The EU's near-term agenda includes three major priorities: introducing a single currency, preparing for new members, and defining its future at the Intergovernmental Conference.

EU organs include the European Parliament (q.v.), the Council of the European Union (q.v.), the Commission of the Union, the Court of Justice of the Union, and the Court of Auditors (q.v.). In addition, there are two advisory bodies that represent economic, social, and regional interests, the Economic and Social Committee (q.v.), the Committee of the Regions; and an European Investment Bank (q.v.) set up to contribute to the balanced development of the EU and the European Monetary Institute, created in 1994 in preparation for monetary union. There are currently 15 members of the EU: Austria, Belgium, Denmark, Finland, France, Germany, Greece, Ireland, Italy, Luxembourg, the Netherlands, Portugal, Spain, Sweden, and the United Kingdom. Norway signed an accession treaty in 1994 that it failed to ratify after voters rejected—for the second time—accession in a referendum. Turkey applied for membership in 1987, Malta and Cyprus in 1990, and Switzerland in 1992. Poland and Hungary applied in 1994, and Bulgaria, Estonia, Latvia, Lithuania, Romania, and Slovakia in 1995. In December 1997, the EU agreed to open membership negotiations with 11 Eastern and Central European countries and enter into a "strategy of rapprochement" with Turkey, a decision that angered the Turkish government. See also Common Agricultural Policy; Council of Ministers; European Community; European Economic Community.

Exclusive Economic Zone (EEZ). Refers to the rights of coastal states to control the living and nonliving resources of the sea within 200 miles off their coasts, while allowing freedom of navigation to other states beyond the 12-mile territorial seas. This was codified as part of the third UN Law of the Sea Treaty.

Expanded Program of Technical Assistance (EPTA). This was the first enlargement of the previous technical assistance activities of the United Nations (UN) (q.v.), following from U.S. President Truman's call for increased aid through the UN. In 1950, the initial 18-month budget was $20 million, with the U.S. pledging 60 percent of that amount. By 1965, the year that it was absorbed into the United Nations Development Program (q.v.), the annual budget was $54 million, with the United States furnishing 40 percent of the total. See Development Assistance Committee.

F

Feed the Children International. Founded in 1993 to serve as the main "switchboard" between the three Feed the Children (FTC) offices in the United States, Canada, and the United Kingdom and the 18 FTC field offices. It works in 14 developing countries (q.v.) and has been actively engaged in the Commonwealth of Independent States (CIS).

Food and Agriculture Organization (FAO). The FAO is the UN Specialized Agency (q.v.) aimed at raising levels of nutrition and increasing efficiency of production and distribution of food and other agricultural products. Established in Quebec, Canada, in 1945 and headquartered in Rome, Italy, it is empowered to (1) promote scientific, technological, social, and economic research related to nutrition, food (q.v.), and agriculture; (2) work toward improvement of appropriate education and relevant administrative practices and the spread of public knowledge of nutritional and agricultural science; (3) ensure conservation of natural resources and adoption of improved methods of agricultural production; (4) encourage adoption of policies for the promotion of adequate agricultural credit; and (5) promote international policies with respect to agricultural commodities.

Criticism of the FAO has focused on claims that it puts too much emphasis on short-term food aid and not enough into long-term agricultural growth to cope with serious food crises. With U.S. support, the World Food Council (q.v.) was set up in 1974 to try to answer criticisms such as these. The FAO was skeptical. The International Fund for Agricultural Development (IFAD) (q.v.) was also established over FAO objections.

Food, shelter, and agriculture. Food, like shelter, is basic to survival. Accordingly, international organizations have long focused on providing food relief to those in need and in disseminating information about ways to make croplands more productive. The former is the main task of such organizations as the World Food Programme (WFP) (q.v.); the latter has been the concern of such organizations as the International Fund for Agricultural Development (IFAD) (q.v.) and the World Bank (q.v.). Much more controversial—although a longstanding topic of discussion at the Food and Agriculture Organization (FAO) (q.v.) and World Food Council (q.v.)—has been establishment of food buffers to stabilize agricultural prices and ensure that food is available when it is needed. While the United Nations (UN) (q.v.) has periodically convened conferences relating to agriculture, its members have come to recognize the interconnectiveness of issues, especially food and population.

The UN's focus on shelter has been less consistent, often reacting to pressure from nongovernmental organizations and centered on debates at UN-sponsored global conferences. See also Asian Coalition for Housing Rights; Comité des Organisations Professionelles Agricoles; Habitat for Humanity International, Inc.; Habitat International Coalition; United Nations Center for Human Settlements; United Nations Commission on Human Settlements.

Freedom House. Since 1941, from its headquarters in New York City, Freedom House has been monitoring the violation of political and civil rights and promoting the growth of democratic institutions around the world. Its Freedom Fund has assisted in providing civic education for election campaigns in Eastern and Central Europe. More than 50 percent of its funding is public in origin. Since its beginning, Freedom House has bestowed a Freedom Award to individuals for outstanding contributions to the cause of human liberty. Past recipients include, among others, Winston Churchill, General Dwight Eisenhower, civil rights leader Medgar Evers (posthumously), Vaclav Havel, and the Dalai Lama. A recent recipient was Dr. Sergei Kovalyov, head of Russia's Human Rights Commission and the most outspoken critic of Moscow's war in Chechnya.

Friends of the Earth International (FoEI). The origins of FoEI can be traced to 1971. Its aims are clear: to protect the Earth against further deterioration and to restore damage already inflicted as a consequence of human activity or negligence. It seeks to achieve these goals by political lobbying, citizen actions, and the global distribution of information. Its lobbying efforts focus on multilateral development banks as well as national governments. It currently counts more than one million people among its members in more than 50 countries. Its headquarters are in Amsterdam, the Netherlands.

Functionalism. The theory that international economic and social cooperation is a prerequisite for the ultimate solution of conflicts and the elimination of war. Functionalists assume that war is the consequence of the inadequacies of the nation-state system and believe that cooperation among functionally specific specialists can lead to its demise.

G

General Agreement on Tariffs and Trade (GATT). GATT aims at the promotion of trade among participating parties by liberalizing and reducing tariffs. It consists of an international set of bilateral trade agreements that are multilateralized through GATT's application of the most favored nation (MFN) (q.v.) clauses in all agreements. It aims at the abolition of trade restrictions among contracting parties. It was signed in Geneva, Switzerland, in 1947 by 23 countries as a preliminary doctrine pending establishment of an International Trade Organization (ITO). But the ITO never came into being, and GATT served for decades in its stead. In the United States, the ITO would have required senatorial approval; the GATT was agreed to by executive agreement.

GATT's work has evolved through periodic rounds of multilateral negotiations: Geneva Round (1947), Annecy Round (1949), Torquay Round (1950), Geneva Round (1956), Dillon Round (1960–1961) (q.v.), Kennedy Round (1964–1967) (q.v.), Tokyo Round (1973–1979) (q.v.), and Uruguay Round (1986–1994) (q.v.). Its focus has evolved from dealing primarily with reducing tariff barriers to restrictions on the use of nontariff barriers (NTBs) and the adoption of codes dealing with specific practices.

GATT's long struggle to gain the support of developing countries (q.v.), which preferred the United Nations Conference on Trade and Development (UNCTAD) (q.v.) as a negotiating arena, reached a climax when the contracting parties adopted Part IV in 1964. It stated that economically less developed countries would not be required to make the same concessions as developed countries on tariffs or on the removal of nontariff barriers, seemingly a fundamental concession to win support from the economically less developed countries. Moreover, in 1971, developed countries were authorized to grant, through a waiver of GATT's most favored nation requirement, preferential treatment (i.e., lower tariffs) to economically less developed countries on a wide range of goods.

The Uruguay Round included agreement on the World Trade Organization (WTO) (q.v.), a comprehensive international trade organization to coordinate international economic activities, as was envisaged in the Havana Charter (i.e., what was to be the basis of the ITO). Among other treaties, it is charged with implementing the GATT, which continues to exist as a substantive agreement, establishing a set of guidelines, rules, and norms of international trade for participating states. Indeed, 25 additional states signed the GATT during the Uruguay Round.

Generalized System of Preferences (GSP). In 1961, the UN General Assembly (q.v.) launched the idea of preferential tariff treatment for economically less developed countries. The GSP is a system through which developed countries can give preferential treatment, for a minimum of 10 years, to manufactured or semifinished exports from economically less developed countries. The United Nations Conference on Trade and Development (UNCTAD) (q.v.), with some assistance from the Organisation for Economic Co-operation and Development (OECD) (q.v.), pursued this idea until it was formally adopted in 1970. GATT (q.v.) subsequently took action to allow this exception to its most favored nation (q.v.) principle.

Genocide Convention. Responding to the horrors of Nazi actions during World War II, the United Nations General Assembly (q.v.) adopted an International Convention on the Prevention and Punishment of the Crime of Genocide in 1948. It went into effect in 1951. Genocide, identified as an international crime, was defined as participation in any of the following acts, committed with the *intent* to destroy, in whole or in part, a national, ethnic, racial, or religious group: (1) killing a member of the group, (2) causing serious bodily or mental harm to a member of the group, (3) deliberately inflicting on the group conditions of life calculated to bring about its physical destruction in whole or in part, (4) imposing measures intended to prevent births within the group, or (5) forcibly transferring children of the group to another group. The convention includes as punishable conspiracy, incitement, directing and planning, attempts, and complicity to commit genocide, as well as overt acts of genocide. The contracting parties agreed that genocide, whether committed in a time of peace or of war, is a punishable crime under international law. The U.S. Senate did not give its advice and consent to the convention until 1986.

Good offices. Good offices is defined as services rendered by an impartial third party to a dispute. It involves communication between two other parties without suggesting any form of settlement or compromise (a contrast to mediation [q.v.]). The notion of good offices is formalized in the Hague Conventions on the Pacific Settlement of Disputes (1899 and 1907) (q.v.). Good offices is not specifically mentioned in the United Nations (q.v.) Charter as one of the methods for peaceful settlement of disputes, although it has been performed by the UN from time to time, as in Cyprus in the mid-1970s and in El Salvador in the early 1990s..

Greenpeace. Greenpeace, an international nongovernmental organization that traces its origins to a Unitarian church in Vancouver, Canada, in 1971, now occupies an uncomfortable position within the international environmental community. Many environmentalists see its direct actions, which include positioning activists between harpooners and whales and floating a hot-air balloon into a nuclear test site, as too confrontational. These critics fear that such actions alienate rather than build support. On the other hand, militant environmentalists see Greenpeace as not radical enough.

Throughout its history, Greenpeace has tried to remain true to its goal of changing the root causes of environmental harm by changing the way people treat the natural world. The organization, whose headquarters are in Amsterdam, the Netherlands, receives funds from over five million supporters in 158 countries. Its staff of over 1,300 work in 43 offices in 30 countries.

Group of Fifteen (G-15). The origins of the G-15 can be traced to the Ninth Conference of the Heads of State or Government of Non-Aligned Countries, which met in Belgrade, Yugoslavia, in September 1989. There it was agreed that there should be an annual meeting of a subset of the globe's nonaligned countries in order to assess the international scene and develop, especially international economic, strategies. Foci of the meetings have included the means for improving South-South trade and increased Southern access to developed country markets. See also Non-Aligned Movement.

Group of Five (G-5). Formerly known as the Library Group because it first met in the White House Library in April 1973 to discuss international monetary negotiations, the G-5 is the name given to meetings of the finance ministers and Central Bank governors of France, Germany, Great Britain, Japan, and the United States. The G-5's agendas are wide ranging, and meetings occur at various times, including during the annual meetings of the World Bank (q.v.) and the International Monetary Fund (q.v.).

Group of Seven (G-7). The origins of the G-7 are often traced to a suggestion by Henry Kissinger, then U.S. secretary of state. In 1974, French President Valéry Giscard d'Estaing invited his colleagues from Germany, Italy, Japan, the United Kingdom, and the United States to the first economic summit. It was held at the Château de Rambouillet in November 1975. A year later, at the summit in Puerto Rico, Canada joined, making it the G-7. Since 1977, the president of the Commission of the European Union (q.v.) and the president of the European Union's Council of Ministers (q.v.), when that post is not held by a member of the G-7, also attend. The Russian president has also been invited to attend of late. Indeed, in 1997, the G-7 was informally referred to as the Summit of the Eight (q.v.). That designation was formalized in 1998.

Group of Ten (G-10) (also known as the Group of Eleven). Established in 1962 by 10 governments offering to supplement International Monetary Fund (q.v.) loan funds through the so-called General Agreements to Borrow (GAB), the G-10 (the later and initially limited participation of the Swiss contributed to the tradition of calling this 11–member state organization the Group of Ten) has continued to provide a venue for the discussions of problems related to the function and structure of the international monetary system. Over the years, the G-10 has gained a reputation for discretion: the communiqués issued at the conclusions of its various meetings are a model of generality.

Group of Twenty-Four (G-24). The G-24 was established by the Group of Seventy-Seven (q.v.) in 1972. It was created to counterbalance the influence of the Group of Ten (q.v.) in the formulation of the recommendations of the Committee of Twenty, which is the Committee on Reform of the International Monetary System and Related Issues—that is, the committee established by the International Monetary Fund's (IMF) (q.v.) board of governors to reform the international monetary system. The G-24, which is composed of eight countries each from Africa, the Americas, and Europe/Asia, discusses international development issues as well as those related to the international monetary system. The IMF provides the G-24 with secretariat assistance.

Group of Seventy-Seven (G-77). Formed by the 77 third world countries that participated at the first United Nations Conference on Trade and Development (UNCTAD) (q.v.) meeting (1964), the G-77 aims to balance the scales of global influence, including in international organizations, tilted toward economically developed states and to create viable economic and trade policies. The G-77 grew to more than 130 countries by the 1990s. It continues to press for better terms of trade (q.v.), more attention to foreign aid, and technical cooperation. It has, however, been plagued by internal conflict, especially given the wide disparity in wealth and economic systems of its members. It mainly functions at the United Nations (q.v.) and related bodies such as UNCTAD.

Gulf Cooperation Council (GCC). See Cooperation Council for the Arab States of the Gulf.

Gutt, Camille (1884–1971). Served as first managing director of the International Monetary Fund (IMF) (q.v.) (1946–1951), following a career in the Belgian finance ministry. Gutt headed the fund during a period in which it was almost moribund, in part because post–World War II European recovery was slower than expected. Gutt tried to get countries to turn to the IMF for assistance but found little interest. The United States was then doing a lot of the IMF's work through bilateral negotiations.

H

Habitat for Humanity International, Inc. Founded in 1977, with its headquarters in Americus, Georgia, Habitat for Humanity International is an international nongovernmental organization that specializes in building and repairing old homes, often in inner cities. Before 1977, it lacked a global orientation. It has ongoing projects in more than 30 less developed countries. What is unique about Habitat for Humanity is that those who will inhabit the homes work alongside the volunteers.

Habitat International Coalition (HIC). Founded in 1976 as the Non-Governmental Organizations (NGOs) Committee on Human Settlements before the 1976 Habitat: United Nations Conference on Human Settlements, HIC continued its activities after the conference. In 1987, HIC reframed its constitution to reorganize itself into a body more representative of community-based organizations and the nongovernmental organizations that support them. The constitutional changes also ensured that HIC was more representative of all regions of the world and functioned as a coalition (i.e., a global umbrella organization of human settlements nongovernmental organizations). Thus, it is dedicated to providing international level leadership to nongovernmental organizations by promoting such issues as housing rights, campaigns against evictions, the roles of women (q.v.), and the linkages between habitat and the environment (q.v.). It acts as a pressure group in defense of the rights of the homeless, poor, and inadequately housed. Its headquarters are in Mexico City.

Hague Peace Conferences. Convened in 1899 and 1907, by Czar Nicholas II of Russia. The first, attended by 26 states, concluded an agreement on arms control and other measures for maintaining peace. It codified international arbitration procedures in its Convention for the Pacific Settlement of Disputes (later revised at the second Hague Conference) and established the Permanent Court of Arbitration (q.v.). The first conference also codified many of the accepted practices of land warfare. The second, at which 44 states participated, sought conventions on the pacific settlement of disputes (q.v.) and other issues related to war and peace. It revised the 1899 convention concerning the rights and duties of belligerents and of neutral status and persons. However, it failed to achieve its goal of decreasing arms levels as a way to deal with the threat of war. The second conference was notable for the equality of participation among small states and great powers, European and non-European countries.

Hammarskjöld, Dag (1905–1961). Second UN secretary-general (q.v.) from 1953 to 1961. Before his terms as secretary-general, he held a series of important posts in the areas of finance and foreign affairs in the Swedish government. Still, he was expected to be a low-key administrator and was sought out, in part, to replace his outspoken predecessor Trygve Lie (q.v.) because of this expectation. An advocate of quiet and preventive diplomacy, he expanded the leadership role of the UN secretary-general more than any other occupant of that position. His most innovative contributions to the development of the United Nations (q.v.) came in the creation and management of two large peacekeeping (q.v.) forces in the Middle East and Congo.

In the Suez crisis of 1956, under a General Assembly (q.v.) directive, he developed a plan for the United Nations Emergency Force (UNEF) of 6,000 lightly armed military personnel from 10 countries to be stationed in a buffer zone in the Sinai on Egyptian territory, to patrol and report on any cease-fire violations by Egypt or Israel. UNEF I came to be viewed as the classic example of UN peacekeeping, a perception reinforced by the guidelines that Hammarskjöld developed for these (and subsequent) forces. The Congo force was the largest deployed to date by the UN (peaking at 20,000 troops from 34 countries). Its charge was to restore internal order in the Congo. Internal chaos led to an expansion of the force's tasks and accusations of a lack of neutrality, and eventually it contributed to Hammarskjöld's death in a plane crash on the way to meet with the secessionist leader of Katanga province. It was also the origin of the UN's financial woes.

Harmal Report. Document approved by the members of the North Atlantic Treaty Organization (NATO) (q.v.) in 1967 that defined the alliance in terms of détente as well as defense. The *Report on the Future of the Alliance* is often credited with initiating NATO's consideration of mutual and balanced force reduction (with the East). See also Joseph M. A. H. Lans.

Havana Charter. The Havana Charter, initially discussed in 1943 and negotiated until 1947, was intended to establish, within the United Nations (q.v.) system, a multilateral organization, the International Trade Organization (ITO), to administer and coordinate economic activities of states and enterprises affecting international trade (q.v.). It was assumed that through the promotion of trade, the ITO would contribute to the UN's goal of global stability and peace. The proposed organization could not gain the support of the United States (owing to opposition in the Senate), and thus this third "sister" of international economic organizations never came to join the World Bank (q.v.) and International Monetary Fund (q.v.).

Health. Because the spread of disease ignores national boundaries, health concerns were among the first issues addressed by intergovernmental organizations. The earliest actors included regional organizations, most notably the Pan American Health Organization (PAHO) (q.v.). In the postcolonial era, the focus of attention of intergovernmental organizations has been on helping poorer countries cope with disease, by the establishment of primary health care facilities, focusing on maternal health and increasing access to affordable medication. The World Health Organization (q.v.) has been the major post–World War II actor in the health field, often working with other UN Specialized Agencies (q.v.) and regional organizations. International nongovernmental organizations have been especially active in assisting in emergency situations. Best known among such organizations are the International Federation of Red Cross and Red Crescent Societies (q.v.) and Médecins sans Frontières (q.v.).

Hebrew Immigrant Aid Society (HIAS). This New York City-based international nongovernmental organization was founded in the late 1800s. Its purpose is to assist in the resettlement of persecuted or oppressed Jews throughout the world. Accordingly, it provides a broad program of services for Jewish refugees (q.v.) and migrants at all stages of the migration process. Many of these services are now also provided to non-Jewish clients under contractual arrangements with the U.S. government.

Helsinki Accord (also known as the Helsinki Final Act and the Helsinki Agreement). A 1975 agreement aimed at achieving peace and security in Europe. It was entered into by the United States, Canada, USSR, and 32 European countries at the end of the Conference on Security and Cooperation in Europe (CSCE) (q.v.) (1973–1975), concluded in Helsinki, Finland. It did not carry the full force and effect of a binding treaty but ameliorated postwar disputes over the German peace settlement of World War II and established a status quo for Europe. It declared as inviolable the frontiers of all signatory states, thus legitimizing the USSR's territorial gains. It also provided for scientific, technological, and cultural exchanges and pledged the signatories to report human rights (q.v.) violations, including those traversing the right to "freedom of thought, conscience, religion or belief." While much of the technological and scientific exchange benefited the USSR, the increased cultural contacts, travel between the East and the West, and the proliferation of press coverage likely contributed to political and philosophical changes within the USSR and advanced democratization in Eastern and Central Europe. Thus, what was initially viewed as, at best, a waste of time and more likely a naïve action on the part of the participating governments may have significantly contributed to the velvet revolutions of 1989.

Hoffman, Paul (1891–1974). Before his assignments in the United Nations (UN) (q.v.), Hoffman worked with the Studebaker corporation for more than 40 years and served as its chief executive officer. He was a U.S. delegate to the UN in 1956–1957. From 1959 until 1965, he was the managing director of the United Nations Special Fund and then served as administrator of the United Nations Development Program (q.v.) (1966–1972).

Human rights. One of the key differences between the Covenant of the League of Nations (q.v.) and the UN (q.v.) Charter is that only the latter mentions human rights. This is usually seen as a reaction against the Nazi holocaust, as are many of the immediate post–World War II actions by the UN and the Council of Europe (q.v.) in the area of human rights. These early post–World War II actions were more often aspirational statements or treaties lacking a sufficient number of signatures to enter into effect. It has only been in the past two decades that international organizations have become active legislators, monitors, and adjudicators in the human rights field. In part, this has come about as a consequence of media attention and actions by international nongovernmental organizations, most notably Amnesty International (q.v.). Along with this change in goals has been a broadening of the human rights agenda. While the United States in particular still resists treating economic rights as equal to civil and political ones, global attention has been focused on the rights of traditionally discriminated against and marginalized peoples, including women (q.v.), indigenous peoples, and those of racial and ethnic minorities. Many states continue to assert their sovereign rights to resist external pressure to alter their human rights practices, sometimes in the name of cultural integrity. International organization machinery is most complex in Europe and least well advanced in Asia. See also All Africa Conference of Churches; Anti-Slavery Society for the Protection of Human Rights; Association Internationale des Juristes Démocrates; Basket Three; European Commission of Human Rights; European Convention on Human Rights; Freedom House; Human Rights Committee; Human Rights Internet; Human Rights Watch; Inter-American Commission on Human Rights; Inter-American Court of Human Rights; International Commission of Jurists; International League for Human Rights; International Lesbian and Gay Association; Roosevelt, (Anna) Eleanor; Survival International; United Nations Center for Human Rights; United Nations Commission on Human Rights; United Nations Special Committee Against Apartheid; Universal Declaration of Human Rights; World Conference on Human Rights.

Human Rights Committee. Pursuant to the entrance into legal effect in 1976 of the International Covenant on Civil and Political Rights, the Human Rights Committee was established as part of the United Nations (q.v.) system. This 18-member state committee is responsible for monitoring the implementation of the covenant. While committee members all serve in their private capacities, this has not prevented the committee from being criticized for having been politicized and not being even-handed in deciding which cases of alleged human rights violations are investigated and commented on most thoroughly.

Human Rights Internet (HRI). HRI, founded in 1976, is an international communications network and clearinghouse on human rights (q.v.). Headquartered in Washington, D.C., HRI is a worldwide organization of over 1,300 individuals and organizations in which more than 75 countries are represented.

Human Rights Watch. The Human Right Watch evolved out of the "Helsinki Watch," which was set up in 1978. The Human Rights Watch coordinates the activities of such related organizations as Africa Watch, Americas Watch, Asia Watch, Helsinki Watch, and Middle East Watch. The purpose of these international nongovernmental organizations is to document violations of clearly accepted international human rights (q.v.) law, including imprisonment without trial, censorship, so-called disappearances, violations of due process of law, poor prison conditions, torture, and violations of the laws of war.

I

Institute of International Law. A nongovernmental society of international law specialists devoted to the development of the law of nations. Founded in 1873 in Ghent, Belgium, it undertakes to clarify general principles and seeks their codification into international law. Membership in the institute is restricted to 60 specialists in the theory or practice of international law and 72 associates. Proceedings are now held in Paris.

Integrated Program for Commodities (IPC). On May 30, 1976, at its fourth session in Nairobi, Kenya, the United Nations Conference on Trade and Development (UNCTAD) (q.v.) adopted a resolution approving the Integrated Program of Commodities (an integrated program to stabilize the price of commodities [q.v.] of export importance to economically less developed countries). Eighteen commodities were initially selected for inclusion in the IPC, encompassing food commodities, agricultural raw materials, and minerals. It was agreed that others could be added later. The resolution allows for such measures as the setting up of international commodity buffer stocks, establishment of pricing arrangements, management measures, compensatory finance facilities, and the improvement of market access. The first new commodity agreement worked out under the IPC was the International Natural Rubber Agreement of 1979.

Inter-African Coffee Organization (IACO). Established in 1960 to study problems of African coffee-exporting countries, including production, processing, and marketing, with the aim of stabilizing production and maximizing price. The IACO assists in the implementation of the various international coffee agreements when they are in effect.

Inter-American Commission of Women. Established in 1928 at the sixth International Conference of American States, the commission has been recognized, since 1953, as an inter-American Specialized Agency, with special relations with the Organization of American States (OAS) (q.v.). It works toward achieving both de facto and de jure equality between the sexes through a series of meetings, research, and leadership training programs.

Inter-American Commission on Human Rights. Promoting the establishment and observance of standards of human rights (q.v.) by members of the Organization of American States (OAS) (q.v.), it was established in 1959 and functions since then as a collateral body supporting the aims of the OAS. The commission, which is composed of seven individuals nominated by member governments and selected by the Permanent Council, makes recommendations on human rights issues to members of the OAS, performs studies, investigates allegations of human rights violations, and encourages members to provide information on their human rights activities. It is the primary implementation mechanism of the American Convention on Human Rights, which entered into effect in 1969 and guarantees 22 basic political and civil rights. The commission uses its influence to issue reports as a kind of sanction: it receives hundreds of complaints every year, but very few cases have resulted in public debate. Through the use of quiet persuasion and threatened media publicity, however, it has been seen to achieve many of its goals. On the other hand, it has been ineffective in influencing the policies of Cuba, Brazil, or Chile. It has no authority to force members to respond to its requests or to enforce its decisions.

Inter-American Court of Human Rights. The court came into effect in 1979, pursuant to the entry into force of the American Convention on Human Rights (also known as the Pact of San José). It is an autonomous judicial institution, acting within the framework of the Organization of American States (OAS) (q.v.). The United States is not a party to the American Convention.

Inter-American Development Bank (IDB). The basic goal of the bank is to contribute to the acceleration of economic development (q.v.) in member countries—individually or collectively—through the financing of economic and social projects. The current membership includes all Latin American countries (except Cuba), Austria, Belgium, Canada, Denmark, the European Union (q.v.), Finland, France, Germany, Israel, Italy, Japan, the Netherlands, Spain, Switzerland, the United Kingdom, and the United States. Established in 1959, it is the oldest regional institution in the field of development finance. By the early 1990s, it had cumulative loans of over $57 billion in support of some 2,000 development projects. Much of its funding comes from the United States, whose influence in the bank has been criticized from time to time. But, of late, the IDB has been successful in securing financing in private capital markets in Europe and Japan, thus easing some of the concern with U.S. dominance. The bank maintains close ties with the World Bank (q.v.).

Inter-American Treaty of Reciprocal Assistance (also known as the Rio Treaty). Adopted in 1947 to safeguard the Western Hemisphere from aggression. It was signed by 19 of the 21 American republics; Ecuador and Nicaragua withheld their signatures. Cuba withdrew from the treaty in 1960. The signatories condemned war and agreed not to resort to the threat or use of force in any manner inconsistent with the UN Charter. The Rio Treaty is best thought of as the military wing of the Organization of American States (OAS) (q.v.). Jurisdictional disputes with the UN (q.v.) have arisen since 1947.

Intergovernmental Organization for International Carriage by Rail. One of the 19th century products of the industrial and transportation (q.v.) revolutions, the organization was established in 1890. Its purpose was to provide for a uniform legal system relating to international rail transport, as it relates to both passengers and freight.

International Air Transport Association (IATA). IATA is the professional organization for the world's airlines; that is, it is the international nongovernmental organization that is charged with promoting safe, regular, and economic air transportation (q.v.). It regulates, through a process of negotiations, the fares that member airlines may charge on international routes. This power, which has often been questioned by various governments, falls under an antitrust immunity. Headquartered in Montreal, Canada, founded in 1919 as the International Air Traffic Association, it was renamed with an expanded mandate in 1945. It is composed of about 200 airlines, with flight paths over 100 countries; most members are publicly owned airlines.

International Alert (IA). Since 1985, IA, which has its headquarters in London, has provided a nongovernmental route to conflict resolution. It works to resolve violent conflicts through person-to-person dialogue and mediation (q.v.). It also sponsors and disseminates research about the causes of conflict and ways to recognize conflicts at an early enough point when dialogue can be fruitful and hopefully prevent an exacerbation of tensions.

International Association for Cultural Freedom (IACF). Founded in June 1950, with headquarters in Paris, the IACF is an international nongovernmental organization composed of writers and other artists, and scholars and intellectuals dedicated to the defense of academic, intellectual, and cultural freedom.

International Association of Lions Clubs. Founded in 1917, with its headquarters in Oak Brook, Illinois, the International Association has as its motto "We serve." More specifically, the association is an international nongovernmental organization aimed to assist refugees (q.v.) by providing funds, food, and shelter. One of its major projects has been Sight First, aimed at sight preservation.

International Association of Trading Organizations for a Developing World (ASTRO). Originally established in 1984 as the International Association of State Trading Organizations of Developing Countries, ASTRO, which adopted its current name in 1992 as it sought to attract additional members, promotes and seeks to strengthen the organizational and professional expertise, and entrepreneurial and managerial capabilities of member trade (q.v.) organizations. This is deemed necessary for them to compete effectively in the international market. It currently has 55 member countries. Its headquarters are in Ljubljana, Slovenia.

International Atomic Energy Agency (IAEA). The IAEA is an autonomous body of the United Nations (UN) (q.v.) that seeks to accelerate and expand the societal contribution of atomic energy for peaceful purposes. Proposed by U.S. President Eisenhower in 1953 and established in 1957, the IAEA's headquarters are in Vienna, Austria. Among other things the IAEA is charged with establishing and administering safeguards to ensure that special fissionable and other materials, services, equipment, facilities, and information are not diverted to military use. It facilitates the teaching of modern technology to scientists of many developing countries (q.v.) and seeks to raise living standards by developing cheap energy sources. It conducts 1,800 on-site inspections annually, at 520 locations around the world. It has formulated basic safety standards for radiation protection and issued regulations and codes of practice for specific types of operations, including the safe transport of radioactive materials. In the aftermath of the Chernobyl nuclear disaster of April 1986, the IAEA adopted the Convention on Early Notification of a Nuclear Accident and the Convention on Assistance in the Case of a Nuclear Accident or Radiological Emergency. Throughout much of the 1990s, it was concerned with ensuring that the Iraqi government did not redevelop a nuclear capacity for military purposes.

International Bank for Economic Cooperation (IBEC). The central focus of the IBEC, which was established in 1963 and has its headquarters in Moscow, Russia, was actually a multilateral system of payments arranged among socialist countries on the basis of "collective currency" (that is, as a transferable ruble). It also worked and works to promote economic cooperation (q.v.) and growth among member countries, its major function after the introduction of market mechanisms, to varying degrees, in its member countries. The current membership includes: Bulgaria, Cuba, the Czech Republic, Hungary, Mongolia, Poland, Romania, Russia, Slovakia, and Vietnam.

International Bank for Reconstruction and Development (IBRD). See World Bank.

International Catholic Migration Commission (ICMC). Founded in 1951 with headquarters in Geneva, Switzerland, the ICMC coordinates the activities of national Catholic migration organizations. It also provides technical assistance concerning the rights of migrants and refugees (q.v.).

International Center for Peace Initiatives (ICPI). The ICPI is a nongovernmental organization established in Bombay, India, in 1990. Its goal is to develop and promote innovative approaches to national, regional, and global peace. It seeks to achieve its aim by serving as a catalyst in partnership with leading institutions with compatible goals. It advocates a nuclear-free world and is actively engaged in seeking the means for conflict resolution in the South Asian region.

International Centre for Settlement of Investment Disputes (ICSID). ICSID was created under the auspices of the World Bank (q.v.) by the Washington Convention of March 18, 1965. Its purpose is to promote increased levels of private investment by assisting in the settlement of disputes between states and nationals of other countries by arbitration (q.v.) or conciliation (q.v.). The jurisdiction of the Washington, D.C.–based center extends to any legal disputes arising directly from an investment between a contracting state, or any of its constituents or agencies acting on its behalf, and another national agency or another contracting state. More than 100 states have agreed to avail themselves of the center's services.

International Chamber of Commerce (ICC). The Paris-based ICC was founded in 1920 but actually traces its origins to a series of periodic conferences of commercial and industrial organizations beginning in 1869. It currently has a membership of more than 5,400 individual corporations and 1,700 organizations, mostly national chambers of commerce. Its goal is to promote free trade (q.v.) and private enterprise at the same time that it provides practical services to its members. It seeks to meet its goals by lobbying at both the national and intergovernmental levels. Its main decision-making bodies are a council and congress. The latter meets every three years; over 2,000 people attend each of its meetings. It operates a Court of Arbitration and a Commercial Crime Service and has established commissions on the environment (q.v.), taxation, air transport, and laws and practices relating to business competition.

International Chamber of Shipping (ICS). The London-based ICS began in 1920 as the International Shipping Conference. It adopted its current name in 1948. Throughout its history, its goal has been to promote the interests of its member national shipping associations. This aim has involved trying to shape legislation and treaties at the national and international levels, including in the areas of maritime safety and pollution control.

International Civil Aviation Organization (ICAO). The ICAO is a UN Specialized Agency (q.v.). In operation since 1947, it is charged with the development and regulation of international air traffic. The ICAO was agreed to at the Chicago Convention of 1944, which adopted the Convention on International Civil Aviation. Headquartered in Montreal, Canada, the ICAO was set up to study and report on such issues as customs facilities, traffic control, aircraft maintenance, and standardization. The ICAO has evolved into a leading contributor to technical assistance, especially in terms of the development of airways, airports, and other facilities in economically less developed countries. It also conducted a highly publicized investigation of the 1983 downing of a Korean airliner by the Soviet air force.

International Cocoa Organization (ICCO). Originally established under the 1972 International Cocoa Agreement, the 37–member state ICCO continues to administer the agreement out of its London headquarters. It functions chiefly through its highest authority, the International Cocoa Council. The agreements that are administered seek to promote the development of the world cocoa economy and to contribute toward the stabilization of the world cocoa market. The ICCO maintains a buffer stock to assist in meeting this latter goal.

International Coffee Organization (ICO). The ICO was established in 1963 in accordance with the 1963 International Coffee Agreement. Headquartered in London, its membership includes 43 coffee exporters as members and 18 importing countries. In 1993, the United States dropped out after decades of participation. Working through its highest authority, the International Coffee Council, the ICO attempts to foster economic diversification in member countries as well as increase their income from coffee. Over the years, the ICO has administered a scheme to stabilize prices for coffee through a system of export quotas linked to an agreed price range, the Diversification Fund to finance projects designed to rationalize coffee production on a country by country basis, and the Promotion Fund that financed a number of programs designed to increase coffee consumption. Since 1973, the ICO has maintained a bibliographic database of studies on coffee or relevant to coffee.

International Commission for Scientific Exploration of the Mediterranean Sea (ICSEM). Established in 1910 to guide and coordinate research programs relating to the Mediterranean and Black seas. The hope of the 22 member countries of this organization, based in Monte Carlo, Monaco, is that if such research is conducted in as objective a manner as possible, including in such politically charged areas as marine radioactivity and protection of endangered species, it will influence international public policy.

International Commission for the Conservation of Atlantic Tunas (ICCAT). In existence since 1969 and with its headquarters in Madrid, the 21-member state ICCAT seeks to maintain the populations of tuna and tunalike species found in the Atlantic Ocean and adjacent areas. Quotas, in accordance with the International Convention for the Conservation of Atlantic Tunas, are set to maximize the *sustainable* catch.

International Commission for the Protection of the Elbe. The commission has been working, since its establishment in 1990, to enable the use of Elbe water, including as drinking water. This has required significant antipollution programs. The commission's headquarters are in Bonn, Germany. Its membership is composed of the Czech Republic, Germany, and Slovakia. Austria, the European Union (EU) (q.v.), and Poland have observer status.

International Commission for the Protection of the Moselle against Pollution. The commission was established in 1963 in Paris, where its headquarters remain. The purpose is to coordinate member state efforts to combat river pollution. Its membership entails France, Germany, and Luxembourg.

International Commission for the Protection of the Rhine against Pollution (ICPRP). Established in 1963, the ICPRP works to identify the sources of pollution and then to develop ways to combat those problems. Its work includes developing and implementing treaties, including the International Convention for the Protection of the Rhine against Chemical Pollution (signed in 1976). Its headquarters are in Koblenz, Germany. Its current membership includes France, Germany, Luxembourg, the Netherlands, and Switzerland.

International Commission for the Protection of the Saar against Pollution. The commission was established in 1961 in Paris, where its headquarters remain. The purpose is to coordinate member state efforts to combat river pollution. It has particularly focused on nitrate levels in the river. France and Germany are members.

International Commission of Jurists (ICJ). The ICJ monitors worldwide observance of the rule of law and due process. It documents systematic violations of human rights (q.v.) and tries to mobilize public opinion against such violations. The ICJ regularly issues judgments on cases in violation of the rule of law and human rights issues and often sends observers to trials. Since 1978, it has maintained the Center for the Independence of Judges and Lawyers. Founded in 1952 in Geneva, Switzerland, the commission's funding comes from lawyers, law firms, individuals, foundations, and governments.

International Committee of the Red Cross (ICRC). Established in 1863 in Geneva, Switzerland, and staffed exclusively by Swiss nationals, the international element of this international nongovernmental organization arises from its mission. Originally it was to help the wounded on the battlefield, but now it also seeks to provide emergency food (q.v.) relief, monitor prison conditions, protect noncombatants, and implement the four Geneva Conventions of 1949. Most recently the ICRC, whose operations are always related to situations of armed conflict, has been active in efforts to ban the use of antipersonnel mines. See also International Federation of Red Cross and Red Crescent Societies.

International commodity agreement (ICA). The name given to a multilateral trade agreement with the following characteristics: (1) it deals with one or more related primary commodities (q.v.); (2) its members include both producers and consumers; (3) its ostensible purpose is to stabilize prices and/or supply, although its real purpose is likely to include some increase in prices; (4) it contains economic provisions such as buffer stocks or quotas or long-term contracts to attain its objectives; and (5) it is administered by a central body representing its members. See also International Coffee Organization; International Grains Council; International Jute Organization; International Sugar Organization; International Tropical Timber Organization.

International Confederation of Free Trade Unions (ICFTU). An international nongovernmental organization founded in London in 1949 with the goal of promoting the interests of working people of the world, through constantly rising standards of living, full employment, social security, and reductions in the gap between the rich and the poor. As its name suggests, it began when some Western trade unions (q.v.) left the rival World Federation of Trade Unions (WFTU). It is composed of 174 affiliated trade unions, totaling 120 million individual members in 124 countries and territories. Most of its members are in Western industrialized countries, the Czech Republic, and Poland, with some in Asia, Africa, and Latin America. In a similar vein, it has not limited its activities to members' worker rights; it has strongly opposed dictatorships and worked for disarmament (q.v.). Its governing body is the Congress, which meets every four years. The organization's headquarters are in Brussels, Belgium.

International Conference on Population and Development. Convened in Cairo, Egypt, in September 1994, the conference built on the 1993 World Conference on Human Rights (q.v.) and previous UN population conferences, most notably the 1974 World Population Conference. In the 1994 conference, however, there was considerable attention to the relationship between population, growth, and sustainable development and the relationship between issues of population and gender equality, equity, and empowerment of women (q.v.).

International Council of Scientific Unions (ICSU). An international forum, dating back to 1919 (when it was called the International Research Council), for planning and organizing cooperative international research projects. The council is a nongovernmental organization composed of 94 multidisciplinary National Scientific Members (scientific research councils or science academies) and 23 international, single-discipline Scientific Unions. It is used by members of the international scientific community as a repository where highly technical advice may be sought and data compared. Its secretariat is in Paris.

International Council of Voluntary Agencies (ICVA). This international nongovernmental organization, based in Geneva, Switzerland, was founded in 1962. It seeks to encourage the growth of voluntary agencies and serves as an information and discussion forum for them. More than 90 international voluntary organizations are its members.

International Court of Justice (ICJ) (also known as the World Court). As the successor to the Permanent Court of International Justice (PCIJ) (q.v.), it was established in 1945 with headquarters in The Hague (although it can and has sat elsewhere). All members of the United Nations (UN) (q.v.) are automatically members of the court; others may become parties to the court's statute. The court is composed of 15 judges, elected for nine-year terms by the UN General Assembly (q.v.) and the Security Council (q.v.). No two judges may come from the same country, although judges are charged with serving in their personal (i.e., nonpolitical) capacity. Rosalyn Higgins, of the United Kingdom, was elected in 1995 as the first woman to sit on the ICJ.

The court has jurisdiction over all cases referred to it, both contentious cases involving states, such as the Corfu Channel case (q.v.)—through the "optional clause" (whereby states can allow all cases involving them to be so resolved), as a consequence of specific treaty obligations or by explicit ad hoc agreement—and advisory opinions, involving organs of the UN (usually by the General Assembly). If the court's decisions are not being implemented, resort to the Security Council is permitted. This has not yet been done. The court's decisions cannot be appealed but can be circumvented (e.g., by turning to the Security Council for action).

The volume of ICJ work has varied considerably over time. In the 1960s, the court's relative inactivity was explained by many as a consequence of its treatment (actually nontreatment) of cases relating to South Africa, whereas its activity in the 1990s is, in part, explained by its decision in the *Nicaragua v. USA* case, which resulted in the U.S. boycotting the decision of the case on its merits and withdrawing its agreement to have cases heard through a (much restricted) optional clause. See also Connally Reservation.

International Criminal Police Organization (INTERPOL). An international nongovernmental organization, established in Vienna, Austria, in 1923 (under the name International Criminal Police Commission), through which police departments around the world cooperate to help prevent and suppress international crime. Currently headquartered in Lyon, France, the police agencies of 176 countries are now members. The principal crimes of interest to INTERPOL include narcotics traffic and counterfeiting operations in Europe.

International Development Association (IDA). An affiliate of the International Bank for Reconstruction and Development, IDA makes "soft loans" to economically less developed countries, usually with per capita GNP of less than $450. Created in 1960, its resources come from contributions of member countries and a small percentage from the IBRD itself. It has 139 members and usually makes loans for 50 years, at no interest and with only a nominal service charge. Membership is open to all members of the IBRD. Voting is weighted (q.v.) according to members' financial contributions. The president of the IBRD serves as the president of the IDA. It is located at the World Bank (q.v.) headquarters in Washington, D.C.

International Energy Agency (IEA). An intergovernmental organization formed in 1974 within the framework of the Paris-based Organisation for Economic Co-operation and Development (OECD) (q.v.) by the industrialized Western countries plus Japan and Turkey to counter the Organization of Petroleum Exporting Countries (OPEC) (q.v.). The IEA has adopted an emergency oil-sharing plan to be put into operation in the event of a reduction in oil supplies to member countries. It has not been resorted to.

International Federation of Red Cross and Red Crescent Societies (IFRC). This Geneva-based organization has been operating since 1919; however, at the time it was known as the League of Red Cross Societies. The federation, whose work is limited to peacetime, has as its goal the inspiration, encouragement, facilitation, and promotion of all forms of humanitarian activities by the 155 national societies. The goal, simply put, is to prevent and alleviate human suffering, believing that to do so is likely to contribute to the achievement and maintenance of peace. See also International Committee of the Red Cross.

International Federation of University Women (IFUW). Composed of national federations and associations, the Geneva-based IFUW was founded in 1919. Its 200,000 members in more than 50 countries are committed to furthering educational and professional opportunities for women (q.v.) and promoting understanding and friendship among female graduates of universities.

International Federation of Women Lawyers (IFWL). Created in 1944 to promote women's (q.v.) rights, the federation's headquarters are in New York City. Its goals include the promotion of the interests of women attorneys. It seeks to achieve these ends through its work at the UN (q.v.) as well as its own conventions and publications.

International Finance Corporation (IFC). This affiliate of the International Bank for Reconstruction and Development (IBRD), established in 1956, is responsible for furthering economic development through investment in *private* enterprises in economically less developed member countries through both lending and equity participation. The IFC invests—without government guarantees—in productive private enterprises in association with investors who can provide competent management. It is empowered to undertake financing on terms that it considers appropriate, taking into consideration the requirements of the borrowing firm and the risks to be assumed by the corporation. The IFC limits its own commitments to no more than 25 percent of each project, acting primarily as a catalyst.

International Fund for Agricultural Development (IFAD). Established as a UN Specialized Agency (q.v.) in 1977, as a follow-up to the 1974 World Food Conference, IFAD's purpose is to offer grants and loans to help increase food (q.v.) production in economically less developed countries. It mobilizes resources to be made available on concessional terms for increased food production. Funds for IFAD come mainly from members of the Organization of Petroleum Exporting Countries (OPEC) (q.v.) and economically advanced, Western states. Financing worked out well until the collapse of oil prices in the 1980s. The Governing Council is unique in that it is divided into three kinds of representation: donor-developed countries, donor-developing countries, and recipient-developing countries.

International Grains Council (formerly the International Wheat Council, IWC). The IWC was established in 1949. It aimed at furthering international cooperation in all aspects of trade in wheat and other grains. It continued until June 30, 1995, when it was succeeded by the International Grains Council, which is designed to further grain market stability and world food security. The council is financed by contributions from member governments that are based on their votes, reflecting shares in international trade in all grains (not wheat alone, as in the past). The council currently has 26 member governments (Algeria, Argentina, Australia, Canada, Côte d'Ivoire, Cuba, Ecuador, Egypt, Holy See, Hungary, India, Iraq, Japan, Jordan, Mauritius, Morocco, Norway, Pakistan, Panama, Russia, South Africa, South Korea, Switzerland, Tunisia, Turkey, and the United States) and the European Union (EU) (q.v.).

International Investment Bank (IIB). As a financial institution, IIB was created in 1970 within the framework of the Council for Mutual Economic Cooperation and Assistance (CMEA or COMECON) (q.v.) to encourage trade (q.v.) and development of centrally planned countries. Historically the IIB granted long-term and medium-term credit, primarily for carrying out projects connected with the socialist division of labor. It is now working to assist member countries in the transition to market economies and integration into the global economy.

International Islamic Organization (IIO). Founded in Bandung, Indonesia, in 1970 as the successor to the Afro-Asian Islamic Organization, the IIO's aim is to work toward the establishment of a new world order that accords with the teachings of Islam. It assists Muslim communities that are seeking independence and promotes the study and use of the Arabic language and the practice of human rights (q.v.) in accordance with the teachings of Islam. Its headquarters are in Jakarta, Indonesia. Its membership is composed of national groups in

23 countries: Afghanistan, Algeria, Australia, Cambodia, China, Cyprus, Egypt, Germany, Hong Kong, India, Indonesia, Iraq, Japan, Laos, Malaysia, Pakistan, the Philippines, Saudi Arabia, Singapore, South Korea, Sri Lanka, Syria, and Thailand.

International Islamic Relief Organization (IIRO). Founded in 1978, with its headquarters in Jeddah, Saudi Arabia, the IIRO is a humanitarian nongovernmental organization. It provides assistance to victims of natural disasters and wars anywhere in the world, offering medical, education, and social support to orphans, refugees (q.v.), and the displaced. It also works with small businesses and sponsors economic projects to assist disaster victims with finding employment.

International Jute Organization (IJO). Headquartered in Dhaka, Bangladesh, since 1984, the IJO has been carrying out its functions through the International Jute Council and the Committee on Projects. The IJO oversees the implementation of the International Agreement on Jute and Jute Products, the purpose of which is to expand and diversify the market for jute and jute products. Its members include five exporting countries (Bangladesh, China, India, Nepal, and Thailand) and 22 importing countries and the European Union (EU) (q.v.).

International Labour Organisation (ILO). The ILO was originally founded in 1919 along with the League of Nations (q.v.). In 1945, it became a UN Specialized Agency (q.v.) with its headquarters remaining in Geneva. Its organizational framework includes the all-member International Labour Conference and the smaller Governing Body. Both are uniquely composed of tripartite delegations: one worker, one employer, and two governmental delegates, each with a separate vote. The ILO's major goals include achieving full employment, raising standards of living, ensuring proper earnings and working conditions, providing adequate training facilities, and obtaining recognition of the right to collective bargaining and social security measures. In 1977, the United States withdrew from the ILO, complaining that it had ignored labor conditions in communist countries. After the issue was resolved to U.S. satisfaction, it resumed membership (in 1980).

International Law Commission (ILC). An agency of the UN General Assembly (q.v.) established in 1947, the ILC is charged with encouraging the development and codification of public international law. The 34 members represent various geographical regions, political views, and legal traditions. The ILC's work at codification has included state and government recognition, state succession, diplomatic immunity, the law of the sea, nationality, aliens, asylum, and arbitral procedures.

International Lead and Zinc Study Group (ILZSG). Founded in 1959 to provide a forum for regular intergovernmental consultations on lead- and zinc-related issues, this London-based organization has no market interventionist power. It has to rely on the dissemination of reliable statistics to achieve its goals. It aims at improving market transparency. Its membership of 29 countries includes Australia, Austria, Belgium, Bulgaria, Canada, China, the Czech Republic, Finland, France, Germany, India, Ireland, Italy, Japan, Morocco, the Netherlands, Norway, Pakistan, Peru, Russia, South Africa, South Korea, Spain, Sweden, Thailand, Tunisia, the United Kingdom, the United States, and the former Yugoslavia.

International League for Human Rights (ILHR). The ILHR, formerly the International League for the Rights of Man, was founded in the early 1940s in New York, where its headquarters remain. Its origins can be traced to the French League for the Rights of Man, founded in 1902, and the International Federation for the Rights of Man, established in 1922. The league is actively involved in the investigation of allegations of human rights (q.v.) abuse. It also works to improve procedures at the international level to redress violations of human rights.

International Lesbian and Gay Association (ILGA). Founded in 1978 as the International Gay Association, the ILGA works for the liberation of lesbians and gay men. It lobbies, coordinates political action, and facilitates the exchange of information. This nonprofit international nongovernmental association is composed of national associations based in more than 60 countries. The association's headquarters are in Brussels, Belgium.

International Maritime Organization (IMO). The IMO is a UN Specialized Agency (q.v.), begun in 1948 as the Intergovernmental Maritime Consultative Organization (IMCO). The new name was adopted in 1982 to underscore its evolution, namely from being merely "consultative" in nature. It focuses on maritime safety, marine pollution, and efficient navigation. Its Legal Committee has sought the codification of laws relating to the protection of the marine environment (q.v.). Among its major accomplishments is the Convention for the Safety of Life at Sea (SOLAS), the most important of all treaties dealing with shipping safety. Its 1994 amendments, focusing on such things as high speed craft, entered into effect in 1996. Most countries in the world belong to the IMO; greater policy influence is granted to states with the largest fleets registered in them. The organization also has an active technical assistance program

International Maritime Satellite Organization (Inmarsat). Since 1979, the London-based Inmarsat has been providing the space segment for maritime, aeronautical, and land mobile communications (e.g., with the assistance of satellites, Inmarsat provides direct-dial telephone, telex, fax, etc., for maritime applications). More than 70 countries take advantage of its activities.

International Meeting on Cooperation and Development. Convened in Cancun, Mexico, on October 22–23, 1981, this meeting had a deliberative, not decision-making purpose. The chief aim of the meeting, attended by the heads of state or government of 22 developed and developing countries (q.v.), was to discuss procedures for future global economic negotiations. Topics for discussion included food (q.v.), energy, trade (q.v.), money, and finance.

International Monetary Fund (IMF). A UN Specialized Agency (q.v.), it was established in 1944. The aim of the IMF is stabilizing international monetary exchange rates. Its operating funds come from its member states. Contributions (and thus voting strength) are related to a country's national income, monetary reserves, trade balance, and other economic indicators.

The IMF has been subjected to considerable criticism for the strict financial conditions that it often attaches to its loans and for its power to negotiate such terms. Terms of conditionality, recently, have also included elements relating to the environment (q.v.), participation of women (q.v.), and governance concerns. Especially notable in this last respect was its July 1997 agreement with Argentina. Critics assert that states that cannot draw funds from the IMF are similarly treated by other potential lending sources, thus compounding the fund's global influence. They also contend the fund has deviated from its charter, which called for making lending decisions strictly on economic bases. See also Camdessus, Michel; de Larosière, Jacques; Gatt, Camille; Jacobsson, Per; Schweitzer, Pierre-Paul; Special Drawing Rights; Witteveen, Henrikus Johannes; World Bank.

International Natural Rubber Organization (INRO). Created under the International Natural Rubber Agreement of 1979, the INRO has its headquarters in Kuala Lumpur, Malaysia. It conducts its business through its highest authority, the International Natural Rubber Council. The key aims of the INRO are to achieve balanced growth between the supply of and demand for natural rubber, stabilize exporting members' earnings, increase exporting members' earnings based on expanding export volumes, and ensure an adequate supply of natural rubber for importing countries. Its members include six exporting countries (Côte d'Ivoire, Indonesia, Malaysia, Nigeria, Sri Lanka, and Thailand) and 21 importing countries and the European Union (q.v.).

International Nickel Study Group (INSG). The INSG, which has its headquarters in The Hague, Netherlands, began operations in 1990. It brings producers and consumers together to collect and disseminate information on the international nickel economy. The group has no market intervention capabilities. Members include the governments of Australia, Canada, Cuba, Finland, France, Germany, Greece, Indonesia, Italy, Japan, the Netherlands, Norway, Russia, and Sweden. The European Union (EU) (q.v.) is also represented.

International Olive Oil Council (IOOC). Headquartered in Madrid, the council is charged with implementing the International Olive Agreement, which provides for the financing of technical cooperation programs in olive cultivation, olive oil extraction and table olive processing. Membership is composed mainly of producing members (Algeria, Cyprus, Israel, Lebanon, Morocco, Tunisia, Turkey, and the former Yugoslavia), partly producing and partly importing members (European Union [q.v.]), and a mainly importing member (Egypt). Many countries, such as the United States, hold observer status.

International Olympic Committee (IOC). Founded in 1894, this international nongovernmental organization is composed of the representatives of the IOC in the 100 individual country Olympic committees. The IOC, whose headquarters are in Lausanne, Switzerland, has full authority on all questions concerning the Olympic games and the Olympic movement. As such, it encourages the coordination, organization, and development of sport and sports competition.

International Organization for Migration (IOM). The IOM was established in 1951 but has its current name only since November 1989 (it was earlier known as the Intergovernmental Committee for European Migration, ICEM). This Geneva-based organization studies the causes of migration; discusses the rights of migrants and solutions to migrants' problems; assists states with managing migration through resettlement, immigration, and return; and helps with the reintegration of migrants into various societies through culture and language training. Most recently, the IOM has been working with the wounded and ill of the former Yugoslavia, Haiti, and Rwanda.

International Organization for Standardization (ISO). Founded in 1947, ISO is a worldwide federation of national standards bodies. The purpose of ISO is to promote the development of standardization and related activities throughout the world with a view to facilitating international exchange of goods and services and to develop cooperation in the sphere of intellectual, scientific, technological, and economic activity. ISO covers standardization in all fields except the electrical and electronic industries. Those are the responsibility of the International Electrotechnical Commission (IEC).

International PEN. Established in 1921, with headquarters in London, International PEN is concerned with freedom of expression and intellectual cooperation between men and women of letters in all countries. It has 121 autonomous centers in 91 countries.

International Planned Parenthood Federation (IPPF). The federation, which was founded in Bombay, India, in 1952, links national autonomous family planning associations in over 150 countries. It is registered as a charity in the United Kingdom—its headquarters are in London—and is the largest nongovernmental organization in the world concerned with family planning and sexual and reproductive health. Its aims include promoting sexual and reproductive health for all; eliminating unsafe abortions; taking affirmative action to gain equity, equality and empowerment for women; and helping young people understand their sexuality and providing services that meet their demands.

International Press Institute (IPI). Tracing its origins to a meeting in New York City in 1950, IPI's headquarters are now in Vienna, Austria. IPI seeks to further and safeguard freedom of the press through such activities as research, seminars, and conferences. More specifically, its goals include ensuring free access to news, regardless of national boundaries; and ensuring the safety of journalists and their ability to report freely. It has members in almost 90 countries.

International Refugee Organization (IRO). An interim (1946–1952) UN Specialized Agency (q.v.), IRO was created to assist persons uprooted and displaced by the events of World War II. It was abolished because of the view that refugee (q.v.) problems were only temporary and owing to severe criticism from the Soviet Union and its allies.

But it had to be replaced by the United Nations High Commissioner for Refugees (UNHCR) (q.v.).

International Research and Training Institute for the Advancement of Women (INSTRAW). Established by the UN General Assembly (q.v.) in 1976, INSTRAW derives its modest budget (approximately $500,000 a year) from governments, private organizations, and individuals. It focuses primarily on the role of women (q.v.) in developing countries (q.v.). It tries to act as a catalyst among other agencies promoting women's rights and welfare.

International Seabed Authority (ISA). ISA was established on November 16, 1994, one year after the Third Law of the Sea Conferences (q.v.)—LOS III—entered into force, after being ratified by the required 60 countries. The ISA is responsible for implementing the various provisions of this wide-ranging and controversial (especially in the U.S.) treaty. Specifically, the authority is the organization through which parties to the LOS III organize and control activities in the international seabed area, beyond the limits of national jurisdiction, particularly with a view to administering the mineral resources of the deep seabed. It is governed by an assembly on which all parties to the convention are represented and a council with elected representatives, carefully balanced to ensure representation by those with a greater financial interest in the seabed's activities, including the largest investors in exploiting the seabed's minerals. In March 1996, Satya N. Nandan, former Fijian special representative of the UN secretary-general for the Law of the Sea, was elected by the authority's assembly as the first ISA secretary-general.

International Sugar Organization (ISO). Headquartered in London since its founding in 1968 and charged with administering the International Sugar Agreement, the ISO's highest authority is the International Sugar Council. The agreement aims at increasing the consumption of sugar, particularly for nontraditional uses, and facilitating trade in sugar by collecting and providing information on the sugar market and other sweeteners. With the entry into force of the Common Fund for Commodities (q.v.), the ISO has been designated an International Commodity Body (ICB), which adds a new function for the ISO to process loan applications for sugar-related projects by its members. There are currently 46 members, including the European Union (EU) (q.v.). These include major sugar producers, such as Cuba, as well as importers, such as Switzerland. The United States is not a member.

International Tea Promotion Association (ITPA). The ITPA was established on February 23, 1979, with headquarters in Nairobi, Kenya. While agreement could not be reached on export restrictions, the association is charged with maintaining and increasing the demand and consumption of tea, fostering the removal of tariff and nontariff barriers as they relate to tea consumption, and gathering and disseminating marketing information. Members include Bangladesh, Indonesia, Kenya, Malawi, Mauritius, Mozambique, Tanzania, and Uganda.

International Telecommunication Union (ITU). The ITU, a Geneva-based UN Specialized Agency (q.v.) since 1947, traces its origins to 1865. The name from its origin until 1934 was the International Telegraph Union. The union's mission now is to promote the improvement and rational use of telecommunications of all kinds. One of its responsibilities is fostering and providing technical assistance to economically and technologically less developed countries. The ITU seeks to fulfill its goals through international conferences and meetings, publication of information, organization of world exhibitions and technical cooperation. Some of the ongoing—and often controversial—functions of the union include allocation and recording of radio frequencies and establishing the lowest possible rates. The real authority of the ITU is more normative than regulatory. It provides opportunities for systems operators and manufacturers from many countries to gather, exchange views, and agree on an extremely broad range of multilateral arrangements. There are currently 187 members of the ITU.

International Telecommunications Satellite Organization (INTELSAT). INTELSAT, which has its headquarters in Washington, D.C., was created on an interim basis in 1964 (and permanently in 1971). Its task was to establish a global commercial telecommunications satellite system. Accordingly, INTELSAT maintains and operates the global satellite system used for public international telecommunications services. It currently provides voice/data and video services to more than 200 countries via a 24-satellite fleet. Some 141 countries belong to INTELSAT.

International Textile, Garment and Leather Workers' Federation. Founded in 1970 to promote the interests of its more than 180 member trade unions (q.v.) that represent the interests of seven million workers in over 80 countries. It gathers and disseminates data on workers' conditions and, when necessary, supports workers on strike.

International Trade Center (ITC). Originally established in March 1964 as a part of the General Agreement on Tariffs and Trade (GATT) (q.v.) secretariat. In 1967, the UN Conference on Trade and Development (UNCTAD) (q.v.) and GATT recommended that the ITC be operated by both organizations, a recommendation that was formally implemented in 1974. It is now legally a joint subsidiary organ of the World Trade Organization (WTO) (q.v.) and the United Nations (q.v.), the latter operating through UNCTAD. The purpose of this Geneva-based organization is to promote the exports of developing countries (q.v.) and economies in transition by providing trade information, advice on marketing, marketing techniques, and training.

International Tropical Timber Organization (ITTO). The ITTO was established in 1983 and has had its headquarters in Yokohama, Japan, since 1986. Its highest authority is the International Tropical Timber Council (ITTC). The organization's aims are to monitor the tropical timber market, providing assistance when needed, and to conduct research, such as market intelligence. It has also set a specific Year 2000 Objective: all tropical timber products traded internationally by its member states shall originate from sustainably managed forests. Its 52 member states include both producer and consumer states: Australia, Austria, Belgium/Luxembourg, Bolivia, Brazil, Cameroon, Canada, China, Colombia, Congo, Côte d'Ivoire, Denmark, Ecuador, Egypt, the European Union (EU) (q.v.), Fiji, Finland, France, Gabon, Germany, Ghana, Greece, Guyana, Honduras, India, Indonesia, Ireland, Italy, Japan, Liberia, Malaysia, Myanmar, Nepal, the Netherlands, New Zealand, Norway, Panama, Papua New Guinea, Peru, the Philippines, Portugal, Russia, South Korea, Spain, Sweden, Switzerland, Thailand, Togo, Trinidad and Tobago, the United Kingdom, Venezuela, and Zaire. The ITTO's members account for 75 percent of the world's tropical rainforests and 90 percent of the trade in tropical timber.

International Union for Conservation of Nature and Natural Resources—World Conservation Union. Established on October 5, 1948 in Fontainebleau, France, the union claims to be the world's oldest conservation organization. Before its establishment, there were several national conservation organizations but none working at the international level. It was established as a union of governments, government agencies, and nongovernmental organizations working together with scientists and experts to conserve nature's integrity and diversity and to provide leadership and promote a common approach to the world conservation movement. Its headquarters are in Vaud, Switzerland.

International Whaling Commission (IWC). The IWC was established in 1948 as a consequence of the entry into force of the 1946 International Convention for the Regulation of Whaling. It encourages research related to the convention's goals, namely the regulation of all species of whales to enable the orderly development of the whaling industry. By 1982, the commission's composition had changed from being pro-whaling to conservationist, and it adopted its first five-year moratorium on commercial whaling in that year. The commission itself can do little to deal with those of its 39 member states that violate its often quite controversial moratoria, most recently Norway. The IWC's secretariat is located in Cambridge, England.

International Wheat Council (IWC). See International Grains Council.

Inter-Parliamentary Union (IPU). An international nongovernmental organization aimed at promoting contacts among members of all national parliaments. Founded in 1889, membership now includes inter-parliamentary national groups in over 100 countries. Its headquarters are in Geneva, Switzerland.

Islamic Development Bank (IDB). Established in Jeddah, Saudi Arabia, in 1973 and functioning since October 20, 1975, the IDB assists Muslim countries and communities with economic development (q.v.) in accordance with Islamic principles. That is, to the extent possible, the IDB follows the *Shariah* in borrowing, lending, and investment practices. It forbids usury, it does not extend loans or credits for interest; and it supports economic and social development by taking equity participation in public and private enterprises. Emergency aid is also extended to Islamic countries and to Muslims in non-Islamic countries. Membership includes all Muslim countries and the Palestine Liberation Organization (PLO).

Ismay, Hastings Lionel Lord (1887–1965). After serving as a general in the British cavalry, Ismay served in a variety of political-military organizations in the British government, culminating in his service as chief of staff to Winston Churchill, when he was prime minister and minister of defense. Lord Ismay—or "Pug," as he was affectionately known to his associates—served as the North Atlantic Treaty Organization's (NATO) (q.v.) first secretary-general from 1952–1957. He is credited with the aphorism explaining that organization's purpose: "to keep Russia out, to keep Germany down, and to keep the U.S. in." As secretary-general, he was able to call upon his wartime experiences and friendships with Churchill and Dwight Eisenhower to try to ease conflicts among the Big Three in the Alliance. His unique strengths proved to be as a conciliator and facilitator on issues ranging from Cyprus to Germany, but they were not sufficient to prevent the Suez Crisis of 1956. He is generally credited with expanding NATO's policy-making role.

J

Jacobsson, Per (1894–1963). Jacobsson was an internationally renowned Swedish economist with extensive experience with the Bank for International Settlements (BIS) (q.v.) before he became managing director of the International Monetary Fund (IMF) (q.v.) in 1956. He was managing director when the IMF really became active, working hard, as he did, to increase the fund's quotas (national contributions), to get all of the European currencies convertible, and to place the French economy on firm grounding at the outset of the Fifth Republic. He remained managing director until 1963.

Junta del Acuerdo de Cartagena (commonly known as the Andean Group, the Andean Pact, the Andean Subregional Group, or the Andean Common Market, Ancom). Founded in 1966 in Bogotá, Colombia (through signing of the Cartagena Agreement) but now headquartered in Lima, Peru, the group owes its origins to the failure of the Latin American Free Trade Association (LAFTA) (q.v.) to form a common market. The Andean Group aims at strengthening the smaller economies of the Andean subregion through trade liberalization, industrial specialization agreements, common policies for regulating foreign investment, a common external tariff, and special arrangements to favor the economically least developed members (Bolivia and Ecuador). Other parties to the accord include Colombia, Peru, and Venezuela. Panama is an associate member. Chile withdrew from the group in 1976, owing to a dispute over foreign investment rules; it wanted more liberal trade rules than were then operative under the Foreign Investment Code known as Decision 24. Peru suspended its participation in August 1992. Still, the group has eliminated almost all internal tariffs. A free trade zone was launched effective January 1, 1992, and a common external tariff was announced in May 1994.

K

Kennedy Round. The name, in honor of U.S. President Kennedy, given the multilateral trade (q.v.) negotiations sponsored by the General Agreement on Tariffs and Trade (GATT) (q.v.) and held in Geneva,

Switzerland, between 1964 and 1967. The talks are credited with having reduced the average level of world tariffs by one-third. They were especially effective in terms of trade reductions between the United States and Western Europe.

Koh, Tommie Thong Bee (1937–   ). A law professor, former dean of the faculty of law at Singapore University (1971–1974), Singapore's permanent representative to the UN (1968–1974 and 1974–1984) and Singapore's ambassador to the United States (1984–1990), Koh is currently ambassador-at-large at the Ministry of Foreign Affairs in Singapore and executive director of the Asia-Europe Foundation. His most notable service at the UN was probably as president (1981–1982) of the Third UN Law of the Sea Conference (q.v.). He also chaired the Singapore Delegation. He is often credited with saving the conference; by his skillful diplomatic maneuvers, he was able to get a final document that most of the world accepted, except the United States. After additional legal maneuverings and changes of administration in the United States, even it came to accept the bulk of the agreement hammered out by Koh.

Kuwait Fund for Arab Economic Development (KFAED). The Kuwait Fund is the oldest of the Arab aid agencies. It was set up in 1961 when Kuwait gained its independence. It has served as a model for subsequent Arab aid agencies. Part of the motivation behind the fund, which has its headquarters in Safat, Kuwait, was for Kuwait to be recognized as a responsible member of the international community. At the outset, all of the fund's money went to Arab states. In 1974, however, the resource base was extended, and loans were made available to other developing countries (q.v.) in Africa, Asia, and Latin America.

L

Latin American Free Trade Association (LAFTA). LAFTA was established in 1960 (by the treaty of Montevideo) to increase trade and foster economic development (q.v.) in Latin America. After initial success in trade negotiations that resulted in a rapid increase in trade (q.v.) among the members, the association hit a number of snags, including those emanating from the members' different levels of economic development, disagreements between large and small members and between rich and poor, and the failure of members to implement the policies they themselves had helped shape. In 1988, LAFTA was replaced by the Latin American Integration Association (q.v.).

Latin American Integration Association (LAIA, Associación Latino-americana de Integración, ALADI). Established in 1980, this organization, based in Montevideo, Uruguay, has as its major goal promoting economic development (q.v.) through the creation of a Latin American common market. It was seen as the successor to the Latin American Free Trade Association (LAFTA) (q.v.), in that its discussions have also focused on infrastructure services, tourism (q.v.), and intraregional trade (q.v.) expansion. Members agreed to a common regional tariff to enter into effect by 1984. There are 11 member countries (Argentina, Bolivia, Brazil, Chile, Colombia, Ecuador, Mexico, Paraguay, Peru, Uruguay, and Venezuela), 15 observer countries, and 5 observer organizations.

Law, diplomacy, and courts. Adjudicatory bodies are among the oldest intergovernmental organizations. The Permanent Court of Arbitration (q.v.), for example, traces its origins to the early years of the 20th century. While the Permanent Court of Arbitration continues to function, the use of arbitral boards has somewhat decreased over the space of this century.

The Permanent Court of International Justice (PCIJ) (q.v.), which was established alongside the League of Nations (q.v.), was deemed so successful that its UN (q.v.) successor, the International Court of Justice (ICJ) (q.v.), is almost structurally identical. The only major difference is that the World Court (q.v.), as most recently established courts, was explicitly connected with an intergovernmental organization, the United Nations in this case. Until the recent surge in International Court of Justice use, most deemed the PCIJ more successful than its successor.

In the post–World War II era, regional courts have proliferated. Most of these have operated within sectoral parameters as well, such as the European Court of Human Rights (q.v.). See also Administrative Tribunal; Advisory Opinions; Cassese, Antonio; common heritage of mankind; Connally Reservation; Corfu Channel case; Court of First Instance; domestic jurisdiction; European Court of Justice; European Patent Organization; Exclusive Economic Zone; Genocide Convention; good offices; Institute of International Law; International Centre for Settlement of Investment Disputes; International Criminal Police Organization; International Law Commission; International Organization for Standardization; International Seabed Authority; Law of the Sea Conferences; mediation; pacific settlement of disputes; preventive diplomacy; quiet diplomacy; United Nations Commission on International Trade Law; United Nations Conference on the Law of the Sea; World Intellectual Property Organization.

Law of the Sea Conferences (1958, 1960, and 1973–1982). The 1958 conference produced four conventions, on (1) the continental shelf, (2) the territorial sea and the contiguous zone, (3) the high seas, and (4) fishing and conservation of the living resources of the high seas. All of these gained sufficient ratifications to enter into force by 1966. The Second Law of the Sea Conference focused on the breadth of the territorial sea; it failed by one vote. The Third Law of the Sea Conference was convened in 1973 to develop a comprehensive treaty, taking into account technological and political changes since the first treaty had been adopted. Because of the scope and complexity of the issues and the clash of diverse national interests (developed vs. developing; coastal vs. landlocked; capitalist vs. state-interventionist, etc.), the negotiations dragged on for nine years. A comprehensive treaty of 320 articles was finally approved by a vote of 130–4–17.

Most prominent among the opposition was the United States, which objected most to provisions relating to deep-sea mining. While the Carter administration appeared ready to ratify the treaty, with reservations, a year-long review by the Reagan administration concluded that the treaty could not be supported. At the same time, the United States took the position that much of the treaty (i.e., the provisions that it supported) were already binding as a part of customary international law (i.e., even in the absence of treaty ratification). As a consequence, the treaty's provisions were widely adhered to, even though it acquired ratifications very slowly. Even most of the advanced, industrialized, capitalist states that had signed the treaty (or abstained on the final vote) chose not to ratify it. In late 1994, the Clinton administration negotiated a sort of compromise accord. This occurred literally as the treaty was coming into effect, having acquired the necessary ratifications. See also Koh, Tommie Thong Bee.

League of Arab States (often called the Arab League). Formed in 1945 as the first pan-Arab organization to involve all Arab countries, its goal was to strengthen unity, coordinate political activities, and promote social, cultural and economic cooperation among member states. Palestine is a member. Egypt was expelled in 1979 because of the Camp David accords but has since been readmitted. The primary governing body is the Majlis, composed of a representative from each member state. Its headquarters were in Cairo, Egypt, until it was expelled and then in Tunis, Tunisia, until January 1, 1991, when its relocation to Cairo was completed. The league meets twice a year. Binding decisions require unanimous agreement. Members have pledged to respect each other's forms of government and not to use force to resolve inter-Arab disputes. For much of its history, anti-Israeli policy was the only really unifying theme. Still, the league is credited with the establishment of the Arab Common Market, the Arab Development Bank, the Arab Press, and the Arab States Broadcasting Union. The league was not able to form a united front during the Gulf War and has disagreed on the softening of the Arab economic boycott of Israel, with members of the Gulf Cooperation Council (GCC) (q.v.) formally abandoning the secondary and tertiary boycotts in 1994.

League of Nations. Formed in 1920 on the basis of 26 articles included in the Treaty of Versailles, which concluded World War I. The principal architect of the League was U.S. President Wilson, but Senate opposition precluded U.S. membership. Its major organs were the assembly, a general conference of all members, the council, the security organ, and the secretariat, headed by a secretary-general with limited powers. The focus of the League was on military security questions. Its key mechanism was a collective security (q.v.) system that aimed at deterring war by threatening the would-be aggressor with the immediate and united response of all other member countries. While the League was successful in defusing some military conflicts in its first decade, its reputation was permanently destroyed by members' inability to take decisive action regarding the Japanese invasion of Manchuria in 1931 and the Italian invasion of Abyssinia (Ethiopia) in 1935. The League was handicapped by the lack of U.S. membership, a unanimity rule for most important decisions, and a lack of resolve by the major European powers. Its activities in the nonmilitary security realm—including with refugees—was much more successful, but insufficient to offset its image as a failed institution. See also Avenol, Joseph; Bruce Report; Drummond, Eric; mandates.

Least developed countries (LLDCs). In 1971 the UN General Assembly (q.v.) drew up a list of those developing countries (q.v.) without significant economic growth, with very low per capita incomes, and with low literacy rates. The list, which includes some three dozen countries, is updated periodically.

Lie, Trygve (1896–1968). First secretary-general (q.v.) of the UN (q.v.) (1946–1953). Before his term as UN secretary-general, Lie had held important posts in the Norwegian government, including that of acting foreign minister. He also headed the Norwegian delegation to the San Francisco conference where the UN Charter was written. Lie had the misfortune of being secretary-general during some of the most intense years of the Cold War. Accordingly, it was his challenge to try to carve out an independent role for the secretary-general, while antagonizing neither the United States nor the Soviet Union.

Lie was not always successful in meeting this challenge. For example, his proposed Twenty-Year Program for Peace was found wanting by both superpowers. More often, however, he alternated in which one of the superpowers he antagonized. In 1946, he reluctantly yielded to U.S. pressure to place on the Security Council's (q.v.) agenda the Soviet Union's failure to promptly withdraw its military forces from northern Iran. Later, however, he refused to support the United States in its contention that the issue should remain on the Security Council agenda until all Soviet troops had been withdrawn. In 1950, he alienated the United States by advocating the seating of the communist Chinese delegates, and then he alienated the Soviets by his support of UN-authorized military action in Korea. For the latter action, the Soviets ostracized him and announced their opposition to his reelection as secretary-general. In 1953, many members of the UN criticized Lie for allowing the (McCarthy-era) United States to use the UN headquarters for carrying out loyalty investigations of U.S. nationals employed in the UN Secretariat (q.v.) and for his dismissal of these employees. This was broadly interpreted as a violation of secretariat independence.

The Soviet veto of Lie's reelection bid was sidestepped by a U.S.-sponsored General Assembly resolution calling for an extension of his term for three years. This extralegal action (nothing in the UN Charter provides for it) turned out to be of little value, as the Soviets refused to deal with Lie in his extended term. Accordingly, he resigned in November 1952, long before he had to under the provisions of the resolution. While the Cold War atmosphere severely constrained what Lie could do as secretary-general, his actions set important precedents for his successors. Among the most notable was his initiative in presenting oral and written statements to the Security Council, whenever he deemed that appropriate.

Liner code (also known as the Convention on a Code of Conduct for Liner Conferences and as the UNCTAD Liner Code Convention). Signed in Geneva, in April 1974 and effective in October 1984, the liner code includes constraints on freight rates and limits on the open registry of ships. It also includes a scheme to allocate more equitably the shipping controlled by the world's shipowner organizations. The code's cargo-sharing ratio reserves 40 percent of the shipping involved in any bilateral trade for the importing country, 40 percent for the exporting country, and 20 percent for third parties to the trading. Countries, such as the United States, that voted against the convention were primarily concerned about these cargo-sharing provisions.

Lomé Convention. An international agreement, initially signed in Lomé, Togo, in February 1975, that established special trading relations between the European Economic Community (EEC) (q.v.) and the so-called African, Caribbean, and Pacific (ACP) (q.v.) countries. The accord replaced the expired Yaoundé Conventions (q.v.) and included Great Britain, then a relatively new member of the EEC. The five-year convention, subsequently renewed and revised, contains a General System of Preferences (q.v.) and an export stabilization scheme called STABEX (q.v.) that supports the prices of a selected list of ACP raw materials exports. There is also a special facility for mining products, SYSMIN, which provides assistance to help overcome adverse consequences of a failure to produce or export copper (and associated cobalt), phosphates, manganese, bauxite (and alumina), tin, or iron ore. The most recent convention, Lomé IV, was negotiated in 1990 for 10 years, with a commitment to a midterm review in 1995. During that review, it became clear that the Lomé process, as it has existed for a generation, is likely to end in 2000. The ACP countries are increasingly diverse in terms of their needs; development assistance is increasingly unpopular in Europe as is the kind of interference with the market that is central to the conventions.

Luns, Joseph M. A. H. (1911–). Luns began his professional career in 1938 as a Dutch foreign service officer, serving his last three years at the United Nations (q.v.). He left the foreign service in 1952 to become minister of foreign affairs, a post he held, with one brief intermission until 1971, when he became secretary-general of the North Atlantic Treaty Organization (NATO) (q.v.). He remained NATO's chief civilian official until 1984, longer than any other holder of that office. Throughout his long term in office, he remained frustrated that the alliance failed to fulfill the military commitments called for in the so-called Harmal Report (q.v.) of 1967, known for the Belgian foreign minister who headed the forward-looking committee. On the other hand, his term of office coincided with the signing of a large number of arms control accords and the successful resolution of a number of serious challenges to the organization. Not the least of these was the debate over the Atlantic Alliance's deployment of intermediate range nuclear forces in Western Europe. He was succeeded by Lord Carrington.

Lusaka Agreement on Cooperative Enforcement Operations Directed in Wild Fauna and Flora. The Lusaka Agreement, which was concluded under the auspices of the United Nations Environment Program (UNEP) (q.v.), entered into force on December 10, 1996, after having obtained the necessary four ratifications and accessions of Lesotho, Tanzania, Uganda, and Zambia. Kenya and the Congo are in the final processes of ratification. The agreement is the first that seeks to reduce and ultimately eliminate illegal international trafficking in African wildlife. It provides for a task force to investigate violations of national laws pertaining to illegal trade in all wildlife and the dissemination of information on activities relating to them. Each party to the agreement also designates or establishes a national bureau responsible for liaison with the task force, and at least one officer from each national bureau is to be seconded to the task force headquarters. See also Convention on International Trade in Endangered Species of Wild Fauna and Flora (CITES).

Luxembourg Agreement (also known as the Luxembourg Compromise or Luxembourg Declaration). An accord of the European Community (EC) (q.v.), announced by its Council of Ministers (q.v.) on January 29, 1966, whereby France agreed to end its six-month-old boycott of the European Commission (q.v.) and the Council of Ministers. The French boycott had come about because of French unwillingness to accept the implementation of the majority vote provisions in the European Community's Treaty of Rome, particularly those relating to the financing of the EC budget. In line with the agreement, members retained the right to veto council decisions on issues of vital importance. While the agreement allowed the European Community to resume its work, it was seen as a major setback on the road to supranational decision making.

M

Maastricht, Treaty of. Drafted in December 1991 by the European Council (q.v.), the Treaty of Maastricht consists of a number of proposals aimed as reinvigorating the European Community's (q.v.) quest for economic and political integration, with special emphasis on the opening of internal borders and a firm commitment to the European Monetary Union (q.v.) by the end of the century. The treaty met with resistance in certain member countries; indeed, in Denmark it was initially rejected by a referendum and was only accepted after a number of key provisions had been changed. See also Delors, Jacques; European Monetary Union.

MacBride Commission (officially the International Commission for the Study of Communication Problems). This report of a commission, sponsored by the United Nations Educational, Scientific and Cultural Organization (UNESCO) (q.v.) and known for its Irish Nobel Prize–winning chair, Sean MacBride, contained 82 recommendations. Some of the recommendations—such as the abolition of press censorship; the rights of individuals to seek, receive, and impart information; the formation of an international center for the study and planning of information; and the call for news about the third world to include more than natural and human disasters—antagonized representatives from both the West and the third world when the report was presented to the UNESCO conference in October 1980. See also New World Information Order.

Mandates. The mandate system of the League of Nations (q.v.), under the leadership of the Permanent Mandates Commission, was devised to improve the lives of those living in colonial possessions. The mandate system placed the colonies of the defeated powers in World War I (chiefly Germany and Turkey) under the guardianship and tutelage of the victors, with oversight by the League Commission. Mandates were classified as follows: Class A mandates (Arab territories formerly under Ottoman rule) were regarded as ready for independence and self-government after a minimum period of time. Class B mandates (East and West African colonies of Germany) were given no promises of early independence. Class C mandates (German South-West Africa and the Pacific Islands) were to be governed as "international portions of the territory" with no promise of ultimate self-rule or independence. Critics portrayed the mandate system as simply a continuation of colonialism under a different name.

Mano River Union. Established in October 3, 1973, as a customs union between Liberia and Sierra Leone, it was an organization that all countries in the West African subregion were invited to join. To date, only Guinea has joined the original two. A common external tariff has been set up, and trade (q.v.) liberalization has begun. The union's headquarters are in Freetown, Liberia.

Mayor, Federico (1934–). Elected director-general of the United Nations Educational, Scientific and Cultural Organization (UNESCO) (q.v.) in November 1987. Before that, Mayor had served in the Spanish government, as a biologist and university official, and as deputy director-general of UNESCO (1978–1981). He is generally credited with restoring administrative and intellectual integrity to the organization. Mayor still found it very difficult to achieve one of his expressed goals, getting the United States to rejoin the organization.

McNamara, Robert S. (1916–). Prior to becoming president of the World Bank (q.v.), McNamara served as president of Ford Motor Company and U.S. secretary of defense. As president of the World Bank from 1968 to 1981, he is often credited with turning it into the world's largest development agency and moving it away from its traditional focus on "bricks and mortar" projects. He expanded its activities in Africa, in the sectors of population planning and rural agriculture. He often spoke of the necessity for the bank to address the needs of the poorest of the poor. Critics of McNamara spoke in terms of his tendency to emphasize large projects and to constantly seek to spend all of the funds at the World Bank's disposal, often without assessing whether such a massive infusion of money was needed or even desirable.

Médecins du Monde (MDM) (Doctors of the World). Created in Paris in 1980, MDM provides assistance to disaster victims throughout the world. It provides assistance in cases of both natural and industrial disasters. Some 60 percent of its funding is private in origin.

Médecins sans Frontières (Doctors without Borders). Founded as a French volunteer organization in 1968, Doctors without Borders is composed of nurses and doctors who are willing to help the sick and hungry, wherever they are, whether their condition is a consequence of war, famine, or the form of political regime under which they live. This international nongovernmental organization has been steadfast in its commitment not to interfere in governmental affairs. This approach is probably not surprising given that one of the impetuses for its founding was a concern that victims of war, famine, and dictatorship cannot rely on or wait for governments to come to their aid. Unlike the Red Cross (q.v.), Doctors without Borders does not wait for government permission before getting involved in an emergency situation. It has missions in more than 60 countries and territories.

Mediation. This is a dispute settlement practice under which the services of a third party are used as a means of reducing differences or bringing about a solution. The Hague Peace Conferences (q.v.) of 1899 and 1907 provided certain procedures for mediation; the League of Nations (q.v.) required that member states submit disputes to the procedures of peaceful settlement.

Mercado Común del Cono Sur (MERCOSUR) (Southern Cone Common Market). Established in 1991 with headquarters in Montevideo, Uruguay, MERCOSUR set its goal as having a regional common market in operation by January 1, 1995. The biggest stumbling block for the founding member states—Argentina, Brazil, Paraguay, and Uruguay—proved to be working out a common external tariff. Members agreed, however, to follow Brazil's suggestion that it negotiate an affiliation agreement with the North American Free Trade

Association (NAFTA), seen by some as a way station to a Free Trade Area of the Americas, to which all are pledged, at least in principle. Members are still considering whether they should eventually combine with the Junta del Acuerdo de Cartagena (q.v.). In the interim, Chile and Bolivia signed free trade accords with MERCOSUR, underscoring how successful the organization has been in increasing trade (q.v.) and investment among its members. MERCOSUR has, however, been much less successful in attracting nonmember foreign investment to the region. Most is going to one country, Brazil. Moreover, member states have thus far not been able to agree on the terms of a MERCOSUR development bank.

Military Staff Committee. Article 47 of the United Nations (UN) (q.v.) Charter provides for a Military Staff Committee composed of the chiefs of staff, or their representatives, of the permanent members of the UN Security Council (q.v.). The committee's purpose was to advise and assist the Security Council on all military matters relating to the council's duties to maintain international peace and security, and to assume strategic direction of any armed forces placed under the direction of the Security Council. With the onset of the Cold War, the major powers never agreed on making such armed forces available. Accordingly, the Military Staff Committee was rendered ineffectual. Proposals to provide a meaningful role have evolved in the post-Cold War era. To date, however, the United States has shown no real interest in such proposals.

MINEX. A commodity price stabilization scheme covering just minerals that was negotiated by the European Economic Community (q.v.) and the African, Caribbean, and Pacific (ACP) (q.v.) states as part of the third Lomé Convention (q.v.). It was signed in December 1984.

Ministates. For much of the history of the United Nations (UN) (q.v.), concern has been expressed about the "problem of ministates"—that is, giving such countries as Monaco, San Marino, and Liechtenstein full voting rights in the General Assembly (q.v.) and access to UN technical assistance funds, even though their contributions to the UN budget are quite minimal. In spite of such concerns, the UN—unlike the League of Nations (q.v.), which denied membership status to some such states—has continued to admit, as full members, states with less than 100,000 people. Suggestions for granting associate membership with limited privileges to ministates have never garnered significant global support, given that sovereign equality is one of the UN Charter's most fundamental principles.

Monnet, Jean (1888–1979). Monnet is sometimes called the father of modern-day Western Europe. After working briefly as a merchant in his native France, Monnet was appointed a deputy director-general of the League of Nations (q.v.). During World War II, he was a member of the Washington-based British Supply Council. In 1947, he drafted what came to be known as the Monnet Plan, which called for the modernization of French industry and agriculture. This led to France's participation in the Marshall Plan and, later, to Monnet's drafting of the Schuman Plan and the establishment of the European Coal and Steel Community (ECSC) (q.v.). Appropriately enough, he was the ECSC's first president. In the 1950s, Monnet organized the Action Committee for a United States of Europe, which supported the development of the European Common Market. He remained active in the movement for European unification for the rest of his life. See also Schuman, Robert.

Morse, Bradford (1921–1994). A member of the U.S. House of Representatives for 12 years before he was appointed United Nations (q.v.) undersecretary-general for Political and General Assembly Affairs (1972–1975) and as administrator of the United Nations Development Program (UNDP) (q.v.) (1976–1986). His years as UNDP administrator were marked by considerable expansion in the activities and prestige of that UN organ.

Most favored nation (MFN). By this principle, equal treatment is to be accorded to the signatories of any trade (q.v.) agreement. It is one of the requirements of all signatories of the General Agreement on Tariffs and Trade (GATT) (q.v.): "to grant each other treatment as favorable as they give to any country in the application and administration of import and export duties and charges."

Most seriously affected (MSA). A term that the United Nations (UN) (q.v.) began to use in the late 1970s to refer to those countries "most seriously affected" by the increased prices of oil in the mid-1970s. These countries, some of which later became major debtors, were also known by some as the "fourth world."

Multifibre Agreement (MFA). Although initially negotiated in 1973 under the auspices of the General Agreement on Tariffs and Trade (GATT) (q.v.), the arrangements regarding international trade (q.v.), and the protocol, the "multifibre agreement," have their own institutional framework. The purpose is to set out the rules and regulations for trade in textiles between the major importing and exporting countries. The objectives of the MFA are to progressively liberalize world trade in textile products, to promote the exports of economically less developed countries, and to encourage adjustment by the economically developed countries in their textile industries. At the same time that it seeks to ensure the orderly and equitable development of the textile market, MFA seeks to avoid market disruption. The structure of MFA includes a textiles committee and a textiles surveillance body, whose responsibilities include the settlement of disputes among participants.

Multilateral Investment Guarantee Agency (MIGA). MIGA, which is legally autonomous of the World Bank (q.v.), is open to all members of the bank. It came into being on April 12, 1988. Its purpose is to promote the flow of foreign investment to and among economically less developed countries. It meets this objective by guaranteeing eligible investments against losses due to currency transfers, expropriation, war or civil disturbances, and breach of contract by host states. It does not provide insurance against the risk of devaluation or currency depreciation.

N

New International Economic Order (NIEO). On May 1, 1974, a special session on development was convened as the Sixth Special Session of the United Nations General Assembly (q.v.) in the aftermath of the Organization of Petroleum Exporting Countries' (OPEC's) (q.v.) initial successes at increasing oil prices. At the session, the economically less developed country members of the General Assembly, in particular, proclaimed, in the Declaration on the Establishment of a New International Economic Order (NIEO), their determination "to work urgently for the establishment of a new international economic order based on equity, sovereignty, interdependence, common interest and co-operation among states, irrespective of their social systems." The stated goals were to correct inequalities, redress existing injustices, eliminate the widening gap between the developed and the economically less developed countries, and ensure steadily accelerating economic development (q.v.).

The Program of Action on the establishment of an NIEO dealt in great detail with the problems and objectives in the NIEO Declaration, but it did not impose legally binding obligations on states. It contains recommendations relating to raw materials, the international monetary system, industrialization, technology transfer, and sovereignty over natural resources. It aimed at a gradual shift in the terms of trade between economically developed and less developed countries and in the greater participation by developing countries (q.v.) in international financial markets and institutions. Subsequent efforts to bring about a new international economic order met with little success, not least of all because of OPEC's lessened threat to the West, divisions within the South, altered relations between the United States and the Soviet Union, and a resurgence of classical liberal economic ideology in the North, especially in the United States and the United Kingdom.

New World Information Order (NWIO) (also known as the New World Information and Communications Order, NWICO). The origins of the NWIO are often traced to the Political Declaration of the Nonaligned Countries' Fifth Summit Meeting (1976), which stated that "a new international order in the fields of information and communication is as vital as a new international economic order." Such an order would include the free and unbiased flow of international news; technology transfer of communications (q.v.) hardware; transborder flows of information and remote sensing, and the issues of state sovereignty connected with those; and the redistribution of the world's available radio frequencies. The NWIO met with stern opposition, not least of all from the U.S. press community, which saw it as a threat to the free flow of information. See also MacBride Commission.

Newly industrialized countries (NICs) (also known as the newly industrializing economies, NIEs). A term first used by the Organisation for Economic Co-operation and Development (OECD) (q.v.) to describe developing countries (q.v.) in the third world that enjoyed very rapid economic growth. While the list varies, it includes such countries as Brazil, Chile, Hong Kong, Malaysia, Singapore, South Korea, Taiwan, and Thailand.

Niger Basin Authority. Established in 1964 as the Niger Basin Commission, the institution's aim remains the same: to promote cooperation among the member states and to ensure the integrated development of the Niger Basin. Its priority projects include reforestation, energy, transportation (q.v.), and communications (q.v.). The authority also helps the states through which the River Niger flows control flooding. Its headquarters are in Niamey, Niger. The member states are Benin, Burkina Faso, Cameroon, Chad, Côte d'Ivoire, Guinea, Mali, Niger, and Nigeria.

Non-Aligned Movement (NAM). A movement whose origins can be traced to the Afro-Asian People's Security Conference (q.v.) held in

Bandung, Indonesia, in 1955. The less developed country members sought to offer a third global force, one that, during the Cold War, was tied to neither the United States nor the Soviet Union. The movement's members—now in excess of one hundred—allowed it to make significant inroads in the appointment process in the United Nations (UN) (q.v.), but its influence has always been limited as it lacks a headquarters and secretariat. Decisions are made at the conference of the heads of state.

Non-self governing. Chapter IX of the United Nations (q.v.) Charter is entitled "Declaration Regarding Non-Self Governing Territories" and provides, in effect, a charter of political, economic, social, and educational rights for all people who, in 1945, were still living under colonial rule. Although most of these territories were not part of the trusteeship system (q.v.), the colonial powers were required to furnish regular reports to the UN on their progressive development.

Nontariff barriers (NTBs). The term used to refer to practices other than the imposition of tariffs that tend to restrain free trade (q.v.). NTBs may be financial, such as internal taxes, countervailing duties or customs fees, or non-financial, such as domestic regulations concerning sanitation or labeling of a product, quotas, or requiring excessive documentation. As tariff barriers to trade have decreased, the focus of attention at the General Agreement on Tariffs and Trade (GATT) (q.v.) and the World Trade Organization (WTO) (q.v.) has shifted to NTBs.

Nordic Council. A regional organization based in Stockholm, Sweden, that, since 1952, has been promoting economic, social and cultural cooperation among the 5 Scandinavian member states, Denmark, Finland, Iceland, Norway and Sweden. The council per se meets in session once a year. But there is also a council of ministers, which has decision-making authority on all Nordic affairs. There are also standing committees dealing with specific issues and two secretariats. In 1976, the council established the Nordic Investment Bank. Recent council concerns have focused on unemployment, social services, and relations with the expanding European Union (EU) (q.v.).

North Atlantic Cooperation Council (NACC). Established in 1991 to serve as the first institutional link, at the ministerial level, between the North Atlantic Treaty Organization (NATO) (q.v.) and Central, Eastern European, and Baltic countries. It served as a body both to facilitate cooperation among the member states and to oversee the development of future cooperation. Russian opposition to NATO

membership by the former members of the Warsaw Treaty Organization (WTO) (q.v.) extended the life of the NACC long beyond what
at least its Eastern and Central European members wished. In May
1997, it was succeeded by the Euro-Atlantic Partnership Council
(q.v.).

North Atlantic Treaty Organization (NATO). A collective defense
organization, initially aimed at keeping the Soviets out of Western
Europe, restraining the Germans from rebuilding their military infrastructure, and keeping the United States firmly committed to the defense of Western Europe. The current members are Belgium, Canada,
Denmark, France, Germany, Greece, Iceland, Italy, Luxembourg, the
Netherlands, Norway, Portugal, Spain, Turkey, the United Kingdom,
and the United States. The North Atlantic Council (NAC), the only
organ whose authority is explicitly derived from the North Atlantic
Treaty, has effective political authority and powers of decision. It consists of permanent representatives of all member countries meeting
together at least once a week. The council also meets at higher levels
involving foreign, defense or treasury ministers or heads of government, but it has the same authority and powers of decision making,
and its decisions have the same status and validity, at whatever level
it meets. The council has an important public profile and issues declarations and communiqués explaining its policies and decisions. The
council itself was given responsibility under the treaty for setting up
subsidiary bodies. Committees and planning groups have since been
created to support the work of the council or to assume responsibility
in specific fields such as defense planning, nuclear planning and military matters.

NATO is credited by many as helping deter the Soviets from
marching into Western Europe. Others contend that the Soviets never
had any intention of doing so. With the end of the Cold War,
many—at least until the Bosnian crisis heated up—wondered whether
NATO should be abolished, a view not widely shared in Washington.
Indeed, Washington tried to breathe new life into NATO by establishing the Partnership for Peace (PfP), which allows for military cooperation with non-NATO members. This was a way to cope with the
demands of Central and Eastern European countries wishing to join
NATO, but significantly Switzerland has also used this arrangement
as a way to edge away from its long nonaligned tradition. NATO
agreed to start talks in 1997 about letting some Eastern and Central
European countries join, in spite of massive Russian opposition. After
working out an agreement with Russian President Yeltsin, NATO issued invitations in July 1997 to the Czech Republic, Hungary, and
Poland to begin the lengthy and costly process of joining. They are

expected to be members in time for the organization's 50th anniversary in 1999. NATO also made clear that it was keeping the door open to others wishing to join, most notably Romania and Slovenia, which had strong support for their applications in 1997 but whose membership lacked the essential support of the United States. Moreover, in July 1997 Ukraine and NATO signed the Charter on a Distinctive Partnership aimed at contributing to a zone of stability and security throughout Europe.

At present NATO is regarded by many as an organization to put out fires and help stabilize Eastern European states. Significantly, in June 1996, France announced that it would rejoin the military structures it pulled out of in 1966, provided the alliance would give European members a stronger role in the organization's leadership. Later in the same year, Spain made a similar declaration, after agreeing to participate fully in the organization for the first time 14 years after it had joined. Simultaneously, NATO agreed to the creation of "combined joint task-forces," as a new means of projecting power beyond the alliance's territory. See also EUROGROUP; European Atomic Energy Community; Harmal Report; Ismay, Hastings Lionel Ismay; Luns, Joseph M. A. H.; Solana, Javier; Spaak, Paul-Henri; Wörner, Manfred.

North-South dialogue. A term used to refer to economic discussions—including, but not limited to, the Conference on International Economic Cooperation (q.v.)—between the North (relatively rich, economically advanced industrialized countries generally located in the Northern Hemisphere) and the South (relatively poor, developing countries [q.v.] located mainly in the Southern Hemisphere).

Nuclear energy. Few intergovernmental organizations have been centrally involved with energy sources. The major exceptions are the European Coal and Steel Community (q.v.) and regional and global organizations relating to the use of nuclear fuel. Such organizations have chiefly two purposes: encouragement of use of nuclear fuel as an alternative to fossil fuels, as they were once believed to be safe, clean, and inexpensive; and oversight of nuclear facilities to ensure that nuclear materials are not diverted to military purposes.

The chief United Nations (UN) (q.v.) body—the International Atomic Energy Agency (IAEA)—charged with nuclear issues, focuses on both of these purposes. That dual mandate is seen by some as dooming the agency to failure in both of them. See also Blix, Hans; CERN; Nuclear Suppliers Group.

Nuclear Suppliers Group (commonly known as the London Nuclear Club or the London Club). The group's origins can be traced to a meeting in London, in November 1975. Its purpose is as simple as it is important: to ensure that cooperation in the peaceful use of nuclear energy does not contribute to the proliferation of nuclear weapons. Members agree to adhere to the International Atomic Energy Agency's (IAEA) (q.v.) safeguards procedures against proliferation but also to additional control accords on the export of nuclear-related dual use goods and technology. Russia and the United States are among its members, as are France and the United Kingdom.

O

Office of the United Nations Disaster Relief Coordinator (UNDRO). UNDRO, which has its headquarters in Geneva, Switzerland, began operations in 1972. Its responsibilities include relief coordination—mobilizing, guiding, and coordinating aid—and prevention and preparedness in disaster-prone areas (see disaster relief). Its funding is all voluntary. Other challenges facing UNDRO include the lack of willingness of some countries to publicize disasters, fearing the negative consequences for foreign investment and tourism (q.v.).

Office of the United Nations High Commissioner for Refugees (UNHCR). Originally set up in 1951 for a three-year period, the Office of the High Commissioner for Refugees has had its mandate renewed for five-year periods since 1954. Based in Geneva, Switzerland, the UNHCR, which was established by the United Nations (UN) (q.v.) General Assembly (q.v.), has over 70 field offices responsible for providing assistance to more than 18 million refugees. The UNHCR's program is carried out under directives issued by the General Assembly and Economic and Social Council (ECOSOC) (q.v.). It sees itself as the catalyst, coordinator, and initiator of refugee programs, which are often supported by individual governments. Although periodically criticized for being overly bureaucratic or insufficiently funded to meet its task, the UNHCR is generally viewed as one of the UN's success stories. It was awarded the Nobel Peace Prize in 1954 and 1981. See also Ogata, Sadako.

Official development assistance (ODA). Formally defined by the Organisation for Economic Co-operation and Development's (OECD) (q.v.) Development Assistance Committee (q.v.) as "those flows to developing countries (q.v.) and multilateral institutions provided by official agencies, including state and local governments, or by their executive agencies, each transaction of which meets the following tests: (a) it is administered with the promotion of the economic development (q.v.) and welfare of developing countries as its main objective and (b) it is concessional in character and contains a grant element of at least 25 percent." ODA is often distinguished from private assistance (e.g., that donated by religious organizations). An often-stated goal of the third world is that each economically developed country should provide ODA in the amount of 0.7 percent of its gross national product.

Ogata, Sadako (1927–   ). Appointed as UN High Commissioner for Refugees (UNHCR) (q.v.) in 1991. Before that, she had served as dean of the Faculty of Foreign Service at Sophia University and in various UN capacities, including as the minister on Japan's mission to the UN in 1978–1979 and chair of the United Nations Children Fund's (UNICEF) (q.v.) executive board. In her appointment as head of UNHCR, she was the first woman to direct a major UN agency.

Oil Companies International Marine Forum (OCIMF). A London-based international nongovernmental organization composed of oil companies having an interest in the transport of oil by sea. Since its founding in 1970, the forum has coordinated policies that, in turn, influence the direction of policy at the International Maritime Organization (q.v.).

Organisation for Economic Co-operation and Development (OECD). In 1961 the OECD replaced the Organisation for European Economic Co-operation (OEEC), which had been set up in 1948 to elicit common action among Marshall Plan recipient countries to aid their recovery from World War II. The OECD is composed of advanced industrialized, capitalist states and has earned the reputation of being the "rich man's club." In 1995, the Czech Republic became the first formerly centrally planned economy to join the organization; Poland followed in 1996. It may also soon have members from among Asia's newly industrialized countries (NICs) (q.v.).

The OECD's members are expected to promote the expansion of world trade (q.v.) on a nondiscriminatory, multilateral basis and to facilitate the processes of economic advance of developing countries (q.v.). It achieves these goals through Working Party 3 (WP-3) in which members discuss and, at times, coordinate fiscal policy and through the Development Assistance Committee (DAC) (q.v.), which serves as a channel through which the major donor countries attempt to coordinate their policies for economic assistance. The OECD's research and publications, relating to the economic and financial status of member countries, are widely circulated and relied upon. Recent studies have focused on structural unemployment and what sort of assistance will be most beneficial to Russia. See also official development assistance.

Organismo para la Proscripción de las Armas Nucleares en la América Latina y el Caribe (OPANAL) (Agency for the Prohibition of Nuclear Weapons in Latin America and the Caribbean). The agency was established by the Treaty of Tlatelolco (Mexico) (q.v.), which was signed by the governments of Bolivia, Brazil, Chile, Ecuador, and Mexico, on February 14, 1967, and can be seen as an outgrowth of the Cuban missile crisis. The treaty entered into force after 11 states had ratified it. The agency's first General Conference was convened on September 2, 1969. The purpose of the agency is to implement the treaty, with a view toward making Latin America a nuclear-free zone. Accordingly, the treaty prohibits all testing, manufacturing, acquisition, installation, and development of new weapons. The agency has been largely successful in acquiring signatories to the treaty as well as to the protocols, which call upon powers from outside Latin America and the Caribbean to renounce nuclear weapon use in the region. The major stumbling block has been Cuba, which traditionally took the position that it would not sign or ratify the treaty until the United States had relinquished Guantánamo Naval Base. More recently, the Castro regime has apparently altered its position and says that it will ratify the accord as soon as the rest of Latin America does. To date 28 Latin American states have ratified the treaty. While Belize, St. Christopher-Nevis and St. Lucia are on the verge of ratification, Guyana has thus far refused even to sign the treaty.

Organization of African Unity (OAU). Formed in 1963, in Addis Ababa, Ethiopia, the OAU seeks to foster African political solidarity, accelerate economic development (q.v.), and provide security for member states. There are currently 53 members—now that South Africa has been admitted—each of which is committed, under the OAU's charter, to noninterference in the internal affairs of member states, peaceful settlement of disputes, and nonalignment with any blocs. The OAU's security provisions have rarely been implemented, but members have agreed to the establishment of a new mechanism for conflict prevention, management, and resolution. Thus far, however, it is so underfunded that it cannot possibly provide the sort of peacekeeping (q.v.) troops its strongest advocates call for. Its social and economic programs have suffered from lack of sufficient funds as well as linguistic and regional differences. Among the OAU's achievements, however, is the establishment of the African Development Bank (ADB) (q.v.). In the United Nations (q.v.), the OAU functions as an effective caucusing group. Members continue to call for an African Common Market by the year 2000 and a complete African Economic Community by the year 2025.

Organization of American States (OAS). Established by the Ninth International Conference of American States in Bogotá, Colombia, in 1948, the OAS has its headquarters in Washington, D.C. The OAS grew out of the earlier Pan American Union (q.v.). It seeks to determine common political, economic, defense (q.v.), and social policies and provide for coordination of various inter-American agencies. The OAS charter reaffirms the principles that "an act of aggression against one American state is an act of aggression against all the other American states" and solemnly proclaims the fundamental rights of individuals regardless of race, nationality, creed, or sex. It is also active in regard to economic development (q.v.) and health (q.v.), through the Pan American Health Organization (PAHO) (q.v.).

The structure of the OAS includes the General Assembly, Meeting of the Consultation of Ministers of Foreign Affairs, Inter-American Juridical Committee, Inter-American Commission on Human Rights, the Inter-American Court of Human Rights (q.v.), and General Secretariat. It has 33 Caribbean, Central, and South American states as well as Canada and the United States as members. Cuba was suspended as a member in 1962.

As the regional superpower, the United States has traditionally played a dominant role in the organization. Still, it was not able to get the OAS to send troops into Haiti; it had to turn to the UN for that. Moreover, its policy regarding the Sandinista government in Nicaragua and support of the Contras was strongly rejected by many Latin American states. They also refused to accept strong measures against Cuba.

Organization of Arab Petroleum Exporting Countries (OAPEC). OAPEC was formed in 1968 to safeguard the interests of member countries—Algeria, Bahrain, Egypt, Iraq, Kuwait, Libya, Qatar, Saudi Arabia, Syria, and the United Arab Emirates—and to determine ways and means to implement mutual cooperation in the Arab oil industry. OAPEC, whose headquarters are in Kuwait City, was instrumental in the success of the 1973–1974 oil embargo of the Organization of Petroleum Exporting Countries (OPEC) (q.v.), but its solidarity fell asunder during the Gulf War.

Organization of Central American States (Organización de Estados Centro-americanos) (ODECA). ODECA was founded in 1951, establishing its headquarters in San Salvador, El Salvador. Costa Rica, El Salvador, Guatemala, Honduras, and Nicaragua comprise its membership. Its current charter dates to December 1962. ODECA's major organs include the meetings of heads of state, conference of ministers of foreign affairs, Executive Council, Legislative Council, Central American Court of Justice, Central American Economic Council, Cultural and Educational Council, and Central American Defense Council. Decisions on substantive matters require unanimity; this is also required in determining whether an issue is substantive or procedural.

The members of ODECA are committed to fostering political, economic, and social cooperation in Central America with their long-term goal as the integration of Central America. The organization has already had some success in fostering regional unity. For example, it has encouraged the establishment of the Central American Bank for Economic Integration (CABEI) (q.v.), Central American University Superior Council of Central America (CSUCA), and the Permanent Secretariat of the General Treaty on Central American Integration (SIECA). But it has been frustrated in its more ambitious political goals.

Organization of Eastern Caribbean States (OECS). The OECS was established in 1981 and has its headquarters in Castries, St. Lucia. Its core is the seven former members of the West Indies Associated States that grouped then British colonies in the eastern Caribbean. Its membership is presently composed of the now-independent states of the region. The organization's central decision-making body is the biannual Authority of Heads of Government meetings. Substantive work is carried out by four committees: Foreign Affairs, Defense and Security, Economic Affairs, and Legal Affairs.

The OECS seeks to increase cooperation among members in their foreign relations; to harmonize their economic, trade (q.v.), and financial policies; and to coordinate defense (q.v.) and security arrangements. The underlying goal is greater subregional integration, and the specific goal is a single economic market. While the organization's noteworthy achievements include the establishment of the Eastern Caribbean Central Bank (in 1983) and discussions about possible political unification, its greatest publicity came at the time of the U.S. intervention in Grenada in 1983. The OECS issued a controversial invitation to the United States to assist it in restoring order to that island member state. The timing and source of the invitation and whether it really accorded with the powers of the organization remain in dispute. To preclude such controversies in the future, the OECS subsequently established a regional security system with the United

States that calls on the United States to help it maintain regional stability.

Organization of Petroleum Exporting Countries (OPEC). OPEC was founded in 1960, but the idea was first broached in 1949. Its headquarters are in Vienna, Austria. OPEC's principal governing body is the conference of all members, which meets once a year. OPEC's ostensible purpose is to ensure the stability of oil production and prices in international markets. But the real purpose is understood by most as attempting to bolster the price of petroleum through a rarely successful policy of limiting members' production. Its major success came with the oil embargoes of 1973–1974 and 1979, which generated sharp rises in prices and oil crises. However, on the whole and after the earlier price rises, oil prices have stabilized and sometimes stagnated. OPEC established the OPEC Fund for International Development in 1976, 16 years after OPEC itself began, but only shortly after it was widely recognized that countries in the South were the major sufferers from the rise of oil prices in the early and mid-1970s.

OPEC has 11 members: Algeria, Gabon, Indonesia, Iraq, Kuwait, Libya, Nigeria, Qatar, Saudi Arabia, the United Arab Emirates, and Venezuela. The success of OPEC has been limited, in part, because some major oil producers, including Russia, the United Kingdom, and the United States, and some major oil exporters, notably Mexico and Norway, have not joined the organization. Others, including Ecuador, dropped out. Some OPEC members have formed the smaller, yet less effective, Organization of Arab Petroleum Exporting Countries (OAPEC) (q.v.). In addition, OPEC has been plagued by rivalries among members, sometimes related to oil revenue, sometimes not. The most obvious of these include those between Iraq and Iran and between Iraq and Kuwait.

Organization of the Islamic Conference (OIC). The OIC was founded in September 1969, with headquarters in Jeddah, Saudi Arabia. Its main aims are to consolidate cooperation among Muslim countries in economic, social, cultural, scientific, and other vital areas of activity; to facilitate consultation among member states in international organizations; to work toward elimination of racial segregation and discrimination; to take measures to support international peace and security; to coordinate efforts for safeguarding holy places; and to support the struggle of the Palestinians. The OIC unsuccessfully sought to mediate the Iran-Iraq war; it was split by the Gulf War. Key unifying themes have included opposition to the state of Israel and its position on the conflict in Bosnia.

Organization on Security and Cooperation in Europe (OSCE) (formerly the Conference on Security and Cooperation in Europe, CSCE). Originally, when known as the Conference on Security and Cooperation in Europe, a series of international conferences on all-European cooperation on security, economics, science and technology, environmental issues, and human rights (q.v.) attended by the United States and Canada and all European countries except Albania. This predecessor organization, the CSCE, was first convened in Helsinki, Finland, in July 1973 and resulted in the Helsinki Accord (q.v.) of August 1, 1975. Formal summit meetings were accompanied by a host of specialized sessions of experts on such topics as arms control, disarmament (q.v.), and confidence-building measures. In 1990, the CSCE agreed to set up a permanent headquarters in Vienna, Austria. More significant, perhaps, were a series of decisions in 1992 to set up an armed peacekeeping (q.v.) force and to further institutionalize the organization. In the latter regard, two organs of the secretariat are particularly noteworthy: the Office of the High Commissioner for National Minorities, located in The Hague, Netherlands, which performs an "early warning" task by identifying problems relating to minorities that might have significant security implications; and the Office of Democratic Institutions and Human Rights (ODIHR), which recently replaced the Office of Free Elections. It is located in Warsaw, Poland. As the change in name suggests, the tasks of that office increased significantly. The Parliamentary Assembly, which meets in Copenhagen, Denmark, held its first session in July 1992. Effective December 1994, the name of the overall organization changed also. This was seen as part of an expansion of tasks reflecting the changing role of the organization and the strengthened secretariat.

The tasks of the OSCE are (1) to serve as a community of values, giving priority to democracy, human rights, the rule of law, and fundamental freedoms; (2) to serve as a permanent forum for dialogue on European security matters; (3) to serve as a forum for arms control and disarmament, and (4) to intervene in regions of conflict. While not always successful, the OSCE has been quite active in offering its good offices (q.v.) and as a mediator in conflict situations in Europe. In accordance with the Dayton Peace Agreement, the OSCE was charged with preparing Bosnia and Herzegovina for elections. It also deployed an assistance group to Chechnya, Russia, in 1995 and is credited with giving the world much of its information about the military crisis there.

OXFAM. Founded in 1942 with headquarters in Oxford, England, and originally called Oxford Committee for Famine Relief, OXFAM's goal is to relieve poverty, distress, and suffering in any part of the world. It also sees as one of its responsibilities to educate the public about the causes of poverty. Its general mode of operation involves providing grants to local agencies and groups in less developed countries. It currently has local committees and field offices in over 70 countries.

P

P-5 (also known as the Perm-5). Term(s) used to refer to the five, veto-wielding members of the UN Security Council (q.v.): China, France, Russia (formerly the Soviet Union), the United Kingdom, and the United States.

Pacific Basin Economic Council (PBEC). Established in 1967 by business leaders from Australia, Canada, Japan, New Zealand, and the United States, PBEC is now composed of some 850 fee-paying firms and business executives from Chile, Fiji, Hong Kong, Malaysia, Mexico, Peru, the Philippines, South Korea, and Taiwan as well as the founders. Annual conferences are held each May to examine regional economic and commercial conditions.

Pacific Economic Cooperation Council (PECC) (formerly the Pacific Economic Cooperation Conference). An international nongovernmental organization whose origins can be traced to the initiatives of Japanese prime minister Masayohsi Ohira and Australian prime minister Malcolm Fraser. Its current name became effective in January 1992. Its composition—academics, business leaders, and state officials from any country, region, or organization that has a commitment to economic cooperation in the Pacific Basin—has become one of its distinguishing characteristics. Its members include representatives from 20 countries, including China and Russia, which also represents other members of the Commonwealth of Independent States (CIS), Chile, Mexico, and Peru. Over the years, both national committees and task forces have been formed. They have reached a consensus on "open regionalism"—that is, regional liberalization that remains consistent with the norms and rules of the General Agreement on Tariffs and Trade (GATT) (q.v.) and the World Trade Organization (WTO) (q.v.) but also embodies a regionally based form of multilateralism. It has also been noteworthy in its ability to facilitate diplomatic negotiations.

Pacific settlement of disputes (also known as peaceful settlement of disputes). This phrase essentially means resolution of international conflicts without recourse to violence or force. There are many techniques for peaceful or pacific settlement, such as arbitration (q.v.), conciliation (q.v.), good offices (q.v.), inquiry, adjudication, mediation (q.v.), and negotiation. The United Nations (UN) (q.v.) unequivocally, especially in Chapter VI of the UN Charter, demands that disputants initially resort to peaceful means for the settlement of disputes. This does not always happen.

Pacific Trade and Development Conference (PAFTAD). Begun in 1968, this international nongovernmental organization has been portrayed as the intellectual driving force behind subsequent intergovernmental regional cooperation. The Japanese Ministry of Foreign Affairs sponsored the first meeting of the conference. It met to discuss a proposed Pacific Free Trade Area (PAFTA). Although those attending the meeting thought the proposal premature, they found a transnational gathering of professional and academic economists valuable and worthy of repetition.

Palme Commission (formally the Independent Commission on Disarmament and Security Issues). Created in 1981 under the leadership of the late Swedish prime minister Olaf Palme, its purpose was to complement the work of the Brandt Commission (q.v.) "by concentrating on security and disarmament (q.v.) measures that can contribute to peace in the 1980s and beyond." Among the recommendations included in its 1982 report, *Common Security: A Blueprint for Survival*, was the call for a nuclear-free zone in Central Europe and a more active UN peacekeeping (q.v.) role. It is, however, probably best known for coining the term "common security" in terms that extend well beyond nuclear strategic issues: by thinking of joint survival rather than mutual destruction; by thinking in terms of global security, not simply the security of the super or major powers. Moreover, and perhaps even more unusually, the commission spoke in terms of security in terms that included the economic well-being of its citizens, which at times was seen possibly to contradict the military security of states.

Pan American Health Organization (PAHO). Set up in 1902 as the International Sanitary Bureau, PAHO promotes and coordinates efforts to combat disease in the Western Hemisphere. It is now a Specialized Agency of the Organization of American States (OAS) (q.v.), with the same membership at the OAS and its headquarters also in Washington, D.C. It is also linked to the World Health Organization (WHO) (q.v.) through its secretariat, which serves as the WHO's regional office for the Americas. Still, because of its long history, it maintains considerable autonomy. Among the PAHO's achievements is its contribution to the eradication of smallpox in the Western Hemisphere and the drastic reduction of yellow fever. It has among its highest priorities providing potable water and basic sanitary conditions to those living within its domain.

Pan American Union (PAU). In 1910 the Pan American Union replaced the Commercial Bureau of the American Republics that had been agreed to at the First International Conference of the American States, convened in 1889 in Washington, D.C. The Commercial Bureau's, and subsequently the PAU's mission focused on the prompt collection and distribution of commercial information. The PAU was replaced in 1948 by the Organization of American States (OAS) (q.v.).

Paris Club. The name given to an international negotiation forum where potential bilateral credits are discussed as is rescheduling and the consolidation of debts given or guaranteed by participating governments. It has no fixed membership but began in 1956 as a forum of 10 Western European countries working together to assist Argentina.

Peace Brigades International (PBI). Founded in 1981 as an international nongovernmental organization with headquarters in London, PBI focuses on conflict resolution. Its work is premised on the belief that a lasting end to violent conflict cannot be imposed from above but must be based on the will and capacity of local people to build a positive peace (q.v.). Accordingly, PBI sends teams to various countries to promote nonviolent peacekeeping, particularly in countries undergoing significant social, economic, and political change. Its teams have recently been dispatched to Colombia, Guatemala, Haiti, and Sri Lanka. It has also worked in concert with the organizations in such places as Croatia, Kosova, Mexico, and Serbia.

Peace, disarmament, and arms control. The League of Nations (q.v.) and the United Nations (q.v.) both saw as their key goal the maintenance of international peace and security. The League sought to achieve this through the means of collective security (q.v.). Its failure led the UN's founders to rely more heavily on a limited collective security system, augmenting the UN with regional collective self-defense organizations, such as the Organization of American States (OAS) (q.v.). Whereas disarmament was central to the League, the UN's founders rested their faith in arms control. This may be because of the League's perceived failure in the peace and security field or because the UN Charter was signed before most of people in the world had witnessed the destructive capacity of atomic weapons.

Especially in the aftermath of the detonation of atomic and nuclear weapons, international nongovernmental organizations, such as the Pugwash Conferences on Science and World Affairs (q.v.), have worked hard to decrease the likelihood of interstate conflict. In the post–Cold War era, additional attention has been devoted to internal conflicts, including the work of the Carter Center (q.v.). See also Conference on Disarmament; Hague Peace Conferences; Helsinki Accord; International Alert; International Center for Peace Initiatives; Organismo para la Proscripción de las Armas Nucleares en la América y el Caribe; Organization on Security and Cooperation in Europe; Palme Commission; Peace Brigades International; peacekeeping forces; Pearson, Lester B.; Pelindaba, Treaty of; Resolution 242; Service Civil International; Tlatelolco, Treaty of; United Nations Disarmament Commission; Uniting for Peace Resolution; War Resisters International; World Federalist Movement.

Peacekeeping forces. Although not provided for in the UN Charter— and thus often referred to Chapter 6½ activities—the use of national forces to contain conflicts is one of the best known of the United Nations' (q.v.) activities. Technically, the term began with the UNEF I, the United Nations Emergency Force in the Middle East at the conclusion of the Suez War. But the term has been loosely applied to just about every non-Chapter VII (i.e., Security Council [q.v.] declared threats to international peace and security) deployment of UN troops, even if their only function is to observe. Although Dag Hammarskjöld (q.v.) articulated a number of quite clear guiding principles for peacekeeping forces, they have been breached more often than followed in subsequent practice. One, however, remains true: UN peacekeeping forces cannot be deployed on a country's territory without that country's explicit permission for that to be done.

Thirty-two peacekeeping operations have completed their missions: First United Nations Emergency Force (in the Middle East) (UNEF I), November 1956–June 1967; United Nations Observation Group in Lebanon (UNOGIL), June 1958–December 1958; United Nations Operation in the Congo (ONUC), July 1960–June 1964; United Nations Security Force in West New Guinea (West Irian) (UNSF), October 1962–April 1963; United Nations Yemen Observation Mission (UNYOM), June 1963–September 1964; Mission of the Representative of the Secretary-General in the Dominican Republic, May 1965–October 1966; United Nations India-Pakistan Observation Mission, September 1965–March 1966; Second United Nations Emergency Force (in the Middle East) (UNEF II), October 1973–July

1979; United Nations Good Offices Mission in Afghanistan and Pakistan (UNGOMAP), April 1988–March 1990; United Nations Iran-Iraq Military Observer Group (UNIIMOG), August 1988–February 1991; United Nations Angola Verification Mission I (UNAVEM I), January 1989–June 1991; United Nations Transition Assistance Group (in Namibia) (UNTAG), April 1989–March 1990; United Nations Observer Group in Central America (ONUCA), November 1989–January 1992; United Nations Angola Verification Mission II (UNAVEM II), June 1991–February 1995; United Nations Observer Mission in El Salvador (ONUSAL), July 1991–April 1995; United Nations Advance Mission in Cambodia (UNAMIC), October 1991–March 1992; United Nations Transitional Authority in Cambodia (UNTAC), March 1992–September 1993; United Nations Protection Force (in the former Yugoslavia) (UNPROFOR), March 1992–December 1995; United Nations Operation in Somalia I (UNOSOM I), April 1992–March 1993; United Nations Operation in Mozambique (ONUMOZ), December 1992–December 1994; United Nations Operation in Somalia II (UNOSOM II), March 1993–March 1995; United Nations Observer Mission Uganda/Rwanda (UNOMUR), June 1993–September 1994; United Nations Mission in Haiti (UNMIH), September 1993–June 1996; United Nations Assistance Mission for Rwanda (UNAMIR), October 1993–March 1996; United Nations Aouzou Strip Observer Group (Chad/Libya) (UNASOG), March 1994–June 1994; United Nations Confidence Restoration Organization in Croatia (UNCRO), March 1995–January 1996; United Nations Verification Mission in Guatemala (MINUGUA), January 1997–May 1997; United Nations Support Mission in Haiti (UNSMIH), July 1996–June 1997; United Nations Angola Verification Mission III (UNAVEM III), February 1995–June 1997; United Nations Observer Mission in Liberia (UNOMIL), September 1993–September 1997; United Nations Transition Mission in Haiti, August 1997–November 1997; United Nations Transitional Administration for Eastern Slavonia, Baranja and Western Sirmium (in Croatia) (UNTAES), January 1996–January 1998.

Current, ongoing peacekeeping operations include (beginning dates provided): United Nations Truce Supervision Organization (in the Middle East) (UNTSO), June 1948; United Nations Military Observer Group in India and Pakistan (UNMOGIP), January 1949; United Nations Peacekeeping Forces in Cyprus (UNFICYP), March 1964; United Nations Disengagement Observer Force (in the Golan Heights) (UNDOF), June 1974; United Nations Interim Force in Lebanon (UNIFIL), March 1978; United Nations Iraq-Kuwait Observation Mission (UNIKOM), April 1991; United Nations Mission for the Referendum in Western Sahara (MINURSO), September 1991; United Nations

Mission of Observers in Tajikistan (UNMOT), December 1994; United Nations Preventive Deployment Force (in the former Yugoslav Republic of Macedonia) (UNPREDEP), March 1995; United Nations Mission of Observers in Prevlaka (in Croatia) (UNMOP), January 1996; United Nations Observer Mission in Angola (MONUA), July 1997; United Nations Civilian Police Mission in Haiti (MIPONUH), December 1997; United Nations Civilian Police Support Group, January 1998; United Nations Mission in the Central African Republic (MINURCR), April 1998. See also Pearson, Lester B.

Pearson, Lester B. (1897–1972). A Canadian prime minister who served as the president of the UN General Assembly (q.v.) in 1952. In 1956, it was his ideas that provided the foundation for what came to be known as UN peacekeeping forces (q.v.), initially in the Sinai. He was awarded the Nobel Peace Prize in 1957 for his idea, which was seized on and concretized by UN secretary-general Dag Hammarskjöld (q.v.). He was also the chair of the Pearson Commission (q.v.) that published a widely cited report, *Partners in Development.*

Pearson Commission (formally the Commission in International Development). Created in 1968 by then World Bank (q.v.) President Robert S. McNamara (q.v.) with a charge to study international development, with a view toward making it more efficient and effective in achieving its ends. The commission's report, *Partners in Development,* recommended increased foreign aid, more aid through multilateral channels, and that it not be considered a replacement for foreign direct investment or increased world trade (q.v.). The commission came to known for its chair, Lester B. Pearson (q.v.), the former Canadian prime minister.

Pelindaba, Treaty of (formally the African Nuclear-Weapon-Free Zone Treaty). Signed on April 11, 1996, in Cairo, Egypt, by more than 40 African countries, the treaty brought to fruition a commitment made 32 years earlier. It also includes protocols to ensure that African denuclearization is supported by the previously acknowledged nuclear powers. It was quickly signed by France, the United Kingdom, and the United States. Pelindaba is the name of the area near Pretoria, South Africa, where a joint UN/Organization of African Unity (OAU) (q.v.) Group of Experts finalized the Treaty on June 2, 1995. Later that same month, it was adopted by the OAU.

Pérez de Cuéllar, Javier (1920–). Fifth secretary-general (q.v.) of the UN (1982–1991). Before his appointment as secretary-general, Pérez de Cuéllar served as the permanent representative of Peru to the UN (1971–1975), as the secretary-general's special representative in Cyprus (1976–1977) and in Afghanistan (1981), and UN undersecretary-general for special political affairs (1979–1981). His first term of office was marked by the growing marginalization of the United Nations (q.v.) during the height of what came to be known as the crisis of multilateralism, not least of all because of U.S. indifference, at best, to the UN and the onset of massive financial difficulties. His second term, however, was marked by increased supportive attention to the UN, partly because of a number of successes credited to the secretary-general himself and the end of the Cold War. Among those successes were the UN's roles in ending of the war between Iran and Iraq and in the Soviet withdrawal from Afghanistan. Likewise, his second term saw a massive proliferation of peacekeeping (q.v.) and peacekeeping-like forces in Central America, Namibia, Angola, the Western Sahara, and Kuwait. His role in response to the Iraqi invasion of Kuwait was both more controversial—accused by some as lacking independence—and more marginal.

Permanent Court of Arbitration. Not permanent and not a court, but actually a panel of international jurists first established in 1900 under the 1899 Hague Peace Conferences (q.v.), providing readily available arbitrators for international disputes. The court is tied to the International Court of Justice (ICJ) (q.v.) in the sense that the members of the ICJ are elected from a list of persons nominated by the national groups in the Permanent Court of Arbitration.

Permanent Court of International Justice (PCIJ). Created by the League of Nations (q.v.) to settle conflicts between states and render advisory opinions on any dispute or question referred to it by the League. The court met beginning in 1922. It did not meet during World War II. Its final session was in 1945, when it was succeeded by the International Court of Justice (q.v.). At no time did a party refuse to accept the PCIJ's judgment (in its 32 contentious cases) or opinion (in its 27 advisory opinions).

Pharmaciens sans Frontières (PSF) (Pharmacists without Borders). Operating since 1985, PSF, which has its headquarters in Paris, provides pharmaceutical assistance in economically developing countries (q.v.), focusing especially on places afflicted by famine and malnutrition. It also assists refugees (q.v.), displaced persons, and war victims.

Plebiscite. Plebiscites—votes to determine the will of an area's population on a particular issue—are among the peaceful means for settlement of disputes used by the United Nations and other bodies. Controversies almost always arise as to the choices and wording of such ballots and, at times, whether the population has been provided sufficient or unbiased information prior to casting their ballots. The UN sponsored plebiscites in several former African trusts (q.v.) as they emerged as independent countries. Others have been proposed but never held, as in Vietnam in 1956 and in India and Pakistan in 1949 about Kashmir.

Plevan Plan. See European Defense Community (EDC).

Prebisch, Raúl (1901–1986). A well-known Argentine economist, especially notable for challenging classical world trade (q.v.) theory in terms of comparative advantage. While serving as executive secretary of the UN Economic Commission for Latin America (ECLA) (q.v.) (1948–1963), he became known as the champion and leading theoretician of developing countries (q.v.), focusing on their negative terms of trade. His popularity reached its zenith prior to the success of the Organization of Petroleum Exporting Countries (OPEC) (q.v.) in raising oil prices. After leaving ECLA, he was appointed as the first secretary-general of the United Nations Conference on Trade and Development (UNCTAD) (q.v.). He held that position from 1963 to 1969. See also Prebisch Report.

Prebisch Report (formally *Towards a New Trade Policy for Development*). The 1964 report written by the secretary-general of the United Nations Conference on Trade and Development (UNCTAD) (q.v.), which came to be the core policy document for the Group of 77 (q.v.). In Raúl Prebisch's (q.v.) view, the economies of developing countries (q.v.) could only develop adequately if exports could be increased, which could happen only if international measures were taken, such as international commodity agreements (q.v.), compensatory finance accords, and tariff preferences. This was because of what Prebisch saw as the inevitable, ongoing negative terms of trade that developing countries all endured, owing to the unfair rules of the international system, colonialism and late industrialization. The success of the member countries of the Organization of Petroleum Exporting Countries (OPEC) (q.v.) and the newly industrialized countries (q.v.) of the South has been seen by many as a refutation of Prebisch's attack on orthodox trade policy.

Preston, Lewis T. (1926–1995). Before becoming president of the World Bank (q.v.) in 1991, Preston had a 40-year career with J. P. Morgan and Company. During the period in which he was president (1991–1995), the World Bank gained 23 new members, including the states of the former Soviet Union. The Bank also initiated economic development (q.v.) programs in the West Bank, Gaza, and South Africa and resumed lending to Vietnam after a 15-year hiatus. Under Preston, the bank made an increased proportion of loans to education, health (q.v.), family planning, and the environment (q.v.). He also sought to make the bank more cost-effective at the same time that he guided it to a larger advisory role in the restructuring of the public sectors of client countries.

Preventive diplomacy. This term was used to refer to UN Secretary-General Dag Hammarskjöld's (q.v.) approach to the handling of disputes. It involved techniques for preventing or forestalling conflicts or preventing their escalation into higher levels of violence, especially in terms of preventing the involvement of the superpowers in regional conflicts.

Public International Unions. This is the term used to refer to the 19th century international agencies concerned with problems in various functional areas, including communications (q.v.) and transportation (q.v.), economics and finance, health (q.v.), science, and art. The unions provided important procedural precedents for the intergovernmental organizations of the 20th century.

Pugwash Conferences on Science and World Affairs. Begun in Pugwash, Nova Scotia, Canada, in 1957, these periodic conferences bring together individuals, in their private capacities, to discuss ways to prevent armed conflict. There are currently national Pugwash Groups in more than 60 countries, all committed to finding better approaches to arms control (q.v.) and tension reduction. Over the years, many have credited the ideas generated at the Pugwash meetings with influencing global policy makers.

Q

Quiet diplomacy. This approach entails negotiation techniques that involve impartiality, tactfulness, persistence, and especially minimal publicity. Initially identified with UN Secretary-General Dag Hammarskjöld (q.v.), it is now used much more generically and commonly.

R

Rainforest Action Network (RAN). Established in 1985 to protect tropical rainforests and to support the rights of indigenous peoples.

To these ends, RAN, which has its headquarters in San Francisco, California, disseminates information, backs direct action campaigns including product boycotts and letter writing, and provides small grants to groups in tropical countries. In 1987, it organized a boycott of Burger King, accusing it of importing cheap beef from tropical countries where rainforests are denuded to provide pasture for cattle. After sales decreased by 12 percent, Burger King canceled $35 million worth of beef contracts in Central America. RAN currently works with environmental and human rights (q.v.) groups in 60 countries.

Red Cross. See International Committee of the Red Cross; see also International Federation of Red Cross and Red Crescent Societies.

Refugees and migrants. International organizations have long been involved with coping with the challenges of refugees. Impressive strides in this area were made by the League of Nations (q.v.). But there has always been the hope that this was a transitory problem. Accordingly, early in its history the United Nations (UN) (q.v.) chose not to set up a permanent Specialized Agency (q.v.), the International Refugee Organization (q.v.), as was initially considered. Rather, it elected to rely on an agency without a permanent budget, the Office of the United Nations High Commissioner for Refugees (UNCHR) (q.v.). A small number of regional intergovernmental organizations work on refugee issues, but much of the "ground work" (i.e., temporary feeding, clothing, housing, legal assistance, acculturation) is done by international nongovernmental organizations, many religious based. See also Aga Khan, Prince Sadruddin; American Refugee Committee; Hebrew Immigrant Aid Society; International Association of Lions Clubs; International Catholic Migration Commission; International Organization for Migration; Ogata, Sadako; United Nations Relief and Works Agency for Palestine Refugees in the Near East.

Regional cooperation. Some intergovernmental organizations have very broad mandates, namely to encourage cooperation across a wide range of sectors. In contrast to functionalism (q.v.), the founders, supporters, and participants in these organizations believe that there are significant advantages in having a broad-based organization where the strengths and needs of member states in one issue area can be traded off for benefits in another. As is true in this book and throughout the study of international organizations, the term *regional* is used loosely (i.e., to refer to any organization that is not open to all countries, not universal). In this vein, the exemplar of a regional cooperation organization is the Commonwealth (q.v.), whose members include countries from throughout the world, whose agendas vary, and which has committees operating on diverse topics. See also Arab Maghreb Union; Asia Pacific Economic Cooperation; Association of Southeast Asian Nations; Black Sea Economic Cooperation; Club du Sahel; Colombo Plan for Cooperative Economic and Social Development in Asia and the Pacific; Conseil de l'Entente; Contadora Group; Cooperation Council for the Arab States of the Gulf; Council of Europe; Council of the Baltic Sea States; Delors, Jacques; European Parliament; League of Arab States; Niger Basin Authority; Nordic Council; North Atlantic Cooperation Council; Organization of African Unity; Organization of American States; Organization of Central American States; Organization of Eastern Caribbean States; Organization of the Islamic Conference; Pacific Basin Economic Council; Pacific Economic Cooperation Council; Pacific Trade and Development Conference; Pan American Union; South Asian Association for Regional Cooperation; South Pacific Commission; South Pacific Forum; South Pacific Forum Secretariat; Southern African Development Community; Southern African Development Coordination Council.

Regional Cooperation for Development (RCD). See Economic Cooperation Organization (ECO).

Rehabilitation International (RI). Founded in 1922 , RI seeks to serve as a forum for the exchange and dissemination of information relating to the rehabilitation of those with disabilities. RI's headquarters are in New York City. Its members are affiliated national organizations in 73 countries. It conducted the first global survey of people with disabilities (estimated at close to 500 million) and organized the first International Conference on Legislation Concerning the Disabled (1971).

Resident representatives. To coordinate United Nations (UN) (q.v.) economic and social projects within each recipient country, the UN appoints a field agent to reside and coordinate activities there. Such an individual is the chief UN representative in the country. As such, he or she is expected to assist a host country in developing its aid requests. Historically, resident representatives—often employees of the United Nations Development Program (UNDP) (q.v.)—have been stymied by the lack of real authority and, often related, problems of cooperation with host governments.

Resolution 242. This UN Security Council (q.v.) resolution, adopted on November 22, 1967, has often been referred to as the "United Nations' blueprint for a settlement of the Arab-Israeli conflict." Its major provisions call for an Israeli withdrawal from occupied territories, acknowledgment of sovereignty of all states in the area, an end to belligerency, and settlement of the refugee (q.v.) problems. Its key provisions are, inevitably and intentionally, open to multiple interpretations.

Rhine River Commission. Formed in 1815 at the Congress of Vienna to promote unrestricted navigation on the Rhine River for ships of all countries. Members of the commission, the first modern intergovernmental organization, include Belgium, France, Germany, the Netherlands, Switzerland, and the United Kingdom. It is notable for the autonomy given to the secretariat, including authority to amend its own rules and to act as a court of appeals for the decisions of local courts.

Roosevelt, (Anna) Eleanor (1884–1962). Eleanor Roosevelt, wife of Franklin D. Roosevelt, president of the United States, served as U.S. delegate to the UN General Assembly (q.v.) (1946, 1949–1952, and 1961), heading the delegation during most of that time. She was a strong advocate of human rights (q.v.), chaired the UN Commission on Human Rights (q.v.) (1947–1951), and is often given credit for having shaped the Universal Declaration of Human Rights (q.v.). With Dwight Eisenhower's election as U.S. president, she resigned from her UN post but continued an active life in the international public sphere, including years of service as head of the American Association for the United Nations.

Rotary International. Founded in 1905, with its current name dating to 1922. In addition to supporting a wide variety of service programs throughout the world (globally there are more than 25,000 Rotary Clubs; they are located in every country in the world), Rotary International runs an active international exchange program for people of all ages and professions. In addition, Rotary International provides grants to teachers to serve in economically developing countries (q.v.) and has a number of special development and technical assistance programs geared to assisting the poor in developing countries. More than a million people in over 155 countries are members of Rotary Clubs. The international headquarters are in Evanston, Illinois.

S

Santer, Jacques (1933–). The Luxembourger, who as president of the Commission of the European Union (EU) (q.v.), has served as the

EU's highest official since January 1995. Before that, he had a long career in the Luxembourg government, including serving as minister of finance, labor and social security (1979–1984); prime minister, minister of state and minister of finance (1984–1989); and prime minister, minister of state, minister for the treasury and minister for cultural affairs (1989–1994). His prior experience in international organizations include serving as governor of the World Bank (q.v.) (1984–1989); governor of the International Monetary Fund (q.v.) (1984–1989); and president of the European Council (q.v.) (in 1985 and in 1991). As president of the commission, his highest priority has been to move forward with the financial integration of the EU.

Saudi Fund for Development (SFD). Established in 1974, the SFD provides "soft" loans (i.e., loans at low rates of interest and long repayments periods) to developing countries (q.v.) in Africa and Asia. There is no restriction that the funds be expended on Saudi goods. The SFD's headquarters are in Riyadh, Saudi Arabia.

Save the Children Alliance (ISCA) (formerly the International Save the Children Alliance). Organized in 1979 to serve as a consultative and coordinating body to help underprivileged children (q.v.) anywhere in the world. Members are 23 autonomous national voluntary organizations that operate in over 100 countries. Its secretariat is in Geneva, Switzerland. The alliance has identified four priority themes: the Convention on the Rights of the Child; children, poverty, and the international economic system; children in armed conflict and displacement; and education.

Save the Children Fund (SCF). Founded in 1919, with its headquarters in London, the Save the Children Fund is an international nongovernmental organization aimed at achieving lasting benefits for children (q.v.) within the communities in which they live. It seeks to do this chiefly by providing technical support and direct implementation of health (q.v.), child welfare, education, and community development programs. Its target groups include refugees (q.v.), displaced persons, asylum seekers, indigenous groups, stateless persons, political detainees, war victims, victims of torture, minority groups, and the physically and mentally disabled. It currently operates programs in 35 countries.

Schuman, Robert (1886–1963). The French finance minister, foreign minister, defense minister and prime minister whose plan—the Schuman Plan, which was drafted by Jean Monnet (q.v.)—eventually became the basis for the European Coal and Steel Community (ECSC) (q.v.). In making his proposal in 1950, Schuman was not only proposing an experiment in economic cooperation (q.v.) and integration, but also conceived of this as the beginning of the political integration of Western Europe. From 1958 to 1960, Schuman served as president of the European Parliamentary Assembly.

Schweitzer, Pierre-Paul (1912–1994). Before becoming managing director of the International Monetary Fund (IMF) (q.v.) in 1963 (where he served for two full terms until 1973), Schweitzer had served in the French treasury and finance ministry. Schweitzer was IMF managing director at a time of international monetary crisis, not least of all brought on by the inability or at least the unwillingness of the United States to raise taxes or devalue the dollar in spite of massive budget deficits deriving from the Vietnam War. Schweitzer's repeated calls for the United States to exercise monetary discipline were not welcomed by the U.S. government, and indeed he had to learn from television of the U.S. decision to end the Bretton Woods System (q.v.) as it had heretofore operated.

Self-determination. Technically, self-determination is the right of a people to choose the political entity under which they would like to live. More commonly (and loosely) it is understood to be the process by which national entities establish themselves as independent states. The right to "self-determination of peoples" is called for in the United Nations (q.v.) Charter (Articles 1 and 55) without any elaboration of what is intended by "peoples" or what means are justified in obtaining it. Since the charter was written, the rights of colonial peoples, at least, to self-determination has generally been understood to have evolved from an international norm to an international legal right.

Service Civil International (SCI) (International Voluntary Service). SCI, which has its headquarters in Bonn, Germany, was founded in 1920. Its aim is to promote international understanding and peace (q.v.). One of its key foci is lobbying for conscientious objection as a basic human right (q.v.). It brings together international groups to work or be trained together on various service projects. It has national branches in 33 countries.

Sierra Club International Program. The Sierra Club's International Program was founded in 1971. Through the 1970s and early 1980s, it operated out of various New York City offices near the United Nations (UN) (q.v.). Its focus then was on the Law of the Sea negotiations, the proposed moratoria on whaling, protection of Antarctica, and various conservationist activities by the Soviet Union and the United States. In 1985, the program relocated to Washington, D.C., and saw as its chief goal fostering a global outlook among grassroots activists in the United States and Canada. It was quite visible at the United Nations Conference on Environment and Development (q.v.), the Earth Summit, underscoring that while its focus is on North America, it is not exclusively so. In this context, it has a special program focused on international population stabilization and another on trade (q.v.) and the environment (q.v.), dealing with activities of the World Trade Organization (WTO) (q.v.) as well as the North American Free Trade Association (NAFTA).

Single European Act (SEA). The name given to the first major revision in the European Community's (q.v.) constitutive document, the Treaty of Rome. It was initially written in 1985, but did not come into force until 1987 after it had been ratified by the legislatures of the member states. The main elements of the SEA were the establishment of an internal market, increased cooperation in foreign and defense policy, and the formal establishment of the European Political Cooperation (EPC) (q.v.). There was also an agreement to strengthen the powers of the European Parliament (q.v.) and to the ease the burden of the European Court of Justice (q.v.).

Sistema Económico Latinoamericana (SELA) (Latin American Economic System). Created in 1975, in the aftermath of the 1974 U.S. Trade Reform Act, SELA aims to coordinate existing integration mechanisms, give new impetus to intraregional cooperation, organize producers of raw materials and basic agricultural products, and coordinate positions and strategies of member states toward the outside world, including the United States. Fearing its overwhelming power, the United States was intentionally not asked to join, contrary to the situation with the Organization of American States (OAS) (q.v.).

This organization, based in Caracas, Venezuela, tries to increase so-called South-South trade (q.v.). It has been fairly successful in building up regional cooperation among Latin American governments on international economic issues, including external debt.

Sixth Special Session. This was the first special session of the United Nations General Assembly (q.v.) called by the third world. The agenda of the session, which met from April 9 to May 2, 1974, quickly went beyond the original focus on trade in raw materials. It expanded to include a broad range of economic concerns for developing countries (q.v.), including the call for a New International Economic Order (q.v.).

Snake. The term used to refer to the joint float (fluctuation) of currencies of member states of the European Economic Community (EEC) (q.v.). It was originally agreed to, in April 1972, among the original six members of the EEC and then was expanded. The participants agreed to limit fluctuations of their own currencies so that the margin between the strongest and weakest currencies would not be more than 4.5 percent. The name "snake" was attached to the scheme because on a graph the narrow band of permitted fluctuation over time resembles a snake. The snake operated within a wider International Monetary Fund (IMF) (q.v.) band, giving rise to the phrase "the snake in the tunnel."

Société Internationale de Télécommunications Aéronautiques (SITA). Created on February 23, 1949, SITA is a global telecommunications organization that provides a variety of services to airlines engaged in public civil air transportation (q.v.). It is owned and operated on behalf of member airlines, whose shares in it are proportionate to their respective use of SITA's services. Its administrative head office is in Neuilly-sur-Seine, France. Currently over 500 airlines and airport transport–related companies use SITA's circuits for seat reservations and other services, including notifying airlines about the location of the clouds of volcanic dust. SITA works with the International Air Transport Association (IATA) (q.v.) on baggage tracing.

Solana, Javier (1942–   ). Solana was elected as secretary-general of the North Atlantic Treaty Organization (NATO) (q.v.) in December 1995, after six weeks of very public and bitter debate on the successor to the Belgian Willy Claes, who had resigned to face charges in an arms-buying scandal while he served in the Belgian cabinet. Before his selection, Solana was the foreign minister of Spain (1992–1995), minister of education and science (1988–1992), minister of culture (1982–1988) and a university professor of solid-state physics. Because he was a member of the Socialist party, his appointment was opposed by a number of Republican senators in the United States.

South Asian Association for Regional Cooperation (SAARC). SAARC was formed in Dhaka, Bangladesh, in 1985 by Bangladesh, Bhutan, India, the Maldives, Nepal, Pakistan, and Sri Lanka. Its goal is to promote regional cooperation (q.v.) on the basis of sovereign equality, political independence, and mutual benefit. In spite of conflicts and postponed meetings, members agreed to the establishment of a modest South Asian Preferential Trade Agreement and a Food Security Reserve. Meetings at the technical level are convened frequently. SAARC also designates thematic years and decades: 1991–2000 focuses on the "Girl-Child."

South Pacific Commission (SPC). Established in 1947 by the six governments which then had colonies in the area—Australia, France, the Netherlands, New Zealand, the United Kingdom, and the United States—with a commitment to promoting the economic and social welfare of the peoples of the South Pacific region. Each of the now 27 member states is represented by two commissioners in the secretariat, which is located in Noumea, New Caledonia. The commission has dealt with such issues as soil and land use, subsistence economies, rural development, youth and community development, the coconut and rice industries, and fisheries. Recently, it has been suggested that perhaps the SPC should become a technical arm of the South Pacific Forum (SPF) (q.v.), especially since the United Kingdom, one of its largest financial backers, left the SPC at the end of 1995.

South Pacific Forum (SPF). Since its first meeting in Wellington, New Zealand, in 1971, the heads of government of the independent and self-governing states of the South Pacific have found the informality associated with the SPF of great value. Lacking even a formal constitution, the SPF operates by consensus, taking up issues of the region as they arise. Among its accomplishments was laying the groundwork for what became the South Pacific Nuclear-Free Zone and the establishment of the South Pacific Forum Fisheries Agency. More recently, discussion has focused on the region's dwindling forest resources.

South Pacific Forum Secretariat. The secretariat is the successor organization to the South Pacific Bureau of Economic Co-operation that had operated out of the headquarters in Suva, Fiji, from 1972 to 1988. The purpose of the organization, which also provides secretariat functions for the South Pacific Forum (SPF) (q.v.), is to improve the economic and social well-being of the people of the South Pacific. It seeks to achieve this goal by increasing cooperation among the members and providing services for the members, such as doing a market survey for Japan and the United States in hopes of identifying trade (q.v.) opportunities for the members.

Southeast Asia Treaty Organization (SEATO). A now-defunct mutual defense alliance that called on the signatories to consult and to meet the common danger of communism (as an internal or external threat). SEATO was created by the Southeast Asia Collective Defense Treaty, signed in Manila, the Philippines, in 1954. Australia, France, New Zealand, Pakistan, the Philippines, Thailand, the United Kingdom, and the United States were members. It evolved as a part of the "pactamania" that typified U.S. foreign policy in the early 1950s and was immediately precipitated by the defeat of the French in Indochina. It was used as one of the justifications for the U.S. military involvement in Vietnam in the 1960s and 1970s. It collapsed after the U.S. withdrawal from Vietnam in 1973 but was not formally dissolved until 1977.

Southern African Development Community (SADC). Established in 1992 by the representatives of the former SADCC (q.v.) states. The goal of this newer organization, with headquarters in Gaborone, Botswana, is to promote economic cooperation eventuating in the establishment of a regional common market. After accepting South Africa as a member in August 1994, the community added regional security issues to its portfolio. Its members now include Angola, Botswana, Lesotho, Malawi, Mozambique, Namibia, South Africa, Swaziland, Tanzania, Zambia, and Zimbabwe.

Southern African Development Coordination Council (SADCC). Established in 1972 as a mechanism for developing southern Africa and reducing the dependency of member states—Angola, Botswana, Lesotho, Malawi, Mozambique, Swaziland, Tanzania, Zambia, Zimbabwe and (later) Namibia—on South Africa. SADCC was a highly decentralized organization; its supreme authority—the annual summit meeting—set overall policy direction. SADCC was dissolved on August 17, 1992, owing to the constitutional reform in South Africa.

Spaak, Paul-Henri (1899–1972). Spaak was a prominent Belgian politician who became, in 1938, the first socialist party premier of Belgium but resigned the following year. He subsequently served as foreign minister with the government-in-exile in London during World War II. In 1946, Spaak was elected president of the first UN General Assembly (q.v.). He served again as Belgian prime minister in 1946 and from 1947 to 1949. Long an advocate of European unification and generally credited with being one of the founders of the European Community (q.v.), he served as chair of the Council for European Recovery (1948–1949) and as president of the consultative assembly of the Council of Europe (q.v.) (1949–1951).

After serving again as Belgian foreign minister (1954–1957), he was selected as secretary-general of the North Atlantic Treaty Organization (NATO) (q.v.), a position he held from 1957 to 1961. This post seemed a natural role for one of that organization's founders and most outspoken advocates. As secretary-general, he vigorously pursued a stronger NATO role in decision making, one where members broadened the scope and deepened the character of their consultation. After serving as secretary-general, he returned to Belgium and served as foreign minister from 1961 until his resignation from Parliament in 1966. While he explained his resignation from NATO as a consequence of internal Belgian politics, others have suggested that it also had to do with his inability to overcome some of the political bickering within the organization, not least of all related to Gaullist nationalism.

Special Drawing Rights (SDRs). SDRs is a term used to describe artificial international reserve units created, initially in 1969, by the International Monetary Fund (q.v.). They were created to supplement the limited supplies of gold and dollars that had been the prime stable international monetary assets up until then. SDRs are used between members to settle balance of payments accounts, as reserve assets and as reserve credits.

Specialized Agencies of the United Nations. These agencies are characterized by Article 57 of the United Nations (q.v.) Charter as "having wide international responsibilities, as defined in their basic instruments, in economic, social, cultural, education, health, and related fields." All are technically responsible to the United Nations Economic and Social Council (ECOSOC) (q.v.), but for some—such as the financial institutions—that means little more than filing an annual report. This reporting requirement contrasts with the arrangement under the League of Nations (q.v.) where analogous bodies—such as the International Labour Organisation (ILO) (q.v.)— were autonomous. This revised arrangement was intended to ensure continued support and praise for the UN, even when its successes in the military security realm lagged. Currently there are 16 Specialized Agencies (all discussed in separate entries in this dictionary): Food and Agricultural Organization (FAO); International Bank for Reconstruction and Development (IBRD); International Civil Aviation Organization (ICAO); International Development Association (IDA); International Finance Corporation (IFC); International Fund for Agricultural Development (IFAD); International Labour Organisation (ILO); International Maritime Organization (IMO); International Monetary Fund (IMF); International Telecommunication Union (ITU); United Nations Educational, Cultural and Scientific Organization (UNESCO); United Nations Industrial Development Organization (UNIDO); Universal Postal Union (UPU); World Health Organization (WHO); World Intellectual Property Organization (WIPO); World Meteorological Organization (WMO).

STABEX. STABEX is the European Community's (EC) (q.v.) compensatory facility for the stabilization of export products. As part of the Lomé Convention (q.v.) of 1975, the EC agreed to a stockpiling and intervention scheme to deal with 12 staple goods exported by the so-called ACP (q.v.) countries, African, Caribbean, and Pacific former colonies of EC member states. These were bananas, cocoa, coconut products, coffee, cotton, groundnut products, palm products, hides and skins, sisal, tea, timber, and iron ore.

Strong, Maurice (1929–   ). Strong is a Canadian business executive who has been the most prominent United Nations (UN) (q.v.) official in the field of environment (q.v.). He was secretary-general of the UN Conference on the Human Environment (q.v.) (UNCHE, Stockholm 1972), executive director of the UN Environment Program (q.v.) (1972–1975), and principal architect and secretary-general of the UN Conference on Environment and Development (q.v.) (UNCED, Rio 1992).

Summit of the Eight (also called the G-8). President Clinton invited President Yeltsin of Russia to participate at the June 1997 meeting of the Group of Seven (G-7) (q.v.) that was convened in Denver, Colorado. Russia participated in all of the meetings, save a one-hour financial conversation. (In 1998, he participated in all of the meetings.) The conferees in Denver called for democratic elections in Hong Kong, peace in the Middle East, peace in Bosnia, and new aid for Africa. But they disagreed on North Atlantic Treaty Organization (NATO) (q.v.) expansion, and the United States refused to join the Europeans in agreeing to specific reductions in carbon dioxide emissions.

Supranationality. An international institution is said to have attained supranational status (or attained elements of supranationality) when member governments can be required to implement decisions that they voted against.

Survival International (SI). Founded in 1972 and with headquarters in London, SI publicizes the problems and aspirations of aboriginal peoples and works to extend the area of international responsibility and recognition of these needs. SI also publicizes the findings of its field work, which focuses on the threats of natural and environmental factors to aboriginal peoples.

T

Thant, U (1909–1974). U Thant served (1961–1971) as the third secretary-general (q.v.) of the United Nations (UN) (q.v.). At the time of his appointment (initially as acting secretary-general), he was the permanent representative of Burma to the UN. His appointment reflected the first move toward choosing a third world top administrator for the UN. His first tasks were to extract the UN from the Congo and to regain the confidence of all of the world's power blocs in the UN. While he never achieved the global influence that his predecessor— Dag Hammarskjöld (q.v.)—had, he was praised for his role in the Congo, West Irian, and the Indo-Pakistani conflicts of both 1965 and 1971. He was criticized for (too) quickly acquiescing to Egyptian demands for the withdrawal of UNEF troops from the Sinai (in 1967). The United States, in particular, was also critical of his frequent (and abortive) attempts to mediate an end to the war in Vietnam. He publicly denounced the 1968 Soviet invasion of Czechoslovakia.

Third World Forum. An independent nongovernmental organization "open to all the social scientists from the Third World with a predominant interest in the development of their societies." The forum was formed at a meeting of third world social scientists (April 23–25, 1973), in Santiago, Chile. Its headquarters are now in Dakar, Senegal.

Tlatelolco, Treaty of. This treaty, formally known as the Treaty for the Prohibition of Nuclear Weapons in Latin America, was signed in Tlatelolco, Mexico, on February 14, 1967. It prohibits the development or deployment of nuclear weapons in Latin America, the Caribbean, and the territorial waters of the countries concerned. The Organismo para la Proscripción de las Armas Nucleares en la América Latina y el Caribe (OPANAL) (q.v.) supervises compliance with the treaty. Countries outside the region were excluded from the treaty itself, but the nuclear powers were invited to adhere to two protocols. Protocol I requested them not to place nuclear weapons in their dependencies within the treaty zone; Protocol II asked them to respect Latin America as a nuclear-free zone. After considerable delay, all announced nuclear powers, save India and Pakistan, have now accepted the protocols.

Tokyo Round. The seventh major multilateral trade (q.v.) negotiations held under the auspices of the GATT (q.v.). These rounds, which lasted from 1973 to 1979, resulted in agreements for an average reduction in tariffs of 33 percent over the following eight years and established new codes of conduct regarding nontariff barriers (NTBs) (q.v.).

Tourism. Although international nongovernmental organizations such as the now-defunct International Union of Official Travel Organizations (IUOTO) long served the interests of tourists and tour companies, it is only relatively recently that intergovernmental organizations have counted tourism among their foci. In part this is a consequence of the recent focus on tourism as one means to accelerate economic growth. Thus, organizations such as the Amazon Pact (q.v.) have added the promotion of tourism to their agendas. In addition, the World Tourism Organization (q.v.) has been expanding its membership base since its establishment in 1975. Some nongovernmental organizations are also concerned about the possible negative social consequences (rise of stratification, prostitution, AIDS, etc.) of relying on the tourist industry as a means for achieving economic growth.

Trade. Working on the presumption that trade contributes to economic growth as well as lessening the chances of interstate conflict, government leaders have spent considerable time, especially in the post–World War II era, concluding trade agreements, some of which have resulted in the establishment of intergovernmental organizations. Most notable in this regard are the General Agreement on Tariffs and Trade (GATT) (q.v.) and the World Trade Organization (WTO) (q.v.). Although both of these institutions are open to all states, the main beneficiaries have been industries located in advanced industrialized, capitalist states. This, in part, explains the origins of the United Nations Conference on Trade and Development (UNCTAD) (q.v.), whose major goal has been to increase the trading opportunities of the economically less developed countries. This involves interfering with the market, a process in tension with the founding principle of the GATT. A similar principle underlies the Lomé Conventions (q.v.), the major beneficiaries of which are the former colonies of the members of the European Union (EU) (q.v.). See also Customs Co-operation Council; Dillon Round; Generalized System of Preferences; International Association of Trading Organizations for a Developing World; International Chamber of Commerce; Sistema Económico Latinoamericana; Tokyo Round; United Nations Commission on International Trade Law; Uruguay Round.

Trade unions and labor. The concern with working conditions is long-standing, as is governments' concern with interstate economic competition. As a consequence, the move to standards for labor practice has a long tradition in international organizations, in terms of both lobbying for those standards, largely the work of numerous trade union (con)federations, and issuing them. The latter is largely the province of the International Labour Organisation (ILO) (q.v.), established in 1919. Among its major achievements have been treaties concerning child labor, maximum hours, and mistreatment of women (q.v.) in the workplace.

The major activities of the key trade union (con)federations, many of which are organized along ideological lines, is assisting workers in less economically advanced countries, who need advice on unionization and defense of rights. See also Charter of Fundamental Social Rights; European Trade Union Confederation; International Confederation of Free Trade Unions; International Textile, Garment and Leather Workers' Federation; World Confederation of Labor; World Federation of Trade Unions.

Transportation. Among the earliest public international unions were those relating to transportation, initially focused on river and rail traffic. Industrialization, initially in Europe, required coordination of schedules, right of access, collection of fees, safety, and other standards, in order to facilitate commerce and thus economic growth. Organizations of this genre proliferated in the 19th century. Many of them established procedural precedents for international organizations in other arenas. Some were nongovernmental, some intergovernmental, and some creative combinations of the two. Some remain operating today, such as those relating to the major river bodies in Europe like the Central Commission for the Navigation of the Rhine (q.v.). While there has been some global coordination, especially in the airlines industry as by the International Air Transport Association (IATA) (q.v.), most cooperation remains geographically delimited. See also Comité Maritime International; Danube Commission; European Civil Aviation Conference; European Organization for the Safety of Air Navigation; Intergovernmental Organization for International Carriage by Rail; International Chamber of Shipping; Kennedy Round; liner code; most favored nation; Multifibre Agreement; nontariff barriers; Oil Companies International Marine Forum; Rhine River Commission.

Trilateral Commission. A nongovernmental organization, begun in 1973 and composed of about 300 citizens from Western Europe, North America, and Japan. Its purpose is to provide a debating forum about the key problems of international public policy confronting those regions of the world. Its members have included prominent statespeople, and some who subsequently became heads of government and foreign ministers.

Troika. This is a term to describe either a Russian carriage drawn by three horses abreast or rule by a group of three persons. In 1960, because of Soviet displeasure over UN secretary-general Dag Hammarskjöld's (q.v.) policies in the Congo, Soviet Premier Khrushchev demanded that Hammarskjöld resign and be replaced by a three-member executive group. These would be representative of socialist, Western, and nonaligned interests, and each would have a veto power over decisions. Many diplomats thought this, in effect, would marginalize the secretary-general (q.v.), if not the entire UN, from global politics. The idea—opposed by the third world, which feared that it too would be further marginalized by such an arrangement—was soundly rejected by the UN General Assembly (q.v.).

Trust territories. Dependent territories, which were former territories of the defeated powers in World War II, that were placed under the United Nations (UN) (q.v.) trusteeship system. The goal of this process was, with the assistance of a designated administering state, to encourage independence. There were two sorts of trusts. Most were under the administration of the UN Trusteeship Council (q.v.). A much smaller number—so-called strategic trusts—were under the authority of the UN Security Council (q.v.). The last remaining dependent territory designated as a trust was Palau, a strategic trust in the western Pacific, administered by the United States until 1994.

Trusteeship Council. The council is one of the six major organs of the United Nations (UN) (q.v.). Its charge is to supervise the administration of trust territories (q.v.). Its composition is specified as an equal number of administering and nonadministering states but also includes automatic membership for the five permanent members of the Security Council. After most trust territories gained independence, the only members of the Trusteeship Council were these five Security Council members, the P-5 (q.v.). The Trusteeship Council performed its functions by reviewing annual reports from the administering authorities, examining petitions from the inhabitants of the territories, and undertaking periodic visiting missions to each trust territory.

The admission to the UN of Palau—the last of the trust territories—led to the formal suspension (effective November 1, 1994) of the Trusteeship Council. This has led to a number of creative suggestions for new missions for it, including overseeing global environmental commons areas, an idea endorsed in 1997 by UN secretary-general Kofi Annan (q.v.). Others have simply suggested that it should be eliminated, but few are keen to begin a UN Charter amendment process for this purpose.

U

Unión de Países Exportadores de Banana (Union of Banana Exporting Countries). The union was formed in 1974 during the post–oil embargo euphoria with commodity cartels. Its goal was to coordinate policy for its member states with regard to the technical and economic development of the banana industry (i.e., promoting exports, finding new, nontraditional markets, rationalizing output, ensuring a good price). Member states include Colombia, Costa Rica, the Dominican Republic, Guatemala, Honduras, Nicaragua, Panama and Venezuela. The headquarters are in Panama City. The key organ is a conference of ministers, composed of the ministers of economy or agriculture of the member states.

Union Douanière et Économique de l'Afrique Centrale (UDEAC) (Central African Customs and Economic Union). Established in 1964 and effective January 1, 1966, UDEAC has its headquarters in Bangui, Central African Republic. It is the successor organization to the Union Douanière Equatoriale (Equatorial Customs Union), which united the member states (Cameroon, Central African Republic, Chad, the Congo, Equatorial Guinea, and Gabon) before they had achieved independence. UDEAC's goal is to establish a customs union. It has been successful in adjusting common external customs and tariffs; in coordinating legislation, regulations, and investment codes; in harmonizing internal taxes, and in developing common industrial projects, development plans, and transportation (q.v.) policies. In 1973, it established the Banque Centrale des Etats d'Afrique Centrale (BEAC), and, 20 years later, members agreed on the establishment of the Communauté Economique et Monétaire de l'Afrique Centrale (CEMAC) (Central African Economic and Monetary Community). But no firm timetable has been set for it.

Union Economique et Monétaire Ouest Africaine (UEMOA) (West African Economic and Monetary Union). The treaty establishing the UEMOA was signed in Dakar, Senegal, on January 10, 1994. The union's supreme decision-making organ is the Conference of Chiefs of State and Heads of Government. It meets at least once a year. The Council of Ministers meets at least twice a year. The key objectives of the union include strengthening competition in the economic and financial activities of the members, ensuring the convergence of members' economic performance and policies, creating a common market, and harmonizing members' sectoral policies and laws, including those relating to taxes. The members include Benin, Burkina Faso, Côte d'Ivoire, Mali, Niger, Senegal, and Togo.

United Nations (UN). The UN is a comprehensive, universal organization (open to all "peace-loving" states in the world) resulting from elaborate planning during World War II. The UN, which officially came into existence on October 24, 1945, has its main headquarters in New York City and subsidiary headquarters in Geneva, Switzerland, and offices in Vienna, Austria. While its primary goal is peace and security, it tried to differentiate itself from the League of Nations (q.v.) that it succeeded by stressing welfare concerns as well. Although membership has grown from 50 to over 184 countries, the major organs remain the same as those stipulated in the UN Charter: General Assembly (q.v.), Security Council (q.v.), International Court of Justice (ICJ) (q.v.), Secretariat (headed by the secretary-general) (q.v.), Economic and Social Council (ECOSOC) (q.v.), and Trusteeship Council (q.v.). All members of the UN are members of the General Assembly, where each has one vote. The Security Council consists of five "permanent members" (P-5) (q.v.) (although proposals abound for increasing the number), each with a veto—China, France, Russia (having replaced the USSR), the United Kingdom, and the United States—and the nonpermanent members, elected by the General Assembly and not eligible for immediate reelection. The official languages of the UN are Arabic, Chinese, English, French, Russian, and Spanish.

United Nations Capital Development Fund (UNCDF). Established in 1966 after five years of preparatory discussion, UNCDF is charged with making grants and long-term loans, at concessionary rates, to very poor countries. The focus of its loan program has been on low-income groups in the least developed countries (q.v.). The administrator of the United Nations Development Program (UNDP) (q.v.) acts as the fund's managing director.

United Nations Center for Human Rights. Not to be confused with the UN Commission on Human Rights (q.v.), the center has, since its founding in 1982, served as the focal point of the United Nations in the field of human rights (q.v.). It assists in the drafting of human rights "legislation" for the UN and follows up and prepares reports on the implementation of human rights. There are, at times, subsequent on-site investigations.

United Nations Center for Human Settlements (UNCHS) (also known as HABITAT). Established in 1978 by the General Assembly (q.v.) as the secretariat to the UN Commission on Human Settlements (q.v.) that, in turn, had succeeded the Committee on Housing, Building and Planning. The center assists countries in solving their habitation problems, especially focusing on the problem of homelessness. It does this by directing funds from the United Nations Development Program (UNDP) (q.v.) to places of need. It was also instrumental in the organization of the second global HABITAT conference that was held in Istanbul, Turkey, in June 1996. Although HABITAT II ran longer than expected, there was no agreement on a number of key issues. The most ambitious goal was the development of a housing treaty. HABITAT I had been held in Vancouver, Canada, in 1976.

United Nations Commission on Crime Prevention and Criminal Justice. The commission was established in 1992, as one of the functional (q.v.) commissions of the Economic and Social Council (ECOSOC) (q.v.). As such, it provides the United Nations (UN) (q.v.) with advice on how to prevent crime. It has focused on organized and transnational criminal activities.

United Nations Commission on Human Rights. This is one of the functional (q.v.) agencies established to assist and report to the Economic and Social Council (ECOSOC) (q.v.). It is responsible for developing recommendations and reports based on alleged violations of human rights (q.v.) and fundamental freedoms. The commission's mandate allows it to appoint special rapporteurs to investigate allegations in particular countries. This has been done in such places as Afghanistan, Chile, El Salvador, Iran, and Romania. Major areas of work have included civil rights, the status of women (q.v.), and freedom of information. Specific recommendations have been developed with regard to so-called disappearances, summary executions and other forms of torture, and religious intolerance. The commission is generally given high marks for its work in standard setting but less praise for the much more difficult task of policy implementation and change. Its major accomplishments include the promulgation of the Universal Declaration of Human Rights (q.v.) (1948) and the Covenants on Civil and Political Rights and on Economic, Social, and Cultural Rights (1966). More routinely, the commission hears testimony from both its own investigators and nongovernmental organizations on charges of gross violations of human rights. See also Roosevelt, Eleanor.

United Nations Commission on Human Settlements. Established in 1978 as the successor to the United Nations Committee on Human Housing, Building, and Planning, the commission's main focus is on homelessness. It hopes to alleviate this problem through the Global Strategy for Shelter by the Year 2000 that was adopted by the United Nations General Assembly (q.v.) in 1988. Accordingly, it funds ongoing technical assistance programs in almost 100 countries. The United Nations Center for Human Settlements (UNCHS) (q.v.) is the secretariat that services the commission.

United Nations Commission on International Trade Law (UNCI-TRAL). UNCITRAL was established by the General Assembly (q.v.) in 1966 to facilitate international trade (q.v.) through "the promotion and progressive harmonization and unification of the law of international trade." Accordingly, this organization, based in Vienna, Austria, prepares and promotes the adoption of new international conventions and model laws. It also monitors the legal development of international law on the municipal level.

United Nations Commission on Narcotic Drugs. This is one of the functional (q.v.) agencies established to assist and report to the UN Economic and Social Council (ECOSOC) (q.v.). It is specifically charged with helping ECOSOC formulate policies on narcotic drugs. Its work has contributed to the codification of international narcotic law.

United Nations Commission on Sustainable Development (CSD). Established in 1993 as a functional agency of the UN Economic and Social Council (ECOSOC) (q.v.) pursuant to the United Nations Conference on Environment and Development (q.v.), the CSD is charged with implementing the conference's wide-ranging and ambitious Agenda 21 (q.v.). Its earliest work was on toxic chemicals, radioactive wastes, and the sustainable use of water, talking positively about the "polluter pays" principle.

United Nations Commission on the Status of Women. The commission was established in 1947 as the successor to the original subcommission by the same name. That was actually a sub-commission of the Commission on Human Rights (q.v.), which was one of the functional (q.v.) commissions of the United Nations Economic and Social Council (ECOSOC) (q.v.). Since 1946, an ECOSOC-designated functional commission in its own right, the commission has sought to advance the rights of women (q.v.) through monitoring, reviewing, and appraising implementation of various national, regional, and global strategies. While the rights of women in most parts of the world have made progress in the years since the commission's establishment, few credit international institutions and fewer still the commission.

The modest credit that is given to international institutions in this arena is usually reserved for the various global ad hoc conferences convened dealing with the rights of women, most notably those held in Mexico City (1975), Nairobi (1985), and Beijing (1995). In each of these instances, as with most global conferences, much of what was achieved occurred prior to the holding of the conference, as country delegations sought to be sure that they would not be embarrassed at the meetings themselves. For example, before the Mexico meetings, many Latin American states took steps to eliminate de jure inequality of women.

Critics of the commission contend, in retrospect, that it may have been a mistake to have women's human rights (q.v.) issues handled separate from other human rights issues, as this allowed them to be marginalized. One of the key consequences of the World Conference on Human Rights (q.v.) (held in Vienna, Austria, in June 1993) was to mainstream the handling of women's issues related to human rights. This has meant that the Commission on Human Rights, which has extensive mechanisms for monitoring the implementation of human rights treaties, has begun to concentrate on women's issues, leaving the Commission on the Status of Women to continue its focus on the role of women in economic development (q.v.), its chief concern since the 1960s.

United Nations Conference on International Organization (UNCIO). The formal name of the San Francisco Conference at which the United Nations (UN) (q.v.) Charter was formally written and adopted. From April 25 to June 26, 1945, almost 300 delegates hammered out the 111-article Charter of the United Nations. Among the more important changes made in the draft during the San Francisco meetings were several intended to accommodate some of the demands of smaller states, which saw the UN as a very hierarchical organization.

United Nations Conference on Environment and Development (UNCED) (also known as the Earth Summit or the Rio Conference). UNCED was held in Rio de Janeiro, Brazil, June 3–14, 1992. It adopted the Rio Declaration on Environment and Development, Agenda 21 (q.v.), an 800-page action program intended to orient environmental (q.v.) practices in the 21st century. It also opened for signature the Climate Change Convention, which addresses so-called "greenhouse" emissions including carbon dioxide; opened for signature the Convention on Biological Diversity; and agreed to a nonlegally binding statement of principles for a global consensus on the management, conservation, and sustainable development of all types of forests. This subsequently came to be called the missing Rio convention.

The Declaration or Charter of Sustainable Development, like UNCED as a whole, tried to reconcile the notions of environmental protection and economic development (q.v.). Nevertheless, some of the proposed measures aroused resistance in certain member states.

For example, the United States initially rejected the United Nations Convention on Biological Diversity (CBD), which aims to conserve biological species, genetic resources, habitats, and ecosystems; to ensure the sustainable use of biological materials; and to provide for the fair and equitable sharing of benefits derived from genetic resources. The United States contended that the treaty was not sufficiently attentive to the rights of intellectual property owners.

United Nations Conference on the Human Environment (UNCHE) (also known as the Stockholm Conference). The first global intergovernmental conference convened to address concerns with the threat of pollution and other environmental (q.v.) hazards. Convened in Stockholm, Sweden, in 1972, the conferees approved a plan for international action as well as agreeing to establish a new United Nations (UN) (q.v.) agency. This idea, which was quickly approved by the General Assembly (q.v.), resulted in the establishment of the United Nations Environmental Program (q.v.), the first major UN agency with its headquarters in the South—namely, Nairobi, Kenya.

United Nations Conference on the Law of the Sea (UNCLOS). See Law of the Sea Conferences. Three major conferences have been convened (1958, 1960, and 1974–1982). Their purposes have been to codify the law of the sea. LOS III resulted in a comprehensive treaty, which is now legally in force, in spite of long-standing opposition by advanced industrialized states, led by the United States. Their objections focused on the convention's provisions regarding deep-sea mining.

United Nations Conference on Trade and Development (UNCTAD). Over the opposition of the economically developed countries, especially the United States, UNCTAD was established on December 30, 1964, as a permanent organ of the United Nations (UN) General Assembly (q.v.). It convenes conferences about every four years. Its purpose is to develop world trade (q.v.) in a way that accelerates economic development (q.v.) (especially of less developed countries), including by provision of lower tariff rates for exports from poor countries and promotion of multilateral trade agreements.

For much of its early history, it was little more than these periodic conferences, at which the numerically dominant less developed country members called for increased foreign aid, lowered shipping insurance rates, and, more generally, revision of the world's trade rules in a way more sympathetic to the needs of the poor. UNCTAD's greatest achievement has been seen as its role as an articulator of the interests of the South. Its secretariat has also been credited with assisting economically less developed states in making their cases for various proposals put forth, including the so-called Common Fund (q.v.) and Integrated Program for Commodities (q.v.).

In recent years, however, especially with the global trend toward free trade and the establishment of the World Trade Organization (q.v.), some have argued that the organization has lost its purpose and direction. Still it takes considerable pride in its initiative leading to the establishment in 1996 of a Trust Fund for Least Developed Countries, to help them integrate into the world economy. Moreover, proponents contend that UNCTAD will have something of a "renaissance," owing to decisions reached at UNCTAD IX in April 1996. These included an agreement that its future work will be organized into four clusters: Globalization and Development Strategies; Investment, Technology, and Enterprise; International Trade and Commodities; and Services for Development and Trade Efficiency. See also Dadzie, Kenneth K. S.; Prebisch, Raúl; Prebisch Report.

United Nations Development Program (UNDP). Established in 1965 as a result of the United Nations General Assembly's (q.v.) decision to merge the Expanded Program of Technical Assistance (q.v.) (set up in 1949) with the Special Fund (set up in 1958). UNDP is chiefly a coordinating mechanism and funding source for most of the UN organs and affiliates engaged in strengthening human resources in economically less developed countries. Its headquarters are in New York City, but it has field offices in over 115 countries. UNDP is generally described as the world's largest agency for multilateral technical and preinvestment cooperation. See also Hoffman, Paul; Morse, Bradford.

United Nations Disarmament Commission (UNDC). Founded in 1952 as a consequence of the merging of two previous commissions (on atomic energy and conventional armaments), the UNDC, which includes all members of the United Nations, meets in New York City each year during the spring. It was formed, in part, to allow smaller states to participate in the arms control (q.v.) and disarmament deliberative process. Although unable to strongly influence the global arms control process, there have been instances in which the policies of the dominant military powers have shifted as a consequence of positions taken in the UN by militarily weaker powers.

United Nations Economic and Social Council (ECOSOC). ECOSOC is one of the six major organs of the United Nations (UN) (q.v.). It is responsible for serving as a central forum for the discussion and formulation of policies relating to global economic and social issues. Accordingly, ECOSOC undertakes studies, convenes global conferences, and (loosely) coordinates activities of the Specialized Agencies (q.v.) and other bodies such as the United Nations Development Program (UNDP) (q.v.), United Nations International Children's Emergency Fund (UNICEF) (q.v.), and United Nations High Commissioner for Refugees (UNHCR) (q.v.). It also influences the work of many nongovernmental organizations that have a consultative status. ECOSOC originally had 18 members, but, as the UN membership grew, it was increased in size to its current 54 in 1973. During most of its history, it held two sessions a year but in 1992 shifted to a single session of about five weeks.

ECOSOC's inability to have a significant impact on global economic and social issues has resulted in it being targeted in many UN reform proposals. Some members have suggested that it simply be abolished, although none is calling for the abolition of the many regional and functional commissions and subcommissions that report to it.

United Nations Educational, Scientific and Cultural Organization (UNESCO). A UN Specialized Agency (q.v.), UNESCO is charged with the promotion of intergovernmental collaboration through education, science, culture, and communications (q.v.). Its constitutive document stresses the belief that education is the means for preventing interstate war. By the nature of its mandate, including work in communications, culture, and education, UNESCO has long been accused of being overly politicized. This occurred first during the Korean War when it was portrayed as serving as an agent of the U.S. government. More recently it was criticized by the United States for being anti-Israeli, pro-Soviet, and biased toward the interests of the developing world, including in its position on the rights of states to restrict the dissemination of information. In 1984, the United States and the United Kingdom withdrew from UNESCO, alleging bureaucratic and managerial incompetence as well as politicization. Singapore also left, simply noting that it was no longer worth belonging to, as most of its policies served the countries in the South. In spite of a significant loss of revenue resulting from these departures, UNESCO continues to convene countless scientific congresses, and works to eradicate illiteracy and to safeguard the natural and built environment (q.v.).

The U.S. government has asserted that the changes within UNESCO now merit its rejoining but that it has to wait for the day when it has sufficient resources to pay for its arrears. With a new Labour majority in control of its government, the United Kingdom returned to the organization, effective July 1, 1997. See also Mayor, Federico.

United Nations Environment Program (UNEP). Established by the UN General Assembly (q.v.) in December 1972 in the aftermath of the United Nations Conference on the Human Environment (UNCHE) (q.v.), UNEP coordinates various programs related to improving the global environment (q.v.). But its greatest contribution, partly owing to necessity as UNEP's budget is quite small by UN standards, is generally taken to be its role in keeping environmental pollution toward the top of member countries' agendas and as a catalyst for action by other organizations. A governing council of 58 member states oversees UNEP. There are 16 seats for members from Africa, 13 for Asia, 6 for Eastern Europe, 13 for Western Europe and other states, and 10 for Latin America and the Caribbean. UNEP has its headquarters in Nairobi, Kenya. See also Strong, Maurice.

United Nations Fund for Drug Abuse Control (UNFDAC). UNFDAC is a trust fund established in 1971 by the UN secretary-general (q.v.). It has its headquarters in Vienna, Austria. Its chief function is to assist countries in complying with their obligations under international drug control treaties. It assists them by designing and implementing programs to combat the production, trafficking, and use of illicit drugs. UNFDAC supports programs of education and information, treatment and rehabilitation, crop replacement and agricultural diversification, research, and drug law enforcement.

United Nations General Assembly (UNGA). The General Assembly is one of the major UN organs, namely, its plenary body. Each member of the UN is entitled to five representatives, but only one votes. Decisions on substantive issues are passed by a simple majority or, if they have been designated as "important questions," by a two-thirds vote. According to the UN Charter, the General Assembly's powers are limited to passing nonbinding resolutions, thus its informal designation as the world's sounding board or debate chamber. The charter's only substantive limitation on topics to be debated by the General Assembly—it was not to discuss any question relating to any international conflict where the situation is currently being discussed by the Security Council (q.v.)—has been obviated by the so-called Uniting for Peace Resolution (q.v.).

The General Assembly holds regular annual sessions of about three months in duration but may meet in both special sessions and emergency sessions, each devoted to a single issue. Among its regular tasks, the assembly approves the UN budget, and chooses members of the Security Council, Economic and Social Council (ECOSOC) (q.v.), and the Trusteeship Council (q.v.). It shares with the Security Council the selection of the secretary-general (q.v.) and the judges of the International Court of Justice (ICJ) (q.v.). It also admits states to UN membership, upon receiving recommendations for membership from the Security Council. The General Assembly also has the leading role in proposing amendments to the UN Charter and has periodically established suborgans that report to it. These include the Office of the United Nations High Commissioner for Refugees (UNCHR) (q.v.), United Nations Conference on Trade and Development (UNCTAD) (q.v.), United Nations Institute for Training and Research (UNITAR) (q.v.), United Nations Disaster Relief Organization (UNDRO), United Nations International Children's Emergency Fund (UNICEF) (q.v.), and the United Nations Population Fund (UNFPA) (q.v.).

United Nations High Commissioner for Human Rights. In April 1994, the post of UN High Commissioner for Human Rights was created, pursuant to the UN General Assembly's (q.v.) decision in the preceding year. The first commissioner was José Ayala Lasso of Ecuador.

The idea for establishing such a post can be traced to the early days of the United Nations (q.v.). It was hoped that such a post would attract a skilled and vigorous champion of human rights who could integrate human rights (q.v.) concerns into the UN's field operations as well as coordinate the panoply of UN human rights activities. Ayala Lasso, who received credit for setting up field offices for monitoring and early warning purposes, was nonetheless criticized by human rights groups for not being active enough in pressing civil rights issues. He resigned midway through his term to become Ecuador's foreign minister. In June 1997, UN Secretary-General Kofi Annan (q.v.) named Irish President Mary Robinson as his successor. Robinson, the first woman elected to be president of Ireland, is an expert in European human rights law and is known as an early advocate of liberalizing Irish divorce and abortion laws and campaigned for the rights of homosexuals.

United Nations Industrial Development Organization (UNIDO). Over the opposition of economically developed states—particularly the United States—UNIDO became a UN Specialized Agency (q.v.), effective 1986. Before that, since 1966, it was an organ of the UN General Assembly (q.v.). Based in Vienna, Austria, UNIDO promotes industrial development. It achieves its ends by convening seminars, sponsoring studies and training programs, and, more generally, applying pressure on rich countries to facilitate the industrial development of less developed countries. Its principal organs are the General Conference and the Industrial Development Board.

Citing U.S. congressional opposition and budgetary considerations, in December 1995 the United States announced that it would no longer be a member of UNIDO after 1996. The United Kingdom has followed the U.S. lead, and other states are considering doing the same thing. This raises serious questions about the viability of the organization, widely recognized for recently making significant progress in reducing its staff and improving its management.

United Nations Institute for Training and Research (UNITAR). As its name implies, this institute, established by the UN General Assembly (q.v.), trains individuals for work in economic and social development (especially technical assistance) and in international negotiations (including work at UN missions and on UN delegations), and conducts studies related to the United Nations' (q.v.) mission.

United Nations International Children's Emergency Fund (UNICEF) (commonly known as the United Nations Children's Fund). Established by the UN General Assembly (q.v.) in 1946 to provide emergency supplies of food (q.v.), clothing, and medicine to destitute children (q.v.) in countries ravaged by World War II. UNICEF, which depends on contributions from governments, individuals, and organizations and on the charitable sale of greeting cards, provides material assistance to nursing mothers, adolescents, and needy children, especially in economically less developed countries. Recent priorities of UNICEF activity have included the administration of mass health (q.v.) campaigns against epidemics that strike young children, often conducted in conjunction with the World Health Organization (WHO) (q.v.); caring for young refugees (q.v.); and overcoming illiteracy among the young. Generally regarded as one of the UN's success stories, UNICEF was awarded the Nobel Peace Prize in 1965.

United Nations International Drug Control Program (UNIDCP). Established in 1991 as a consequence of the integration of the three former UN drug control units: Division of Narcotic Drugs, International Narcotics Control Board, and United Nations Drug Control Program. The goal of UNIDCP is to become the worldwide center of expertise and information on drug abuse. It works with other United Nations (UN) (q.v.) (and national government) organs to try to suppress illicit drug traffic and use. UNIDCP has served as the focal point for promoting the UN Decade against Drug Abuse (1991–2000).

United Nations Non-Governmental Liaison Service (NGLS). NGLS was established in 1975 to strengthen ties between nongovernmental organizations focusing on the area of economic development (q.v.) and the United Nations (UN) (q.v.). NGLS seeks to accomplish its goals, in part, through a publication series and by maintaining data-bases for nongovernmental organizations. It is widely seen as an ad-vocate of the South on development issues.

United Nations Population Fund (UNFPA) (formerly known as the Trust Fund for Population Activities, and the United Nations Fund for Population Activities). Established in 1967 as a trust fund; subsequently made a subsidiary body of the UN General Assembly (q.v.). The current name was adopted in 1987, but the former abbrevi-ation was retained. The fund assists governments in over 130 coun-tries in developing population goals and then funds programs to assist in their achievement. The fund's willingness to continue to provide funds to countries that allow abortions has led the U.S. Congress, initially under the Reagan administration, to cut off its financial sup-port. UNFPA is generally credited with assisting many governments in decreasing the rate of their population growth. Over 25 percent of international population assistance to developing countries (q.v.) is channeled through UNFPA.

United Nations Relief and Works Agency for Palestine Refugees in the Near East (UNRWA). The agency was set up in 1949 as a tempo-rary, nonpolitical body to help refugees (q.v.) who lost their homes and livelihood as a result of the Arab-Israeli conflict of 1948. UNRWA continues to this day to provide a wide range of social ser-vices, including education, training, and health (q.v.) to Palestinians in Jordan, Lebanon, Syria, and the Israeli-occupied territories of the West Bank and the Gaza Strip. Over two million refugees are regis-tered with the agency.

United Nations Research Institute for Social Development (UN-RISD). UNRISD was set up in 1963 as an autonomous body within the United Nations (UN) (q.v.) system, although it receives no sub-vention from the regular UN budget. Its research agenda focuses on issues of practical concern to economically developing countries (q.v.). For example, it has produced work on sustainable development and on the consequences of structural adjustment programs.

United Nations Secretariat. The secretariat is one of the six major organs of the United Nations (UN) (q.v.). The international civil ser-vants who comprise the secretariat serve under the direction of the secretary-general (q.v.). They are recruited internationally in accor-dance with the UN provision for "securing the highest standards of efficiency, competence, and integrity" with due regard to geographical distribution. The last provision differentiated UN secretariat recruitment from that of the League of Nations (q.v.). The UN goal was to garner insights from the world's diverse cultures and experiences. Charter principles also underscore the importance of these individuals' neutrality. The total staff of the secretariat numbers about 30,000, more than half of whom are assigned to field agencies. Under massive budgetary (and political) pressures to do so, throughout the 1980s and 1990s, the secretary-general has sought to implement administrative reforms: reorganizing, cutting staff, freezing salaries, offering competitive exams for lower-level positions, and establishing and empowering a UN inspector-general. One example of this reorganization was the establishment, in 1998, of the post of deputy secretary-general. Louise Fréchette of Canada was appointed as the first to hold the position.

United Nations secretary-general. The secretary-general is the chief administrative officer of the United Nations (UN) (q.v.). He or she is chosen by the UN General Assembly (q.v.) on the recommendation of the UN Security Council (q.v.). The secretary-general's term of office is five years; appointment to a second term is the norm. Many recommendations have been voiced lately to counter the trend in which the election process is increasingly politicized.

The secretary-general's power and influence are derived from a number of sources (and largely exceed those of the League of Nations' [q.v.] secretary-general): serving as the organization's chief administrative officer, under Article 99 having power to place before the Security Council items relating to peace and security, preparing the agenda for major UN organs, and compiling a budget and expending UN funds. The General Assembly chose Trygve Lie (q.v.) of Norway as the first secretary-general. See also Annan, Kofi; Boutros-Ghali, Boutros; Hammarskjöld, Dag; Pérez de Cuéllar, Javier; Thant, U; Waldheim, Kurt.

United Nations Security Council. The principal organ of the United Nations (UN) (q.v.) chiefly responsible for maintaining international peace (q.v.) and security. It is composed of five permanent members (the P-5 [q.v.])—China, France, Russia (replacing the USSR), the United Kingdom, and the United States—and 10 nonpermanent members, with five elected each year by the General Assembly (q.v.) for two-year terms and not eligible for immediate reelection. According to a general understanding concerning the nonpermanent seats, Asia and Africa have five, Central Europe one, Latin America two, and Western Europe two. Any state that is not a member of the Security Council may be invited to participate in the council's deliberations if it is a party to the dispute under consideration.

A member directly involved in a dispute must abstain from voting when questions concerning peaceful settlement are brought to a vote. Voting decisions in the Security Council are made by vote of any nine members of the council on procedural matters. On substantive questions, however, the minimum of nine cannot adopt the measure if one of the permanent members casts a negative vote. It can abstain. Unlike the General Assembly, the Security Council is empowered to take actions that all members are obliged to carry out. Such actions can include the imposition of economic sanctions or even the deployment of military troops (so-called Chapter VII activities).

United Nations Special Committee against Apartheid. The United Nations Special Committee against Apartheid was established in 1962, initially as the Special Committee on the Policies of Apartheid of the Government of South Africa, then the United Nations Special Committee on Apartheid. The current title was adopted in 1974. The committee is given considerable credit for keeping apartheid on the United Nations' (q.v.) and thus the globe's agenda. It did this, in part, by sponsoring UN resolutions and reporting on what was learned on the basis of site visits.

United Nations Special Committee on the Situation with Regard to the Implementation of the Declaration on the Granting of Independence to Colonial Countries and Peoples (also known as the Committee of Twenty-Four or the Special Committee). The Special Committee was set up in 1961 pursuant to the passage, by the UN General Assembly (q.v.), of the landmark United Nations Declaration on the Situation with Regard to the Implementation of the Declaration on the Granting of Independence to Colonial Countries and Peoples (q.v.). The committee is credited by many with keeping the UN's attention, for several decades, focused on decolonization as a high-priority concern and thus with accelerating the pace of decolonization. The committee often formulated UN General Assembly resolutions. More recently, it has been under pressure to vote itself out of office, something its members have steadfastly refused to do. There remain 17 countries before the committee, most of which are not seeking independence: American Samoa, Anguilla, Bermuda, the British Virgin Islands, the Cayman Islands, East Timor, the Falklands, Gibraltar, Guam, Montserrat, New Caledonia, Pitcairn, Tokelu, Turks and Caicos, St. Helena, the United States Virgin Islands, and the Western Sahara.

United Nations University (UNU). Established by the UN General Assembly (q.v.) in 1973 and based in Tokyo, Japan, the UNU links together scholars throughout the world to work on research projects of relevance to the United Nations (UN) (q.v.) agenda. None of the UNU's funding comes from the UN's regular budget. The Japanese government donated its headquarters.

United Nations Volunteers (UNV). Established in 1970 by the UN General Assembly (q.v.), this program involves approximately 2,000 field workers on two-year contracts in more than 100 developing countries (q.v.). Emphasis has been placed on the economically least developed countries (q.v.). Although the volunteers are highly qualified within their specialties, they receive only modest stipends. The largest project to date, involving 400 volunteers, was election supervision in Cambodia in 1992–1993.

Uniting for Peace Resolution. Adopted by the UN General Assembly (q.v.) in 1950, the resolution allows that body to take action if the UN Security Council (q.v.), because of a lack of unanimity of its permanent members, fails to act against an aggressor. The resolution was passed because of fear by the United States and its allies that the Soviet Union would prevent effective Security Council action in response to the North Korean invasion of South Korea. Critics of the resolution see it as amending the UN charter without going through the charter's amendment processes.

Universal Declaration of Human Rights. This is a UN General Assembly (q.v.) proclamation declared on December 10, 1948. It was passed by a vote of 48–8–0 (six Eastern European members, Saudi Arabia, and South Africa voted against it). The declaration—which was explicitly declared *not* to be binding international law at the time of its adoption—proclaims that people everywhere are humans entitled to a wide range of human rights (q.v.). Five decades later, it is generally believed (and has been attested to by municipal and international courts) that many of its items have subsequently become legally binding through the process of customary international law. Others remain only aspirations. See also Roosevelt, Eleanor.

Universal Postal Union (UPU). A UN Specialized Agency (q.v.) since 1948, the UPU's origins can be traced back to the Bern Treaty of 1874. In addition to solving the many dilemmas of international mail (who collects the fee, on what basis it is charged, etc.), the UPU has evolved into an effective technical assistance agency helping countries with the development of cost-effective, expeditious mail-handling systems. Its headquarters are in Bern, Switzerland.

Urquhart, Sir Brian E. (1919–   ). A British public servant who served longer in the UN Secretariat (q.v.) (1946–1986) than any other person. His responsibilities included overseeing peacekeeping (q.v.) operations. Since leaving the UN, he has been an articulate spokesperson for UN (especially secretariat) reform.

Uruguay Round. The largest trade negotiation ever, the (Punta del Elste) Uruguay round took seven and half years (1986–1994), almost twice the original schedule. The 125 countries negotiated in this General Agreement on Tariffs and Trade (GATT) (q.v.) sponsored negotiation that covered almost all trade, from toothbrushes to pleasure boats, from banking to telecommunications, from the genes of wild rice to AIDS treatments. Among the key elements of the final accord were agreements on the creation of the World Trade Organization (WTO) (q.v.) and on some aspects of services and intellectual property.

V

Volunteers in Technical Assistance (VITA). Founded in 1959 and operating with more than 500 volunteers in developing countries (q.v.), VITA aims to make available to individuals and groups in economically developing countries a variety of information and technical resources aimed at fostering self-sufficiency. Its recent activities have included communications (q.v.) technology. It also runs Disaster Information Resources Program. VITA's headquarters are in Arlington, Virginia.

W

Waldheim, Kurt (1918–   ). Waldheim was the fourth secretary-general (q.v.) of the United Nations (UN) (q.v.), serving from 1972 to 1981. Waldheim was a prominent Austrian politician both prior to his service in the UN (including as foreign minister) and subsequent to it (including as president). Waldheim's major accomplishments in the office were in the field of quiet diplomacy (q.v.). He assisted in the development of a number of peacekeeping (q.v.) operations in the Middle East and played an active (yet ultimately unsuccessful) role in trying to negotiate a solution to the Cyprus problem. While generally supportive of third world demands for a New International Economic Order (q.v.), little significant progress in redressing economic (and political) inequities was made during his term in office. Subsequent to his service in the UN, serious questions were raised about his role in World War II, and specifically possible connections with German war crimes in Yugoslavia and Greece. His own autobiographical writings had made no mention of the activities that came to the surface in the mid-1980s.

War Resisters International (WRI). With its headquarters in Brussels, Belgium, WRI is an international nongovernmental organization that traces its origins to 1921. It is dedicated to the struggle for peace (q.v.) throughout the world. It does this by assisting pacifists, conscientious objectors, and peace organizations in their work for peace, social choice, the abolition of conscription, and disarmament (q.v.). It has affiliates in almost 20 countries.

Warsaw Treaty Organization (WTO) (also known as the Warsaw Pact). A now-defunct regional military alliance established in 1955 to ensure joint defense of Central and Eastern Europe. From its origins, its members—Albania, Bulgaria, Czechoslovakia, the German Democratic Republic (East Germany), Hungary, Poland, Romania, and the Soviet Union—contended that it was simply meant as a counter to the North Atlantic Treaty Organization (NATO) (q.v.) and that it would close up shop as soon as NATO did. In fact, it was abolished in 1991 as a consequence of the collapse of the Soviet Union and the velvet revolutions in Central and Eastern Europe. Before that, Albania had left (in 1968), and the East German membership ended when that country ceased to exist. Throughout its 35-year existence, it was dominated by the Soviet Union.

Weighted voting. While equality of voting (each sovereign state getting an equal vote) is the general principle for voting in intergovernmental organizations, it is not the only voting principle operating. In some institutions, a distribution of voting rights that more accurately reflects differences in power or national interests operates. Oftentimes, this pattern of distribution is referred to as weighted voting. For example, in some organizations whose primary function is the handling of money, such as members of the World Bank Group (q.v.) and the International Monetary Fund (q.v.), voting power is governed by amount of contribution. In councils established by international commodity agreements (q.v.), votes are often allocated according to the volume of imports and exports of a commodity. In the Central Commission for the Navigation of the Rhine (q.v.), voting rights are roughly proportional to river frontage. In other organizations, where this sort of weighted voting is not acceptable, differences among members are often recognized by the creation of special executive or deliberative bodies of limited membership. The UN Security Council (q.v.) is the most prominent of these.

West African Development Bank (Banque Ouest Africaine de Développement). Established in 1973, with operations beginning in 1976, the West African Development Bank aims to increase the chances of balanced development through, in part, economic cooperation and integration (q.v.). It does this through loans, some at unusually low interest rates. Priority is on projects in the least developed countries (q.v.) that are members and rural development programs, including village water supplies.

Western European Union (WEU). The WEU, an organization concerned with European defense matters, was established in 1955 after the French rejection of the European Defense Community (EDC) (q.v.). Moribund throughout much of its history, the WEU has been revived of late because of the presence of France as a full member and the absence of the United States. Thus, it was looked on as a possible alternative or complement to the North Atlantic Treaty Organization (NATO) (q.v.) and to the European Community's (EC) (q.v.) defense and foreign policy activities. This was especially so because it lacks NATO's problem with coordinating actions out-of-area (i.e., beyond the area specifically called for in its constitutive document). The WEU worked with NATO during the Iran-Iraq War and the Gulf War. It was much less successful in dealing with problems related to the former Yugoslavia.

The WEU's Parliamentary Assembly is purely consultative, providing recommendations to the council. Under the Maastricht Treaty (q.v.), the WEU became an integral part of the European Union (EU) (q.v.), essentially the institution through which the EU is to implement its Common Foreign and Security Policy (CFSP). Accordingly, the WEU now has four membership categories: full members, which are members of both the EU and NATO; associate members, which include European members of NATO but that are not members of the EU; observers, which (except for Denmark) are traditionally neutral countries, and are members of the EU but not NATO; and associate partners, which are countries that have concluded "Europe Agreements" with the EU—that is, those Central and Eastern European countries that intend to become EU members. This complicated membership arrangement underscores why many suspect that the WEU will remain organizationally distinct from the EU. On the other hand, the transfer of the WEU's Permanent Council from London to Brussels was seen as both a substantively and symbolically meaningful occurrence.

Witteveen, Henrikus Johannes (1921–). Witteveen is a Dutch economist and politician who served as managing director of the International Monetary Fund (IMF) (q.v.) from 1973 to 1978, the years when the international monetary system was under particular stress owing to massive increases in the price of oil. Witteveen's initiatives, which came to be connected with his name (i.e., the Witteveen facility), included increasing access to IMF funds to cope with the balance of payments deficits connected to the increase in the price of barrels of oil.

Wolfensohn, James (1933–   ). Following a successful career as a Wall Street investment executive, he became president of the World Bank (q.v.) in June 1995. His announced intention was to change the way the bank did its work. Taking a cue from business, he focused on learning from the bank's clients in ways that would make the bank more efficient and effective. Wolfensohn has invested heavily in staff training and accelerated the loan approval process. Critics wonder what his substantive vision is for the bank's future.

Women. Issues relating to women have long been on the agendas of international organizations, including the International Labour Organisation (ILO) (q.v.) and the United Nations Commission on the Status of Women (q.v.). But rarely were they treated as high-priority items. Even after three United Nations-convened conferences on the status of women, there still is no high-level UN institution focusing on women.

Attention on the regional level has also been slow in coming. Notable strides in addressing issues of gender inequality have been taken in the European Union (q.v.) and the Organization of American States (OAS) (q.v.). But significant, persistent and ongoing attention to the rights of women, including those in the third world, has only been evidenced by international nongovernmental organizations, like Development Alternatives with Women for New Era (DAWN) (q.v.). See also Inter-American Commission of Women; International Federation of University Women; International Federation of Women Lawyers; International Research and Training Institute for the Advancement of Women; Women's International Information and Communication Service; World Young Women's Christian Association.

Women's International Information and Communication Service (ISIS). The ISIS is a resource and documentation center. It was set up in 1974 by a collective of women (q.v.) to gather materials from local women's groups and the feminist movement and to make these resources available to other women. The ISIS, which has its headquarters in Geneva, Switzerland, coordinates the International Feminist

Network (IFN), a communication channel through which women can mobilize international support for each other.

Woods, George (1901–1982). Although Woods's presidency at the World Bank (q.v.) (1963–1968) is often ignored because of the much greater personal fame of his successor—Robert S. McNamara (q.v.)—and the greater growth of the bank during the McNamara years, many of the dramatic changes for which the McNamara years at the bank are known were actually presaged by actions taken during the latter part of Woods's term. In part, this is because Woods was the first World Bank president who headed not simply the International Bank for Reconstruction and Development but also the International Finance Corporation (q.v.) and, most importantly, the International Development Association (q.v.) (established in 1960). In part, it is because Woods was nominated for the job by President Kennedy as part of Kennedy's plans for transforming and expanding foreign assistance.

Woods came to the World Bank with years of successful experience in the private banking sector but also with some international experience, owing to overseas missions he had gone on for his predecessor, Eugene Black (q.v.). Under Woods's leadership, the bank began to serve a new constituency, the third world. It also moved beyond its traditional "bricks and mortar" type loans. It is probably not inaccurate to say that under Woods's leadership the World Bank was transformed from a relatively passive investment organization, owned by many governments, to a development assistance institution that actively sought more and better ways to assist economically less developed countries throughout the world.

World Administrative Radio Conference (WARC). WARC is the conference regularly convened by the International Telecommunication Union (q.v.) to allocate and regulate radio frequencies for the purposes of television and radio broadcasting, data communications, navigation, maritime and aeronautical communication, and satellite broadcasting. Third world countries have strongly protested the traditional "first come, first served" principle of frequency allocation, which they claim privileges the already technologically advanced.

World Alliance of Young Men's Christian Associations (YMCA). Founded in 1855, the World Alliance is a confederation of national YMCAs in 60 countries. The World Alliance, which has its headquarters in Geneva, Switzerland, sponsors activities in the fields of education, recreation, sports, special programs (homeless children, delinquent youth, etc.), Bible studies, and religious activities.

World Bank (formally the International Bank for Reconstruction and Development, IBRD). The World Bank is a United Nations (UN) (q.v.) Specialized Agency (q.v.) created to provide capital for rebuilding countries devastated by World War II and for development programs in economically less developed countries. It was established at Bretton Woods in 1944 and began operation in 1946. It makes loans for projects and relies for its funding on its ability to borrow in the international capital markets and to secure contributions from member states. The voting power of its members is proportionate to their capital subscriptions (i.e., weighted voting [q.v.]). The World Bank has made 3,000 loans totaling over $150 billion. Loan decisions are ostensibly made on economic criteria alone. See also Black, Eugene; Bretton Woods System; McNamara, Robert S.; Preston, Lewis T.; Wolfensohn, James; Woods, George.

World Bank Group. The World Bank Group is composed of five organizations: the International Bank for Reconstruction and Development (IBRD), commonly called the World Bank (q.v.), the International Development Association (IDA) (q.v.), the International Finance Corporation (IFC) (q.v.), the Multilateral Investment Guarantee Agency (MIGA) (q.v.), and the International Centre for Settlement of Investment Disputes (ICSID) (q.v.).

World Confederation of Labor (WCL). Founded in Brussels, Belgium, in 1920 as the International Federation of Christian Trade Unions (IFCTU), the confederation went out of existence in 1940 owing, in part, to the suppression of unions by fascist Germany and Italy. But it was reconstituted after the war and changed its name to World Confederation of Labor in 1968. The WCL claims more than 21 million members in 102 countries. It now has Protestant, Buddhist, and Muslim member confederations as well as its mainly Roman Catholic members. Most members are in Western Europe and Latin America, although there are a small number in Africa and Asia.

World Conference on Human Rights. Convened in Vienna, Austria, June 14–25, 1993, almost 7,000 participants attended the conference including representatives of more than 800 nongovernmental organizations. Its final document, the Vienna Declaration and Programme of Action for Human Rights, called for the establishment of a High Commissioner for Human Rights (q.v.), the appointment of a Special Rapporteur on Violence against Women, and the universal ratification, by 1995, of the Convention on the Rights of the Child. It also recommended the proclamation by the UN General Assembly (q.v.) of an international decade of the world's indigenous peoples.

World Council of Churches (WCC). This Geneva-based nongovernmental organization was formally constituted in 1948. Its goal is to promote cooperation among Christian churches and to clarify the bases for unity among churches. It is open to all churches that acknowledge "the Lord Jesus as God and savior according to the Scriptures and therefore seek to fulfill together their common calling to the glory of one God, Father, Son and Holy Spirit." The WCC has 335 member churches in over 100 countries. Although the Roman Catholic Church is not a member, it does possess observer status at the WCC's meetings.

World Court. See International Court of Justice.

World Federalist Movement. Begun in 1946 in Luxembourg, the movement now has national organizations in 17 countries. Its goal is world governance through the rule of international law, developed by an international legislature. It militates in favor of world peace (q.v.) and supports United Nations (UN) (q.v.) efforts seen to be leading in that direction. On the other hand, it supports revision of the UN Charter to enhance that organization's ability to deal with global conflict and poverty.

World Federation of Trade Unions (WFTU). Headquartered in Prague, the Czech Republic (formerly in Paris) and established in 1945, this organization has as its goal to consolidate and unite trade unions (q.v.) throughout the world. It currently has over 90 million members in 119 countries and territories. Before 1989, most of its members were in Central and Eastern Europe. Because of its connections for some time with the World Peace Council—seen by some as a communist front organization—it has had difficult relations with some "capitalist" labor unions, such as the American Federation of Labor.

World Food Council (WFC). Established by the UN General Assembly (q.v.) in 1974, the WFC seeks to raise the political priority of food (q.v.) and hunger issues, to coordinate food assistance, and to assist in the defining of an international food policy that can promote food security.

World Food Programme (WFP). Established by the UN General Assembly (q.v.) in 1961 and jointly sponsored by the UN and the Food and Agricultural Organization (FAO) (q.v.), the WFP provides emergency relief in the form of food (q.v.). The initial plan was to establish a system that would redistribute agricultural surpluses. Now, member countries make voluntary contributions of commodities, cash, and services (especially shipping) to the program. Food aid is provided, primarily, to people in low-income, food-deficit countries and to those suffering from disaster, whether natural or caused by human beings. The program is regarded as one of the most successful involving the United Nations (UN) (q.v.), although some scholars express concern about the long-term effects of food aid on countries' achievement of food self-sufficiency. If they know they can get multilateral aid when they need it, food prices may be suppressed and governments may not provide sufficient funds to get their own agricultural industries working.

World Health Organization (WHO). A United Nations (UN) (q.v.) Specialized Agency (q.v.) since 1948, the WHO is one of the largest international organizations. It is headquartered in Geneva, Switzerland. Its primary goal is to help countries strengthen their health (q.v.) systems by increasing an awareness of health needs and services and by creating and developing health institutions, referral systems and technology. The WHO sponsors conferences and research. For the past decade, many of its human and financial resources have been focused on coping with the AIDS pandemic, not least of all getting governments to admit its existence as a problem. Its goal (which no one really believes is wholly achievable) is Health for All by the Year 2000.

World Intellectual Property Organization (WIPO). Established as a United Nations (UN) (q.v.) Specialized Agency (q.v.) in 1974, the origins of WIPO can be traced back to the 1883 Paris Convention for the Protection of Industrial Property and the 1886 Bern Convention for the Protection of Literary and Artistic Works. WIPO's sometimes controversial mission is to harmonize policies concerning proprietary rights so that knowledge can be effectively shared, widely used, and fairly compensated. Just how contentious and important this can be was underscored in 1996 when it adopted treaties to crack down on the flow of unauthorized information over electronic data networks. WIPO also assists economically less developed countries through the transfer of technology. One of WIPO's most important achievements has been in standard setting and international registration.

World Meteorological Organization (WMO). A United Nations (UN) (q.v.) Specialized Agency (q.v.) since 1957, the WMO traces its origins back to the International Meteorological Organization (IMO) set up in 1873. Headquartered in Geneva, Switzerland, the WMO is charged with coordinating activities to ensure reliable weather data. Its supreme body is the World Meteorological Congress that meets every four years. Its current agenda, which is oriented around the

World Weather Watch, includes attention to issues related to global warming and the use of space-based observation systems and satellite communications.

World Summit for Social Development (also known as the People's Summit). Convened in Copenhagen, Denmark, March 6–12, 1995. The ambitious goal of this conference was to find a way to make extreme poverty seem as intolerable to the 21st century as slavery has become to the 20th. Stated otherwise, it aimed to find the means for eradicating poverty in the world by finding the way for everyone to attain secure and sustainable livelihoods through freely selected work.

World Tourism Organization (WTO). Established as an intergovernmental organization in 1975, the WTO replaced an international non-governmental organization, the International Union of Official Travel Organizations (IUOTO) that had been in place for the previous five decades. WTO's purpose is to promote world tourism (q.v.) as a means to economic development (q.v.). It is the only intergovernmental organization whose activities cover all aspects of tourism on a worldwide basis. In seeking to achieve its goal, it provides economically developing countries (q.v.) with technical assistance, including that related to providing security to tourists. More than 120 countries belong to the organization, whose headquarters are in Madrid. One of its members' key preoccupations is drafting of a treaty to facilitate international travel and tourist stays. Affiliate membership in the WTO is open to organizations from all tourism-related sectors. Affiliate members include airlines and other transportation companies, hotels and restaurants, tour operators and travel organizations, educational institutions, and other tourism industry interests in 70 countries.

World Trade Organization (WTO). The WTO was established effective January 1, 1995, in accordance with agreement at the Uruguay Round (q.v.) of the General Agreement on Tariffs and Trade (GATT) (q.v.). Its purpose is to replace the GATT with a more permanent, structured and effective organization with the same goals, liberalizing and expanding world trade (q.v.). Accordingly, it is responsible for administering multilateral trade agreements negotiated by its members, in particular the GATT, the General Agreement on Trade in Services (GATS), and the Agreement on Trade-Related Intellectual Property Rights (TRIPs). The WTO itself does not embody substantive rules regarding government policies. It is a formal institutional structure under whose auspices member states negotiate and implement treaty agreements. The WTO's basic underlying philosophy is that of open markets and the belief that nondiscrimination and competition in global trade are conducive to the national welfare of all countries.

World Vision International. World Vision International was founded in 1950 as an international nongovernmental organization aimed at assisting children (q.v.) and their families by providing emergency relief, developing self-reliance, and strengthening leadership. This is done largely by providing training programs in community and child-focused development projects in less developed countries. World Vision International has its headquarters in Monrovia, California.

World Wide Fund for Nature (WWF). Initially called the World Wildlife Fund, a name it still uses in North America, the WWF began its activities in 1951. Based in Geneva, Switzerland, the WWF's basic purpose has been conservation, that is, to stop and eventually to reverse the degradation of the Earth's natural environment. It focuses its efforts on projects such as sustainable forestry and reducing greenhouse gas emissions. WWF promotes the conservation of the ecosystem and biodiversity. Much of its impact has been at the local level.

World Young Women's Christian Association (YWCA). Founded in 1894, the association coordinates its affiliates in more than 100 countries from its headquarters in Geneva, Switzerland. It holds international and regional conferences and studies social and economic questions, especially those concerned with the status of women (q.v.) and youth, family, migration, and interracial relationships.

Wörner, Manfred (1934–1994). Before becoming secretary-general of the North Atlantic Treaty Organization (NATO) (q.v.), a post he held from 1988 to 1994, Wörner was the speaker of the German Federal Parliament and German minister of defense. During his leadership at NATO, the Germanies reunited and the Soviet Union imploded. He was an early supporter of opening up NATO to Central and European states and worked to ease NATO's transition into the post–Cold War era. The most frustrating moments on his watch were those related to NATO's reaction to fighting in the former Yugoslavia. He died of cancer before the fighting had ceased.

Y

Yaoundé Conventions. The conventions were a series of trade agreements between the European Economic Community (q.v.) and 18 African countries. The first was signed in Yaoundé, Cameroon, on July 20, 1963. They were superseded by the Lomé Conventions (q.v.).

Bibliography

The topic of international organizations is enormous, especially when it is defined as in this work, namely, including international nongovernmental organizations. Accordingly, it was necessary to establish some guiding principles for inclusion and exclusion of works in the bibliography that follows.

The first principle that was adhered to relates to inaccessibility. This bibliography is restricted to books, and, for the most part, they are secondary sources. The reason for omitting journal articles and for not focusing on the publications by international organizations (including so-called house organs) is because those materials are becoming increasingly accessible, especially by the use of electronic databases and those produced on CD-ROM. What the electronic finding guides have not done as well is to list books and bibliographies of books in the field, which therefore is the focus here.

The second principle is to focus on recent works, partly because of the emphasis in this series. Thus, for example, the key works on the League of Nations and on the founding of the United Nations are included, as are some works that cover the origins of the various organs of what is now the European Union. However, there is much more coverage on the UN of the 1990s and the contemporary European Union. This principle also reflects the fact that many of the bibliographies cited in this book and the recent books included here have bibliographies of their own that include older works. Thus, if the intent of the reader is to get access to a broader listing than contained here, then this bibliography can assist that reader in taking the first step down that path as well.

The third principle is to focus on works from a variety of ideological perspectives. Admittedly, limiting the bibliography to works published in English is somewhat in tension with this principle, but great efforts were expended to include works that are both supportive and critical of various international organizations. The works on the World Bank and the International Monetary Fund illustrate this, as well as those on the major organs of the UN.

The fourth principle relates to the breadth of coverage. Especially in the section on regional organizations, as wide a variety of organizations as possible was covered. In some instances, that has meant that the coverage of some institutions is much thinner than of others; in other cases, organizations are only represented by relatively outdated works. Works on all international organizations go in spurts, but some institutions get much more attention than others. In addition, despite the emphasis on academic works, there are also included a number of works that interested laypersons will find of value.

Finally, the bibliography includes a number of general and classic works on international organization.

The following paragraphs highlight a few works from each section and explain why they are included and why particular attention was drawn to them.

The general works section of the bibliography includes both functionally specific works and those that transcend a single function. Included here, for example, is Inis Claude's classic text *Swords into Plowshares*. It provides an eloquent introduction to the subject of intergovernmental organizations. Other more recent texts are noted, including A. LeRoy Bennett's frequently revised and easy to read *International Organizations: Principles and Issues*. They should be turned to if the goal is up-to-date information especially on the United Nations, but none of these others has the breadth of coverage, historical and theoretical, that Claude's does. Also found in this section of the bibliography is David Mitrany's theoretical masterpiece, *A Working Peace System*. Its classic articulation of the notion of functionalism in international organization explains the particular faith that many put in the UN's Specialized Agencies and the various component parts of what is now the European Union. Ernst B. Haas's *Beyond the Nation State*, found in the section on Specialized Agencies because it includes an in-depth study of the International Labour Organisation, begins with an extended essay on neofunctionalism. It is the best statement of that refinement of Mitrany available anywhere. Haas's book also demonstrates the ability to write both an in-depth case study and a work of major theoretical import.

There is no single great book on the United Nations. Goodrich, Hambro, and Simons remains the definitive study of the UN Charter, however. And Gordenker and Rovine have provided essential works on the UN secretaries-general. Both are outdated, however, and must be supplemented by the many monographs, autobiographies, and biographies in the UN section of the bibliography. No biography is better done than Urquhart's of Hammarskjöld.

M. J. Peterson's work on the General Assembly is comprehensive but could use a revised edition. Fortunately, Bailey has published a revision of his work on the Security Council, as time had taken a larger toll on his work than on Peterson's. There are several recent works on the International Court of Justice, including a recent edition of Shabtai Rosenne. The bibliography is peppered with works on UN reform and with works on the specific functions of the UN, including human rights, gender equity and peacekeeping, including the UN's own recently revised work, *The Blue Helmets: A Review of United Nations Peace-keeping.*

There are, unfortunately, few works on the relationship between member countries and the UN. Krause and Knight's *State, Society and the UN System: Changing Perspectives on Multilateralism*; Alger, Lyons, and Trent's *The United Nations System and the Politics of Member States*; and Karns and Mingst's *The United States and Multilateral Institutions: Patterns of Changing Instrumentality and Influence* each in its own way begins to fill this gap. Krause and Knight also begin to address the UN from a state-society perspective, and Karns and Mingst offer some useful insights into often-overlooked United Nations Specialized Agencies.

When it was first published, everyone praised both the goal and execution of Cox and Jacobson's comparative and theoretically important work, *Anatomy of Influence*. Its focus was on power and influence within the UN's Specialized Agencies. In spite of its praise, no one has published a successor volume in the generation since. Instead most of the attention has been focused on a relatively few Specialized Agencies, particularly the Bretton Woods twins, the World Bank and the International Monetary Fund. Included in the bibliography are both "house" histories (Mason and Asher's and Kapur, Lewis and Webb's for the World Bank Group and Horsefield's and De Vries's for the IMF) and quite critical works, including Bruce Rich's on the World Bank's environmental record and the volume edited by Dharam Ghai on the IMF's practices of conditionality in its loans to the third world. Cheryl Payer's widely cited, quite critical works on both organizations are also noted here.

As the bibliography reflects, works on regional organizations—aside from the European Union and to a lesser extent NATO—are not too numerous. Even less frequent are works covering organizations from more than one region, much less comparing them. The most recent comparative regional works, *Regionalism and World Order* edited by Andrew Gamble and Anthony Payne, and *Regionalism in World Politics: Regional Organizations and International Order* edited by Louise Fawcett and Andrew Hurrell, include considerable information about international organizations in various regions of the world, but that is not their focus, much less their exclusive focus.

The early years of European economic integration are best approached by reading Ernst B. Haas's magisterial work, *The Uniting of Europe*. The study of economic integration in Europe and beyond is best pursued by reading the various chapters in *Regional Integration*, edited by Leon Lindberg and Stuart Scheingold. They provide useful insights into reasons for the unparalleled success of the Western European experiment. That is, they are useful for their theoretical insights rather than as up-to-date case studies. Details on the current state of integration in Europe are readily available from such standard works as Dennis Swann's *European Economic Integration*. While the regional section includes a number of useful works on NATO's origins, policy and process books seem to be timed to coincide with that organization's ten-year anniversaries. Thus, a spate of such works should be expected prior to the end of the century.

The section on non-UN, nonregional intergovernmental organizations includes the "must reads" about the League of Nations. F. P. Walters's definitive work, *A History of the League of Nations*, is where everyone should turn first. It is usefully supplemented, however, with F. S. Northedge's more recent *The League of Nations: Its Life and Times, 1920–1946*.

Scholarly attention has only recently returned to international nongovernmental organizations. But there are now two fine, relatively comprehensive works: Peter Willetts's *"The Conscience of the World"* and Leon Gordenker and Thomas G. Weiss's *NGOs, the UN, and Global Governance*. Both are edited volumes and, as such, provide a range of perspectives on nongovernmental organizations, but none as skeptical as David Hulme's books: *Beyond the Magic Bullet: NGO Performance and Accountability in the Post Cold War World* and a coedited volume (with Michael Edwards), *NGOs, States, and Donors: Too Close for Comfort*. Also included in the section on international nongovernmental organization are some monographs on individual organizations and those within a single issue area. Attention in the latter regard is drawn to *Ecological Resistance Movements*, edited by Bron Raymond Taylor. It takes up the organizations infrequently studied and rarely invited to global conferences.

Readers interested in further information on international organizations might refer to the more specialized volumes in the Historical Dictionaries of International Organization by Scarecrow Press, all of which are included in the relevant sections of the bibliography. These include books on aid and development organizations, the European Community, European organizations, inter-American organizations, international food agencies, international organizations in sub-Saharan Africa, multinational peacekeeping, UNESCO, the United Nations, refugee and disaster relief organizations, the World Bank, and the World Health Organization. In addition, mention is made of several volumes in the series on religions, philosophies and movements that provide information on related international organizations.

General Works on International Organizations

Works with No Specific Functional Focus

Ali, Sheikh Rustom. *The International Organizations and World Order Dictionary*. Santa Barbara, Calif.: ABC-Clio, 1992.

Amerasinghe, C. F. *Principles of the International Law of International Organizations*. Cambridge: Cambridge University Press, 1996.

Archer, Clive. *International Organizations*. 2nd ed. New York: Routledge, 1992.

Armstrong, David, Lorna Lloyd, and John Redmond. *From Versailles to Maastricht: International Organization in the Twentieth Century*. The Making of the Twentieth Century. New York: St. Martin's, 1996.

Armstrong, J. D. *The Rise of the International Organisation: A Short History*. New York: St. Martin's, 1982.

Arnold, Guy. *Historical Dictionary of Aid and Development Agencies*. International Organization Series No. 10. Lanham, Md.: Scarecrow, 1996.

Baer, George W. *International Organizations: A Guide to Research and Research Materials, 1918–1945*. Rev. ed. Wilmington, Del.: Scholarly Resources, 1991.

Bekker, Peter H. F. *The Legal Position of Intergovernmental Organizations: A Functional Necessity Analysis of Their Legal Status and Immunities*. Boston: Kluwer Law International, 1994.

Bennett, A. LeRoy. *International Organizations: Principles and Issues*. 6th ed. Upper Saddle River, N.J.: Prentice Hall, 1995.

Bertrand, Maurice, and Daniel Warner (Eds.). *A New Charter for a Worldwide Organisation?* Nijhoff Law Specials, Vol. 22. Boston: Kluwer Law International, 1997.

Chuang, Richard. *The IATA: A Case Study of a Quasi-Governmental Organization*. Leiden: Sitjhoff, 1972.

Claude, Inis L. *Swords into Plowshares: The Problems and Progress of International Organization*. 4th ed. New York: Random House, 1984.

Colas, Bernard (Ed.). *Global Economic Co-operation: A Guide to Agreements and Organizations*. 2nd ed. Tokyo: United Nations University Press, 1994.

Commission on Global Governance (Eds.). *Issues in Global Governance: Papers Written for the Commission on Global Governance*. Cambridge: Kluwer Law International, 1995.

Commission on Global Governance. *Our Global Neighborhood: The Report of the Commission on Global Governance*. New York: Oxford University Press, 1995.

Diehl, Paul F. (Ed.). *The Politics of Global Governance: International*

Organizations in an Interdependent World. Boulder, Colo.: Rienner, 1996.

Diehl, Paul F. (Ed.). *The Politics of International Organizations: Patterns and Insights.* Chicago: Dorsey, 1989.

Dijkzeul, Dennis. *The Management of Multilateral Organizations.* Boston: Kluwer Law International, 1997.

Feld, Werner J., and Robert S. Jordan. *International Organizations: A Comparative Approach.* 3rd ed. Westport, Conn.: Praeger, 1994.

Haas, Ernst B. *When Knowledge Is Power: Three Models of Change in International Organizations.* Berkeley: University of California Press, 1990.

Hajnal, Peter I. (Ed.). *International Information: Documents, Publications, and Information Systems of International Governmental Organizations.* 2nd ed. Englewood, Colo.: Libraries Unlimited, 1997.

Hirsch, Moshe. *Responsibility of International Organizations toward Third Parties: Some Basic Principles.* Boston: Nijhoff, 1995.

Jacobson, Harold K. *Networks of Interdependence: International Organizations and the Global Political System.* 2nd ed. New York: Knopf, 1984.

Jordan, Robert S. (Ed.). *International Administration: Its Evolution and Contemporary Applications.* New York: Oxford University Press, 1971.

Kaufman, Johan. *Conference Diplomacy: An Introductory Analysis.* Basingstoke Hants, England: Macmillan, 1996.

Kirgis, Frederic L., Jr. *International Organizations in Their Legal Setting.* 2nd ed. St. Paul, Minn.: West, 1993.

Louis-Jacques, Lyonette, and Jeanne S. Korman (Eds.). *Introduction to International Organizations.* Dobbs Ferry, N.Y.: Oceana, 1996.

Luard, Evan (Ed.). *The Evolution of International Organizations.* New York: Praeger, 1966.

Martin Martinez, Magdalena M. *National Sovereignty and International Organizations.* Legal Aspects of International Organizations, Vol. 25. Boston: Kluwer Law International, 1996.

Mitrany, David. *A Working Peace System: An Argument for the Functional Development of International Organizations.* London: Royal Institute of International Affairs, 1944.

Muller, A. Sam. *International Organizations and Their Host States: Aspects of Their Legal Relationship.* Boston: Kluwer Law International, 1996.

Murphy, Craig N. *International Organization and Industrial Change.* New York: Oxford University Press, 1994.

Sabel, Robbie. *Procedures at International Conferences: A Study of the Rules of Procedure of International Inter-Governmental Conferences.* Cambridge: Cambridge University Press, 1997.

Schechter, Michael G. (Ed.). *Future Multilateralism: The Political and Social Framework*. London: Macmillan for the United Nations University Press, 1998.

Schechter, Michael G. (Ed.). *Innovation in Multilateralism*. London: Macmillan for the United Nations University Press, 1998.

Schiavone, Giuseppe. *International Organizations: A Dictionary and Directory*. 3rd ed. New York: St. Martin's, 1993.

Schraepler, Hans-Albrecht. *Directory of International Organizations*. Washington, D.C.: Georgetown University Press, 1996.

White, Nigel. *The Law of International Organisations*. Studies in International Law. Manchester: Manchester University Press, 1996.

Yasutomo, Dennis. *The New Multilateralism in Japan's Foreign Policy*. New York: St. Martin's, 1995.

Functionally Specific General Works

Ball, Nicole, and Tammy Halevy. *Making Peace Work: The Role of the International Development Community*. Baltimore: Johns Hopkins University Press, 1996.

Bates, Robert H. *Open-Economy Politics: The Political Economy of the World Coffee Trade*. Princeton, N.J.: Princeton University Press, 1997.

Benedick, Richard E. *Ozone Diplomacy: New Directors in Safeguarding the Planet*. Cambridge: Oxford University Press, 1991.

Boczek, Boleslaw Adam. *Historical Dictionary of International Tribunals*. International Organization Series No. 5. Metuchen, N.J.: Scarecrow, 1994.

Bulterman, M. K., and M. Kuijer. *Compliance with Judgements of International Courts: Proceedings of the Symposium Organized in Honour of Professor Henry G. Schermers by Mordenate College and the Department of International Public Law of Leiden University*. Boston: Nijhoff, 1996.

Compa, Lance A., and Stephen F. Diamond (Eds.). *Human Rights, Labor Rights, and International Trade: Law and Policy Perspectives*. Philadelphia: University of Pennsylvania Press, 1996.

De Menil, Georges, and Anthony M. Solomon. *Economic Summitry*. New York: Council on Foreign Relations, 1983.

Docherty, James. *Historical Dictionary of Organized Labor*. Religions, Philosophies, and Movements Series No. 10. Lanham, Md.: Scarecrow, 1996.

Dunn, David H. (Ed.). *Diplomacy at the Highest Level: The Evolution of International Summitry*. New York: St. Martin's, 1996.

Esman, Milton J., and Telhami Shibley (Eds.). *International Organiza-*

tions and Ethnic Conflict. Ithaca, N.Y.: Cornell University Press, 1995.

Fani, Riccardo, and Enzo Grilli. *Multilateralism and Regionalism after the Uruguay Round.* New York: St. Martin's, 1997.

Ferris, Elizabeth G. (Ed.). *Refugees and World Politics.* New York: Praeger, 1985.

Finlayson, Jock A., and Mark W. Zacher. *Managing International Markets: Developing Countries and the Commodity Trade Regime.* New York: Columbia University Press, 1988.

Gorman, Robert F. *Historical Dictionary of Refugee and Disaster Relief Organizations.* International Organization Series No. 7. Metuchen, N.J.: Scarecrow, 1994.

Gorman, Robert F., and Edward Mihalkanin. *Historical Dictionary of Human Rights and Humanitarian Organizations.* Lanham, Md.: Scarecrow, 1997.

Haas, Peter M., Robert O. Keohane, and Marc A. Levy (Eds.). *Institutions for the Earth: Sources of Effective International Environmental Protection.* Cambridge, Mass.: MIT Press, 1993.

Jackson, John H. *The World Trading System: The Law and Policy of International Economic Relations.* Cambridge, Mass.: MIT Press, 1989.

Jönsson, Christer. *International Aviation and the Politics of Regime Change.* New York: St. Martin's, 1987.

Kahler, Miles. *International Institutions and the Political Economy of Integration.* Washington, D.C.: Brookings Institution, 1995.

Keohane, Robert O., and Marc A. Levy (Eds.). *Institutions for Environmental Aid: Pitfalls and Promise.* Cambridge, Mass.: MIT Press, 1996.

Khan, K. R. *The Law and Organization of International Commodity Agreements.* Dordrecht: Nijhoff, 1982.

Kimball, Lee. *Forging International Agreements: Strengthening Inter-Governmental Institutions for Environment and Development.* Washington, D.C.: World Resources Institute, 1992.

Leninza, Umberto, et al. *The Future of International Telecommunications: The Legal Regime of Telecommunications by Geostationary Orbit Satellite.* Dobbs Ferry, N.Y.: Oceana, 1992.

McCoubrey, Hilary, and Nigel D. White. *International Organizations and Civil Wars.* Brookfield, Vt.: Dartmouth, 1995.

Mikesell, Raymond F., and Lawrence F. Williams. *International Banks and the Environment, from Growth to Sustainability: An Unfinished Agenda.* San Francisco: Sierra Club Books, 1992.

Robertson, A. H. *Human Rights in the World: An Introduction to the Study of International Protection of Human Rights.* 3rd ed. New York: St. Martin's, 1990.

Smith, M. L. *International Regulation of Satellite Communication*. Dordrecht: Nijhoff, 1960.

Solomon, Robert. *The International Monetary System, 1945–1981*. New York: Harper & Row, 1982.

Stein, Robert. *Banking on the Biosphere? Environmental Procedures and Practices of Nine Multilateral Development Agencies*. Lexington, Mass.: Lexington, 1979.

Stienstra, Deborah. *Women's Movements and International Organizations*. New York: St. Martin's, 1994.

Suskind, Lawrence E. *Environmental Diplomacy: Negotiating More Effective Global Agreements*. New York: Oxford University Press, 1991.

Van der Bent, Ans Joachim. *Historical Dictionary of Ecumenical Christianity*. Religions, Philosophies, and Movements Series No. 3. Metuchen, N.J.: Scarecrow, 1994.

Wells, Edward R., and Alan M. Schwartz. *Historical Dictionary of North American Environmentalism*. Religions, Philosophies, and Movements Series No. 14. Lanham, Md.: Scarecrow, 1997.

United Nations (Major Organs)

General Works

Alger, Chadwick R., Gene M. Lyons, and John E. Trent (Eds.). *The United Nations and the Politics of Member States*. Tokyo: United Nations University, 1995.

Baehr, Peter R., and Leon Gordenker. *The United Nations in the 1990s*. 2d ed. New York: St. Martin's, 1994.

Bailey, Sydney D., and Sam Daws. *The United Nations: A Concise Political Guide*. London: Macmillan, 1995.

Baratta, Joseph P. *Strengthening the United Nations: A Bibliography*. New York: Greenwood, 1987.

Baratta, Joseph P. (Ed.). *United Nations System*. International Organization Series, Vol. 10. New Brunswick, N.J.: Transaction, 1995.

Bardonnet, Daniel (Ed.). *The Adaptation of Structures and Methods at the United Nations*. Lancaster: Nijhoff, 1986.

Barnaby, Frank (Ed.). *Building a More Democratic United Nations*. London: Cass, 1991.

Bartos, Adam, and Christopher Hitchens. *International Territory: The United Nations 1945–95*. London: Verso, 1994.

Beigbeder, Yves. *The Internal Management of United Nations Organizations: The Long Quest for Reform*. New York: St. Martin's, 1997.

Beigbeder, Yves. *Management Problems in United Nations Organizations: Reform or Decline.* New York: St. Martin's, 1987.

Beker, Avi. *The United Nations and Israel.* Lexington, Mass.: Lexington, 1988.

Bennett, A. LeRoy. *Historical Dictionary of the United Nations.* International Organization Series, No. 8. Lanham, Md.: Scarecrow, 1995.

Bertrand, Maurice. *Some Reflections on Reform in the United Nations.* Geneva: United Nations Joint Inspection Unit, 1985.

Bertrand, Maurice. *The United Nations: Past, Present and Future.* Boston: Kluwer Law International, 1997.

Bourantonis, Dimitri, and Marios Evriviades (Eds.). *A United Nations for the Twenty-First Century: Peace, Security, and Development.* Boston: Kluwer Law International, 1996.

Bourantonis, Dimitri, and Jarrod Wiener (Eds.). *The United Nations in the New World Order: The World Organization at Fifty.* New York: St. Martin's, 1995.

Boutros-Ghali, Boutros. *An Agenda for Democratization: Report of the Secretary-General.* A/51/761 (20 Dec. 1996); reprinted, DPI/1867. New York: United Nations, 1996.

Broms, Bengt. *The United Nations.* Helsinki: Suomalainen Tiedeakatemia, 1990.

Bustelo, Mara R., and Philip Alston (Eds.). *Whose New World Order: What Role for the United Nations?* Annandale, NSW, Australia: Federation Press, 1991.

Childers, Erskine, and Brian Urquhart. *Renewing the United Nations System:* Uppsala: Dag Hammarskjöld Foundation, 1994.

Childers, Erskine, and Brian Urquhart. *Towards a More Effective United Nations.* Uppsala: Dag Hammarskjöld Foundation, 1990.

Claude, Inis L., Jr. *The Changing United Nations.* New York: Random House, 1967.

Coate, Roger A. (Ed.). *United States Policy and the Future of the United Nations.* New York: Twentieth Century Fund, 1994.

Dallin, Alexander. *The Soviet Union and the United Nations.* New York: Praeger, 1962.

Dell, Sidney. *The United Nations and International Business.* Durham: Duke University Press, 1990.

Documents of the United Nations Conference on International Organization. 16 vols. San Francisco: 1945. New York: United Nations Information Organization, 1945–1946.

Eichelberger, Clark Mell. *Organization for Peace: A History of the Founding of the UN.* New York: Harper & Row, 1977.

Elmanadjra, Mahdi. *The United Nations System: An Analysis.* London: Faber, 1973.

Evans, Gareth. *Cooperating for Peace: The Global Agenda for the*

1990s and Beyond. St. Leonards, NSW, Australia: Allen & Unwin, 1993.

Everyone's United Nations. New York: United Nations, 1986.

Falk, Richard, Samuel S. Kim, and Saul H. Mendlovitz. *The United Nations and a Just World Order*. Boulder, Colo.: Westview, 1991.

Fawcett, Eric, and Hanna Newcombe (Eds.). *United Nations Reform: Looking Ahead after Fifty Years*. Toronto: Science for Peace, University of Toronto, 1995.

Finkelstein, Lawrence S. (Ed.). *Politics in the United Nations System*. Durham, N.C.: Duke University Press, 1988.

Finkelstein, Marina S., and Lawrence S. (Eds.). *Collective Security*. San Francisco: Chandler, 1966.

Finger, Seymour Maxwell. *Your Man at the UN: People, Politics and Bureaucracy in Making Foreign Policy*. New York: New York University Press, 1980.

Franck, Thomas M. *Nation against Nation: What Happened to the UN Dream and What the U.S. Can Do about It*. New York: Oxford, 1985.

Fromuth, Peter J. (Ed.). *A Successor Vision: The United Nations of Tomorrow*. Lanham, Md.: University Press of America, 1988.

Gati, Toby I. (Ed.). *The US, the UN, and the Management of Global Change*. New York: New York University Press, 1983.

Goodrich, Leland M. *The United Nations in a Changing World*. New York: Columbia University Press, 1974.

Goodrich, Leland M., Edvard Hambro, and A. P. Simons. *Charter of the United Nations. Commentary and Documents*. 3rd rev. ed. New York: Columbia University Press, 1969.

Goodrich, Leland, Edvard Hambro, and Anne Patricia Simons. *Charter of the United Nations*. New York: Columbia University Press, 1969.

Goodrich, Leland M., and Anne P. Simons. *The United Nations and the Maintenance of International Peace and Security*. Washington, D.C.: Brookings Institution, 1955.

Gordenker, Leon. *The UN Tangle: Policy Formation, Reform, and Reorganization*. Cambridge, Mass.: World Peace Foundation, 1996.

Gordenker, Leon (Ed.). *The United Nations in International Politics*. Princeton, N.J.: Princeton University Press, 1971.

Gordenker, Leon, and Thomas G. Weiss. *Soldiers, Peacekeepers and Disasters*. London: Macmillan, 1992.

Gordon, Wendell. *The United Nations at the Crossroads of Reform*. Armonk, N.Y.: Sharpe, 1994.

Gregg, Robert W. *About Face? The United States and the United Nations*. Boulder, Colo.: Rienner, 1993.

Gross, Ernest A. *The United Nations Structure for Peace*. New York: Harper, 1962.

Haas, Ernst B. *Why We Still Need the United Nations: The Collective*

Management of International Conflict, 1945–1984. Berkeley: Institute of International Studies, University of California, 1986.

Hajnal, Peter I. *Guide to UN Organization, Documentation, and Publishing for Students, Researchers, Librarians*. Dobbs Ferry, N.Y.: Oceana, 1978.

Hajnal, Peter I. (Compiler). *Directory of United Nations Documentary and Archival Sources*. Millwood, N.Y.: Kraus International, 1991.

Harrod, Jeffrey, and Nico Schrijver (Eds.). *The UN Under Attack*. Aldershot: Gower, 1988.

Hazzard, Shirley. *Defeat of an Ideal: A Study of the Self-Destruction of the United Nations*. Boston: Little, Brown, 1973.

Hilderbrand, Robert C. *Dumbarton Oaks: The Origins of the United Nations and the Search for Postwar Security*. Chapel Hill: University of North Carolina Press, 1990.

Hill, Martin. *The United Nations System: Coordinating Its Economic and Social Work*. Cambridge: Cambridge University Press, 1979.

Hoffmann, Walter (Ed.). *A New World Order*. [New York?]: World Federalist Association, 1991.

Holtje, James. *Divided It Stands: Can the United Nations Work?* Atlanta: Turner, 1995.

Hoopes, Townsend, and Douglas Brinkley. *FDR and the Creation of the UN*. New Haven, Conn.: Yale University Press, 1997.

Hovet, Thomas. *Annual Review of United Nations Affairs: A Chronology and Factbook of the United Nations 1941–1979*. Dobbs Ferry, N.Y.: Oceana, 1979.

Hovet, Thomas. *Bloc Voting in the United Nations*. Cambridge, Mass.: Harvard University Press, 1960.

Hovet, Thomas, and Waldo Chamberlain. *The Chronology and Fact Book of the UN, 1941–1979*. Dobbs Ferry, N.Y.: Oceana, 1979.

Hudson, W. J. *Australia and the New World Order: Evatt at San Francisco, 1945*. Canberra: Australian National University, 1993.

Hüfner, Klaus (Ed.). *Agenda for Change: New Tasks for the United Nations*. Opladen: Leske & Burich, 1995.

Independent Working Group on the Future of the United Nations. *The United Nations in Its Second Half-Century*. New York: Ford Foundation, 1995.

Jackson, Richard. *The Non-aligned, the UN and the Superpowers*. New York: Praeger for the Council on Foreign Relations, 1983.

Janello, Amy, and Brennon Jones. *A Global Affair: An Inside Look at the United Nations*. New York: Jones & Janello, 1995.

Jensen, Erik, and Thomas Fisher (Eds.). *The United Kingdom—The United Nations*. London: Macmillan, 1990.

Kapteyn, Paul Joan George, et al. (Eds.). *International Organization and Integration: Annotated Basic Documents and Descriptive Direc-*

tory of International Organizations and Arrangements. Vol. 1A: *The United Nations Organization*. Vol. 1B: *Organizations Related to the United Nations*. The Hague: Nijhoff, 1981, 1982.

Kaufman, Johan. *United Nations Decision-Making*. Rockville, Md.: Sijthoff & Noorhoff, 1981.

Kay, David A. *The New Nations in the United Nations 1960–1967*. New York: Columbia University Press, 1970.

Kaye, David. *United Nations Military Forces: The UN Charter and the United States Constitution*. Public Service Monograph Series No. 5. Washington, D.C.: Division of Public Affairs, American Bar Association, 1994.

Kent, Randolph. *Anatomy of Disaster Relief: The International Network in Action*. London: Pinter, 1987.

Kim, Samuel S. *China, the United Nations, and World Order*. Princeton, N.J.: Princeton University Press, 1979.

Kinninen, Tapio. *Leadership and Reform: The Secretary-General and the UN Financial Crisis of the Late 1980s*. Legal Aspects of International Organization, Vol. 22. Boston: Kluwer Law International, 1995.

Krasner, Stephen. *Structural Conflict: The Third World against Global Liberation*. Berkeley: University of California Press, 1985.

Krause, Keith, and W. Andy Knight (Eds.). *State, Society and the UN System: Changing Perspectives on Multilateralism*. Tokyo: United Nations University Press, 1995.

Kunugi, Tatsuro, et al. *Towards a More Effective UN*. Tokyo: PHP Research Institute, March 1996.

Lall, Arthur. *The UN and the Middle East*. New York: Columbia University Press, 1970.

Lorenz, Joseph P. *The UN after the Cold War*. Boulder, Colo.: Westview, 1997.

Luard, Evan. *A History of the United Nations*. 2 vols. New York: St. Martin's, 1982.

Luard, Evan. *The United Nations: How It Works and What It Does*. 2nd ed. New York: St. Martin's, 1994.

Mayor, Frederico. *The New Page*. Brookfield, Vt.: Dartmouth, 1995.

Meisler, Stanley. *United Nations: The First Fifty Years*. New York: Atlantic Monthly Press, 1995.

Melvern, Linda. *The Ultimate Crime: Who Betrayed the UN and Why*. London: Allison & Busby, 1995.

Mendolvitz, Saul H., and Burns H. Weston (Eds.). *Preferred Futures for the United Nations*. Irvington-on-Hudson, N.Y.: Transnational, 1995.

Mingst, Karen A., and Margaret P. Karns. *The United Nations in the Post–Cold War Era*. Boulder, Colo.: Westview, 1995.

Misra, Kashi Prasad. *The Role of the United Nations in the Indo–Pakistan Conflict of 1971*. Delhi: Vikas, 1973.

Moore, Jonathan. *The UN and Complex Emergencies: Rehabilitation in Third World Transitions*. Geneva: UN Research Institute for Social Development, 1996.

Moskowitz, Moses. *The Roots and Reaches of United Nations Actions and Decisions*. Rockville, Md.: Sijthoff & Noorhoff, 1980.

Moynihan, Daniel Patrick. *A Dangerous Place*. New York: Berkley, 1980.

Müller, Joachim W. *The Reform of the United Nations*. 2 vols. New York: Oceana, 1992.

Muller, Robert, and Douglas Roche. *Safe Passage into the Twenty–First Century: The United Nations' Quest for Peace, Equality, Justice and Development*. New York: Continuum, 1995.

Murphy, John F. *The United Nations and the Control of International Violence*. Totowa, N.J.: Allanheld, Osmun, 1983.

Narasimhan, C. V. *History of the United Nations University: A Personal Perspective*. Tokyo: United Nations University Press, 1994.

Nicholas, H. G. *The United Nations as a Political Institution*. 4th ed. New York: Oxford University Press, 1971.

Nolan, Cathal J. *Principled Diplomacy*. Westport, Conn.: Greenwood, 1993.

Noyes, John E. (Ed.). *The United Nations at 50: Proposals for Improving Its Effectiveness*. Washington, D.C.: American Bar Association, 1997.

Ogata, Shijuro, and Paul Volker. *Financing an Effective United Nations: A Report of the Independent Advisory Group on UN Financing*. New York: Ford Foundation, 1993.

Osmanczyk, Jan Edmund. *Encyclopedia of the United Nations and International Relations*. 2nd ed. London: Taylor & Francis, 1990.

Parsons, Anthony. *From Cold War to Hot Peace: UN Interventions 1947–1994*. London: Michael Joseph, 1995.

Patil, Aiyali V. *The UN Veto in World Affairs, 1946–1990*. Sarasota: Unifo-Marshall, 1992.

Peck, Connie. *The United Nations as a Dispute Settlement System: Improving Mechanisms for the Prevention and Resolution of Conflict*. Boston: Kluwer Law International, 1996.

Pérez de Cuéllar, Javier. *Anarchy or Order—Annual Reports 1982–1991*. New York: United Nations, 1991.

Pellopää, Matti, and David D. Caron. *The UNCITRAL Arbitration Rules as Interpreted and Applied: Selected Problems in Light of the Practice of the Iran–United States Claims Tribunal*. Helsinki: Finnish Lawyers' Publishing, 1995.

Pines, Burton Yale (Ed.). *A World without a UN: What Would Happen If the UN Shut Down?* Washington, D.C.: Heritage Foundation, 1984.

Protheroe, David. *The UN and Its Finances: A Test for Middle Powers.* Ottawa: North-South Institute, 1988.

Rae, Heather, and Chris Reus-Smit. *The United Nations: Between Sovereignty and Global Governance? Report on the International Conference Held at La Trobe University, Melbourne 2–6 July 1995.* Melbourne: School of Public Affairs, La Trobe University, 1996.

Rajan, M. S., V. S. Mani, and C. S. R. Murthy. *The Nonaligned and the United Nations.* New Delhi: South Asia, 1987.

Renniger, John P. (Ed.). *The Future Role of the United Nations in an Interdependent World.* Boston: Nijhoff, 1989.

Richardot, Jean. *Journeys for a Better World: A Personal Adventure in War and Peace, An Inside Story of the United Nations by One of Its First Senior Officers.* Lanham, Md.: University Press of America, 1994.

Riggs, Robert E., and Jack C. Plano. *The United Nations: International Organization and World Politics.* Belmont, Calif.: Wadsworth, 1988.

Righter, Rosemary. *Utopia Lost: The United Nations and World Order.* New York: Twentieth Century Fund, 1995.

Rittberger, Volker, Hans von Mangoldt, and Frank Knipping. *The United Nations System and Its Predecessors: Basic Documents.* 2 vols. Oxford: Oxford University Press, 1997.

Roberts, Adam, and Benedict Kingsbury. *Presiding over a Divided World: Changing UN Roles, 1945–1993.* Boulder, Colo.: Rienner, 1994.

Roberts, Adam, and Benedict Kingsbury (Eds.). *United Nations, Divided World: The UN's Role in International Relations.* 2nd ed. Oxford: Clarendon, 1993.

Rochester, J. Martin. *Waiting for the Millennium: The United Nations and the Future World Order.* Columbia: University of South Carolina Press, 1993.

Rosenau, James N. *The United Nations in a Turbulent World.* Boulder, Colo: Rienner, 1992.

Rossi, Josphen Samuel. *American Catholics and the Formation of the United Nations.* Vol. IV. Melville Studies in Church History. Lanham, Md.: University Press of America and the Department of Church History, Catholic University, 1993.

Russell, Ruth B., and Jeannette E. Muther. *A History of the United Nations: The Role of the United States, 1940–1945.* Washington, D.C.: Brookings Institution, 1958.

Segall, Jefrey J., and Harry H. Lerner (Eds.). *CAMDUN-2: The United Nations and a New World Order for Peace and Justice: Report of* the Second International Conference for a More Democratic United Nations (Vienna 1991). New York: CAMDUN Project, 1992.

Simma, Bruno, et al. (Eds.). The Charter of the United Nations: A Commentary. New York: Oxford University Press, 1994.

Simons, G. L. The United Nations: A Chronology of Conflict. New York: St. Martin's, 1994.

Simons, Geoff. UN Malaise: Power, Problems, and Realpolitik. New York: St. Martin's, 1995.

South Commission. Reforming the United Nations: A View from the South. Geneva: South Centre, 1995.

Stevenson, Adlai. Looking Outward: Years of Crisis at the United Nations. New York: Harper & Row, 1963.

Stoessinger, John G. Financing the United Nations System. Washington, D.C.: Brookings Institution, 1964.

Stone, Julius. Conflict through Consensus: United Nations Approaches to Aggression. Baltimore: Johns Hopkins University Press, 1977.

Stremlau, John. Sharpening International Sanctions: Toward a Stronger Role for the United Nations. Washington, D.C.: Carnegie Commission on Preventing Deadly Conflict, November 1996.

Sung-Joo, Han (Ed.). The United Nations: The Next Fifty Years. Seoul: Ilnin International Institute, Korea University, 1996.

Sutterland, James S. The United Nations and the Maintenance of International Security: A Challenge to Be Met. Westport, Conn.: Praeger, 1994.

Swisher, Karin L. The United Nations. San Diego, Calif.: Greenhaven, 1997.

Taylor, Paul, and A. J. R. Groom (Eds.). Global Issues in the United Nations Framework. London: Macmillan, 1989.

Thakur, Ramesh (Ed.). The United Nations at Fifty: Retrospect and Prospect. Canberra: Peace Research Centre, Australian National University, 1996.

Twitchett, Kenneth J. (Ed.). The Evolving United Nations: A Prospect for Peace? New York: Europa, 1971.

United Nations. Everyone's United Nations: A Handbook on the World of the United Nations. 10th ed. New York: United Nations, 1986.

United Nations. Special Edition of the Yearbook of the United Nations. The Hague: Nijhoff, 1995.

United Nations. UN 21—Better Service, Better Value, Better Management: Progress Report of the Efficiency Board to the Secretary-General. New York: Author, 1996.

United Nations. UN Yearbook. New York: United Nations, annual.

United Nations. The United Nations and Nuclear Non-Proliferation. New York: United Nations Department of Public Information, 1995.

United Nations. Department of Public Information. Image and Reality:

Questions and Answers about the United Nations and How It Works and Who Pays for It. New York: United Nations, 1993.

United Nations Volunteers. *Volunteers against Conflict*. New York: United Nations University Press, 1996.

Vincent, Jack E. *Support Patterns at the United Nations*. Lanham, Md.: University Press of America, 1991.

Weiler, Lawrence L., and Anne Patricia Simons. *The United States and the United Nations*. New York: Manhattan, 1967.

Weiss, Thomas G. (Ed.). *Collective Security in a Changing World*. Boulder, Colo.: Rienner, 1993.

Weiss, Thomas G. (Ed.). *The United Nations and Civil Wars*. Boulder, Colo.: Rienner, 1995.

Weiss, Thomas G. (Ed.). *The United Nations in Conflict Management: America, Soviet and Third World Views*. New York: International Peace Academy, 1990.

Weiss, Thomas G., David P. Forsythe, and Roger A. Coate. *The United Nations and Changing World Politics*. 2nd ed. Boulder, Colo.: Westview, 1997.

Weiss, Thomas G., and Leon Gordenker. *Soldiers, Peacekeepers, and Disasters*. New York: St. Martin's, 1991.

Whitaker, David J. *United Nations in Action*. Armonk, N.Y.: Sharpe, 1995.

White, N. D. *Keep the Peace: The United Nations and the Maintenance of International Peace and Security*. Manchester: Manchester University Press, 1995.

Williams, Ian. *The UN for Beginners*. New York: Writers & Readers, 1995.

Williams, Phil, and Ernesto U. Savona (Eds.). *The United Nations and Transnational Organized Crime*. London: Cass, 1996.

Winslow, Anne (Ed.). *Women, Politics, and the United Nations*. Westport, Conn.: Greenwood, 1995.

General Assembly

Alker, Hayward R., Jr., and Bruce M. Russett. *World Politics in the General Assembly*. New Haven, Conn.: Yale University Press, 1965.

Bailey, Sydney. *The General Assembly of the United Nations*. Rev. ed. London: Pall Mall, 1964.

Peterson, M. J. *The General Assembly in World Politics*. Boston: Allen & Unwin, 1986.

Russell, Ruth B. *The General Assembly: Patterns/Problems/Prospects*. New York: Carnegie Endowment for International Peace, 1970.

Sloan, Blaine. *United Nations General Assembly Resolutions in Our Changing World*. Irvington-on-Hudson, N.Y.: Transnational, 1991.

United Nations Association of the United States of America. *Issues before the General Assembly of the United Nations.* New York: Author, annual (since 1977).

International Court of Justice

Alexandrov, Stanimir. *Reservations in Unilateral Declarations Accepting the Compulsory Jurisdiction of the International Court of Justice.* Dordrecht: Kluwer Academic, 1995.

Bloed, A., and P. van Dijk. *Forty Years of International Court of Justice: Jurisdiction, Equity and Equality.* Utrecht: Europa Institutt, 1988.

Bodie, Thomas J. *Politics and the Emergence of an Activist International Court of Justice.* Westport, Conn.: Praeger, 1995.

Damrosch, Lori Fisler (Ed.). *The International Court of Justice at a Crossroads.* Dobbs Ferry, N.Y.: Transnational, 1987.

Elias, T. O. *The International Court of Justice and Some Contemporary Problems: Essays on International Law.* Boston: Kluwer Law International, 1983.

Elkind, Jerome B. *Non-Appearance before the International Court of Justice: Functional and Comparative Analysis.* Boston: Kluwer Law International, 1984.

Eyffinger, Arthur. *The International Court of Justice, 1946–1996.* Boston: Kluwer Law International, 1996.

Franck, Thomas M. *Judging the World Court.* New York: Priority Press for Twentieth Century Fund, 1986.

Lowe, Vaughan, and Malgosia Fitzmaurice (Eds.). *Fifty Years of the International Court of Justice: Essays in Honour of Sir Robert Jennings.* New York: Cambridge University Press, 1995.

McWhinney, Edward. *The International Court of Justice and the Western Tradition of International Law.* The Paul Martin Lectures in International Relations and Law. Boston: Kluwer Law International, 1987.

Muller, A. S., D. Raic, and J. M. Thuránsky (Eds.). *The International Court of Justice: Its Future Role after Fifty Years.* Boston: Nijhoff, 1996.

Rosenne, Shabtai. *The World Court: What It Is and How It Works.* 5th ed. Boston: Nijhoff, 1995.

Shahabuddeen, Mohamed. *Precedent in the World Court.* Cambridge: Cambridge University Press, 1996.

Szafraz, Renata. *The Compulsory Jurisdiction of the International Court of Justice.* Dordrecht: Kluwer Academic, 1993.

United Nations. *World Court: What It Is and How It Works.* New York: Author, 1989.

Secretariat (Including Secretary-General)

Bailey, Sydney D. *The Secretariat of the United Nations.* New York: Carnegie Endowment for International Peace, 1962.

Barros, James. *Trygve Lie and the Cold War: The UN Secretary General Pursues Peace, 1946–1953.* DeKalb: Northern Illinois University Press, 1989.

Beigbeder, Yves. *Threats to the International Civil Service.* London: Pinter, 1988.

Cordier, Andrew W., Wilder Foote, and Max Harrelson. *The Public Papers of the Secretaries-general of the United Nations.* 8 vols. New York: Columbia University Press, 1969–1977.

Foote, Wilder (Ed.). *The Servant of Peace: A Selection of the Speeches and Statements of Dag Hammarskjöld.* London: Bodley Head, 1962.

Fosdick, Raymond R. *The League and the United Nations after Fifty Years: The Six Secretaries-General.* Newtown, Conn.: Fosdick, 1972.

Gordenker, Leon. *The UN Secretary-General and the Maintenance of Peace.* New York: Columbia University Press, 1967.

Graham, Norman A., and Robert S. Jordan. *The International Civil Service: Changing Role and Concepts.* New York: Pergamon, 1980.

Hazzard, Shirley. *Countenance of Truth: The United Nations and the Waldheim Case.* New York: Viking, 1990.

Jones, Barlett C. *Flawed Triumphs: Andy Young at the United Nations.* Lanham, Md.: University Press of America, 1996.

Jordan, Robert S. (Ed.). *Dag Hammarskjöld Revisited: The UN Secretary-General as a Force in World Politics.* Durham, N.C.: Carolina Academic Press, 1983.

Kelen, Emergy. *Hammarskjöld.* New York: Putnam, 1966.

Lash, Joseph P. *Dag Hammarskjöld: Custodian of the Brushfire Peace.* New York: Doubleday, 1961.

Lie, Trygve. *In the Cause of Peace: Seven Years with the United Nations.* New York: Macmillan, 1954.

Lillich, Richard B. *The United Nations Compensation Commission.* Irvington, N.Y.: Transnational, 1995.

Marks, Edward. *Complex Emergenices: Bureaucratic Arrangements in the UN Secretariat.* Washington, D.C.: National Defense University Press, 1996.

Meron, Theodor. *The United Nations Secretariat.* Lexington, Mass.: Heath, 1977.

Nassif, Ramses. *U Thant in New York, 1961–1971: A Portrait of the Third UN Secretary-General.* London: Hurst, 1988.

Pitt, David, and Thomas George Weiss (Eds.). *The Nature of United Nations Bureaucracies.* London: Croom Helm, 1987.

Ramcharan, B. G. *Humanitarian Good Offices in International Law:*

The Good Offices of the United Nations Secretary-General in the Field of Human Rights. The Hague: Nijhoff, 1982.

Ramcharan, B. G. *The International Law and Practice of Early-Warning and Preventive Diplomacy: The Emerging Global Watch.* Boston: Nijhoff, 1991.

Rikyhe, Indar Jit. *Military Adviser to the Secretary General: UN Peacekeeping and the Congo Crisis.* Washington, D.C.: Institute of World Affairs, 1993.

Rivlin, Benjamin, and Leon Gordenker (Eds.). *The Challenging Role of the UN Secretary-General: Making "The Most Impossible Job in the World" Possible.* Westport, Conn.: Praeger, 1993.

Rovine, Arthur W. *The First Fifty Years: The Secretary-General in World Politics, 1920–1970.* Leiden: Sitjhoff, 1970.

Schwebel, Stephen M. *The Secretary-General of the United Nations: His Political Powers and Practice.* Cambridge, Mass.: Harvard University Press, 1952.

Thant, U. *Portfolio for Peace. Excerpts from the Writings and Speeches of U Thant, 1961–1968.* 2nd ed. New York: United Nations, 1970.

Thant, U. *Toward World Peace: Addresses and Public Statements, 1957–1963.* New York: Yoseloff, 1964.

Thant, U. *View from the UN.* Garden City, N.Y.: Doubleday, 1978.

Urquhart, Brian. *Hammarskjöld.* New York: Knopf, 1972.

Urquhart, Brian. *A Life in Peace and War.* New York: Harper & Row, 1987.

Urquhart, Brian. *Ralph Bunche: An American Life.* New York: Norton, 1993.

Urquhart, Brian, and Erskine Childers. *Towards a More Effective United Nations.* Uppsala: Dag Hammarskjöld Foundation, 1992.

Urquhart, Brian, and Erskine Childers. *A World in Need of Leadership: Tomorrow's United Nations.* Uppsala: Dag Hammarskjöld Foundation, 1990.

Waldheim, Kurt. *Building the Future Order.* New York: Free Press, 1980.

Waldheim, Kurt. *The Challenge of Peace.* New York: Rawson, Wade, 1980.

Waldheim, Kurt. *In the Eye of the Storm: The Memoirs of Kurt Waldheim.* London: Weidenfeld & Nicolson, 1985.

Wellens, Karel C. (Ed.). *Resolutions and Statements of the UN Security Council (1946–1992): A Thematic Guide.* 2nd enlarged ed. Boston: Nijhoff, 1993.

Security Council

Bailey, Sydney D. *The UN Security Council and Human Rights.* New York: St. Martin's, 1994.

Bailey, Sydney D., and Sam Daws. *The Procedures of the UN Security Council*. 3rd ed. Oxford: Oxford University Press, 1997.

Boyd, Andrew. *Fifteen Men on a Powder Keg: A History of the United Nations Security Council*. New York: Stein & Day, 1971.

Kleg, Mary-Honor L., and Dick A. Leurdijk. *Decision-making by the Security Council: The Case of Former Yugoslavia*. 2nd ed. Clingendael: The Netherlands Institute of International Relations, November 1993.

Nicol, Davidson (Ed.). *Paths to Peace: The UN Security Council and Its Presidency*. New York: Pergamon, 1981.

Pogany, Istvan. *The Security Council and the Arab-Israeli Conflict*. New York: St. Martin's, 1984.

Russell, Ruth B. *The United Nations and United States Security Policy*. Washington, D.C.: Brookings Institution, 1968.

Russett, Bruce (Ed.). *The Once and Future Security Council*. New York: St. Martin's, 1997.

Trusteeship Council

Toussant, Charmian E. *The Trusteeship System of the United Nations*. Westport, Conn.: Greenwood, 1976.

Economic, Environmental, Financial, and Social Issues

Borgese, Elizabeth Mann. *Ocean Governance and the United Nations*. Halifax: Centre for Foreign Policy Studies, Dalhousie University, 1995.

Boutros-Ghali, Boutros. *An Agenda for Development: Report of the Secretary General*. A/48/935 (6 May 1994). New York: United Nations, 1995.

Chapelier, Georges, and Hamid Tabatabai. *Development and Adjustment: Stabilization, Structural Adjustment and UNDP Policy*. New York: United Nations Development Program, 1989.

Conca, Ken, Michael Alberty, and Geoffrey Dabelko (Eds.). *Green Planet Blues: Environmental Politics from Stockholm to Rio*. Boulder, Colo.: Westview, 1995.

Corea, Gamani. *Taming Commodity Markets: The Integrated Program and the Common Fund in UNCTAD*. New York: St. Martin's, 1992.

El-Ayouty, Yassin. *The United Nations and Decolonization: The Role of Afro-Asia*. The Hague: Nijhoff, 1971.

Fraser, Arvonne S. *The UN Decade for Women: Documents and Dialogue*. Boulder, Colo.: Westview, 1987.

Gardner, Richard N. *Negotiating Survival: Your Priorities after Rio*. New York: Council on Foreign Relations, 1985.

Gordenker, Leon. *International Aid and National Decisions.* Princeton, N.J.: Princeton University Press, 1976.

Gordenker, Leon. *Refugees in International Politics.* London: Croom Helm, 1989.

Gosovic, Branislav. *The Quest for World Environmental Cooperation: The Case of the UN Global Environment Monitoring System.* New York: Routledge, 1992.

Gosovic, Branislav. *UNCTAD: A Political Analysis.* Washington, D.C.: Carnegie Endowment, 1968.

Jackson, Robert. *A Study Capacity of the UN Development System.* 2 vols. New York: United Nations, 1969.

Jacobson, Harold K. *The USSR and the UN's Economic and Social Activities.* Notre Dame, Ind.: University of Notre Dame Press, 1963.

Johnson, Stanley. *The Politics of Population: The International Conference on Population and Development, Cairo 1994.* London: Earthscan, 1995.

Kurbayashi, Tado, and Edward L. Miles (Eds.). *The Law of the Sea in the 1990s: A Framework for Further International Cooperation.* Honolulu: Law of the Sea Institute, University of Hawaii, 1992.

Levitsky, Melvyn. *UN Coordination for a Global Drug Strategy.* Washington, D.C.: U.S. Department of State, 1990.

Micholak, Stanley. *The United Nations Conference on Trade and Development: An Organization Betraying Its Mission.* Washington, D.C.: Heritage Foundation, 1983.

Minear, Larry. *The Challenge of Famine Relief: Emerging Operation in the Sudan.* Washington, D.C.: The Brookings Institution, 1992.

Minear, Larry, and Thomas G. Weiss. *Humanitarian Action in Times of War: A Handbook for Practitioners.* Boulder, Colo.: Rienner, 1993.

Minear, Larry, and Thomas G. Weiss. *Humanitarianism under Siege: Operation Lifeline Sudan.* Lawrenceville, N.J.: Red Sea Press, 1991.

Mower, A. Glenn, Jr. *International Cooperation for Social Justice.* Westport, Conn.: Greenwood, 1985.

Murphy, Craig. *The Emergence of the NIEO Ideology.* Boulder, Colo.: Westview, 1984.

Platzöder, Renate (Ed.). *The 1994 United Nations Convention and the Law of the Sea: Basic Documents with an Introduction.* Boston: Nijhoff, 1995.

Redgwell, Catherine, and Michael Bowman (Eds.). *International Law and the Conservation of Biological Diversity.* Cambridge: Kluwer Law International, 1995.

Robie, David. *The United Nations Development Programme in the South Pacific.* Wellington: NZCTD, 1984.

Rocha, Geise Maria. *In Search of Namibian Independence: The Limitations of the United Nations.* Boulder, Colo.: Westview, 1984.

Rotberg, Robert I. (Ed.). *Namibia: Political and Economic Perspectives.* Lexington, Mass.: Lexington, 1983.

Rothstein, Robert L. *Global Bargaining: UNCTAD and the Quest for a New International Economic Order.* Princeton, N.J.: Princeton University Press, 1979.

Soons, Alfred, and Barbara Kwiatkowska (Eds.). *International Organizations and the Law of the Sea: Documentation Yearbook 1994.* Boston: Graham & Trotman/Martinus Nijhoff, 1996.

United Nations Conference on Environment and Development. *The Global Partnership for Environment and Development: A Guide to Agenda 21.* Geneva: Author, 1992.

United Nations Development Program. *Generation, Portrait of the United Nations Development Program.* New York: Author, 1985.

United Nations Public Information and United Nations International Drug Control Programme. *The United Nations and Drug Abuse Control.* New York: United Nations, 1992.

Weiss, Thomas G. *Multilateral Development Diplomacy in UNCTAD.* London: Macmillan, 1986.

Weiss, Thomas G., and Robert S. Jordan. *The World Food Conference and Global Problem Solving.* New York: Praeger, 1976.

Whitman, Jim, and David Pocock. *After Rwanda: The Coordination of United Nations Humanitarian Assistance.* London: Macmillan, 1996.

Williams, Marc. *Third World Co-operation: The Group of 77 in UNCTAD.* New York: St. Martin's, 1991.

Human Rights

Alston, Philip (Ed.). *The United Nations and Human Rights: A Critical Reappraisal.* Oxford: Clarendon, 1992.

Banton, Michael. *International Action against Racial Discrimination.* Oxford: Clarendon, 1996.

Deng, Francis M. *Protecting the Dispossessed: A Challenge for the International Community.* Washington, D.C.: Brookings Institution, 1993.

Deng, Francis M., and Larry Minear. *The Challenges of Famine Relief.* Washington, D.C.: Brookings Institution, 1992.

Donnelly, Jack. *Human Rights and International Relations.* Boulder, Colo.: Westview, 1993.

Donnelly, Jack. *International Human Rights.* Boulder, Colo.: Westview, 1993.

Donnelly, Jack. *Universal Human Rights in Theory and Practice.* Ithaca, N.Y.: Cornell University Press, 1989.

Forsythe, David P. *Human Rights and Peace: International and National Dimensions.* Lincoln: University of Nebraska Press, 1993.

Forsythe, David P. *Human Rights and World Politics*. 2nd ed. Lincoln: University of Nebraska Press, 1989.

Forsythe, David P. *The Internationalization of Human Rights*. Lexington, Mass.: Lexington, 1991.

Henkin, Alice H. (Ed.). *Honoring Human Rights and Keeping the Peace. Lessons from El Salvador, Cambodia, and Haiti*. Washington, D.C.: Aspen Institute, 1995.

Henkin, Louis. *The International Bill of Rights: The Covenant on Civil and Political Rights*. New York: Columbia University Press, 1981.

Human Rights Watch. *The Lost Agenda: Human Rights and UN Field Operations*. New York: Author, 1993.

Humphrey, John P. *Human Rights and the United Nations: A Great Adventure*. Dobbs Ferry, N.Y.: Transnational, 1983.

Kaufman, Natalie Hevener. *Human Rights Treaties and the Senate*. Chapel Hill: University of North Carolina Press, 1990.

Lauren, Paul Gordon. *Power and Prejudice: The Politics and Diplomacy of Racial Discrimination*. 2nd ed. Boulder, Colo.: Westview, 1996.

Lillich, Richard. *International Human Rights*. Boston: Little, Brown, 1991.

Loescher, Gil, and Laila Monahan (Eds.). *Refugees and International Relations*. New York: Oxford University Press, 1989.

McGoldrick, Dominic. *The Human Rights Committee: Its Role in the Development of the International Covenant on Civil and Political Rights*. Oxford: Clarendon, 1991.

Meron, Theodor (Ed.). *Human Rights Law-Making in the United Nations: A Critique of Instruments and Process*. Oxford: Clarendon, 1986.

O'Flaherty, Michael. *Human Rights and the UN: Practice before the Treaty Bodies*. London: Sweet & Maxwell, 1996.

Pietila, Hikka, and Jeanne Vickers. *Making Women Matter: The Role of the United Nations*. 3rd ed. London: Zed, 1996.

Tolley, Howard J. *The UN Commission on Human Rights*. Boulder, Colo.: Westview, 1987.

United Nations. *Human Rights: A Compilation of International Instruments*. New York: Author, 1993.

United Nations. *The United Nations and Apartheid, 1948–1994*. New York: Author, 1994.

United Nations. *The United Nations and Human Rights, 1945–1995*. New York: Author, 1995.

United Nations. *The United Nations and the Advancement of Women, 1948–1996*. 3rd ed. New York: Author, 1996.

United Nations High Commissioner for Refugees. *The State of the*

World's Refugees: In Search of Solutions. New York: Oxford University Press, 1995.

United Nations Reference Guide in the Field of Human Rights. Geneva: UN Centre for Human Rights, 1993.

Van Boven, Theo. *People Matter.* Amsterdam: Meulenhoff Nederland, 1982.

Legal Issues

Al-Nauimi, Najeeb, and Richard Meese (Eds.). *International Legal Issues Arising under the United Nations Decade of International Law.* Proceedings of the Qatar International Law Conference 1994. Boston: Nijhoff, 1995.

Bassiouni, M. Cherif, and Peter Manikas. *The Law of the International Criminal Tribunal for the Former Yugoslavia.* Irvington-on-Hudson, N.Y.: Transnational, 1996.

Bedard, Ralph, and Dilys Hill (Eds.). *Economic, Social and Cultural Rights: Progress and Achievement.* London: Macmillan, 1992.

Bowett, Derek W. *United Nations Forces: A Legal Study of United Nations Practice.* London: Stevens, 1964.

Briggs, Herbert W. *The International Law Commission.* Ithaca, N.Y.: Cornell University Press, 1965.

Cassese, Antonio (Ed.). *United Nations Peacekeeping: Legal Essays.* Alphen aan den Rijn: Sijthoff & Noorhoof, 1978.

Cassese, Antonio (Ed.). *The Current Legal Regulation of the Use of Force 40 Years after the UN Charter.* Lancaster: Nijhoff, 1986.

Chayes, Abram, and Antonia Handler Chayes. *The New Sovereignty: Compliance with International Regulatory Agreements.* Cambridge, Mass.: Harvard University Press, 1995.

Clark, Roger S. *The United Nations Crime Prevention and Criminal Justice Program: Formulation of Standards and Efforts at Their Implementation.* Philadelphia: University of Pennsylvania Press, 1994.

Clark, Roger S., and Madeleine Sann. *The Prosecution of International Crimes: A Critical Study of the International Tribunal for the Former Yugoslavia.* New Brunswick, N.J.: Transaction, 1996.

Conforti, Benedotto. *The Law and Practice of the United Nations.* Boston: Kluwer Law International, 1996.

Craven, Matthew. *The International Covenant on Economic, Social and Cultural Rights: A Perspective on Its Development.* New York: Oxford University Press, 1995.

Dugard, John. *Recognition and the United Nations.* Cambridge: Grotius, 1987.

Ferencz, Benjamin B. *New Legal Foundations for Global Survival: Security through the Security Council.* New York: Oceana, 1994.

Gowland-Debbas, Vera. *Collective Responses to Illegal Acts in International Law: United Nations Action in the Question of Southern Rhodesia.* Dordrecht: Nijhoff, 1990.

Higgins, Rosalyn. *The Development of International Law through the Political Organs of the United Nations.* New York: Oxford University Press, 1963.

Joyner, Christopher C. (Ed.). *The United Nations and International Law.* Cambridge: Cambridge University Press, 1997.

Kirgis, Frederic L. *International Organizations in Their Legal Setting.* 2nd ed. St. Paul, Minn.: West, 1993.

LeBlanc, Lawrence J. *The Convention on the Rights of the Child: United Nations Lawmaking on Human Rights.* Lincoln: University of Nebraska Press, 1995.

LeBlanc, Lawrence J. *Negotiating the Convention on the Rights of the Child.* Lincoln: University of Nebraska Press, 1994.

LeBlanc, Lawrence J. *The United States and the Genocide Convention.* Durham, N.C.: Duke University Press, 1991.

Lijnzaad, Lieseth (Ed.). *Reservations to the UN Human Rights Treaties: Ratify and Ruin?* Dordrecht: Nijhoff, 1995.

Lillich, Richard (Ed.). *Humanitarian Intervention and the United Nations.* Charlottesville: University Press of Virginia, 1973.

MacPherson, Bryan F. *An International Criminal Court: Applying World Law to Individuals.* Washington, D.C.: Center for UN Reform Education, 1992.

McWhinney, Edward. *United Nations Law Making: Cultural and Ideological Relativism and International Law Making for an Era of Transition.* New York: Holmes & Meier, 1984.

Morris, Virginia, and Michael P. Scharf. *An Insider's Guide to the International Tribunal for the Former Yugoslavia: A Documentary History and Analysis.* 2 vols. Irvington-on-Hudson, N.Y.: Transnational, 1995.

Mower, A. Glenn, Jr. *The United States, the United Nations and Human Rights.* Westport, Conn.: Greenwood, 1979.

Nkala, Jericho. *The United Nations, International Law and the Rhodesian Independence Question.* Oxford: Clarendon, 1985.

Schachter, Oscar, and Christopher C. Joyner (Eds.). *United Nations Legal Order.* 2 vols. Cambridge: Cambridge University Press, 1995.

Sohn, Louis B. (Ed.). *Cases on United Nations Law.* Brooklyn: Foundation Press, 1967.

Tahzib, Behiyyih G. *Freedom of Religion or Belief: Ensuring Effective International Legal Protection.* International Studies in Human Rights, Vol. 44. Boston: Nijhoff, 1996.

Tomuschat, Christian (Ed.). *The United Nations at Age Fifty: A Legal Perspective.* Legal Aspects of International Organization, Vol. 23. Boston: Kluwer Law International, 1995.

Weller, Marc (Ed.). *The Haiti Crisis in International Law*. New York: Cambridge University Press, 1996.

Wolfrum, Rüdiger (Editor-in-Chief). *United Nations: Law, Policies, and Practice*. New, rev. ed. 2 vols. Boston: Nijhoff, 1995.

Peacekeeping

Abi-Saab, Georges. *The United Nations Operation in the Congo 1960– 1964*. New York: Oxford University Press, 1978.

Acuña, Tathiana Flores. *The United Nations Mission in El Salvador: A Humanitarian Perspective*. Nijhoff Law Specials, Vol. 14. Boston: Kluwer Law International, 1995.

Allard, Kent. *Somalia Operations: Lessons Learned*. Washington, D.C.: National Defense University Press, 1995.

Allen, James H. *Peacekeeping: Outspoken Observations by a Field Officer*. Westport, Conn.: Praeger, 1996.

Anstee, Margaret Joan. *Orphan of the Cold War: The Inside Story of the Collapse of the Angolan Peace Process*. New York: St. Martin's, 1996.

Azimi, Nassrine (Ed.). *The Role and Functions of Civilian Police in United Nations Peace-Keeping Operations: Debriefing and Lessons*. Report and Recommendations of the International Conference, Singapore, 1995. Boston: Kluwer Law International, 1996.

Azimi, Nassrine (Ed.). *The United Nations Transitional Authority in Cambodia (UNTAC): Debriefing and Lessons*. Report and Recommendations of the International Conference, Singapore, 1994. Boston: Kluwer Law International, 1995.

Bailey, Kathleen. *The UN Inspections in Iraq: Lessons for On-Site Verification*. Boulder, Colo.: Westview, 1995.

Bailey, Sydney. *How Wars End: The United Nations and the Termination of Armed Conflict 1946–1964*. 2 vols. Oxford: Oxford University Press, 1982.

Berridge, G. R. *Return to the UN: UN Diplomacy in Regional Conflicts*. London: Macmillan, 1991.

Boutros-Ghali, Boutros. *An Agenda for Peace: Preventive Diplomacy, Peacemaking, and Peace-keeping*. A/47/277; S/24111 (17 June 1992). New York: United Nations, 1992.

Boutros-Ghali, Boutros. *The 50th Anniversary Annual Report on the World of the United Nations*. New York: United Nations, 1996.

Boutros-Ghali, Boutros. *Supplement to An Agenda for Peace: Position Paper of the Secretary-General on the Occasion of the Fiftieth Anniversary of the United Nations*. A/50/60-S/1995/1 (3 Jan. 1995). New York: United Nations, 1995.

Charters, David A. (Ed.). *Peacekeeping and the Challenge of Civil Con-*

flict Resolution. Fredericton, Canada: Centre for Conflict Studies, University of New Brunswick, 1994.

Childers, Erskine (Ed.). *Challenges Facing the United Nations: Building a Safer World*. New York: St. Martin's, 1995.

Clarke, Walter, and Jeffrey Herbst. *Learning from Somalia: The Lessons of Armed Humanitarian Intervention*. Boulder, Colo.: Westview, 1997.

Connaughton, Richard M. *Military Intervention in the 1990s: Multilateral Military Intervention as a Collective Security Measure in the 1990s*. New York: Routledge, 1992.

Cox, David, and Albert Legault. *United Nations Rapid Reaction Capabilities, Requirements and Prospects*. Toronto: Canadian Institute of Strategic Studies, 1995.

Daniel, Donald C. F., and Bradd C. Hayes (Eds.). *Beyond Traditional Peacekeeping*. New York: St. Martin's, 1995.

De Marco, Guido, and Michael Bartolo. *A Second Generation United Nations: For Peace in Freedom in the 21st Century*. London: Kegan Paul International, 1996.

De Rossanet, Bertrand. *Peacemaking and Peacekeeping in Yugoslavia*. Nijhoff Law Specials, Vol. 17. Boston: Kluwer Law International, 1996.

Diehl, Paul. *International Peacekeeping*. Baltimore: Johns Hopkins University Press, 1993.

Doyle, Michael W. *UN Peacekeeping in Cambodia: UNTAC's Civil Mandate*. Boulder, Colo.: Rienner, 1995.

Doyle, Michael W., Ian Johnstone, and Robert C. Orr (Eds.). *Keeping the Peace: Multidimensional UN Operations in Cambodia and El Salvador*. New York: Cambridge University Press, 1997.

Durch, William J. (Ed.). *The Evolution of UN Peacekeeping: Case Studies and Comparative Analysis*. New York: St. Martin's, 1993.

Durch, William J. (Ed.). *UN Peacekeeping, American Policy, and the Uncivil Wars of the 1990s*. A Henry L. Stimon Center Book. New York: St. Martin's, 1996.

Fabian, Larry L. *Soldiers without Enemies: Preparing the United Nations for Peacekeeping*. Washington, D.C.: Brookings Institution, 1971.

Falk, Mattias. *The Legality of Humanitarian Intervention: A Review in Light of Recent UN Practice*. Stockholm: Juristförlaget, 1996.

Fetherstone, A. B. *Towards a Theory of United Nations Peacekeeping*. New York: St. Martin's, 1994.

Findlay, Trevor. *Cambodia: The Legacy and Lessons of UNTAC*. New York: Oxford University Press, 1995.

Goodrich, Leland M. *Korea: A Study of U.S. Policy*. New York: Council on Foreign Relations, 1956.

Harbottle, Michael. *The Blue Berets*. Harrisburg: Stackpole Books, 1972.

Harrelson, Max. *Fires All around the Horizon: The UN's Uphill Battle to Preserve the Peace*. New York: Praeger, 1989.

Harrison, Selig S., and Masashi Nishihar (Eds.). *UN Peacekeeping: Japanese and American Perspectives*. Washington, D.C.: Carnegie Endowment for International Peace, 1995.

Heininger, Janet E. *Peacekeeping in Transitions: The United Nations in Cambodia*. New York: Twentieth Century Fund Press, 1994.

Higgins, Rosalyn. *United Nations Peacekeeping, 1946–1967. Documents and Commentary*. 4 vols. New York: Oxford University Press, 1980.

International Peace Academy. *Peacekeeper's Handbook*. New York: Pergamon, 1984.

James, Alan. *Peacekeeping in International Politics*. London: Macmillan, 1990.

James, Alan. *The Politics of Peace-keeping*. New York: Praeger, 1969.

Jockel, J. J. *Canada and International Peacekeeping*. Washington, D.C.: Center for Strategic and International Studies, 1994.

Johnstone, Ian. *Aftermath of the Gulf War: An Assessment of UN Action*. Boulder, Colo.: Rienner, 1992.

Johnstone, Ian. *Rights and Reconciliation: UN Strategies in El Salvador*. Boulder, Colo.: Rienner, 1995.

Kaloudis, George Stergiou. *The Role of the UN in Cyprus from 1964 to 1989*. New York: Lang, 1991.

Lee, John M., Robert van Pagenhardt, and Timothy W. Stanley. *To Unite Our Strength: Enhancing the United Nations Peace and Security System*. Lanham, Md.: University Press of America, 1992.

Lefever, Ernest W. *Crisis in the Congo: A United Nations Force in Action*. Washington, D.C.: Brookings Institution, 1965.

Leurdijk, Dick A. *The United Nations and NATO in Former Yugoslavia, 1991–1996: Limits to Diplomacy and Force*. The Hague: Netherlands Institution of International Relations, "Clingedael," 1997.

Liu, F. T. *United Nations Peacekeeping and the Non-use of Force*. Boulder, Colo.: Rienner, 1992.

Mackinlay, John. *The Peacekeepers: An Assessment of Peacekeeping Operations on the Arab-Israeli Interface*. London: Unwin Hyman, 1989.

Makinda, Samuel M. *Seeking Peace from Chaos: Humanitarian Intervention in Somalia*. Boulder, Colo.: Rienner, 1993.

Mays, Terry. *Historical Dictionary of Multinational Peacekeeping*. International Organization Series, No. 9. Lanham, Md.: Scarecrow, 1996.

McCoubrey, Hilaire, and Nigel D. White. *The Blue Helmets: Legal Reg-*

ulation of United Nations Military Operations. Aldershot: Dartmouth, 1996.

Miller, Linda B. *World Order and Local Disorder: The United Nations and Internal Conflicts*. Princeton, N.J.: Princeton University Press, 1967.

Murphy, Sean D. *Humanitarian Intervention: The United Nations in an Evolving World Order*. Philadelphia: University of Pennsylvania Press, 1996.

Nachmani, Amikam. *International Intervention in the Greek Civil War: The United Nations Special Committee on the Balkans, 1947–1952*. New York: Praeger, 1990.

O'Brien, Connor Cruise. *To Katanga and Back*. New York: Simon & Schuster, 1962.

O'Brien, Connor Cruise, and Feliks Topolski. *The United Nations: Sacred Drama*. London: Hutchinson, 1968.

Pugh, Michael (Ed.). *Maritime Security and Peacekeeping*. Manchester: Manchester University Press, 1994.

Ratner, Steven R. *The New UN Peacekeeping: Building Peace in Lands of Conflict after the Cold War*. New York: St. Martin's, 1995.

Rikhje, Indar Jit. *The Future of Peacekeeping*. New York: International Peace Academy, 1989.

Rikhje, Indar Jit. *The Theory and Practice of Peacekeeping*. London: Hurst, 1984.

Rikhje, Indar Jit, and Kjell Skelsbaek (Eds.). *The United Nations and Peacekeeping, Results, Limitations and Prospects: The Lessons of 40 Years of Experience*. New York: St. Martin's, 1991.

Shaw, Mark, and Jakkie Cilliers. *South Africa and Peacekeeping in Africa: Vol. I*. Halfway House, South Africa: Institute for Defence Policy, 1995.

Siekmann, Robert D. R. *Basic Documents on United Nations and Related Peace-keeping Forces*. 2nd enlarged ed. Dordrecht: Nijhoff, 1989.

Siilasvuo, Ensio. *In the Service of Peace in the Middle East, 1967–1979*. New York: St. Martin's, 1992.

Skogomo, Bjorn. *UNIGIL: International Peacekeeping in Lebanon, 1978–1988*. Boulder, Colo.: Rienner, 1989.

Sköld, Nils. *United Nations Peacekeeping after Suez: UNEF 1—The Swedish Involvement*. New York: St. Martin's, 1996.

Smith, Hugh (Ed.). *Australia and Peacekeeping*. Canberra: Australian Defence Studies Centre, 1990.

Sommer, John. *Hope Restored? Humanitarian Aid in Somalia 1990–1994*. Washington, D.C.: Refugee Policy Group, 1995.

Stegenga, James A. *The United Nations Force in Cyprus*. Columbus: Ohio State University Press, 1968.

Thakur, Ramesh. *International Peacekeeping in Lebanon: United Nations Authority and Multinational Force.* Boulder, Colo.: Westview, 1987.

Thakur, Ramesh, and Carlyle A. Thayer. *A Crisis of Expectations: UN Peacekeeping in the 1990s.* Boulder, Colo.: Westview, 1995.

United Nations. *The Blue Helmets: A Review of United Nations Peacekeeping.* 3rd ed. New York: Department of Public Information, United Nations, 1996.

United Nations. *The United Nations and Cambodia, 1991–1995.* New York: Author, 1995.

United Nations. *The United Nations and El Salvador, 1990–1995.* New York: Author, 1995.

United Nations. *The United Nations and Mozambique, 1992–1995.* New York: Author, 1995.

United Nations. *The United Nations and Rwanda, 1993–1996.* New York: Author, 1996.

United Nations. *The United Nations and Somalia, 1992–1996.* New York: Author, 1996.

Verrier, Anthony. *International Peacekeeping: United Nations Forces in a Troubled World.* New York: Penguin, 1981.

Von Horn, Carl. *Soldiering for Peace.* New York: McKay, 1966.

Wainhouse, David W. *International Peacekeeping at the Crossroads: National Support—Experience and Prospects.* Baltimore: Johns Hopkins University Press, 1973.

Wiseman, Henry (Ed.). *Peacekeeping: Appraisals and Proposals.* New York: Pergamon, 1983.

Wolfrum, Rüdiger, and Christiane Philipp (Eds.). *United Nations: Law, Policies and Practice.* Rev. English ed. Boston: Beck/Nijhoff, 1995.

Women's Studies Quarterly. Vol. 24, Nos. 1 & 2 (Spring/Summer 1996). Special issue: Beijing and Beyond: Toward the Twenty-First Century of Women.

World Commission on Environment and Development (Bruntland Commission Report). *Our Common Future.* Oxford: Oxford University Press, 1987.

Wronka, Joseph M. *Human Rights and Social Policy in the Twenty-First Century: A History of the Idea of Human Rights and Comparison of the United Nations Universal Declaration of Human Rights with United States Federal and State Constitutions.* Lanham, Md.: University Press of America, 1992.

Yeselson, Abraham, and Anthony Gaglione. *A Dangerous Place: The United Nations as a Weapon in World Politics.* New York: Grossman, 1974.

Yoder, Amos. *The Evolution of the United Nations System.* 2nd ed. Washington, D.C.: Taylor & Francis, 1993.

Zacarias, Agostinho. *The United Nations and International Peacekeeping*. New York: St. Martin's, 1996.

Zacher, Mark W. *Dag Hammarskjöld's United Nations*. New York: Columbia University Press, 1970.

Zacher, Mark W. *International Conflicts and Collective Security, 1946–1977*. New York: Praeger, 1979.

Zammit Cutajar, Michael (Ed.). *UNCTAD and the South-North Dialogue: The First Twenty Years: Essays in Memory of W.R. Malinowski*. Elmsford, N.Y.: Pergamon, 1985.

Specialized and Related Agencies of the United Nations

General

Ahlurvalia, Kuljit. *The Legal Status, Privileges and Immunities of the Specialized Agencies of the United Nations and Certain Other International Organizations*. New York: International, 1964.

Alexandrowicz, Charles H. *Law Making Functions of the Specialized Agencies of the United Nations*. Littleton, Colo.: Rothman, 1973.

Ameri, Houshang. *Politics and Process in the Specialized Agencies of the United Nations*. Aldershot: Gower, 1982.

Cox, Robert W. (Ed.). *The Politics of International Organization: Studies in Multilateral Social and Economic Agencies*. New York: Praeger, 1970.

Cox, Robert W., Harold K. Jacobson, et al. *The Anatomy of Influence: Decision Making in International Organization*. New Haven, Conn.: Yale University Press, 1973.

Imber, Mark. *The USA, ILO, UNESCO and IAEA: Politicization and Withdrawal in the Specialized Agencies*. New York: St. Martin's, 1989.

Karns, Margaret P., and Karen A. Mingst. *The United States and Multilateral Institutions: Patterns of Changing Instrumentality and Influence*. Boston: Unwin Hyman, 1990.

Luard, Evan. *International Agencies: The Emerging Framework of Interdependence*. London: Macmillan, 1977.

Osakwe, Chris. *Participation of the Soviet Union in Universal Organization: A Political Analysis of Soviet Strategies and Aspirations Inside ILO, UNESCO, and WHO*. Atlantic Highlands, N.J.: Humanities, 1973.

Sewell, James P. *Functionalism and World Politics*. Princeton, N.J.: Princeton University Press, 1966.

Wells, Robert N., Jr. *Peace by Pieces—United Nations Agencies and Their Roles: A Reader and Selective Bibliography*. Metuchen, N.J.: Scarecrow Press, 1991.

Williams, Douglas. *The Specialized Agencies of the United Nations: The System in Crisis.* New York: St. Martin's, 1987.

Communications and Transportation

Codding, George A. *The International Telecommunication Union.* Dedham, Mass.: Artech House, 1972.

Codding, George A. *The Universal Postal Union.* New York: New York University Press, 1964.

Codding, George A., and Anthony M. Ruthkowski. *The International Telecommunication Union in a Changing World.* Dedham, Mass.: Artech House, 1982.

Henry, Cleopatra Elmira. *The Carriage of Dangerous Goods by Sea: The Role of the International Maritime Organization in International Legislation.* New York: St. Martin's, 1985.

Mankabady, Samir (Ed.). *The International Maritime Organization.* Baltimore: Croom Helm, 1984.

Savage, James G. *The Politics of International Telecommunication Regulation.* Boulder, Colo.: Westview, 1989.

White, Rita Laura, and Harold M. White, Jr. *The Law and Regulation of International Space Communication.* Dedham, Mass.: Artech House, 1988.

Zacher, Mark W., with Brent A. Sutton. *Governing Global Networks: International Regimes for Transportation and Communications.* Cambridge: Cambridge University Press, 1996.

Economic Development and Finance

Aufricht, Hans. *The International Monetary Fund: Legal Bases, Structure, Functions.* New York: Praeger, 1964.

Ayok, Chol Anthony. *IMF and the Underdeveloped Countries.* Dar es Salaam: Sameja, 1984.

Ayres, Robert. *Banking on the Poor: The World Bank and World Poverty.* Cambridge, Mass.: MIT Press, 1983.

Baker, James C. *The International Finance Corporation: Origin, Operations and Evaluations.* New York: Praeger, 1968.

Bhatnagar, Bhuvan, James Kearns, and Debra Sequeria (Eds.). *The World Bank Participation Sourcebook.* Washington, D.C.: World Bank, 1996.

Bird, Graham. *IMF Lending to Developing Countries: Issues and Evidence.* London: Routledge, 1995.

Brown, Bartram S. *The United States and the Politicization of the World Bank: Issues of International Law and Policy.* New York: Kegan Paul International, 1992.

Brydon, Lynne, and Karen Legge. *Adjusting Society: The World Bank, the IMF and Ghana.* London: Tauris, 1996.

Buvinic, Mayra, Catherine Gwin, and Lisa M. Bates. *Investing in*

Women: Progress and Prospects for the World Bank. ODC Policy Essay, 19. Washington, D.C.: Overseas Development Council, 1996.

Caufield, Catherine. *Masters of Illusion: The World Bank and the Poverty of Nations.* A Marian Wood Book. New York: Holt, 1996.

Chandavarkar, Anand G. *The International Monetary Fund: Its Financial Organization and Activities.* Washington, D.C.: International Monetary Fund, 1984.

Chossudovsky, Michel. *The Globalisation of Poverty: Impacts of IMF and World Bank Reforms.* London: Zed, 1997.

Clapp, Jennifer. *Adjustment and Agriculture in Africa: Farmers, the State and the World Bank in Guinea.* New York: St. Martin's, 1997.

Commins, Stephen K. (Ed.). *Africa's Development Challenges and the World Bank: Hard Questions, Costly Choices.* Boulder, Colo.: Rienner, 1988.

Dam, Kenneth. *The Rules of the Game: Reform and Evolution in the International Monetary System.* Chicago: University of Chicago Press, 1982.

De Vries, Margaret Garritsen. *Balance of Payments Adjustment, 1945 to 1986: The IMF Experience.* Washington, D.C.: International Monetary Fund, 1987.

De Vries, Margaret Garritsen. *The IMF in a Changing World, 1945–85.* Washington, D.C.: International Monetary Fund, 1986.

De Vries, Margaret Garritsen (Ed.). *International Monetary Fund, 1966–1971: The System under Stress.* 2 vols. Washington, D.C.: International Monetary Fund, 1976.

De Vries, Margaret Garritsen (Ed.). *International Monetary Fund, 1972–1978: Cooperation on Trial.* 3 vols. Washington, D.C.: International Monetary Fund, 1985.

Denters, Erik. *Law and Policy of IMF Conditionality.* Boston: Kluwer Law International, 1996.

Edwards, Sebastian. *The IMF and the Developing Countries: A Critical Evaluation.* Carnegie-Rochester Conference Series on Public Policy, No. 31. Washington, D.C.: North Holland, 1989.

Ferguson, Tyrone. *The Third World and Decision Making in the International Monetary Fund.* Geneva: Graduate Institute of International Studies, 1987.

Finch, David C. *The IMF: The Record and Prospect.* Essays in International Finance, No. 175. Princeton, N.J.: International Finance Section, Department of Economics, Princeton University, 1989.

Ghai, Dharam (Ed.). *The IMF and the South: The Social Impact of Crisis and Adjustment.* London: Zed, 1991.

Gold, Joseph. *Interpretation: The IMF and International Law.* Boston: Kluwer Law International, 1996.

Griesgraber, Jo Marie, and Bernhard G. Gunter (Eds.). *Development:*

New Paradigms and Principles for the Twenty-First Century. Rethinking Bretton Woods, Vol. 2. East Haven, Conn.: Pluto, with Center of Concern, 1995.

Griesgraber, Jo Marie, and Bernhard G. Gunter (Eds.). *Promoting Development: Effective Global Institutions for the Twenty-First Century.* Rethinking Bretton Woods, Vol. 1. East Haven, Conn.: Pluto, with Center of Concern, 1995.

Griesgraber, Jo Marie, and Bernhard G. Gunter (Eds.). *The World Bank: Lending on a Global Scale.* Rethinking Bretton Woods, Vol. 3. Chicago: Pluto, 1996.

Gwin, Catherine, and Richard E. Feinberg (Eds.). *The International Monetary Fund in a Multipolar World: Pulling Together.* Washington, D.C.: Overseas Development Council, 1989.

Gylfason, Thorvaldur. *Credit Policy and Economic Activity in Developing Countries with IMF Stabilization Programs.* Studies in International Finance, No. 60. Princeton, N.J.: Princeton University, 1987.

Hanlon, Joseph. *Peace without Profit: How the IMF Blocks Rebuilding in Mozambique.* Portsmouth, N.H.: Heinemann, 1996.

Haq, Mahbub ul, et al. (Eds.). *The UN and the Bretton Woods Institutions: New Challenges for the Twenty-First Century.* New York: St. Martin's, 1995.

Helleiner, Gerald K. (Ed.). *Africa and the International Monetary Fund.* Washington, D.C.: International Monetary Fund, 1983.

Heller, Peter S., et al. *The Implications of Fund-Supported Adjustment Programs for Poverty.* Occasional Paper No. 58. Washington, D.C.: International Monetary Fund, 1988.

Holland, Stuart. *Toward a New Bretton Woods: Alternatives for the Global Economy.* Nottingham, U.K.: Spokesman, 1994.

Honeywell, Martin (Ed.). *The Poverty Brokers, the IMF and Latin America.* London: Latin America Bureau, 1983.

Horsefield, J. Keith (Ed.). *The International Monetary Fund, 1945–1965: Twenty Years of Monetary Cooperation.* 3 vols. Washington, D.C.: International Monetary Fund, 1969.

Humphreys, Norman K. *Historical Dictionary of the International Monetary Fund.* International Organizations Series, No. 2. Metuchen, N.J.: Scarecrow, 1993.

Hurni, B. S. *The Lending Policy of the World Bank in the 1970s: Analysis and Evaluation.* Boulder, Colo.: Westview, 1980.

Jacobson, Harold K., and Michel Okensberg. *China's Participation in the IMF, the World Bank, and GATT: Toward a Global Economic Order.* Ann Arbor: University of Michigan Press, 1990.

James, Harold. *International Monetary Cooperation since Bretton Woods.* New York: Oxford University Press, 1996.

Kapur, Devesh, John P. Lewis, and Richard Webb (Eds.). *The World*

Bank: Its First Half Century. Vol. 1. History. Washington, D.C.: Brookings Institution, 1997.

Kapur, Devesh, John P. Lewis, and Richard Webb (Eds.). *The World Bank: Its First Half Century*. Vol. 2. Perspectives. Washington, D.C.: Brookings Institution, 1997.

Kenen, Peter B. *Managing the World Economy: Fifty Years after Bretton Woods*. Washington, D.C.: Institute for International Economics, 1994.

Killick, Tony (Ed.). *The IMF and Stabilization: Developing Country Experiences*. New York: St. Martin's, 1984.

Killick, Tony. *IMF Programmes in Developing Countries: Design and Impact*. New York: Routledge, 1995.

Killick, Tony (Ed.). *The Quest for Economic Stabilisation: The IMF and the Third World*. New York: St. Martin's, 1984.

King, John A. *Economic Development Projects and Their Appraisal: Cases and Principles from the Experience of the World Bank*. Baltimore: Johns Hopkins University Press, 1967.

Körner, Peter, et al. *The IMF and the Debt Crisis: A Guide to the Third World's Dilemma*. London: Zed, 1986.

Kraske, Jochen. *Bankers with a Mission: The Presidents of the World Bank, 1946–91*. New York: Oxford University Press, 1996.

Lister, Frederick K. *Decision-Making Strategies for International Organizations: The IMF Model*. Denver: Graduate School of International Studies, University of Denver, 1984.

Mason, Edward S., and Robert E. Asher. *The World Bank since Bretton Woods*. Washington, D.C.: Brookings Institution, 1973.

Matecki, B. E. *Establishment of the International Finance Corporation and United States Policy: A Case Study in International Organization*. New York: Praeger, 1957.

Miller, Morris. *Coping Is Not Enough: The International Debt Crisis and the Roles of the World Bank and the International Monetary Fund*. Homewood, Ill.: Dow Jones–Irwin, 1985.

Morley, Samuel A. *Poverty and Inequality in Latin America: The Impact of Adjustment and Recovery in the 1980s*. Baltimore: Johns Hopkins University Press, 1995.

Mosley, Paul, Jane Harrigan, and John Toye. *Aid and Power: The World Bank and Policy-Based Lending*. 2 vols. New York: Routledge, 1991.

Myers, Robert J. (Ed.). *The Political Morality of the International Monetary Fund*. New Brunswick, N.J.: Transaction Books, 1987.

Narasimham, M. *Bretton Woods—Forty Years On*. Bombay: Forum of Free Enterprise, 1984.

Norton, Joseph J. (Ed.). *Emerging Financial Markets and the Role of International Financial Organizations*. Boston: Kluwer Law International, 1996.

Oliver, Robert W. *George Woods and the World Bank*. Boulder, Colo.: Rienner, 1995.

Onimode, Bade (Ed.). *The IMF, the World Bank and the African Debt*. 2 vols. London: Zed, 1989.

OXFAM. *Africa Make or Break: The Failure of IMF/World Bank Policies*. Oxford: Author, 1993.

Pastor, Manuel. *The International Monetary Fund and Latin America: Economic Stabilization and Class Conflict*. Boulder, Colo.: Westview, 1987, ©1986.

Payer, Cheryl. *The Debt Trap: The IMF and the Third World*. New York: Monthly Review Press, 1974.

Payer, Cheryl. *The World Bank: A Critical Analysis*. New York: Monthly Review Press, 1982.

Peace, Stanley. *The Hobbled Giant: Essays on the World Bank*. Boulder, Colo.: Westview, 1984.

Polak, Jacques J. *The World Bank and the International Monetary Fund: A Changing Relationship*. Washington, D.C.: Brookings Institution, 1994.

Reid, Escott. *Strengthening of the World Bank*. Chicago: University of Chicago Press, 1976.

Salda, Anne C. (Compiler). *International Monetary Fund* [Bibliography]. International Organization Series, Vol. 4. New Brunswick, N.J.: Transaction, 1992.

Salda, Anne C. (Compiler). *The World Bank* [Bibliography]. International Organization Series, Vol. 9. New Brunswick, N.J.: Transaction, 1995.

Schadler, Susan, et al. *IMF Conditionality: Experience under Stand-By and Extended Arrangements*. Pts. 1 and 2. Occasional Papers No. 128 and 129. Washington, D.C.: International Monetary Fund, 1995.

Schild, Georg. *Bretton Woods and Dumbarton Oaks: American Economic and Political Post-War Planning in the Summer of 1944*. New York: St. Martin's, 1995.

Schydlowsky, Daniel M. (Ed.). *Structural Adjustment: Retrospect and Prospect*. Westport, Conn.: Praeger, 1995.

Shihata, Ibrahim F. I. *MIGA and Foreign Investments: Origins, Operations, Policies, and Basic Documents of the Multilateral Investment Guarantee Agency*. Boston: Nijhoff, 1988.

Shihata, Ibrahim F. I. *The World Bank in a Changing World: Selected Essays and Lectures*. 2 vols. Cambridge: Kluwer Law International, 1991, 1995.

Shihata, Ibrahim F. I. *The World Bank Inspection Panel*. New York: Oxford University Press, 1995.

Siddell, Scott R. *The IMF and Third World Instability: Is There a Connection?* London: Macmillan, 1988.

Simha, S. L. N. *Fifty Years of Bretton Woods Twins (IMF and World Bank)*. Chennai, India: Institute for Financial Mangement and Research, 1996.

Solomon, Robert. *The IMF, 1945–1976: An Insider's View*. New York: Harper & Row, 1977.

Szobó-Pelsöczi, Mikós (Ed.). *Fifty Years After Bretton Woods: The New Challenge of East-West Partnership for Economic Progress*. Brookfield, Vt.: Avebury, 1996.

Tew, Brian. *International Monetary Cooperation, 1945–1970*. 10th rev. ed. London: Hutchinson, 1970.

Torfs, Marijke. *Effects of the IMF Structural Adjustment Programs on Social Sectors of Third World Countries*. Washington, D.C.: Friends of the Earth/Environmental Policy Institute/Oceanic Society, May 1991.

Ul Haq, Mahbub, et al. (Eds.). *The UN and the Bretton Woods Institutions: New Challenges for the Twenty-First Century*. New York: St. Martin's, 1995.

Van de Laar, Aart. *The World Bank and the Poor*. The Hague: Nijhoff, 1980.

Van Dormael, Armand. *Bretton Woods: Birth of a Monetary Order*. New York: Holmes & Meier, 1978.

Weaver, James H. *The International Development Association: A New Approach to Development*. New York: Praeger, 1965.

Williamson, John (Ed.). *IMF Conditionality*. Washington, D.C.: Institute for International Economics, 1983.

Wilson, Carol R. *The World Bank Group: A Guide to Information Sources*. New York: Garland, 1991.

World Bank. *Adjustment Lending: An Evaluation of Ten Years of Experience*. Washington, D.C.: Author, 1989.

World Bank. *The Evolving Role of IDA*. Washington, D.C.: Author, 1989.

World Bank. *Governance: The World Bank's Experience*. Washington, D.C.: International Bank for Reconstruction and Development, 1994.

World Bank. *IDA in Retrospect: The First Two Decades of the International Development Association*. New York: Oxford University Press, 1982.

World Bank. *The International Bank for Reconstruction and Development, 1946–1953*. Baltimore: Johns Hopkins University Press, 1954.

World Bank. *The World Bank and International Finance Corporation*. Washington, D.C.: Author, April 1986.

World Bank. [Bibliography]. Oxford: Clio, 1995.

Zulu, Justin B., and Saleh M. Nsouli. *Adjustment Programs in Africa: The Recent Experience*. Washington, D.C.: International Monetary Fund, 1985.

Environment

Bank Information Center. *Funding Ecological and Social Destruction: The World Bank and International Monetary Fund.* Washington, D.C.: Author, 1990.

Brack, Duncan. *International Trade and the Montreal Protocol.* London: Royal Institute of International Affairs, 1996.

Le Prestre, Philippe. *The World Bank and the Environmental Challenge.* London: Associated University Presses, 1989.

M'Gongile, Michael, and Mark Zacher. *Pollution, Politics, and International Law: Tankers at Sea.* Berkeley: University of California Press, 1979.

Rich, Bruce. *Mortgaging the Earth: The World Bank, Environmental Impoverishment and the Crisis of Development.* Boston: Beacon, 1994.

Talbot, Ross B. *Historical Dictionary of the International Food Agencies: FAO, WFP, IFC, IFAD.* International Organizations Series, No. 6. Metuchen, N.J.: Scarecrow Press, 1994.

United Nations Environment Program. *Two Decades of Achievement and Challenge.* Nairobi: Author, October 1992.

Food, Health, and Shelter

Abbott, John. *Politics and Poverty: A Critique of the Food and Agriculture Organization of the United Nations.* London: Routledge, 1992.

Berkov, Robert. *The First Ten Years of the World Health Organization.* Albany, N.Y.: World Health Organization, 1958.

Berkov, Robert. *The Second Ten Years of the World Health Organization.* Albany, N.Y.: World Health Organization, 1968.

Chisholm, Brock. *Prescription for Survival.* Irvington, N.Y.: Columbia University Press, 1957.

Food and Agriculture Organization of the United Nations. *Activities of International Organizations Concerned with Fisheries.* Rome: Author, 1987.

Hoole, Francis W. *Politics and Budgeting in the World Health Organization.* Bloomington: Indiana University Press, 1976.

Marchisio, Sergio, and Antonietta DiBiase. *The Food and Agriculture Organization.* Boston: Nijhoff, 1991.

Siddiqi, Javed. *World Health and World Politics: The World Health Organization and the UN System.* London: Hurst, 1995.

Talbot, Ross B. *The Four World Food Agencies in Rome.* Ames: Iowa State University Press, 1990.

Labor and Human Rights

Alcock, Antony. *The History of the International Labour Organisation.* London: Macmillan, 1970.

Bartolomei de la Cruz, Hector G., et al. *The International Labor Organization: The International Standards System and Basic Human Rights*. Boulder, Colo.: Westview, 1996.

Galenson, Walter. *The International Labor Organization: An American View*. Madison: University of Wisconsin Press, 1981.

Ghebali, Victor Yves, Roberto Ago, and Nicolas Valticos. *The International Labour Organization: A Case Study on the Evolution of UN Specialized Agencies*. Dordrecht: Nijhoff, 1989.

Haas, Ernst B. *Beyond the Nation State: Functionalism and International Organization*. Stanford, Calif.: Stanford University Press, 1964.

Haas, Ernst B. *Human Rights and International Action: The Case of Freedom of Association*. Stanford, Calif.: Stanford University Press, 1970.

Jenks, Wilfred C. *Social Justice in the Law of Nations: The ILO Impact after Fifty Years*. New York: Oxford University Press, 1970.

Johnston, G. A. *The International Labour Organization: Its Work for Social and Economic Progress*. London: Europa, 1970.

Lubin, Carol Riegelman, and Anne Winslow. *Social Justice for Women: The International Labor Organization and Women*. Durham, N.C.: Duke University Press, 1990.

Morse, David. *The Origin and Evolution of the ILO and Its Role in the World Community*. Ithaca: New York State School of Industrial and Labor Relations, Cornell University, 1969.

Nuclear Energy

Scheinman, Lawrence. *The International Atomic Energy Agency and World Nuclear Order*. Washington, D.C.: Resources for the Future, 1987.

Schiff, Benjamin N. *International Nuclear Technology Transfer: Dilemmas of Dissemination and Control*. Lanham, Md.: Rowman & Allanheld, 1983.

Szasz, Paul C. *The Law and Practices of the International Atomic Energy Agency*. Vienna: International Atomic Energy Agency, 1970.

Social, Cultural and Educational

Coate, Roger. *Unilateralism, Ideology and United States Foreign Policy: The US In and Out of UNESCO*. Boulder, Colo.: Rienner, 1988.

Evans, Luther H. *The United States and UNESCO*. Dobbs Ferry, N.Y.: Oceana, 1971.

Giffard, C. Anthony. *UNESCO and the Media*. New York: Longman, 1989.

Hajnal, Peter I. *Guide to UNESCO.* New York: Oceana, 1983.

Haves, Walter A. C., and Charles A. Thomson. *UNESCO: Purpose, Progress, Prospects.* Bloomington: Indiana University Press, 1957.

Hoggart, Richard. *An Idea and Its Servants: UNESCO from Within.* New York: Oxford University Press, 1987.

Huxley, Julian. *UNESCO: Its Purpose and Philosophy.* Washington, D.C.: Public Affairs Press, 1978.

Jones, Phillip W. *International Policies for Third World Education: UNESCO, Literacy and Development.* New York: Routledge, 1988.

Maheu, Rene. *UNESCO in Perspective.* Lanham, Md.: Unipublishers, 1974.

Preston, William, Edward S. Herman, and Herbert I. Schiller. *Hope and Folly: The United States and UNESCO*: Minneapolis: University of Minnesota Press, 1992.

Sewell, James P. *UNESCO and World Politics: Engaging in International Relations.* Princeton, N.J.: Princeton University Press, 1975.

Singh, Nihal. *The Rise and Fall of UNESCO.* Calcutta: Allied, 1987.

Spaulding, Seth, and Lin Lin. *Historical Dictionary of the United Nations Educational, Scientific and Cultural Organization (UNESCO).* International Organizations Series, No. 13. Lanham, Md.: Scarecrow Press, 1997.

Wells, Clare. *The UN, UNESCO and the Politics of Knowledge.* London: Macmillan, 1987.

Trade

Collins, Susan M., and Barry P. Bosworth (Eds.). *The New GATT: Implications for the United States.* Brookings Occasional Papers. Washington, D.C.: Brookings Institution, 1994.

Croome, John. *Reshaping the World Economy: A History of the Uruguay Round.* Geneva: World Trade Organizations, 1995.

Dam, Kenneth. *The GATT: Law and International Economic Organization.* Chicago: University of Chicago Press, 1977.

Dennin, Joseph F. *Law and Practice of the World Trade Organization.* Dobbs Ferry, N.Y.: Oceana, 1995.

GATT: What It Is, What It Does. Geneva: GATT, 1991.

Hoekman, Bernard M., and Michael M. Kostecki (Eds.). *The Political Economy of the World Trading System: From GATT to WTO.* Oxford: Oxford University Press, 1995.

Hudec, R. E. *The GATT Legal System and World Trade Diplomacy.* 2nd ed. Salom: Butterworth Legal, 1990.

Jackson, John H. *Implementing the Uruguay Round.* Oxford: Oxford University Press, 1997.

Jackson, John Howard. *The World Trading System: Law and Policy of International Economic Relations.* 2nd ed. Cambridge, Mass.: MIT Press, 1997.

Kasto, Jalil (Ed.). *The Function and Future of the World Trade Organization: International Trade Law between GATT and WTO*. Hounslow: Jalil Kasto, 1996.

Kock, Karin. *International Trade Policy and the GATT: 1947–1967*. Stockholm: Almquist & Wilsell, 1969.

Long, Oliver. *Law and Its Limitations in the GATT Multilateral Trade System*. Dordrecht: Nijhoff, 1985.

Low, Patrick. *Trading Free: The GATT and U.S. Trade Policy*. New York: Twentieth Century Fund, 1993.

Petersmann, Ernst Urlich. *The GATT/WTO Dispute Settlement System: International Law, International Organizations and Dispute Settlement*. Boston: Kluwer Law International, 1996.

Preeg, Ernest H. *Trade in a Brave New World: The Uruguay Round and the Future of the International System*. Chicago: University of Chicago Press, 1995.

Qureshi, Asif H. *The World Trade Organization: Implementing International Trade Norms*. Melland Schill Studies in International Law. Manchester: Manchester University Press, 1996.

Raworth, Philip, and Linda Reif. *The Law of the World Trade Organization: Final Text of the GATT Uruguay Round Agreements, Summary* (with Autobook Diskette). Dobbs Ferry, N.Y.: Oceana, 1995.

Schott, Jeffrey J. *WTO 2000: Setting the Course for the World Trading System*. Washington, D.C.: Institute of International Economics, 1996.

Schott, Jeffrey J., assisted by Johanna W. Buurman. *The Uruguay Round: An Assessment*. Washington, D.C.: Institute of International Economics, 1994.

Stewart, Terence P. (Ed.). *The World Trade Organization: The Multilateral Trade Framework for the 21st Century and U.S. Implementing Legislation*. Chicago: American Bar Association and Section of International Law and Practice, 1996.

Swacker, Frank W., Kenneth R. Redden, and Larry B. Wenger. *World Trade without Barriers: The World Trade Organization (WTO) and Dispute Resolution*. Charlottesville: Michie, Butterworth Law, 1995.

Tussie, Diana. *The Less Developed Countries and the World Trading System: A Challenge to the GATT*. New York: St. Martin's, 1987.

Van Dijck, Pitou, and Gerrit Faber. *Challenges of the New World Trade Organization*. Cambridge: Kluwer Law International, 1996.

Whally, John. *The Future of the World Trading System*. Washington, D.C.: Institute for International Economics, 1993.

Wiener, Jarrod. *Making Rules in the Uruguay Round of the GATT*. Aldershot: Dartmouth, 1995.

Winham, Gilbert R. *International Trade and the Tokyo Round Negotiations*. Princeton, N.J.: Princeton University Press, 1986.

Regional Organizations

General

Akindele, R. A. *The Organization and Promotion of World Peace: A Study of Universal-Regional Relationships.* Toronto: University of Toronto Press, 1976.

Andemicael, Berhanykun (Ed.). *Regionalism and the United Nations.* Dobbs Ferry, N.Y.: Oceana Publications for UNITAR, 1979.

Cantori, Louis J., and Steven L. Spiegel. *The International Relations of Regions: A Comparative Approach.* Englewood Cliffs, N.J.: Prentice Hall, 1970.

Chayes, Abram, and Antonia Handler Chayes (Eds.). *Preventing Conflict in the Post-Communist World: Mobilizing International and Regional Organizations.* Brookings Occasional Papers. Washington, D.C.: Brookings Institution, 1996.

Faini, Riccardo, and Enzo Grilli (Eds.). *Multilateralism and Regionalism after the Uruguay Round.* New York: St. Martin's, 1997.

Fawcett, Louise, and Andrew Hurrell. *Regionalism in World Politics: Regional Organizations and International Order.* New York: Oxford University Press, 1995.

Fishlow, Albert, and Stephan Haggard. *The United States and the Regionalization of the World Economy.* Paris: Organisation for Economic Co-operation and Development, March 1992.

Gamble, Andrew, and Anthony Payne. *Regionalism and World Order.* New York: St. Martin's, 1996.

Hawdon, James. *Emerging Organizational Forms: The Proliferation of Regional Intergovernmental Organizations in the Modern World-System.* Contributions to Sociology, No. 119. Westport, Conn.: Greenwood, 1996.

Hong, Ki-Joon. *The CSCE Security Regime Formation: An Asian Perspective.* New York: St. Martin's, 1997.

Lindberg, Leon, and Stuart Scheingold (Eds.). *Regional Integration.* Oxford: Oxford University Press, 1971.

Marashi, S. H. *Activities of Regional Fishery Bodies and Other International Organizations Concerned with Fisheries.* Rome: Food and Agriculture Organization, 1993.

Nierop, Tom. *Systems and Regions in Global Politics: An Empirical Study of Diplomacy, International Organization and Trade, 1950–1991.* New York: Wiley, 1994.

Nye, Joseph S. *International Regionalism: Readings.* Boston: Little, Brown, 1968.

Nye, Joseph S. *Peace in Parts: Integration and Conflict in Regional Organization.* Boston: Little, Brown, 1971.

Russett, Bruce. *International Regions and the International System.* Chicago: Rand McNally, 1967.

Tow, William. *Subregional Security Cooperation in the Third World.* Boulder, Colo.: Rienner, 1990.

Africa

Adibe, Clement, and Mike MacKinnon. *Managing Arms in Peace Processes: Liberia.* UNIDIR/96/32. Geneva: United Nations Institute for Disarmament and Research (UNIDIR), 1996.

Agbi, Sunday O. *The Organization of African Unity and African Diplomacy, 1963–1979.* Agodi: Impact Publishers Nigeria, 1986.

Amate, C. O. C. *Inside the OAU: Pan-Africanism in Practice.* Basingstoke: Macmillan, 1986.

Ankumah, Evelyn A. *The African Commission on Human and Peoples' Rights.* Cambridge: Kluwer Law International, 1996.

Asanta, S. K. B. *The Political Economy of Regionalism in Africa: A Decade of ECOWAS.* New York: Praeger, 1986.

Bhatia, Rattan J. *The West African Monetary Union: An Analytic Review.* IMF Occasional Paper Number 35. Washington, D.C.: International Monetary Fund, 1985.

DeLancey, Mark W., and Terry M. Mays. *Historical Dictionary of International Organizations in Sub-Saharan Africa.* International Organizations Series No. 3. Metuchen, N.J.: Scarecrow, 1994.

El-Ayouty, Yassin (Ed.). *Organization of African Unity after Thirty Years.* Westport, Conn.: Praeger, 1994.

English, E. Phillip, and Harris M. Mule. *The African Development Bank.* Boulder, Co.: Rienner, 1996.

Ezenwe, Uka. *ECOWAS and the Economic Integration of West Africa.* New York: St. Martin's, 1983.

Fredland, Richard A. *A Guide to African International Organization.* New York: Zell, 1990.

Fredland, Richard A., and Christian P. Potholm (Eds.). *Integration and Disintegration in East Africa.* Lanham, Md.: University Press of America, 1980.

Harris, Gorden. *The Organization of African Unity* [Bibliography]. Oxford: CLIO, 1994.

Hazelwood, Arthur. *Economic Integration: The East African Experience.* London: Heinemann, 1975.

Hazelwood, Arthur (Ed.). *African Integration and Disintegration: Case Studies in Economic and Political Union.* London: Oxford University Press, 1967.

Mingst, Karen A. *Politics and the African Development Bank.* Lexington: University Press of Kentucky, 1990.

Mwase, Ngila. *The East African Community: A Study of Regional Disintegration*. Paper No. 77. Dar es Salaam: Economic Research Bureau, University of Dar es Salaam, 1979.

Naldi, Gino J. *The Organization of African Unity: An Analysis of Its Role*. London: Mansell, 1989.

Nye, Joseph S. *Pan-Africanism and East African Integration*. Cambridge, Mass.: Harvard University Press, 1965.

Nyong'o, Anyang' (Ed.). *Regional Integration in Africa: Unfinished Agenda*. Nairobi: African Academy of Sciences, 1990.

Onwuka, Ralph I. *Development and Integration in West Africa: The Case of the Economic Community of West African States (ECOWAS)*. Ife, Nigeria: University of Ife Press, 1982.

Plessz, Nicholas G. *Problems and Prospects of Economic Integration in West Africa*. Montreal: McGill University Press, 1968.

Robson, Peter. *Economic Integration in Africa*. Evanston, Ill.: Northwestern University Press, 1968.

Wolfers, Michael. *Politics in the Organization of African Unity*. London: Methuen, 1976.

Woronoff, Jon. *Organizing African Unity*. Metuchen, N.J.: Scarecrow, 1969.

Asia

Anwar, Dewi. *Indonesia in ASEAN: Foreign Policy and Regionalism*. New York: St. Martin's, 1994.

ASEAN Centre. *ASEAN-Japan Statistical Pocketbook*. Tokyo: ASEAN Promotion Centre on Trade, Investment and Tourism, 1993.

Asia Pacific Economic Community. *A Vision for APEC: Towards an Asian Pacific Economic Community: Report of the Eminent Persons Group to APEC Ministers*. Singapore: Author, October 1993.

Australia Department of Foreign Affairs and Trade. *The APEC Region: Trade and Investment*. Canberra: Author, 1993.

Beckovitch, Jacob (Ed.). *ANZUS in Crisis: Alliance Management in International Affairs*. New York: St. Martin's, 1988.

Broinowski, Alison (Ed.). *ASEAN into the 1990s*. New York: St. Martin's, 1990.

Broinowski, Alison. *Understanding ASEAN*. New York: St. Martin's, 1982.

Bundy, Barbara, Stephen Burns, and Kimberly Weichel (Eds.). *The Future of the Pacific Rim: Scenarios for Regional Cooperation*. New York: Praeger, 1994.

Clements, Kevin (Ed.). *Peace and Security in the Asia Pacific Region*. Tokyo: United Nations University Press, 1993.

Drysdale, Peter, and Hugh Patrick. *An Asian Pacific Regional Economic*

Organization. Congressional Research Paper. Washington, D.C.: Library of Congress, 1979.

Economic Group Meeting on Feasible Forms of Economic Co-operation and Integration in Western Asia. *Economic Integration in Western Asia*. New York: St. Martin's, 1985.

Funabashi, Yoichi. *Asia-Pacific Fusion: Japan's Role in APEC*. Washington, D.C.: Institute for International Economics, 1995.

Garnut, Ross, and Peter Drysdale (Eds.). *Asia Pacific Regionalism: Readings in International Economic Relations*. Pymble, Australia: Harper Educational, 1994.

Imada, Pearl, and Seiji Naya (Eds.). *AFTA: The Way Ahead*. Singapore: Institute of Southeast Asian Studies, 1992.

Leifer, Michael. *ASEAN and the Security of South-East Asia*. London: Routledge, 1989.

Lim, Hua Sing. *Japan's Role in ASEAN: Issues and Prospects*. Singapore: Times Academic Press, 1994.

Mahathir bin Mohamad. *Regionalism, Globalism and Spheres of Influence: ASEAN and the Challenge of Changes in the 21st Century*. Singapore: Institute of Southeast Asian Studies, 1989.

McIness, Colin, and Mark G. Rolls (Eds.). *Post Cold War Security Issues in the Asia-Pacific Region*. Ilford, U.K.: Cass, 1994.

McIntrye, David W. *Background to the ANZUS Pact: Strategy and Diplomacy, 1945–55*. New York: St. Martin's, 1995.

Palmer, Norman D. *The New Regionalism in Asia and the Pacific*. Lexington, Mass.: Lexington, 1991.

Robertson, David (Ed.). *East Asian trade after the Uruguay Round*. Cambridge: Cambridge University Press, 1997.

Sandhu, Kernial, et al. *The ASEAN Reader*. Singapore: Institute for Southeast Asian Studies, 1992.

Scalapino, Robert S., et al. (Eds.). *Asian Security Issues: Regional and Global*. Berkeley: Institute of East Asian Studies, University of California, 1988.

Wilson, John S. *Standards and APEC: An Action Agenda*. Policy Analyses in International Economics, No. 42. Washington, D.C.: Institute for International Economics, 1995.

Europe

Anderson, Svein S., and Kjell A. Eliassen. *Making Policy in Europe*. London: Sage, 1993.

Archer, Clive. *Organizing Western Europe: The Institutions of Integration*. 2nd ed. New York: Arnold, 1994.

Archer, Clive, and Fiona Butler. *The European Union*. 2nd ed. New York: St. Martin's, 1995.

Arter, David. *The Politics of European Integration in the Twentieth Century.* London: Dartmouth, 1993.

Artis, Mike, and Norman Lee. *The Economics of the European Union: Policy and Analysis.* New York: Oxford University Press, 1994.

Aubert, Jean-François, et al. *Democracy and Federalism in European Integration.* Bern: Stämpfli + Cie, 1995.

Austin, Dennis. *The Commonwealth and Britain.* London: Routledge & Kegan Paul, 1988.

Baker, Susan, Kay Milton, and Steven Yearly (Eds.). *Protecting the Periphery: Environmental Policy in Peripheral Regions of the European Union.* Portland, Oreg.: Cass, 1994.

Baldassarri, Mario, and Robert Mundell. *Building the New Europe.* New York: St. Martin's, 1993.

Baun, Michael J. *An Imperfect Union: The Maastricht Treaty and the New Politics of European Integration.* Boulder, Colo.: Westview, 1996.

Beddard, Ralph. *Human Rights and Europe: A Study of the Machinery of Human Rights Protection of the Council of Europe.* 2nd ed. London: Sweet & Maxwell, 1980.

Beloff, Max. *Britain and the European Union: Dialogue of the Deaf.* New York: St. Martin's, 1996.

Betten, Lammy, and Delma MacDevitt. *The Protection of Fundamental Social Rights in the European Union.* Boston: Kluwer Law International, 1996.

Bourke, Thomas. *Japan and the Globalisation of European Integration.* Brookfield, Vt.: Dartmouth, 1996.

Bradley, Anthony W., Mark W. Janis, and Richard S. Kay. *European Human Rights Law: Text and Materials.* Oxford: Clarendon, 1995.

Brine, Jenny (Ed.). *COMECON: The Rise and Fall of an International Socialist Organization* [Bibliography]. International Organizations, Vol. 3. New Brunswick, N.J.: Transaction, 1993.

Budd, Stanley A., and Alun Jones. *The EEC: A Guide to the Maze.* 4th ed. London: Kogan Page, 1991.

Bulmer, Simon, and Andrew Scott (Eds.). *Economic and Political Integration in Europe: Internal Dynamics and Global Context.* Cambridge: Blackwell, 1994.

Cafruny, Alan W., and Carl Lankowski. *Europe's Ambiguous Unity: Conflict and Consensus in the Post-Maastricht Era.* Boulder, Colo.: Rienner, 1996.

Cafruny, Alan W., and Glenda G. Rosenthal. *The State of the European Community, Vol. 2. The Maastricht Debates and Beyond.* Boulder, Colo.: Rienner, 1993.

Cahen, Alfred. *The Western European Union and NATO: Building a*

European Defence Identity within the Context of Atlantic Solidarity.
London: Brassey's, 1989.

Calingaert, Michael. *European Integration Revisited: Progress, Prospects, and U.S. Interests.* Boulder, Colo.: Westview, 1996.

Carr, Fergus, and Kostas Ifantis. *NATO and the New European Order.* New York: St. Martin's, 1996.

Clawson, Robert W., and Lawrence S. Kaplan (Eds.). *The Warsaw Pact: Political Purpose and Military Means.* Wilmington, Del.: Scholarly Resources, 1982.

Coffey, Peter. *The Future of Europe.* Brookfield, Vt.: Elgar, 1995.

Cox, Andrew W. *A Modern Guide to the European Community: A Guide to Key Facts, Institutions and Terms.* Brookfield, Vt.: Elgar, 1992.

Corbett, Richard. *The Treaty of Maastricht: From Conception to Ratification.* New York: Longman, 1993.

Crawford, Beverly, and Peter W. Schulze (Eds.). *European Dilemmas after Maastricht.* Berkeley: International and Area Studies, Center for German and European Studies, University of California at Berkeley, 1993.

Crawford, Malcolm. *One Money for Europe? The Economics and Politics of Maastricht.* 2nd ed. New York: St. Martin's, 1996.

Delors, Jacques. *Our Europe: The Community and National Development.* London: Verso, 1992.

De Nooy, Gert (Ed.). *Cooperative Security, the OSCE, and Its Code of Conduct.* Nijhoff Law Specials, Vol. 24. Boston: Kluwer Law International/Netherlands Institute of International Relations "Clingendael," 1996.

De Wilde, Jaap, and Hakan Wiberg. *Organized Anarchy in Europe: The Role of States and Intergovernmental Organizations.* Tauris Academic Studies. New York: St. Martin's, 1996.

Deutsch, Karl, Sidney A. Burrell, and Robert A. Kann. *Political Community in the North Atlantic Area.* Princeton, N.J.: Princeton University Press, 1958.

Dinan, Desmond. *Ever Closer Union? An Introduction to the European Community.* Boulder, Colo.: Rienner, 1994.

Dinan, Desmond. *Historical Dictionary of the European Community.* International Organizations Series, No. 1. Metuchen, N.J.: Scarecrow, 1993.

Edward, David A. O., and Robert C. Lane. *European Community Law: An Introduction.* Edinburgh: Butterworths, Law Society of Scotland, 1995.

Ellis, Evelyn. *European Community Sex Equality Law.* New York: Oxford University Press, 1991.

Elman, R. Amy (Ed.). *Sexual Politics and the European Union: The New Feminist Challenge*. Oxford: Berghahn, 1996.

European Banking Law: A Guide to Community and Member State Legislation. Brussels: Coopers & Lybrand Europe, 1990.

Eyal, Jonathan. *The Warsaw Pact and the Balkans: Moscow's Southern Flank*. New York: St. Martin's, 1989.

Fabricius, Fritz. *Human Rights and European Politics: The Legal-Political Status of Workers in the European Community*. New York: Berg, 1992.

Fagerberg, Jan, and Lars Lundberg (Eds.). *European Economic Integration: A Nordic Perspective*. Brookfield, Vt.: Avebury, 1993.

Faini, Riccardo, and Richard Portes (Eds.). *European Union Trade with Eastern Europe: Adjustment and Opportunities*. London: Center for Economic Policy Research, 1995.

Featherstone, Kevin, and Roy Ginsburg. *The United States and the European Union in the 1990s*. 2nd ed. New York: St. Martin's, 1996.

Feld, Werner J. *The Future of European Security and Defense Policy*. Boulder, Colo.: Rienner, 1993.

Fodor, Neil. *The Warsaw Treaty Organization: A Political and Organizational Analysis*. New York: St. Martin's, 1990.

Francis, Geoffrey Jacobs. *European Parliament*. 3rd ed. London: Cartermill, 1994.

Freeman, John. *Security and the CSCE Process: The Stockholm Conference and Beyond*. New York: St. Martin's, 1991.

Frid, Rachel. *The Relations between the EC and International Organizations: Legal Theory and Practice*. Legal Aspects of International Organizations, Vol. 24. Boston: Kluwer Law International, 1995.

Garcia-Ramon, Maria Dolores, and Janice Monk (Eds.). *Women of the European Union: The Politics of Work and Daily Life*. New York: Routledge, 1996.

Gardner, Anthony Laurence. *A New Era in US-EU Relations? The Clinton Administration and the New Transatlantic Agenda*. Brookfield, Vt.: Avebury, 1997.

George, Stephen. *Politics and Policy in the European Union*. 3rd ed. New York: Oxford University Press, 1996.

Gillespie, Richard (Ed.). *The Euro-Mediterranean Partnership: Political and Economic Perspectives*. Newbury Park, Essex: Cass, 1997.

Goldsmith, Michael J. F., and Kurt K. Klausen (Eds.). *European Integration and Local Government*. Brookfield, Vt.: Elgar, 1997.

Goyder, D. G. *EC Competition Law*. 2nd ed. New York: Oxford University Press, 1992.

Grilli, Enzo R. *The European Community and the Developing Countries*. Cambridge: Cambridge University Press, 1993.

Gros, Daniel, and Niels Thygesen. *European Monetary Integration.* New York: St. Martin's, 1992.

Grosser, Alfred. *The Western Alliance: European-American Relations Since 1945.* New York: Continuum, 1980.

Haas, Ernst B. *The Uniting of Europe: Political, Economic and Social Forces, 1950–1957.* Stanford, Calif.: Stanford University Press, 1958.

Harrop, Jeffrey. *Structural Funding and Employment in the European Union: Financing the Path to Integration.* Lyme, N.H.: Edward Elgard, 1996.

Hayes-Renshaw, Fiona, and Helen Wallace. *The Council of Ministers.* New York: St. Martin's, 1996.

Heller, Francis H., and James R. Gillingham (Eds.). *The United States and the Integration of Europe.* The Franklin and Eleanor Roosevelt Institute Series on Diplomatic and Economic History. New York: St. Martin's, 1996.

Heraclides, Alexis. *Helsinki-II and Its Aftermath: The Making of the CSCE into an International Organization.* London: Pinter, 1993.

Hitiris, Theodore. *European Community Economics.* 2nd ed. New York: Harvester Wheatsheaf, 1991.

Holland, Martin. *European Community Integration.* London: Pinter, 1993.

Holland, Martin. *European Union Common Foreign Policy: From EPC to CFSP Joint Action and South Africa.* New York: St. Martin's, 1995.

Hollins, Steve, and Richard Macrory. *A Source Book of European Community Environmental Law.* New York: Oxford University Press, 1995.

Howard, Jack (Ed.). *The Crisis of Representation in Europe.* Portland, Oreg.: Cass, 1995.

Hurwitz, Leon, and Christian Lequesne (Eds.). *The State of the European Community, Vol. 1: Policies, Institutions, and Debates in the Transition Years.* Boulder, Colo.: Rienner, 1991.

Jacobs, Francis G. *The European Convention on Human Rights.* 2nd ed. Oxford: Oxford University Press, 1996.

Janis, Mark, Richard Fay, and Anthony Bradley. *European Human Rights Law: Text and Materials.* New York: Oxford University Press, 1995.

Jeffrey, Charlie. *The Regional Dimension of the European Union: Towards a Third Level in Europe?* Newbury Park, Essex: Cass, 1997.

Jones, Robert A. *The Politics of the European Union: An Introductory Text.* Lyme, N.H.: Elgar, 1996.

Jovanovic, Miroslav N. *European Economic Integration: Limits and Prospects.* London: Routledge, 1997.

Kaniel, Moshe. *The Exclusive Treaty-Making Power of the European*

Community up to the Period of the Single European Act. Boston: Kluwer Law International, 1996.

Kaser, Michael. *Comecon: Integration Problems of the Planned Economies*. 2nd ed. New York: Oxford University Press, 1967.

Kazakos, Panos, and P. C. Ioakimidis (Eds.). *Greece and EC Membership Evaluated*. EC Membership Evaluated Series. New York: St. Martin's, 1995.

Kenen, Peter. *EMU after Maastricht*. Washington, D.C.: Group of Thirty, 1992.

Keohane, Robert O., and Stanley Hoffmann (Eds.). *The New European Community: Decision-Making and Institutional Change*. Boulder, Colo.: Westview, 1991.

Kirchner, Emil Joseph. *Decision-Making in the European Community: The Council Presidency and European Integration*. New York: Manchester University Press, 1992.

Kirchner, Emil Joseph. *Future of European Security*. Brookfield, Vt.: Dartmouth, 1994.

Landau, Alice, and Richard Whitman (Eds.). *Rethinking the European Union: Institutions, Interests and Identities*. New York: St. Martin's, 1996.

Leonardi, Robert. *Convergence, Cohesion, and Integration in the European Union*. New York: St. Martin's, 1995.

Levine, Norman (Ed.). *The US and the EU: Economic Relations in a World of Transition*. Lanham, Md.: University Press of America, 1996.

Liefferink, J. D., P. D. Lowe, and A. J. P. Mol (Eds.). *European Integration and Environmental Policy*. New York: Belhaven, 1993.

Lindberg, Leon. *Europe's Would-be Polity: Patterns of Change in the European Community*. Upper Saddle River, N.J.: Prentice Hall, 1970.

Lindberg, Leon. *The Political Dynamics of European Economic Community*. Stanford, Calif.: Stanford University Press, 1963.

Lodge, Juliet (Ed.). *The European Community and the Challenge of the Future*. 2nd ed. London: Pinter, 1994.

Marks, Gary, et al. (Eds.). *Governance in the European Union*. Thousand Oaks, Calif.: Sage Publications, 1996.

Mayne, Richard J. *The Community of Europe*. New York: Norton, 1963.

Mayne, Richard J. *The Recovery of Europe: From Devastation to Unity*. London: Weidenfeld & Nicolson, 1970.

Mazey, Sonia, and Jeremy Richardson. *Lobbying in the European Community*. New York: Oxford University Press, 1993.

McCormick, John Spencer. *The European Union: Politics and Policies*. Boulder, Colo.: Westview, 1996.

Mény, Yves, Pierre Muller, and Jean-Louis Quermonne (Eds.). *Adjust-*

ing to Europe: The Impact of the European Union on National Institutions and Policies. New York: Routledge, 1996.

Merrills, J. G. The Development of International Law by the European Court of Human Rights. 2nd ed. Manchester: Manchester University Press, 1993.

Morgan, Roger, and Clare Tame. Parliaments and Parties: The European Parliament in the Political Life of Europe. New York: St. Martin's, 1996.

Mortensen, Jorgen (Ed.). Improving Economic and Social Cohesion in the European Community. New York: St. Martin's, 1994.

Murray, Philomena, and Paul Rich (Eds.). Visions of European Unity. Boulder, Colo.: Westview, 1996.

Nelsen, Brent F., and Alexander C.-G. Stubb (Eds.). The European Union: Readings on the Theory and Practice of European Integration. Boulder, Colo.: Rienner, 1994.

Neuwahl, Nanette, and Allan Rosas. The European Union and Human Rights. Boston: Nijhoff, 1995.

Newman, Michael. Democracy, Sovereignty and the European Union. London: Hurst, 1996.

Nicoll, William, and Trevor C. Salmon. Understanding the New European Community. 2nd ed. New York: Harvester Wheatsheaf, 1994.

Nielsen, Ruth, and Erika Szyszczak. The Social Dimension of the European Community. 2nd ed. Copenhagen: Handelshøjskolens, 1993.

Nugent, Neil (Ed.). At the Heart of the Union: Studies of the European Commission. London: Macmillan, 1997.

Nugent, Neil. The Government and Politics of the European Union. 3rd ed. Durham, N.C.: Duke University Press, 1994.

Nuttall, Simon J. European Political Co-operation. New York: Oxford University Press, 1995.

Ockenden, Jonathan, and Michael Franklin. European Agriculture: Making the CAP Fit the Future. London: Pinter, 1995.

Page, Edward C. People Who Run Europe. Oxford: Clarendon, 1997.

Papademetriou, Demetrios G. Coming Together or Pulling Apart? The European Union's Struggle with Immigration and Asylum. International Migration Policy Program, Vol. 5. Washington, D.C.: Carnegie Endowment for International Peace, 1996.

Paxton, John (Ed.). European Communities [Bibliography]. International Organizations, Vol. 1. New Brunswick, N.J.: Transaction, 1992.

Piening, Chrisopher. Global Europe: The European Union in World Affairs. Boulder, Colo.: Rienner, 1997.

Pilkington, Colin. Britain in the European Union Today. Manchester: Manchester University Press, 1995.

Raworth, Philip. Foreign Trade Law of the European Union. Dobbs Ferry, N.Y.: Oceana, 1995.

Redwood, John. *Our Currency, Our Country, the Dangers of the European Monetary Union: Should Britain Join the European Single Currency?* London: Penguin, 1997.

Rees, G. Wyn. *The Western European Union and the European Security Debate.* Boulder, Colo.: Westview, 1997.

Regelsberger, Elfriede, Philippe de Schoutheete, and Wolfgang Wessels. *Foreign Policy of the European Union: From EPC to CFSP and Beyond.* Boulder, Colo.: Rienner, 1996.

Rhodes, Carolyn, and Sonia Mazey (Eds.). *The State of the European Union, Vol. 3: Building a European Polity?* Boulder, Colo.: Rienner, 1995.

Richardson, Jeremy (Ed.). *European Union: Power and Policy-Making.* New York: Routledge, 1996.

Robertson, A. H., and J. G. Merrills. *Human Rights in Europe: A Study of the European Convention on Human Rights.* 3rd ed. Manchester: Manchester University Press, 1995.

Rometsch, Dietrich, and Wolfgang Wessels (Eds.). *The European Union and Member States: Towards Institutional Fusion?* European Policy Research Unit Series. Manchester: Manchester University Press, 1996.

Salmon, Trevor, and Sir William Nicoll. *Building European Union? A Documentary History and Analysis.* New York: Manchester University Press, 1997.

Sbragia, Alberta (Ed.). *Euro-Politics: Institutions and Policymaking in the "New" European Community.* Washington, D.C.: Brookings Institution, 1993.

Schiavone, Guiseppe. *The Institutions of Comecon.* London: Macmillan, 1981.

Schneider, Gerald, Patricia A. Weitsman, and Thomas Bernauer. *Towards a New Europe: Stops and Starts in Regional Integration.* Westport, Conn.: Praeger, 1995.

Smith, Dale L., and James Lee Ray (Eds.). *The 1992 Project and the Future of Integration in Europe.* Armonk, N.Y.: Sharpe, 1993.

Smith, Hazel. *European Union Foreign Policy in Central America.* London: Macmillan, 1995.

Smith, Peter H. (Ed.). *The Challenge of Integration: Europe and the Americas.* New Brunswick, N.J.: Transaction, 1992.

Springer, Beverly. *The European Union and Its Citizens: The Social Agenda.* Westport, Conn.: Greenwood, 1994.

Stone, Peter. *Copyright Law in the United Kingdom and the European Community.* European Community Law Series, No. 1. Atlantic Highlands: Athlone, 1995.

Stuyck, Jules (Ed.). *Financial and Monetary Integration in the Euro-*

pean Economic Community: Legal, Institutional and Economic Aspects. Boston: Kluwer Law and Taxation, 1993.

Swann, Dennis. *European Economic Integration: The Common Market, European Union and Beyond*. Lyme, N.H.: Elgar, 1996.

Szawalowski, Richard. *The System of International Organizations of the Communist Countries*. Leyden: Sijthoff, 1976.

Taylor, Paul. *The European Union in the 1990s*. New York: Oxford University Press, 1996.

Thompson, Helen. *The British Conservative Government and the European Exchange Rate Mechanism, 1974–1994*. London: Pinter, 1996.

Thomson, Ian. *The Documentation of the European Communities: A Guide*. New York: Mansell, 1989.

Treverton, Gregory F. *The Shape of the New Europe*. New York: Council on Foreign Relations Press, 1992.

Treves, Tullio, and Laura Pineschi (Eds.). *The Law of the Sea: The European Union and its Member States*. Publications on Ocean Development, Vol. 28. Boston: Nijhoff, 1997.

Tsoukalis, Loukas. *The New European Economy: The Politics and Economics of Integration*. 2nd ed. New York: Oxford University Press, 1993.

United States Commission on Security and Cooperation in Europe. *The Conference on Security and Cooperation in Europe: An Overview of the CSCE Process, Recent Meetings, and Institutional Development*. Washington, D.C.: The Commission on Security and Cooperation in Europe, 1992.

Urwin, Derek W. *Historical Dictionary of European Organizations*. International Organizations Series, No. 4. Metuchen, N.J.: Scarecrow, 1994.

Van Brabant, Jozef M. *Remaking Eastern Europe—On the Political Economy of Transition*. Boston: Kluwer Academic, 1990.

Van Tartwijk-Novey, Louise B. *The European House of Cards: Towards a United States of Europe?* New York: St. Martin's, 1995.

Waaldijk, Kees, and Andrew Clapham. *Homosexuality, a European Community Issue: Essays on Lesbian and Gay Rights in European Law and Policy*. Boston: Nijhoff, 1993.

Wallace, William. *The Dynamics of European Integration*. London: Frances Pinter, 1992.

Wallace, William. *Regional Integration: The West European Experience*. Washington, D.C.: Brookings Institution, 1995.

Wallace, William V., and Roger A. Clarke. *COMECON, Trade and the West*. London: Pinter, 1986.

Weatherill, Stephen. *Law and Integration in the European Union*. Oxford: Clarendon, 1995.

Weigall, David, and Peter Stirk (Eds.). *The Origins and Development of the European Community.* Leicester: Leicester University Press, 1992.

Welsh, Michael. *Europe United? The European Union and the Retreat from Federalism.* New York: St. Martin's, 1996.

Wilkes, George (Ed.). *Britain's Failure to Enter the European Community 1961–63: The Enlargement Negotiations and Crises in European, Atlantic and Commonwealth Relations.* Newbury Park, Essex: Cass, 1997.

Williams, Alan M. *The European Community: The Contradictions of Integration.* Oxford: Blackwells, 1994.

Winters, L. Alan, and Anthony J. Venables (Eds.). *European Integration: Trade and Industry.* New York: Cambridge University Press, 1993.

Wise, Mark, and Richard Gibb. *Single Market to Social Europe: The European Community in the 1990s.* New York: Wiley, 1993.

Wyatt-Walter, Holly. *The European Community and the Security Dilemma, 1979–92.* New York: St. Martin's, 1996.

Ziegler, Andreas R. *Trade and Environmental Law in the European Community.* Oxford: Clarendon, 1996.

Zwass, Adam. *The Council for Mutual Economic Assistance: The Thorny Path from Political to Economic Integration.* Armonk, N.Y.: Sharpe, 1989.

Latin and North America

Ball, M. Margaret. *The OAS in Transition.* Durham, N.C.: Duke University Press, 1969.

Barrett, John. *The Pan-American Union: Peace, Friendship and Commerce.* Washington, D.C.: Pan American Union, 1911.

Bulmer-Thomas, Victor, Nikki Craske, and Monica Serrano. *Mexico and the North American Free Trade Agreement: Who Will Benefit?* London: Macmillan, 1994.

De Palacius Puyana, Alicia. *Economic Integration among Unequal Partners: The Case of the Andean Group.* New York: Pergamon, 1982.

Gale, Edward G. *Latin American Free Trade Association: Progress, Problems, Prospects.* Washington, D.C.: Department of State, Office of External Research, 1969.

Garcia-Ambador, Francisco G. *The Inter-American System: Treaties, Conventions and Other Documents.* 2 volumes. New York: Oceana, 1982–1983.

Gauhar, Altaf (Ed.). *Regional Integration: The Latin American Experience.* Boulder, Colo.: Westview, 1985.

Glick, Leslie Alan. *Understanding the North American Free Trade*

Agreement: Legal and Business Consequences of NAFTA. Boston: Kluwer Law and Taxation, 1993.

Grunwald, Joseph, Miguel S. Wionczek, and Martin Carnoy. *Latin American Economic Integration and US Policy.* Washington, D.C.: Brookings Institution, 1972.

Haverstock, Nathan A. *"OAS": Organization of American States: The Challenges of the Americas.* New York: Coward-McCann, 1966.

Hufbauer, Gary Clyde, and Jeffrey J. Schott. *NAFTA: An Assessment.* Washington, D.C.: Institute for International Economics, 1993.

Inter-American Development Bank. *Economic and Social Progress in Latin America: Economic Integration.* Washington, D.C.: Author, Annual.

Lowenthal, Abraham F., and Gregory Treverton (Eds.). *Latin America in a New World Order.* Boulder, Colo.: Westview, 1994.

Lustig, Nora, Barry P. Bosworth, and Robert Z. Lawrence. *North American Free Trade: Assessing the Impact.* Washington, D.C.: Brookings Institution, 1992.

Quebec and the North American Free Trade Agreement. Québec: Ministère des Affaires Internationales, 1993.

Rubin, Seymour J., and Dean J. Alexander (Eds.). *NAFTA and Investment.* Cambridge: Klwuer Law International, 1995.

Scott, James B. *The International Conferences of American States, 1889–1954.* 3 vols. New York: Oxford University Press, 1938–1956.

Sheinin, David. *The Organization of American States* [Bibliography]. International Organizations, Vol. 11. New Brunswick, NJ.: Transaction, 1995.

Sheman, L. Ronald. *The Inter-American Dilemma: The Search for Inter-American Cooperation at the Centennial of the Inter-American System.* New York: Praeger, 1988.

Stoetzer, O. Carlos. *The Organization of American States.* 2nd ed. New York: Praeger, 1993.

Tussie, Diana. *The Inter-American Development Bank.* Boulder, Colo.: Rienner, 1995.

U.S.–Mexico Trade: The Maquiladora Industry and U.S. Employment. Washington, D.C.: Government Printing Office, 1993.

Vaky, Viron L., and Heraldo Muñoz. *The Future of the Organization of American States.* New York: Twentieth Century Fund, 1993.

Welch, Thomas L. *The Organization of American States: A Bibliography.* Washington, D.C.: Columbus Memorial Library, Organization of American States, 1990.

Wilson, Larman C., and David W. Dent. *Historical Dictionary of Inter-American Organizations.* International Organizations Series, No. 14. Lanham, Md.: Scarecrow, 1997.

Wionczek, Miguel S. (Ed.). *Economic Integration in Latin America,*

Asia, and Africa: A Handbook of Documents. Cambridge, Mass.: MIT Press, 1969.

Wionczek, Miguel S. (Ed.). *Latin American Economic Integration: Experiences and Prospects.* New York: Praeger, 1966.

Middle East

Ahrari, Mohammed E. *OPEC: The Failing Giant.* Lexington: University Press of Kentucky, 1985.

Al-Chalabi, Fadhil J. *OPEC at the Crossroads.* New York: Pergamon, 1989.

Ansari, Mohammed Iqbal. *The Arab League, 1945–1955.* Aligarh: Bligarh Muslim University, Institute of Islamic Studies, 1968.

Clements, Frank A. (Ed.). *Arab Regional Organizations* [Bibliography]. International Organizations, Vol. 2. New Brunswick, N.J.: Transaction, 1992.

El Mallakh, Ragei. *OPEC: Twenty Years and Beyond.* Boulder, Colo.: Westview, 1982.

Flowers, E. C., Jr. *The Arab League in Perspective.* The Citadel Monograph Series, No. 1. Charleston: Citadel, 1961.

Gomaa, Ahmad Mohmoud H. *The Foundation of the League of Arab States: Wartime Diplomacy and Inter-Arab Politics, 1941 to 1945.* London: Longman, 1977.

Griffin, James M., and David J. Teece. *OPEC Behavior and World Oil Prices.* Boston: Allen & Unwin, 1982.

Gueicoueru, Adda. (Ed.). *The Problems of Arab Economic Development and Integration.* Boulder, Colo.: Westview, 1984.

Hassouna, Hussein A. *The League of Arab States and Regional Disputes: A Study of Middle East Conflicts.* Dobbs Ferry, N.Y.: Oceana, 1975.

Khali, Muhammed (Ed.). *The Arab States and the Arab League.* 2 vols. Beirut: Khayat's, 1962.

Luciana, Guiacomo, and Ghassan Salame. *The Politics of Arab Integration.* London: Croom Helm, 1988.

Maachou, Abdelkader. *OAPEC: An International Organization for Economic Cooperation and an Instrument for Regional Integration.* Paris: Berger-Levrault, 1982.

McDonald, Ronald W. *The League of Arab States: A Study in the Dynamics of Regional Organization.* Princeton, N.J.: Princeton University Press, 1965.

Meenal, S. A. *The Islamic Development Bank: A Case Study of Islamic Cooperation.* London: Kegan Paul International, 1989.

Nakhleh, Emile A. *Gulf Cooperation Council: Policies, Problems and Prospects.* New York: Praeger, 1986.

Peterson, Erik R. *The Gulf Cooperation Council: Search for Unity in a Dynamic Region.* Boulder, Colo.: Westview, 1988.

Podeh, Elie. *The Quest for Hegemony in the Arab World: The Struggle over the Baghdad Pact.* New York: Brill, 1995.

Pogany, Istvan. *The Arab League and Peacekeeping in Lebanon.* Aldershot, U.K.: Avebury, 1987.

Ramazani, R. K. *The Gulf Cooperation Council: Record and Analysis.* Charlottesville: University Press of Virginia, 1988.

Seymour, Ian. *OPEC: Instrument of Change.* London: Macmillan, 1980.

Skeet, Ian. *OPEC: Twenty-five years of Prices and Policies.* New York: Cambridge University Press, 1988.

Terzian, Pierre. *OPEC: The Inside Story.* London: Zed, 1985.

Tetreault, Mary Ann. *The Organization of Arab Petroleum Exporting Countries: History, Policies and Prospects.* Westport, Conn.: Greenwood, 1981.

Twinam, J. Wright. *The Gulf, Co-operation and the Council: An American Perspective.* Washington, D.C.: Middle East Policy Council, 1992.

Union of International Associations. *Arab and Islamic International Organization Directory, and Participation in Other International Organizations, 1984/85.* New York: Saur, 1984.

Other (Commonwealth, NATO, Organisation for Economic Co-operation and Development)

Blair, David J. *Trade Negotiations in the OECD: Structures, Institutions and States.* London: Kegan Paul International, 1993.

Bland, Douglas L. *The Military Committee of the North Atlantic Alliance: A Study of Structure and Strategy.* New York: Praeger, 1991.

Chan, Stephen. *Twelve Years of Commonwealth Diplomatic History: Commonwealth Summit Meetings, 1979–1991.* Lewiston, Maine: Mellen, 1992.

Chernoff, Fred. *After Bipolarity: The Vanishing Threat, Theories of Cooperation, and the Future of the Atlantic Alliance.* Ann Arbor: University of Michigan Press, 1995.

Cook, Don. *The Forging of an Alliance: NATO 1945–1950.* New York: Arbor House/Morrow, 1989.

Doxey, Margaret P. *The Commonwealth Secretariat and the Contemporary Commonwealth.* New York: St. Martin's, 1989.

Duffield, John S. *Power Rules: The Evolution of NATO's Conventional Force Posture.* Stanford, Calif.: Stanford University Press, 1995.

Gordon, Philip H. (Ed.). *NATO's Transformation: The Changing Shape of the Atlantic Alliance.* Lanham, Md.: Rowman & Littlefield, 1996.

Gregory, Shaun R. *Nuclear Command and Control in NATO: Nuclear Weapons Operations and the Strategy of Flexible Response.* New York: St. Martin's, 1995.

Haftendorn, Helga. *NATO and the Nuclear Revolution: A Crisis of Credibility, 1966–1967.* Oxford: Clarendon, 1996.

Hall, H. Duncan. *Commonwealth: A History of the British Commonwealth.* New York: Van Nostrand Reinhold, 1971.

Heller, Francis H., and James R. Gillingham (Eds.). *NATO: The Founding of the Atlantic Alliance and the Integration of Europe.* New York: St. Martin's, 1992.

Jordan, Robert S. *Political Leadership in NATO: A Study in Multinational Diplomacy.* Boulder, Colo.: Westview, 1979.

Judd, Dennis, and Peter Slinn. *The Evolution of the Modern Commonwealth.* London: Macmillan, 1982.

Kaplan, Lawrence S. *American Historians and the Atlantic Alliance.* Kent, Ohio: Kent State University Press, 1991.

Kaplan, Lawrence S. *A Community of Interest: NATO and the Military Assistance Program, 1948–1951.* Washington, D.C.: Office of Secretary of Defense, Historical Office, 1980.

Kaplan, Lawrence S. *NATO after Forty Years.* Wilmington, Del.: Scholarly Resources, 1990.

Kaplan, Lawrence S. *NATO and the Mediterranean.* Wilmington, Del.: Scholarly Resources, 1985.

Kaplan, Lawrence S. (Ed.). *NATO and the Policy of Containment.* Boston: Heath, 1968.

Kaplan, Lawrence S. *NATO and the United States: The Enduring Alliance.* Twayne's International History Series, No. 1. Boston: Twayne, 1988.

Kaplan, Lawrence S. *NATO and the United States: The Formative Years.* Lexington: University Press of Kentucky, 1984.

Keeton, George W. (Ed.). *The British Commonwealth: Its Laws and Constitutions.* 9 vols. London: Stevens, 1951.

Larby, Patrick, and Harry Hannam (Compilers). *The Commonwealth* [Bibliography]. International Organizations, Vol. 5. New Brunswick, N.J.: Transaction, 1992.

Maxwell, W. Harold, and Leslie F. *Sweet and Maxwell's Legal Bibliography of the British Commonwealth of Nations.* 2 vols. 2nd ed. London: Rees, 1989.

McIntyre, W. D. *The Significance of the Commonwealth, 1965–90.* London: Academic and Professional, 1991.

Moore, R. J. *Making the New Commonwealth.* Oxford: Clarendon, 1987.

Osgood, Robert E. *NATO, The Entangling Alliance.* Chicago: University of Chicago Press, 1962.

Papacosma, S. Victor, and Mary Ann Heiss (Eds.). *NATO in the Post-Cold War Era: Does It Have a Future?* New York: St. Martin's, 1995.

Papadopoulos, Andrestinos N. *Multilateral Diplomacy within the Commonwealth: A Decade of Expansion.* The Hague: Nijhoff, 1982.

Shea, Jamie. *NATO 2000: A Political Agenda for a Political Alliance.* London: Brassey's, 1990.

Sloan, Stanley R. *NATO's Future: Toward a New Transatlantic Bargain.* Washington, D.C.: National Defense University Press, 1985.

Smith, Arnold. *Stitches in Time: The Commonwealth in World Politics.* London: Deutsch, 1981.

Smith, Joseph (Ed.). *The Origins of NATO.* Exeter: Exeter University Press, 1990.

Stuart, Douglas, and William Tow. *The Limits of Alliance: NATO's Out-of-Area Problems Since 1949.* Baltimore, Md.: Johns Hopkins University Press, 1990.

Thompson, Kenneth W. (Ed.). *NATO and the Changing World Order: An Appraisal by Scholars and Policymakers.* Lanham, Md.: University Press of America, 1996.

Williams, Phil. *NATO* [Bibliography]. International Organizations, Vol. 8. New Brunswick, N.J.: Transaction, 1994.

Non–United Nations, Nonregional Intergovernmental Organizations (Includes the League of Nations)

League of Nations

Baer, George W. *Test Case: Italy, Ethiopia and the League of Nations.* Stanford, Calif.: Hoover Institution Press, 1976.

Barros, James. *Betrayal from Within: Joseph Avenol, Secretary-General of the League of Nations, 1933–1940.* New Haven, Conn.: Yale University Press, 1969.

Barros, James. *Office without Power: Secretary General Sir Eric Drummond, 1919–1933.* New York: Oxford University Press, 1979.

Cecil, Robert. *A Great Experiment.* New York: Oxford University Press, 1939.

Dexter, Byron. *The Years of Opportunity: The League of Nations, 1920–1926.* New York: Viking, 1967.

Dore, Isaak I. *The International Mandate Systems and Namibia.* Boulder, Colo.: Westview, 1985.

Gill, George. *The League of Nations from 1929 to 1946.* Partners for Peace Series, Vol. 2. Garden City Park, N.Y.: Avery, 1996.

Hudson, Manley O. *The Permanent Court of International Justice, 1920–1942.* New York: Macmillan, 1943.

League of Nations. *The Development of International Cooperation in Economic and Social Affairs.* Geneva: League Secretariat, 1939.

Miller, David Hunter. *The Drafting of the Covenant.* 2 vols. New York: Putnam, 1928.

Morrison, Herbert S., et al. *The League and the Future of the Collective System.* London: Allen & Unwin, 1937.

Northedge, F. S. *The League of Nations: Its Life and Times, 1920–1946.* New York: Holmes & Meier, 1986.

Ostrower, Gary B. *The League of Nations From 1919 to 1929.* Garden City. N.Y.: Avery, 1996.

Scott, George. *The Rise and Fall of the League of Nations.* London: Hutchinson, 1973.

Skran, Claudena M. *Refugees in Inter-war Europe: The Emergence of a Regime.* Oxford: Clarendon, 1995.

Walters, F. P. *A History of the League of Nations.* 2 vols. New York: Oxford University Press, 1952.

Zimmern, Alfred. *The League of Nations and the Rule of Law.* 2nd, rev. ed. London: Macmillan, 1945.

Other Non-United Nations, Nonregional Intergovernmental Organizations

Bonnet, Roger M., and Vittorio Manno. *International Cooperation in Space: The Example of the European Space Agency.* Cambridge, Mass.: Harvard University Press, 1994.

Hajnal, Peter I. (Compiler and Ed.). *The Seven-Power Summit: Documents from the Summits of Industrialized Countries, Supplement. Documents from the 1990 Summit.* White Plains, N.Y.: Kraus International, 1989.

Hajnal, Peter I. (Compiler and Ed.). *The Seven-Power Summit: Documents from the Summits of Industrialized Countries, 1975–1989.* White Plains, N.Y.: Kraus International, 1989.

Lister, Frederick K. *The European Union, the United Nations, and the Revival of Confederal Governance.* Westport, Conn.: Greenwood, 1996.

Majid, Amin A. *Legal Status of International Institutions: SITA, IN-MARSAT and EUROCONTROL Examined.* Brookfield, Vt.: Dartmouth, 1996.

Peters, Ingo (Ed.). *New Security Challenges: The Adaptations of International Institutions, Reforming the UN, NATO, EU, and CSCE since 1989.* New York: St. Martin's, 1996.

Pomerance, Michla. *The United States and the World Court as a "Su-*

preme Court of Nations": Dreams, Illusions and Disillusion. Legal Aspects of International Organization, Vol. 26. Boston: Nijhoff, 1996.

Putnam, Robert D., and Nicholas Bayne. *Hanging Together: Co-operation and Conflict in the Seven-Power Summits*. Rev. and enlarged ed. Cambridge, Mass.: Harvard University Press, 1987.

Reinsch, Paul Samuel. *Public International Unions: Their Work and Organization: A Study in International Administrative Law*. Boston: Ginn, 1911.

Sauvant, Karl P. *The Group of 77: Evolution, Structure, Organization*. New York: Oceana, 1981.

International Non-Governmental Organizations

Alliband, Terry. *Catalysts of Development: Voluntary Agencies in India*. Hartford, Conn.: Kumarian, 1983.

Annis, Sheldon, and Peter Hakim (Eds.). *Direct to the Poor: Grassroots Development in Latin America*. Boulder, Colo.: Rienner, 1989.

Asian NGO Coalition for Agrarian Reform and Rural Development. *NGO Initiatives in Rural Nutrition and Health*. Manila, The Philippines: Author, September 1986.

Berry, Nicholas A. *War and the Red Cross: The Unspoken Mission*. New York: St. Martin's, 1997.

Boardman, Robert. *International Organizations and the Conservation of Nature*. London: Macmillan, 1981.

Brown, Michael, and John May. *The Greenpeace Story*. Scarborough, Ontario: Prentice Hall, 1989.

Buchanan, Ian, and Bill Mallon. *Historical Dictionary of the Olympic Movement*. Religions, Philosophies, and Movements Series No. 7. Lanham, Md.: Scarecrow, 1995.

Bussey, Gertrude, and Margaret Tims. *The Women's International League for Peace and Freedom, 1915–1965*. London: Allen & Unwin, 1965.

Caribbean Network for Integrated Rural Development. *Developing the Rural Network: A Directory of Rural Development Resources in the Caribbean*. St. Augustine, Trinidad and Tobago: Author, 1989.

Carroll, Thomas F. *Intermediary NGOs: The Supporting Link in Development*. Hartford, Conn.: Kumarian, 1992.

Checci and Company Consulting, Inc. *Final Report: Evaluation of Experience of USAID Missions with PVO Umbrella Groups in Costa Rica, Guatemala, Honduras and Haiti*. Washington, D.C.: Author, 1989.

Clark, John. *Democratizing Development: The Role of Voluntary Organizations*. London: Earthscan, 1991.

Development Centre of the Organisation for Economic Co-operation and Development. *Directory of Non-Governmental Organisations Active in Sustainable Development. Part I: Europe.* Paris: Author, 1996.

Development Centre of the Organisation for Economic Co-operation and Development. *Human Rights, Refugees, Migrants & Development: Directory of NGOs in OECD Countries.* Paris: Author, 1993.

Douglas, James. *Why Charity? The Case for a Third Sector.* Beverly Hills, Calif.: Sage, 1983.

Downs, Charles, et al. *Social Policy from the Grassroots: Nongovernmental Organizations in Chile.* Boulder, Colo.: Westview, 1989.

Egeland, Jan, and Thomas Krebs (Eds.). *Third World Organisational Development: A Comparison of NGO Strategies.* HDI Series on Development, Vol. 1. Geneva: Henry Dunant Institute, 1987.

Environment and Development in the Third World OECD Development Centre. *Directory of Non-Governmental Environment and Development Organisations in OECD Member Countries.* Paris: Organisation for Economic Co-operation and Development, 1992.

Farringdon, John, and Anthony Bebbington. *Reluctant Partners? Non-Governmental Organizations, the State and Sustainable Agricultural Development.* London: Routledge, 1993.

Fisher, Julie. *Agrarian Reform in Peru and El Salvador: Technoserve's Experience.* Norwalk, Conn.: Technoserve, Replication and Policy Analysis Division, 1989.

Fisher, Julie. *The Road from Rio: Sustainable Development and the Non-governmental Movement in the Third World.* Westport, Conn.: Praeger, 1993.

Foster, Catherine. *Women for All Seasons: The Story of the Women's International League for Peace and Freedom.* Athens: University of Georgia Press, 1989.

Gehring, Thomas. *Dynamic International Regimes: Institutions for International Environmental Governance.* Frankfurt: Lang, 1994.

Gomes, P. I. (Ed.). *Rural Development in the Caribbean.* New York: St. Martin's, 1985.

Gordenker, Leon, et al. *International Cooperation in Response to AIDS.* New York: Pinter, 1995.

Gordenker, Leon, and Thomas G. Weiss (Eds.). *NGOs, the UN, and Global Governance.* Boulder, Colo.: Rienner, 1996.

Gorman, Robert F. (Ed.). *Private Voluntary Organizations as Agents of Development.* Boulder, Colo.: Westview, 1984.

Heyzer, Noeleen, James V. Riker, and Antonio B. Quizon (Eds.). *Government-NGO Relations in Asia: Challenges for Improving the Policy Environment for People-Centered Development.* International Political Economy Series. New York: St. Martin's, 1995.

Hirschman, Albert O. *Getting Ahead Collectively: Grassroots Experiences in Latin America.* New York: Pergamon, 1984.

Hulme, David. *Beyond the Magic Bullet: NGO Performance and Accountability in the Post Cold War World.* Hartford, Conn.: Kumarian, 1996.

Hulme, David, and Michael Edwards (Eds.). *NGOs, States and Donors: Too Close for Comfort.* New York: St. Martin's, 1996.

Hutchinson, John F. *Champions of Charity: War and the Rise of the Red Cross.* Boulder, Colo.: Westview, 1996.

Independent Sector (Washington, D.C.). *The Non-Profit Sector (NGOs) in the United States and Abroad: Cross Cultural Perspectives.* Boston: Author, March 15–16, 1990.

International Tree Project Clearinghouse. *A Directory: NGOs in the Forestry Sector.* 2nd ed. New York: Non-Governmental Liaison Service, United Nations, 1987.

Jean, François (Ed.). *Life, Death and Aid: The Médecins Sans Frontières Report on World Crisis Intervention.* New York: Routledge, 1993.

Korten, David. *Getting to the 21st Century: Voluntary Action and the Global Agenda.* Hartford, Conn.: Kumarian, 1990.

Lee, Marth. *Earth First! Environmental Apocalypse.* Syracuse, N.Y.: Syracuse University Press, 1995.

Lefever, Ernest W. *Nairobi to Vancouver: The World Council of Churches and the World, 1975–87.* Washington, D.C.: Ethics and Public Policy Center, 1988.

Leonard, David K., and Dale Rogers Marshall (Eds.). *Institutions of Rural Development for the Poor: Decentralization and Organizational Linkages.* Berkeley: Institute of International Studies, University of California, 1982.

Livezey, Lionel W. *Non-Governmental Organizations and the Idea of Human Rights.* Princeton, N.J.: Center for International Studies, Princeton University, 1988.

McAllister, Ian. *Sustaining Relief with Development: Strategic Issues for the Red Cross and Red Crescent.* Boston: Nijhoff, 1993.

McCarthy, Kathleen D. *The Nonprofit Sector in the Global Community.* San Francisco: Jossey-Bass, 1989.

Nelson, Paul J. *The World Bank and Non-Governmental Organizations: The Limits of Apolitical Development.* London: Macmillan, 1995.

Organisation for Economic Co-operation and Development. *Voluntary Aid for Development: The Role of Non-Governmental Organizations.* Paris: Author, 1988.

Organization of American States, Inter-American Commission on Women. *Non-Governmental Women's Organizations and National Machinery for Improving the Status of Women: A Directory for the Caribbean Region.* Washington, D.C.: Author, 1990.

Paul, Samuel. *Community Participation in Development Projects: The World Bank Experience*. World Bank Discussion Papers No. 6. Washington, D.C.: The World Bank 1987.

Pei-heng, Chiang. *Non-Governmental Organizations in the United Nations: Identity, Role and Function*. New York: Praeger, 1981.

Population Institute. *The Nairobi Challenge: Global Directory of Women's Organizations Implementing Population Strategies*. Washington, D.C.: Author, 1988.

Princen, Thomas, and Matthias Finger (Eds.). *Environmental NGOs in World Politics: Linking the Local and the Global*. New York: Routledge, 1994.

Red Cross. *The League of Red Cross and Red Crescent Societies 1919–1989*. Geneva: League of Red Cross and Red Crescent Societies, 1989.

Rice, Andrew (Ed.). *The Role of Non-Governmental Organizations in Development Cooperation, Liaison Bulletin between Development Research and Training*. Paris: Organisation for Economic Co-operation and Development, Development Center, 1983.

Riddell, Roger C. *Non-Governmental Organizations and Rural Poverty Alleviation*. New York: Oxford University Press, 1995.

Riddell, Roger C. *Promoting Development by Proxy: The Development Impact of Government Support to Swedish NGOs*. Stockholm: Swedish International Development Agency, 1995.

Ritchey-Vance, Marion. *The Art of Association: NGOs and Civil Society in Colombia*. Country Focus Series No. 2. Washington, D.C.: Inter-American Foundation, 1991.

Robins, Dorothy B. *Experiments in Democracy: The Story of U.S. Citizen Organizations in Forging the Charter of the UN*. New York: Parkside, 1971.

Rotberg, Robert I. *Vigilance and Vengeance: NGOs Preventing Ethnic Conflict in Divided Societies*. Washington, D.C.: Brookings Institution, 1996.

Rowlands, Ian H. *The Politics of Global Atmospheric Change*. Manchester: Manchester University Press, 1995.

Sandberg, Eve (Ed.). *The Changing Nature of Non-Governmental Organizations and African States*. Westport, Conn.: Praeger, 1994.

Smith, Brian H. *More than Altruism: The Politics of Private Foreign Aid*. Princeton, N.J.: Princeton University Press, 1990.

Sogge, David (Ed.). *Compassion and Calculation: The Business of Private Foreign Aid*. London: Pluto, 1996.

Taylor, Bron Raymond (Ed.). *Ecological Resistance Movements: The Global Emergence of Radical and Popular Environmentalism*. Albany: State University of New York Press, 1995.

Theunis, Sjif (Ed.). *Non-governmental Development Organizations of Developing Countries: And the South Smiles.* Boston: Nijhoff, 1992.

Thoolen, Hans, and Bewrth Verstappen. *Human Rights Missions: A Study of the Fact-finding Practice of Non-governmental Organizations.* Boston: Nijhoff, 1986.

Tongsawate, Maniemai, and Walter E. J. Tips. *Coordination between Governmental and Non-Governmental Organizations in Thailand's Rural Development.* Monograph No. 5. Bangkok: Division of Human Settlements Development, Asian Institute of Technology, 1985.

Trzna, Thaddeus C., et al. (Eds.). *World Directory of Environmental Organizations.* 5th ed. Sacramento: California Institute of Public Affairs, 1989.

United Nations, Non-Governmental Liaison Service. *Non-Governmental Organizations and Sub-Saharan Africa.* Geneva: Author, July 1988.

Vermaat, J. A. Emerson. *The World Council of Churches and Politics, 1975–1986.* New York: Freedom House, 1989.

Visser t'Hooft, William Adolph. *The Genesis and Formation of the World Council of Churches.* Geneva: World Council of Churches, 1982.

Wapner, Paul. *Environmental Activism and World Civic Politics.* Albany: State University of New York Press, 1996.

Welch, Claude E., Jr. *Protecting Human Rights in Africa: Strategies and Roles of Non-Governmental Organizations.* Philadelphia: University of Pennsylvania Press, 1995.

Wellard, Kate, and James G. Copestake. *Non-Governmental Organizations and the State in Africa: Rethinking Roles in Sustainable Agricultural Development.* London: Routledge, 1993.

White, Lyman Cromwell. *International Non-Governmental Organizations.* New Brunswick, N.J.: Rutgers University Press, 1951.

Willetts, Peter. *"The Conscience of the World": The Influence of Non-Governmental Organisations in the UN System.* Washington, D.C.: Brookings Institution, 1996.

Willetts, Peter (Ed.). *Pressure Groups in the Global System: The Transnational Relations of Issue-Oriented Non-Governmental Organisations.* London: Pinter, 1982.

Wiseberg, Laurie S., and Harry M. Scoble (Compilers). *Human Rights Directory: Latin America, Africa, Asia.* Washington, D.C.: Human Rights Internet, 1981.

Wiseberg, Laurie S., and Harry M. Scoble (Compilers). *North American Human Rights Directory 1980 Human Rights Internet.* Washington, D.C.: Human Rights Internet, 1980.

Woods, Lawrence T. *Asia Pacific Diplomacy: Non-Governmental Organisations and International Relations.* Vancouver: University of British Columbia Press, 1993.

About the Author

MICHAEL G. SCHECHTER (B.A. University of Wisconsin, Madison; M.Phil. Columbia University; Ph.D. Columbia University) is a professor in James Madison College of Michigan State University. An award winning teacher of international relations, he has taught about international law and organization for more than 20 years. Early in his academic career (1978–81) he served as the international organization editor of *The Political Handbook of the World*. More recently, he has served as a project director for the United Nations University's Multilateralism and the United Nations System (MUNS) Programme. He has edited two volumes based on symposia he organized as a part of that program: *Innovation in Multilateralism* (Macmillan for the United Nations University Press, 1998) and *Future Multilateralism: The Political and Social Framework* (Macmillan for the United Nations University Press, 1998). He also wrote the international organization entry in the *Encyclopedia of Democracy* (Congressional Quarterly Press, 1995) and has published numerous articles and chapters of books in his field of specialization of global governance. He also served as an officer in the International Studies Association, the Academic Council on the United Nations System (ACUNS), and the American Society of International Law.